Also by Judith Dupré

Skyscrapers

Bridges

Churches

MONUMENTS

HERNANDEZ · NICHOLAS R TUNNY · SMITH
NALD R SOLES · J C DAVIS
T E BARNHILL · CHARLES V DONOHO
D FISHER · HERMINIO G CENTENO
HUGH J SHEVLIN · CHRISTOPHER W MORGENS
REX L FRAZIER · WILLIAM K VADEN
E MUNIZ GARCIA · RONALD E GERSTNER
DEWALT GARCIA · HARRY I PETERSEN
WALDEMAR S GRZESKOWIAK
RICHARD · RONALD E GARLAND
LES G HUGHES · DANIEL I JEDNEAK
YCE L ADDINGTON · JOSE G BARRERA
OLE · FREDDIE L DACUS · TITUS L EPPS
H · JESSE L KESTLER · JOE BILLY McNETT
ED · CRAIG T RESKA · WILLIAM L AIKEN
FARNSWORTH Jr · ROBERT H GUMM Jr
ALVIN J SCOTT · JOHN G STRACHOTA
AMS · LEONARD P ALLEN · PAUL T COE
ERT SILAS ROCHA · FRANK R HITESHUE
AMES M MEEHAN · PERRY A MITCHELL
MUDIO Jr · CLARENCE R PRITCHARD Jr
NT L ROSSI Sr · RICHARD W SALMOND
ROBERT G DRAPP · BRUCE L HANKINS
OMBAS · JAMES F RILEY · JOHN M ROE
NNETH D ADKINS · JOSEPH CARTER Jr
SSELL G DANIELS · RICHARD R BUTTRY
A DONNELL II · CLEVELAND R HARVEY
ANDALL P MANELA · BENTON L MILLER
JAMES E STOLZ Jr · ROBERT E TUCKER
HOMAS R BIERLINE · JOHN R GRISARD
AS L OSTEEN Jr · WILLIAM J PERRYMAN
FRANKLIN R AKANA · PHILLIP J BARBA
LIAM E FLEMING Jr · THEODORE ISOM
LE · ROBERT L SHRINER · RAY E TANNER
MAS E BRADLEY · CURTERS J BURNETT
TOMMY BOWENS · JEFFREY A COFFIN
ROBERT D KAVICH · MARK A LARSON
JGLASS T WHELESS · DANIEL J CHAVEZ
VERNON G ZORNES · IAN McINTOSH
AMES E ESKRIDGE · NORMAN F EVANS
N H MOBLEY · BENJAMIN J ANTHONY
WILLARD G STORIE · FRANK D TINSLEY
LAWRENCE E SCOTT · LYLE D HAYES
DAVID E KILLIAN · PHILIP E RICHARD
LEN J BODIN · RAMON A HERNANDEZ
REDERICK R NEEF · WILLIAM B O'KIEFF
CHARLES F CREAMER III · GARY E FIELD
AMES B POWELL Jr · EUGENE PRINCE Jr
MS · GARY ANDERSON · JOHN R BEAN
NKLIN D DEFENBAUGH · JACK R GIBBS
ALD R GREENHOUSE · RALPH S GUCK
B JOHNSON · WILLIAM D KENNEDY III
LEE ROY E LINTON · SAMMIE J LONG
AS H PARRIS · NORBERT A PODHAJSKY
ER · BOBBY D SEAY · DONALD A SLATE
HARRY A WATSON · JAMES B YOUNG
GLAS S BRIDGERS · CHARLES R COILEY
ROBERT S GEER · DONALD L GOLDEN
NELSON Jr · PATRICK J PAULICH
WALL · ROBERT L BLACKWELL

DOUGLAS O FORD · WILLARD E LILLEY · LOUIS E STEWART · WICK · PATRIC
KRUG · JOE H LILLIE · LEWIS S HALL · BARRY H BERGER · CLINTON C RO
RICHARD · EDWARDS · ROBERT D BLACK Jr · CORNELIUS H RAM · CECIL E CAL
CLODFELTER · S HUGGINS · THOMAS F IRVIN · RICHARD V BLACKBURN · JACKIE LEE SAWNEY · JAMES T
JOSE R SANDOVAL · WILLIAM E STRACNER · WILLIAM F JOHNSON · LEE W CLORE · ALLEN
STEPHEN E HENDRICKS · EDWARD J STRACNER · FRANCIS J KAPUSTA · DAVID L MEYER · ALLEN
DEANY RAY EASTER · ROBERT D HERTZ · HAROLD E CARR · BILLY RAY THORPE · REX A
RUDOLPH C THOMAS · EDGAR L WEST Jr · JERRY LEE PRICE Jr · ROBERT L
DANIEL F COX · JOSEPH W GAA Jr · JAMES A HARWOOD · BILLY RAY MOFFETT · ROBERT R
WILLIAM · ENFANT · CURTIS W MOORE · WILLIAM NAKI III · GERALD F KINSMAN · DAVID
ROBERT E SHARPE · WILLIAM R ZEYEN · JEFF T BARNETT Sr · DELBERT R PORTER · BRIAN P
PAUL DARBY · JOHN E DAVIS · DONALD G DETRICK · CHARLES R BESS · DEWAINE L BR
HERBERT S HINSON · ROGER G HOLLER · JOHN M GRAHAM · LARRY
TERRY MEZERA · EARL NELSON · REINALDO REIN RODRIGUEZ · MARTIN JIM Jr · PAUL E LEARY Jr · CARLTON J M
LEE D STUART Jr · CHARLES D StCLAIR · WILLIAM H THIGPEN · JOHNNY N WARD Jr · JOHN S
WILLIAM B BLACKMON Jr · ALBERT L BROWN · DAVID W COON · ROY RODRIGUEZ SALINAS · BRUCE C
JOHN GEDDINGS · MALCOLM J LYONS · ROBERT H MIRRER · JESSE E NIXON · JAMES M
PERRY M SMITH · CECIL W SOUTHERLAND · JOSEPH S TIDWELL · WILLIAM F AARONSON IV · RONN
JOSHUA M DANIELS · EUGENE T GILMORE · BILLY JOE PLASTER Jr · LARRY J PRICE · WILBUR D
GLENN R ETHINGTON · JESUS A GONZALES · STEPHEN A ALTSCHAFFL · RONALD D ROWSEY · WILLIA
ARTHUR S NABBEN · RONALD D STEPHENSON · JAMES R GARTEN · TOMMY H IVEY · ROBERT P M
GREGORY S KARGER · EUGENE J LEVICKIS · LOUIS A TRAVERS · RONALD M GARRISON · ROBERT H
RONNIE G VAUGHAN · LARRY D BEAN · FRANK A CELANO · ROG JOHNSON · KENNETH L
HUGH D OPPERMAN · GREGORY L PEFFER · MICHAEL E PETTY · DENNIS R SCHOSSOW · WILLIAM H SE
DONALD L SENTI · FREDERICK A VIGIL · ALFONSO A BRITO · JERRY W CUTTING · GEORGE
RONALD J REVIS · JAMES L COLWYE · STEPHEN L LINDSAY · CALVIN E MILAM · WILLIAM J
RICHARD C PORTER · MERRELL E BRUMLEY Jr · WILLIAM O CREECH Jr · JUAN E GONZALES · GERALD
JAMES P MARKEY II · WILLIAM D NICODEMUS · GEORGE L ROBERTSON · ROBERTO L CANAS · JOH
DEWIGHT E NORTON · STEVEN J OLCOTT · WILLIAM F RECHERT · JAMES E WEATHERSBY · GARNEY H
DEAN A HARRIS · RONALD M RIGDON · ARTHUR A SMITH · MICHAEL E WILLIAMS · HAROLD B U
DAVID I MIXTER · ROBERT L PULLIAM · JEFFREY L BARLOW · HAROLD E BIRKY · JAMES F
ALLEN C ELL · RAFAEL GARCIAPAGAN · RONALD W HACKNEY · RONALD N JASINSKI
JOHN R MILLER · ROBERT A SISK · JOHNNY C SPEARS · JOHNNY E TIVIS · PATRICK G CARTWRIGHT · LARR
JOSEPH W CASINO · CLYDE W COBLE · GORDON L CRAWFORD · JAMES C HARRIS · LOREN
KEITH M JACKSON · WALTER X MENDEZ · THOMAS C MILLER · STEPHEN A MOORE · STEPHEN
RICHARD D RANDOLPH · KEITH A STODDARD · MICHAEL P AUSTIN · DARRELL W COWAN · ROBERT
FRANK S McCUTCHEON III · FLOYD RICHARDSON Jr · JOHN C STRAUSER · PHILIPP R V
LUTHER N BAGNAL III · MARTIN J BURNS · MILFRED R GREEN · LENNART G LANGHORNE · THOMAS
ROBERT L STANDERWICK Sr · JOSEPH L STONE · WALLIS W WEBB · TERRENCE W WELDON · ROBERT
JACKIE LEE DENNY · SAMUEL H EBERHART · GREGORY S SOMERS · LARRY H MARSHALL · DANIEL
ANDRES LOPEZ RAMON · NELSON G RICHARDSON · DAYLE R HALL · STEPHEN M TRAYNOR · PATRICK
CLIFTON E CALLAHAN · DAVID C JOHNSON · CLIFTON C NEWCOMB · JAMES L PAUL · DAVID A
CARL M WOOD · LARRY A WOODBURN · RICHARD A AARON · DAVID L ALEXANDER · KENNETH W BO
FRANK J GASPERICH Jr · AMBERS A HAMILTON · ROBERT P JACQUES · MICHAEL J KERL · CARR
WILLIAM B RHODES · ROBERT J ROGERS · JOSEPH A TERESINSKI · CURTIS L WILLIAMS · THEODOR
BRIAN R FOLEY · THOMAS P B KING · RICHARD S KULWICKI · WILLIAM A LARGEN
RUSSELL G BLOCHER · DONALD L MEEHAN Jr · CHARLES L PEACE · JOSE MARIE ROCHA · DOUGLAS H
LEWIS R YATES · ROLAND D TROYANO · BRUCE A VANDAM · CHARLES E WITHERSPOON · HARRY H
THOMAS A SONY · RAFAEL RIVERA BENITEZ · CHARLES G BOBO · TYRONE C BRADLEY · BARRY
LONALD R COLEMAN · THOMAS P DOODY · MICHAEL B FIRST · DAVID N FOX · JO
KYLE C HOLFELTZ · RANDALL L HARRIS · KEVIN P KNIGHT · DALE W MEAD · LEWIS D MEYER Jr · JOSE
LENOX L RATCLIFF · JOHN E ROBERTSON · CHARLES L SOULE · PAUL C STEWART · JOHN
GERALD J TWOREK · GREG R CARTER · BRUCE A CHRISTENSEN · SHELBY L HENSLEY
MELVIN J FELTON · EDMOND S BLACKBURN Jr · EDGAR McDANIEL · STEVEN D DOWELL
FRED D PAKELE · NORMAN J PEARSON · PHILLIP J SANDO
MICHAEL C LAWSON · JAMES E COLLINS · DONALD A MACKEY
MARK J ROBERTSON · MONETTE V WHITE · JOSEPH R ANTHONY · CHARLES
OLAN D COLEMAN · JAMES F CONNOR Jr · GEORGE G HUTSON
CLYDE W HANSON · ROY L HELBERT · WAYNE D PATTERSON
RICHARD W OKEEFE · WILLIAM L WILLIAMS
WILLIS G UHLS
WILLIE GARDNER
ARTHUR E McLEOD · JAMES E SPEARS
MICHAEL D ADKINS · STEVEN
HEINZ S SEIBERLING

MONUMENTS

AMERICA'S HISTORY
IN ART AND MEMORY

JUDITH DUPRÉ

Random House
New York

Published in the United States by Random House,
an imprint of The Random House Publishing Group,
a division of Random House, Inc., New York.

RANDOM HOUSE and colophon are registered trade-
marks of Random House, Inc.

Library of Congress Cataloging-in-Publication Data

Dupré, Judith
Monuments / Judith Dupré.
p. cm.
Includes bibliographical references and index.
ISBN: 978-1-4000-6582-0

1. Monuments—United States. 2. Monuments—
United States—Pictorial works. 3. Historic sites—
United States. 4. Historic sites—United States—
Pictorial works. 5. United States—History, Local.
6. United States—History, Local—Pictorial works.
7. Architecture and society—United States.
8. Memory—Social aspects—United States. I. Title.

E159.D86 2006
973—dc22
2006047356

Printed in Italy on acid-free paper

www.atrandom.com

987654321

First Edition

Designed by Allison G. Russo,
Alleycat Design, Inc.

Cover Illustrations: All images are copyrighted by
the photographers or lending institutions, and have
been used with permission. Clockwise from top:
Memorial to Matthew Diaz: David Finn/Library of
Congress; Shaw Memorial: Richard Benson and the
Eakins Press Foundation; Straus Memorial, Figure
of Memory: Lee Sandstead; Lincoln Memorial: Lee
Sandstead; Mount Rushmore National Memorial,
Courtesy of the National Park Service; Liberty Bell:
ESTO/Courtesy of Bohlin Cywinski Jackson; Statue
of Liberty: Reed Kaestner/Corbis. Stonework,
Westerleigh, photograph by Richard Rhodes,
Courtesy of Steven and Diana Steinman and
Rhodes Architectural Stone. Title typeface drawn by
Nicholas Benson, John Stevens Shop.

"Empty Sky" by Bruce Springsteen. Copyright
© 2002 Bruce Springsteen (ASCAP). Reprinted by
permission. International copyright secured. All
rights reserved.

To my beloved son Brendan

*and in memory of
Marine Lance Cpl.
Richard Anthony Caruolo,
1945–1966*

Contents

Foreword

The very process of deciding how an event should be remembered allows reconciliation with the event itself, and in doing so frees history to move forward.

Driving over the Triborough Bridge, the panorama of Manhattan's skyline unfolding before me in its thrilling way, I could see the Trade Towers' square profiles blurred by the humidity, and knew the day was going to be a sizzler. It was September 10, 2001. I was on my way to a meeting to discuss a new book I wanted to write about American memorials. Reluctantly, because "Americans aren't much for the past," my publisher at the time capitulated to my proposal. The next day, the towers fell from the air and dropped in on themselves in seconds.

Like everyone, I was numb. History had exploded into the present moment and Americans, within hours, had become invested in memorializing the events of that day. This book took on new meaning for me.

Although only a fraction of these pages concerns the 9/11 memorial at Ground Zero, which has yet to be realized, that unfolding story has been an invaluable context for the writing of this book. It allowed me to witness the complexities of raising any monument, while the design, location, and budget of a major American landmark was debated. It became clear that Americans are very much for remembering the past and finding new forms and rituals that honor its memory.

Greek temple architecture, epitomized by the Parthenon, influenced the neoclassical stylings of many commemorative works in America.

Opposite page, inset One-hundred-sixty-feet tall, the steel façade of One World Trade Center that remained upright after the blast was disassembled into twenty-five pieces weighing forty tons apiece so it could be stored for future exhibitions.

17,000 B.C.

c. 17,000–15,000 B.C.
Prehistoric people in Lascaux, France, paint images on cave walls for utilitarian and ritualistic purposes

4000 B.C.

The Blau Monuments, two small shale plaques made by the Sumerians, are the earliest
known objects to combine words and pictures

4000–3000 B.C.

Small arches built in Egypt, Mesopotamia, and the Indus
Valley

Given that the vast majority of our species is below earth, we the living have devoted a good deal of time to thinking about ways to remember those who are no longer here. In his eloquent *The Dominion of the Dead,* scholar Robert Pogue Harrison tells readers to be grateful for the "hiding and receiving power of their terraqueous globe" which has "reabsorbed the dead into its elements for so many millions upon millions of years." But we are more than mere compost. Our legacy is a living memory that is marked, for most of us, by a headstone or an urn, and for the nation as a whole in our monuments and memorials.

Monuments are history made visible. They are shrines that celebrate the ideals, achievements, and heroes that existed in one moment in time. They commemorate singular individuals, heroic accomplishments, or the millions of lives swept away by war or disaster. They reflect the politics of remembering, and the subtle comparisons our bodies make when looking up or down at effigies of others. The best of them are redemptive, allowing us to understand the past in a way that is meaningful in the present.

Monuments are not about death, as I first assumed, nor are they wholly about life. Rooted in the Latin *monere,* which means to remind or admonish, monuments are not necessarily about remembering, either. More often than not, they allow us to forget. Much like filing away a paper in a cabinet, erecting a monument can reinforce the slim illusion that the memories associated with it can be retrieved when desired at some later date. The very process of deciding how an event should be remembered allows reconciliation with the event itself, and in doing so frees history to move forward. Ultimately, monuments are about resolution, the outward sign that finally all has been said and done.

By voicing and sealing the identity of the collective, monuments codify the values of a given time.

Lee Friedlander (b. 1934) comments on America's crowded commemorative landscape in witty photographs such as *Father Duffy* (1974), taken in Times Square. Duffy's memorial, like much urban statuary, competes for attention with traffic, noise, and billboards.

The earliest known written records, Sumerian clay tablets incised with pictographs, contain the seeds of writing

In Egypt, pictographs evolve into hieroglyphics, a monumental language system of word-pictures that cover temples, tombs, clothing, and jewelry

Their meaning, and so their form, shifts and evolves, as is apparent in the chronological overview provided here. Representing a broad spectrum of commemorations erected over two centuries, the works in this book illuminate the issues typically involved in a monument's creation and how the monuments in turn have shaped the national psyche.

Quite a bit of lip service is paid to the difference between the words "monument" and "memorial." The former is more closely associated with large-scale civic works that celebrate a triumphalist history, while the latter speaks to commemorations that are interwoven with death and loss. Since both types mark resolution, and don't speak exclusively of death, life, triumph, or loss, but proffer a message that combines all these elements overlaid with the element of time, I use both terms interchangeably. Because I am interested in how the community, and by extension the nation, perceives monuments, most of the works here presented are large-scale civic works.

One cemetery, Mount Auburn, is included for its innovative design; another, Arlington National Cemetery, for its symbolic importance to the nation. Both acknowledge that the individual headstones and tablets that mark the final resting places of our loved ones move us most profoundly.

The monument-building campaign in the United States today rivals the one that followed the Civil War, when America, having survived a nearly fatal wound to her union, reached a new maturity as a nation. The current proliferation of monuments speaks to our second national maturity, and to the growing awareness that the nation's history, for better or for worse, is worth preserving. Their construction is also a response to the velocity of time. The public no longer hears about tragedies days or weeks later, but often watches them unfold in real time. Our reaction to a sense of out-of-control time has been a profusion of memorials thrown out as anchors, milestones, something, anything, to mark time as it was once understood.

Like everything else, monuments require attention in order to retain their meaning; when neglected, they erode, crumble, and disappear from conscious-ness, if not from view. Grant's Tomb in Manhattan's Morningside Heights—today best known for the old chestnut, "Who's buried in Grant's tomb?" (Grant and his wife, Julia Dent)—attracted upwards of a million visitors annually in its heyday at the turn of the nineteenth century. Now, though beautifully restored, it is largely ignored. Monuments that once stood proudly on a prominent piece of civic property have been relegated by urban development to the sidelines, where they gather trash and graffiti. In his landmark book, *American Monuments,* photographer Lee Friedlander addresses this peculiar invisibility which influences the way we look at monuments today.

The only guarantee of a monument's continuing viability is placement on the National Mall in Washington, D.C. I have included essays on Native American (Little Bighorn Battlefield), Japanese American (Manzanar), and African American (*Amistad* schooner) monuments, each established well after the events they commemorate, but it is impossible to ignore that these constituencies have no official monuments on the National Mall.

Pierre L'Enfant's 1791 plan for the nation's capital, itself a monument, transformed the city into an empty slate waiting for the infant capital's monumental sculpture and architecture. That plan, rich in circles, parks, and spacious boulevards, was overlaid with the 1901 McMillan Plan that made Washington a commemorative city without peer. Of the ongoing debate about "what belongs on the Mall," architectural critic James S. Russell said that what makes that sacrosanct piece of turf "so fine a work of civic art is its resilience; as the Vietnam memorial has shown." That resiliency was tested, if not checked, in 2003 when Congress deemed the Reserve—the great cross-axis of the Mall which extends from the Capitol to the Lincoln Memorial and from the White House to the Jefferson Memorial—to be a "substantially completed work of civic art" and passed legislation that prohibited building new commemorative works there. Exceptions to the law have been subsequently made.

Monuments encompass endings and beginnings. The appropriately phallic Washington Monument honors the father of the nation and the birth of

Monuments beget monuments. Boston's Leonard P. Zakim Bunker Hill Bridge (2003) is dominated by two illuminated wishbone-shaped towers that rise 270 feet (81 m) above the deck and echo the tapering form of the nearby Bunker Hill obelisk. Designed by FIGG Engineering Group and HNTB Corporation after a concept by engineer Christian Menn, the bridge is dedicated to Zakim, a modern civil rights activist, and the Revolutionary War patriots.

Architect Rodney Léon (b. 1969), an African American of Haitian descent, designed the Ancestral Libation Chamber, a memorial to mark what was once the resting place for more than fifteen thousand enslaved and free Africans who historians say lived in New York City from about 1640 to 1795. The African Burial Ground was discovered accidentally in 1991 when the foundation for a new federal building was being excavated in Lower Manhattan. In 1993, the exhumed remains and artifacts of 419 persons were reinterred at the site. Léon's complex and elegant design incorporates elements inspired by African peoples, stories, and cultures. It remembers, Mr. Léon says, "all those who were lost, all those who were stolen, all those who were left behind, all those who are not forgotten." Ground was broken on the memorial in 2005, and it was declared a national monument in February 2006.

the United States. The Vietnam Veterans Memorial, also on the Mall, was the first of many monuments, some new, others revised, that initiated a healing process. The idea that healing can begin once the end is acknowledged and reconciled undergirds this book. Marking a beginning also means that the beginning is over. The completion of the Washington Monument, significantly not finished until the end of the Civil War, signaled the end of the birthing of the new nation.

The role of the temporary memorial is also considered. These temporary works, created in the immediate wake of a tragic event and lost to history once an official memorial is built, are early attempts to reconcile what is to be commemorated, and always influence what is eventually built. The role the temporary memorials of September 11, 2001, have played at Ground Zero parallels the roles of those created at other times and other places of memory, and sheds valuable light on the many issues associated with constructing a permanent memorial.

Daniel Chester French's first major work, *Minute Man* (1871–75), became an icon of monument portraiture.

Attempts to encapsulate an official version of events generate controversy because what is being argued is history itself. The finished monument represents the majority opinion about how an event should be remembered. The process of erecting a monument is strikingly similar no matter what the period or site: Overwhelming consensus that an event should be commemorated is followed by criticism of the bureaucracies charged with selecting a design and of the architects, designers, and artists commissioned to realize it; interminable public discussion and argument follows, much of it acrimonious; the memorial design is dissected, reconfigured, tweaked, adjusted, and,

somehow, miraculously, built. On the dedication day, or sometimes a few weeks later, the controversy is tamped and the monument extolled.

Whether or not one agrees with the aesthetics of the commemoration, the vast majority will accept the monument narrative as "the way things were." Over time, the monument fades into the fabric of the landscape, until one day it disappears and no one sees it anymore. You might say that what is finally built is only a marker of the soul-searching process that brought it into being.

Memorials that today seem benign bordering on the narcotic caused firestorms of controversy while in the planning stages. When the public learned in 1938 that some of the cherry trees in Washington given by the Japanese would have to be removed to make room for the new Jefferson Memorial, it started a "cherry tree rebellion." President Roosevelt himself had to placate women who had chained themselves to the trees, others who recited Joyce Kilmer's "Trees" outside the White House, and even his wife, Eleanor, who penned her opposition in a *Reader's Digest* article. To spare the trees, the site was moved. When the Japanese attacked Pearl Harbor three years later, all thought of their gift disappeared.

Memorials are only built if the public, abetted by the media, places importance on a given tragedy. *Time* reporter Roger Rosenblatt has pointed out that the public nature of the 1995 bombing in Oklahoma City, combined with the desire of many who were not personally affected to commemorate the tragedy, led to the construction of a memorial. There are no monuments at Waco, Texas, he contends, because of general antipathy

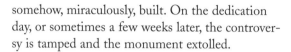

c. 2600 B.C.

Egyptian builders use a try square, a triangular form with 3:4:5 proportions, to make a perfect right angle

c. 2465–2325 B.C.

Egyptian temple accounts, the earliest writing on paper, are written in ink on papyrus, a paperlike material made by laminating strips taken from the papyrus plant toward the fringe ethos of the eighty Branch Davidians who died there on April 19, 1993, nor outside the Happy Land Social Club in the Bronx, where eighty-seven souls, most of them Honduran immigrants, were lost in 1990.

There is something about a monument that wants to be useless. The commemorative function of monuments that do double duty as bridges, hospitals, or libraries is diluted by their practical utility. Yet monuments risk becoming yet another piece of urban furniture, competing with the visual chaos of traffic signals, billboards, cars, and shop windows for our attention. Ordinarily, we don't pay them much attention, but look around you—they are everywhere. Daniel Chester French's *Minute Man* (1875), honoring the Battle of Concord at North Bridge, was a forerunner of

the ubiquitous World War I doughboy statues erected on village greens throughout the nation. Almost a century later, the doughboy figures illuminate the growing importance since World War I of acknowledging the individual's contribution to the cause. As a genre, however, these historical figures do not call our attention to a particular individual or a group, nor even to the Great War, but instead serve as historical markers whose primary function is to remind us that our legacy is to be part of life's continuum.

Monuments have become a staple of cultural tourism that seeks historically enriched travel destinations. Their caretakers must compete with other forms of entertainment and find new ways to engage visitors. In the past decade, a you-are-there intensity pervades the educational experi-

Michael Elmgreen (b. 1961) and Ingar Dragset (b. 1969), Scandinavian-born artists who live in Berlin, collaborate on works about history and memory. *Monument to Short-Term Memory: Robert Indiana Version* (2004) conjures with sardonic humor monuments' inherent contradictions. An oversized restatement of Robert Indiana's *Love*, a staple of the Pop Art era, *Short-Term Memory* parodies the notion of monumentality and, placed in a landscape populated only by unconcerned sheep, the limited attention that monuments command.

SO NIGH IS GRANDEUR TO OUR DUST
SO NEAR IS GOD TO MAN
WHEN DUTY WHISPERS LOW "THOU MUST"
THE YOUTH REPLIES "I CAN"

A skateboarder makes use of the
base of the World War I Monument
(1929) in Providence, Rhode Island,
which is carved with words from
Ralph Waldo Emerson: *When duty
whispers low, "Thou must"/The youth
replies, "I can."*

ence that is frequently provided in proximity to the actual monument. A monument's primary task is to bear witness, yet the storytelling impulse, strong in contemporary monuments, asks us to do something rather than to feel something. Ideally, monuments do not verify, teach, or quench curiosity, but exist solely so that we might, as T. S. Eliot put it in "Little Gidding," "kneel where prayer has been valid."

This educational impulse has changed how monuments are conceived. To engage the visitor's imagination, a wide range of first-person stories have been incorporated into the memorial narrative, many of them influenced by the filmmaker Ken Burns's compelling approach to making history come alive. Some of these narratives challenge us to rethink triumphalist versions of American histo-

ry. Throughout the country, monuments such as the Little Bighorn Battlefield are being built or amended to reflect differing political perspectives.

Building monuments is political, since what is selected to be preserved tells us everything about what is valued by the majority of the population at a given moment in history. Achieving such consensus is becoming increasingly difficult as the prerequisite for public memorialization—a shared set of values—no longer exists. In response to the need to publicly address divergent understandings of history and ways of private remembrance, commemoration design often takes the form of what I call the "compound memorial," a collection of outdoor rooms and experiences that, much like a miniature city, synthesizes elements from the existing urban fabric with newly constructed components. As the

c. 2000 B.C.
Sundials used in Egypt

In 1901, the nation's most eminent architects and artists revised Pierre L'Enfant's 1791 plan for Washington, D.C. The resulting McMillan Plan, illustrated in a 1902 rendering by Francis L.V. Hoppin, transformed the National Mall. The "kite plan" created two axes anchored on each end by national icons: the Capitol, Lincoln Memorial, White House, and Jefferson Memorial.

multipart commemoration in Atlanta's Sweet Auburn neighborhood where Dr. Martin Luther King, Jr., lived makes clear, these ensembles can powerfully evoke a life and a legacy.

My town has been engaged in a heated, years-long argument about moving the Kemper Memorial, a granite slab honoring ninety-nine local residents who died in the Second World War, to make room for a new high school soccer field. The memorial, which has stood for sixty years, is not particularly distinguished; in fact, its nondescript design makes it a poster child for every other generic monument out there. Until recently, it was overlooked except on Memorial Day and Veterans Day, when officials gathered and placed wreaths on it. In the current disagreement, one side argues that sports are important, and in this congested suburb of New York City, there isn't another place for the field. The other side points out that the soldiers' sacrifice ensured the democracy that makes the athletic programs possible. A resolution has not been reached.

What is being argued, though perhaps not consciously, is the nature of sacred ground. No one is buried at the site, nor does it have a battlefield's historic importance. What makes one spot and not another holy? And which do we value more, the past or the future? This particular piece of land is sacred because for decades the sacrifice of the dead has been recalled on that specific spot, and each retelling consecrates it anew. The dispute makes it clear why monuments are so intriguing: Far more than just marble or granite, they are constructs that are created by, and exist most fully in, the human mind and heart.

An R.I.P. mural honoring the rapper Big Pun, who died in 2000, was spray-painted in the Hunts Point neighborhood of the Bronx by TATS CRU, a group of Bronx-based muralists who have raised graffiti into an art form. Memorial walls, such as this one, emerged in the 1980s, primarily in urban Latino communities.

Bringing any abstract vision into being requires humility and courage. When the work of art is a monument or a memorial that must also address the personal and collective need for solace, inspiration, and enlightenment, an even greater challenge exists. Art will always be imperfect; that is the nature of making thought physical, and the nature too of human beings. In the end, what inspires us is the nobility of the quest. Architect Daniel Libeskind, who has fought his own very public collaborative battles, said that building a memorial is the "reverse of what the romantic Germans thought—that the most ethereal art was music and therefore was closest to spirituality. On the contrary, what is heaviest, what is the most burdensome, what is written in stone, gives us a form of liberty."

Monuments express what is most noble and transcendent about human nature. They put forth the goals we aspire to, individually and as a nation, even though we may not attain them. Monuments address our primary and primal concerns as human beings: Why am I here? Where am I going? Will I be remembered?

Monuments urge us to find ways to give meaning to our brief time here and, in the face of loss, to reach for the grace that will allow us to rededicate ourselves to life. They help us perform these necessary psychological tasks. However unfathomably diminished, life goes on. It must, and mysteriously does, continue. This sure truth arrives as I contemplate my son's small hand, an uncanny replica of my own, a hand that will wave in the future.

DESIGN

Page design

We are visual creatures, understanding from birth the world first and best with our eyes, and with language later. Odd, isn't it, that the moment we master reading—a major milestone that deserves reward—illustrations are pruned from our books with punishing rapidity? An ingrained puritanical distrust of beauty lingers. The sheer pleasure of seeing legitimizes the activity, just as an idea gains currency by the simple beauty of its expression. The visual world is my preferred means of deciphering life; an image is just as likely to inspire me as something I read or hear, and these pages reflect that predilection.

To understate it, the way we read text and photographs has evolved quickly since the advent of electronic media. Each page of this book, laden with deep-captioned photographs, floating quotations, and sidebar explorations, is uniquely designed to pay homage to the venerable tradition of the illuminated book and its material presence. Moreover, the page layouts suggest a kinetic reading experience beyond that of turning successive pages, and have been purposely conceived to invite readers to create an experience of their choosing when reading the photographs, essays, and marginal commentaries—just as monuments evoke a similar, highly individualized response.

Timeline

Running through the book is a timeline of events that are related to monuments, time, and memory. Milestones in the history of photography and books are emphasized because they, like monuments, form the collective memory. In fact, the earliest illustrated books were communications between the living and dead. *Chia-ku-wen*, early Chinese calligraphy dating from about 1800 B.C. made by branding shells with red-hot metal, formed messages thought to be communications from the dead, whether gods or ancestors. About two hundred years later, in 1580 B.C., the Egyptians combined pictures and hieroglyphics on papyrus sheets that were the first illustrated manuscripts. Intended to accompany the deceased into the afterlife, *The Book of the Dead*, as they were known, was actually many books that were created for and buried with individuals—guides to the afterlife, heaven on $5 a day, as it were.

Photography

Monuments showcases the work of an international roster of photographers. The photographs run the gamut from Ansel Adams's classic black-and-white documentation of the Japanese internment camp at Manzanar to Steve Miller's painting inspired by traditional memento mori still lifes using X-rays of microbes. One essay examines the ever-expanding role played by photography and the complexity and fluidity introduced by digital photography. The Shaw Memorial narrative is illustrated with the photographs that

caused the existing monument to be modified nearly a century after its dedication.

Photographs relate a powerful narrative, one that seems to help us remember but does not quite say just what transpired. Most of us have had the experience of looking at a group photo ablaze with toothy smiles while recalling the fights that occurred, or the hilarity that played out, just beyond the picture frame. In that quality, photos are much like monuments. Both are mnemonic devices that freeze a moment and trigger its memory—but that memory is open to a host of possible interpretations, all of them subjective and many elusive.

The cover

The mark of the human hand is the first step in creating a monument. Inscriptions that identify those honored or provide uplifting texts are often deeply incised into a memorial, whether an individual headstone or a civic commemoration of great magnitude. Running one's fingertips along a name that has been cut into stone is an innately human and compelling act, a timeless action that transcends language, and the most ancient form of remembrance.

This activity is commemorated in the cover's title letters, which were drawn by Nicholas Benson, of the tenth generation of stone-carvers to work from the John Stevens Shop, established three centuries ago in Newport, Rhode Island. An interview with Benson that follows the World War II Memorial essay, for which he designed and cut the inscriptions, provides insight into this venerable art.

The cover of *Monuments* consists of a collage made from fragments of American landmarks and a photograph of ancient stones taken from villages along China's Yangtze River that will be flooded over once the Three Gorges Dam opens. The cover is ruggedly fabricated to replicate cut stone and underscores the meaning that arises from the physical confrontation with these forms. We attempted not an interpretive but a semantic use of materials and typography. The carved image cannot be duplicated on a computer screen. It can only be experienced when you hold the book in your hands.

Cemetery memorials at the U.S. Military Academy, West Point, include an eagle-topped gazebo honoring Major General Daniel Butterfield, whom some credit with composing "Taps," the haunting air played at military funerals and memorial services. The adjacent, pyramidal tomb is that of Brigadier General Egbert Viele, a West Point graduate and chief engineer of New York's Central and Prospect parks. Before his death in 1902, Viele demanded a buzzer and a light for his vault so that he could call for help in the event of a resurrection; they were finally turned off during World War II, presumably not to the occupant's disadvantage.

c. 1900 B.C.

Stonehenge monumental stone circle built with about twenty bluestones from previous circles at the same site in England

c. 1800 B.C.

The earliest examples of Chinese calligraphy, called *chia-ku-wen* and made by branding shells with red-hot metal, were read as messages from the dead and tied to the art of divination

MONUMENTS

Robert Graham's *Olympic Gateway* (1984) commemorates the Games of the XXXIII Olympiad, held in Los Angeles. It is permanently installed at the entrance to the Los Angeles Memorial Coliseum. The idealized headless figures represent all races and nationalities.

Monuments are our response to the collective need to remember, revisit, and delineate the dreams of history. The best memorials are not mere relics, but extraordinarily rich communications from the past, living history books that illuminate societal, political, and cultural values at specific moments in time. Because consensus about historical events, shared values, and appropriate visual vocabularies is increasingly rare, monuments must find new ways to inspire and console. The unspoken directive today is to read into a memorial what you will.

1792–1750 B.C.

The Code of Hammurabi, 282 divinely inspired laws, is inscribed on oversized stones that are erected in Babylon and other cities

c. 1700 B.C.

Phoenicians produce the first true alphabet containing twenty-two letters

Once proudly ascendant or low and tomblike, the forms of monuments are changing, as are the materials from which they are made. Public works that now are revered created controversy and encountered resistance when their unfamiliar forms were first unveiled. In the last century, abstract art and architecture have allowed designers to sidestep a specific or heroic message. This stance was exemplified by the minimalist design for the Vietnam Veterans Memorial by Maya Lin which, although it met bitter opposition when first proposed, is now recognized as a milestone of commemorative architecture against which future monuments must be measured.

The
Evolving Monument

Similarly, marble and limestone, once sacrosanct materials of Western commemoration, are giving way to ephemeral materials such as light and other nonpermanent elements. The genius of the gay rights activists who conceived of the AIDS Quilt in 1985 was recognizing the quilted form as a way to tap into a familiar yet subversive tradition that has existed for centuries in the shadow of the dominant male culture. Soft, domestic, intimate yet epic, the AIDS Quilt is made of fabric and other materials more vulnerable than stone or steel.

Glass and light have long been employed in buildings to express transcendence, but have been used less frequently in memorial design. Reflective and translucent monuments such as *Luminous Manuscript* as well as the Kennedy Space Center's Astronaut Memorial Space Mirror (1991), which honors the American astronauts who died in the quest to explore space, suggest the wide metaphoric possibilities of glass. Even more ephemeral are works created solely from light, and portable monuments that are no longer rooted in one place.

Above John Lennon's life and music is remembered in Strawberry Fields, a three-acre garden in Manhattan's Central Park that opened on October 9, 1985. A circular black-and-white mosaic with the word "Imagine" in the center of an ancient starburst pattern was a gift from Lennon's fans in Italy.

c. 1580 B.C.

The Egyptians, the first to produce illustrated manuscripts that combine images and hieroglyphics, produce texts on papyrus known as *The Book of the Dead,* to accompany the deceased into the afterlife

c. 1500–1001 B.C.

The Rigveda, the most ancient Hindu sacred verses, are written down

At Chesterwood, his summer home and studio in Stockbridge, Massachusetts, Daniel Chester French created canonical works in the Beaux-Arts tradition, including the Statue of Lincoln for the Lincoln Memorial.

Some memorials exist only in cyberspace, with increasingly popular online sites featuring photos of and quotes from the deceased as well as virtual guest books for recording remembrances. After September 11, 2001, millions gathered online to express grief, prayers, and political commentary. The rapidly emerging Web with its seemingly infinite pages, sites, and hyperlinks allows the world to do what it most often needs in order to heal: talk together.

A rusticated granite pyramid (1869) designed by Charles Dimmock in Richmond, Virginia's Hollywood Cemetery is dedicated to the eighteen thousand Confederate soldiers who are buried there, along with twenty-five Confederate generals.

Recent, heavily publicized competitions have exposed the huge cultural and political stakes at play in the manufacture of monuments. The competition's function is not limited to getting a monument built. In fact, getting something built is often beside the point. Competitions raise public consciousness about what can and should be built, and expand the notion of what is possible. They also promote the idea that the proposed memorial should be funded and help raise funds. Additionally, they fulfill a significant conciliatory role by helping a potential memorial's myriad stakeholders come to terms with the event itself. The World Trade Center Memorial Competition, announced in April 2003, was the largest design competition in history, generating 5,201 submissions from 63 nations, most from nonprofessionals who, despite the low odds of winning, were moved to express their feelings.

PYRAMIDS AND OBELISKS

Ancient builders intuitively understood the first-and-last-on-earth status that stones enjoy. In sites around the world, they artfully unearthed rocks or dragged them into position to amplify the concept of the eternal, of infinite memory, as expressed by stones in the landscape.

They also honored death to an extent unimaginable today. The Egyptians, the Chinese, the Maya, and other classic civilizations were obsessed with the construction of gargantuan funereal structures. Permanence, not life, motivated them. Life was merely a probationary period, a temporal prelude to eternity, and far less important than death.

Today, it is difficult to look at these shells of the past as symbols of eternity. We know too much, for starters, about how they were built, the fading and faults of the civilizations that built them, the erosive vulnerability of stone, and, more recently, the ever-present possibility of instantaneous obliteration.

Pyramidal stone forms never found a wide popular audience in America, a country settled by Puritans who were eager to quickly raise wooden meeting houses and get on with the business of worship. An intriguing exception is the pyramid in Richmond, Virginia's Hollywood Cemetery that is dedicated to Confederate soldiers and generals, including Jefferson Davis, J.E.B. Stuart, and George E. Pickett. The 90-foot (27.4 m) pyramid was built of massive stones positioned without mortar. At the time of its construction, the severe profile of the unadorned stones must have seemed reflective of the hard times experienced in the antebellum South, but those same qualities make it appear powerful and fresh today.

In 1998, artist Krzysztof Wodiczko projected monumental images onto Boston's Bunker Hill Monument and transformed a Revolutionary War memorial into a contemporary statement about the ongoing struggle against tyranny.

Another commemorative form favored by the ancients was the obelisk, a tapering stone column capped with a pyramidal top. Originally, obelisks were used to mark land ownership, usually acquired through force, and evolved into symbols of power. The obelisk's long appeal in the West might be explained by its form. While pyramids hug the ground and look like elements of the earth, the obelisk, like a standing human being, defies the law of gravity. Architect Cesar Pelli, who has built skyscrapers around the world, observed, "Obelisks are an attempt not to recreate the human form, but to recreate the verticality that is the nature of the human form. They are extremely vertical. Humans are tenuously vertical—indeed, if you fall asleep or dead, you're down." Indeed.

The Bunker Hill Monument in the Charlestown area of Boston, Massachusetts, designed in 1825 and dedicated in 1843, presaged the design of the Washington Monument. In September 1998,

however, as part of the Vita Brevis "Let Freedom Ring" program organized by Boston's Institute of Contemporary Art, this historic monument briefly became a contemporary memorial. Conceptual artist Krzysztof Wodiczko projected onto the 221-foot obelisk the faces, hands, and words of Charlestown residents, enlarged to monumental scale, who spoke of their personal experience of violence, freedom, and tyranny. According to the artist, adding human images and voices to the obelisk made its abstract form into a giant figure that spoke freely about the struggle for "life, liberty, and the pursuit of happiness."

TRIUMPHAL ARCHES AND GATEWAYS

Ancient Roman builders developed and mastered the arch, a crucial structural development that was born of the need to construct bridges and aqueducts. Two enormously influential triumphal arches, the Arch of Titus (A.D. 81) at the entrance to the Roman Forum and the Arch of Constantine (A.D. 312–15), located along a processional route between the Colosseum and Palatine Hill, are examples of freestanding barrel-vaulted arches that celebrate military victories.

The much larger Arc de Triomphe (1806–36) in Paris, probably the best-known triumphal arch, is modeled after the Arch of Titus and was conceived by Napoleon to flaunt his imperial conquests. A key cultural and patriotic symbol of Paris, it was seen by the myriad American artists and architects who flocked to Paris in the nineteenth century to study at the Ecole des Beaux-Arts. Upon their return home, they adapted such monuments for American cities, whose residents were demanding new art forms and parks to beautify their public spaces and rival those of the European capitals.

To honor the fallen Union veterans of the Civil War, Brooklyn mayor Seth Low sponsored a competition for a monument to be built on Grand Army Plaza at the northern entrance to Prospect

The centerpiece of Brooklyn's Grand Army Plaza is the Soldiers' and Sailors' Memorial Arch (1892), a colossal triumphal arch designed by John H. Duncan, architect of Grant's Tomb.

Artists Christo and Jeanne-Claude tapped the historic form of the triumphal arch to create *The Gates*, an evanescent artwork installed in New York's Central Park for sixteen days in 2005. *The Gates* updated the concept of traditional stone triumphal arches with brilliant orange curtains hung from 7,500 minimal steel frames.

Top The Gateway Arch in St. Louis, Missouri, was designed in 1965 by architect Eero Saarinen (1910–1961) to mark the nation's westward expansion. At 630 feet (192 m), the arch is the tallest national monument. Shunning the opulent ornament typical of triumphal arches, its beauty arises from its thrillingly minimal structure made of shimmering stainless steel. A classic catenary curve—the form assumed by a chain suspended between two points—the arch frames both the city and the Mississippi River on which it flourished.

Park. Architect John H. Duncan (1855–1929), who would later design Grant's Tomb, won the 1889 commission with a colossal granite Roman-style arch. Civil War general William Tecumseh Sherman laid the Soldiers' and Sailors' Memorial Arch cornerstone in 1889, and the granite arch, 80 feet (24.3 m) high and 80 feet (24.3 m) wide, was dedicated in 1892 "To the Defenders of the Union, 1861–1865." Frederick MacMonnies (1863–1937), an eclectic Brooklyn-born sculptor who apprenticed with Augustus Saint-Gaudens (1848–1907) and then studied at the Ecole des Beaux-Arts, was commissioned in 1894 to create heroic statuary to further adorn the arch. MacMonnies's bronze quadriga, a four-horse Roman chariot and a classic symbol of triumph, was cast in Paris and installed on top of the arch in 1899.

The first purely decorative public architecture in Manhattan—a temporary arch constructed of wood, decorated with papier-mâché wreaths, garlands, and two stuffed eagles, and topped with a wooden statue of George Washington—was designed by architect Stanford White (1853–1906) to commemorate the 1889 centennial of the first president's inauguration in New York City. It proved so popular that plans were put in motion to erect a permanent arch one hundred feet south: Washington Square Arch (1895), an iconic symbol of Greenwich Village,

also designed by White (1853–1906), with much of the ornamentation sculpted by MacMonnies.

Retired Air Force brigadier general Wilma L. Vaught led the campaign to build the only major national memorial honoring the servicewomen of the United States Armed Forces, past, present, and future. Architects Marion Weiss (b. 1959) and Michael Manfredi (b. 1953) transformed the Hemicycle, a decorative semicircular gateway to Arlington National Cemetery, which was designed by McKim, Mead and White and dedicated in 1932 but never completed or used, into a new memorial honoring the more than two million enlisted women who have served the country. The Women in Military Service for America Memorial (1997) exemplifies creative architectural reuse. The memorial reconfigured the existing neoclassical façade and reclaimed its intended role as a ceremonial entrance.

The designers scooped out 37,000 square feet of earth behind the façade for new construction that includes exhibition spaces, an auditorium, conference rooms, a computerized registry, and a Hall of Honor. The most dramatic feature is a canted roof constructed of 138 glass tablets held aloft with minimalist stainless steel mounts that have been inscribed with quotations from women who have served. On sunny days, the inscriptions on the skylight are projected onto and animate the gleaming white marble wall below. The glass ceiling is a metaphor for the struggles of enlisted women to gain recognition for their contributions.

The new memorial taps into the historically significant axial relationships that connect Arlington to the great monuments of American democracy, including the Capitol, the Washington Monument, and the Lincoln Memorial. At Arlington, the women's memorial provides views up the hill to the John F. Kennedy plot, which holds the tombs of the assassinated president, Jacqueline Kennedy Onassis, and those of two of their children, and the eternal flame. That site is itself located on axis with the Arlington House with its plump Greek columns, Robert E. Lee's home for more than thirty years.

Left In an inspired act of commemorative recycling, architects Michael Manfredi and Marion Weiss created the Women in Military Service for America Memorial (1997) by excavating the land behind the existing ceremonial entrance to Arlington National Cemetery.

Above On the roof level of the Women in Military Service for America Memorial, expansive vistas open to endless rows of grave markers set in the rolling Virginia hills that once comprised the estate of Robert E. Lee.

There are three casts of Clark Mills's portrait of Andrew Jackson (1848–53), the first American equestrian statue. This one is the first cast, sited across from the White House.

EQUESTRIAN MONUMENTS

In every war until the First World War, when tanks were introduced, horses were the primary means of military mobility. It naturally followed that military heroes were portrayed in the manner in which they led their troops in the field—on horseback. As horses were replaced with other means of transportation, the time-honored equestrian symbol of leadership faded away, with the exception of the riderless horse, which remains a haunting feature of ceremonial state funerals.

Although it does not always hold true, the standard iconography of equestrian statuary is, generally speaking, this: When a rider is mounted on a horse with all four hooves on the ground, the rider survived the conflict; three hooves indicate the rider was wounded in battle; two hooves, that the rider died during battle; and when the rider stands beside the horse, both horse and rider were killed in battle.

The jaunty statue of Andrew Jackson (1767–1845), a popular war hero and the seventh president of the United States, is shown astride an equally spirited horse. Sculpted by Clark Mills (1815–1883), it is the oldest equestrian statue in the United States. Three copies of the bronze were cast; the first was erected across from the White House in Washington, one stands in Lafayette Square in New Orleans, and the third was placed in the plaza of the state capitol in Nashville, Tennessee.

Mills's accomplishment is made more extraordinary by virtue of the fact that the statue was his first major commission, his first portrait of a horse, and his first large-scale bronze. A self-taught jack-of-all-trades, Mills never went to Europe and preferred naturalistic renderings over more formal portraits. At that time, however, the United States still looked to Europe for its sculpted portraits—the exception being Horatio Greenough's colossal

630 B.C.
Zoroaster, founder of Persian religion, born (d. 546 B.C.)

c. 604 B.C.
Lao-tzu, Chinese philosopher, born (d. c. 531 B.C.); believed to have written earliest document in the history of Taoism

The Other Monument by Judith Shea (American, b. 1948) was a temporary installation sponsored by the Public Art Fund, a New York City–based nonprofit organization that has introduced contemporary outdoor art projects into the civic realm. Displayed on the southern edge of Central Park, Shea's equestrian monument explores what it means to be outside the mainstream societal conventions that defined nineteenth-century commemorations.

Right Meredith Bergmann's Boston Women's Memorial (2003) portrays, from left to right, Lucy Stone, Abigail Adams, and Phillis Wheatley—working American women from the last three centuries who exemplified the ongoing struggle of independent, creative women to break through societal limitations and those of their own imagination.

Below Planners for the Lincoln Memorial first considered installing a replica of the Lincoln statue (1906) by Augustus Saint-Gaudens that graces Chicago's Grant Park.

sculpture of George Washington—not believing that native talent was sophisticated enough. But, as art historian Wayne Craven has noted, when Mills arrived in the capital in the mid-nineteenth century, major sculpture commissions were beginning to trickle down to American artists.

Mills decided to depict the dashing and vital Jackson, "Old Hickory," on a rearing horse, which, because of the difficulty in balancing an extremely heavy, asymmetrical sculpture on two slim hind legs, had never been attempted. It could only be constructed in bronze, a material strong enough to support the sculpture's weight, some of which came from a cannon Jackson had captured in New Orleans. Mills is not remembered for his artistry so much as for his engineering skills and inventive gifts that made his large-scale monuments possible.

ON AND OFF THE PEDESTAL

The elevation of a monument, whether on or off a pedestal, up or down stairs, plays a key role in shaping the viewer's experience. At one time monumental statuary was placed high above the ground to reinforce who was the king or queen, and who was not (you). The trend in contemporary memorial design is to place everything at pavement level to announce the monument's democratic intentions. But, Witold Rybczynski observed, there is nothing like climbing upward to produce a sense of having arrived at somewhere important.

A seated figure was a time-hallowed way in Western art of representing a dead statesman or king. *Seated Lincoln* (1906) in Chicago's Grant Park by Augustus Saint-Gaudens, the canonical portraitist of Lincoln until Daniel Chester French (1850–1931), was so revered that those who planned the Lincoln Memorial first considered replicating the Chicago Lincoln and placing that in the temple on the Mall.

In the decades following the Civil War, American sculptors made a definitive transition away from European subjects and techniques toward an art that was distinctly American. This shift in emphasis, as French's biographer Michael Richman notes, was coupled with the growing technical capability of domestic foundries, which easily moved from making military hardware to the peacetime production of sculpture, enabled by 1874 legislation that permitted confiscated bronze Civil War cannons to be melted for cast sculptures.

551 B.C.
Confucius (K'ung-Fu-tzu), Chinese philosopher, born (d. 479 B.C.)

550 B.C.
Siddhartha (Gautama Buddha, called Sakyamuni), founder of Buddhism, born (d. 480 B.C.)

The country's increasing economic muscle, especially in the victorious North, freed funds for the enthusiastic construction of civic monuments, which, proliferating in towns and villages, inaugurated a golden age of American public sculpture.

In the Boston Women's Memorial by Meredith Bergmann (b. 1955) the bronze figures of First Lady and correspondent Abigail Adams, abolitionist and suffragist Lucy Stone, and poet Phillis Wheatley literally step down from their pedestals and use them as work surfaces. The slightly larger-than-life figures occupy the last empty spot on Boston's Commonwealth Avenue Mall, which is peopled with monumental figures, all of them male. Realizing this, Bergmann decided to rethink nineteenth-century commemorative conventions. With great wit, she subverted the pedestal's traditional aggrandizing role: Her women do not stand in "heroic idleness," but have climbed down to earth and put their plinths to good use. Bergmann writes, "Stone has attempted to subdue and steer her pedestal, Adams leans in companionable, almost spousal co-existence on hers, and Wheatley has made hers into a desk, the object that symbolizes the privacy that she won with her talent while still a slave."

THE PSYCHOLOGICAL MOMENT

The Burghers of Calais (modeled 1884–95) by the French sculptor Auguste Rodin (1840–1917) pioneered the psychologically realistic monument. Commissioned by the French town of Calais in 1884, and Rodin's first major public commission, the cast bronze stands 7 feet 11 inches (217 cm). It depicts the six wealthy burghers, or noblemen, who in 1347 offered themselves as hostages to Edward III, King of England, to end the bloody siege of Calais during the Hundred Years' War. The men are portrayed as penitents, wearing voluminous sackcloths, with ropes around their necks, their feet and heads bare. Rodin portrays them as they leave Calais for their presumed deaths, which they were spared after Edward's wife dreamed their murder would bode ill for her unborn child.

Rodin depicted the men not as heroes idealized on a high pedestal, but as living beings set low on a plinth at a moment of intense psychological awareness. Stripped of their typical finery, the burghers are portrayed as ordinary mortals, fearful and anguished as they leave Calais and proceed to their doom. Even though their bodies are visually intertwined, each twists and turns inwardly in private agony.

Rodin made multiple copies of his many sculptural works. His insistence on replication is regularly debated, although the unparalleled fame and

Of *The Burghers of Calais* (1884–95), sculptor Auguste Rodin is reported to have said to his biographer Paul Gsell, "I have not shown them grouped in a triumphant apotheosis, such glorification of their heroism would not have corresponded to anything real. On the contrary, I have, as it were, threaded them one behind the other, because in the indecision of the last inner combat which ensues between their cause and their fear of dying, each of them is isolated in front of their conscience."

500 B.C.

480 B.C.
An early war monument—raised after 300 Spartans fought to the last man defending the Thermopylae pass against Xerxes' army of 200,000—is inscribed: "Go and tell the Spartans, stranger passing by, / That here, obedient to their laws, we lie."

400 B.C.

400 B.C.
The catapult, the forerunner of modern artillery, invented in Greece

approbation he enjoyed during and after his lifetime are not. He made three casts of *The Burghers* while alive, followed by eight posthumous castings, that are on view in Washington, D.C.; Philadelphia; Omaha, Nebraska; Calais; London; Paris; and elsewhere. As has been noted, the multiple copies of *The Burghers,* mounted in various locations, opened up the notion that a monument did not necessarily have to be planted in one spot. More crucial than location was the intangible yet powerful intention to commemorate.

MULTICULTURAL VISTAS

Nina Akamu created *Golden Cranes,* a gold-plated bronze sculpture that depicts two cranes struggling to free themselves from barbed wire, for the National Japanese American Memorial (2000) in Washington, D.C.

America's monuments are changing as her history is reconsidered from the perspective of those once overlooked, and now reflect the demands that voice be given to those once marginalized. Often these monuments have been particularly divisive because they have required acknowledging the racist and exploitive attitudes that brought them into being.

The *Amistad* schooner, which in 1839 carried away fifty-three free Africans who were later shown to have been illegally enslaved by greedy slave traders, was recreated in 1998 at Mystic Seaport, a century and a half after the incident. A handful of buildings have been restored or recreated at Manzanar, one of ten World War II Japanese internment camps, in order to salvage this dark piece of America's history.

With the addition of a Native American memorial at Montana's Little Bighorn Battlefield, the site redresses the earlier version of the battle and underscores a monument's potential as an instrument of reconciliation. History, although it cannot be rewritten, can be retold in a way that invites all voices and stories into the circle.

SPONTANEOUS MEMORIALS

The spontaneous memorial—a memorial that arises when strangers place personal objects at the actual site of a tragic event or at sites closely related to the event—seems to be a new expression of commemoration, but the practice of leaving offerings has a long tradition in Native American and Hispanic American culture. Now a codified and important part of the commemorative canon, these temporary shrines are indicative of the sea change in how communities mourn and remember.

The first widespread attention paid to such memorials occurred in 1997 after the death of Diana Princess of Wales, when a vast sea of personal tributes were left at the front gates of Kensington Palace, her London home. This commemorative practice was seen earlier at Oklahoma City in 1995, and affirmed by the tragedy at Columbine High School in 1999 and the death of John F. Kennedy, Jr., that same year. Each event inspired massive banks of flowers, notes, and trinkets. Seemingly overnight, the spontaneous memorial had become a new commemorative genre.

In earlier times, when grief was a personal burden, one not borne into the television sets and psyches of all, it was a given that the memorial was a marker, no more or less, of a life. It was understood too that no column of stone,

On February 20, 2003, fire suddenly erupted at The Station, a Rhode Island nightclub, killing a hundred people and injuring more than two hundred. A spontaneous memorial grew along the chain-link fence surrounding the site.

356–323 B.C.

In his brief thirty-two years, Alexander the Great carries Hellenistic culture throughout the ancient world and forms libraries, including a major one in the Egyptian port of Alexandria

351 B.C.

Tomb of Mausolus, Persian satrap, ruler over Caria (c. 376–353 B.C.), completed at Halicarnassus (the first mausoleum)

heroic figure, shard of light, or reflecting pool could begin to approximate the life of the one lost, and monuments were not expected to fulfill that role. With the instant availability of information in quantities once unimaginable, however, we have become virtual albeit temporary participants in tragedies around the globe. The resulting need for cathartic communal ritual has fueled the creation of the spontaneous memorial.

By now we are well familiar with its form: A boundary fence, often chain-linked, is covered with teddy bears, carnations, key chains, American flags, personal notes, and other commentaries that paradoxically achieve universality by their specificity. Such items gather for weeks, and then, after the public has moved on to a new tragedy, these fragile heaps rot, fade, and are carted away. One exception is those items left at the Vietnam Veterans Memorial in Washington, D.C., where non-organic tributes are gathered daily and archived by the National Park Service. Another exception is found in Oklahoma City, where the tributes left on the fence form the basis of an educational program.

The everyday objects piled upon the spontaneous memorial recall the quotidian objects—food, tools, clothing—that were buried with the dead by the Egyptians, who believed such items would ease the afterlife. It would be a stretch to say the key chains and teddy bears will be of use beyond the comfort they provide to those who left them in tribute, but taken as a whole, they represent the gamut of small and necessary objects that define our lives.

TEMPORARY MONUMENTS

This same spirit—of community, impermanence, and speed—has liberated traditional forms of commemoration. Temporary monuments allow almost instantaneous commentaries and expressions of emotion and have been realized in forms that are malleable, easily distributed, and inexpensive to produce. This ease has in turn inspired still more experimentation.

To honor Rosa Parks and the fiftieth anniversary of the Montgomery bus boycott in 2005, the American Public Transportation Association (APTA) electronically distributed artwork that could be printed as posters or seat decals. The APTA encouraged its fifteen-hundred-member organizations to exhibit the poster above the front seat in each bus, and tens of thousands of bus riders took part in the one-day tribute.

Seat dedication in honor of
Rosa Parks
1913-2005

On December 1, 2005, the American Public Transportation Association commemorated the fiftieth anniversary of Rosa Parks's historic refusal to give up her seat on a segregated bus by issuing this decal, a temporary memorial to be affixed to the front seat of a bus for one day.

Newspapers, too, are tools of temporary commemoration. Just as World War II provoked patriotic coverage and unusual page layouts, the attacks of September 11, 2001, extended the boundaries of graphic design. At that time, stores ran out of their stock of American flags in a matter of days, so newspapers printed flags—full-color pages that were ready to clip—to meet the sudden desire to display this symbol; for months afterward, newsprint flags, scorched yellow, were visible in car and building windows.

"Portraits of Grief," more than twenty-two hundred thumbnail profiles of 9/11 victims, ran daily in *The New York Times* from September 15 to December 31, 2001, and continued sporadically into 2003. The profiles featured stamp-size photographs and impressionistic biographies that revealed those lost—traders, firefighters, new parents, gourmet chefs, literary escapists, fanatical golfers—in all their lovable idiosyncrasy. It evolved into a national shrine of sorts.

Every monument—tomb, column, arch, plaque, park—is rooted in past expressions of commemoration. Whether places of glory or grief, constructed of stone or light, all of them over time become creatures of memory. What follows is a look at selected landmark monuments that have evolved from traditional and newer types of commemoration.

343 B.C.
Ch'ü Yüan, earliest of the Chinese poets, born (d. 277 B.C.)

300 B.C.

300 B.C.
Ctesibius of Alexandria invents a water clock, called a clepsydra, to measure time more precisely

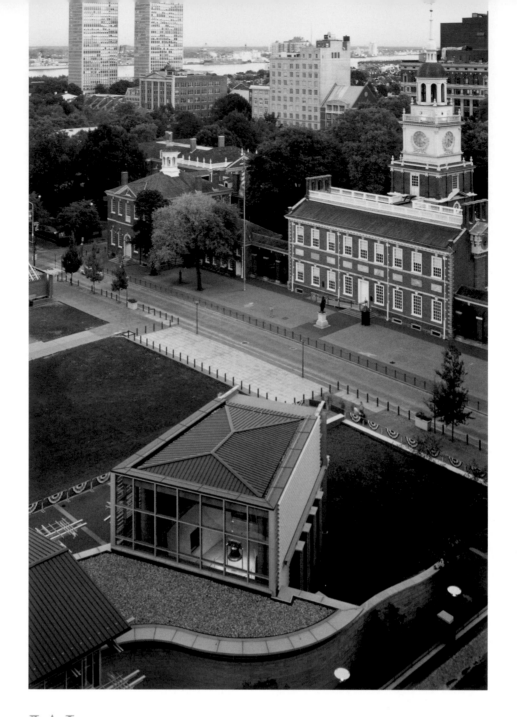

We cannot fully appreciate today the passionate attachment to and dependence on bells in the eighteenth century, when the Liberty Bell was cast at London's Whitechapel Foundry. A bell's powerful impact on communal identity, its marking of both time and space and regulation of nearly every aspect of life, has dribbled away in the last two centuries, its contemporary resonance drowned out by the cacophony of traffic and alarm clocks and the instantaneous availability of news.

The Liberty Bell

LOCATION	DEDICATION	DESIGNER	COMMEMORATION
Philadelphia, Pennsylvania	*1753 and 2003*	*Whitechapel Bell Foundry, Pass and Stow*	*Liberty*

Needing a bell to alert legislators and the public to important events, Pennsylvania Assembly speaker Isaac Norris commissioned one in 1751 from London, asking that the bell be inscribed "Proclaim Liberty throughout all the land unto all the inhabitants thereof Lev. XXV X." The reference to Leviticus 25:10, a biblical passage, was typical of the practice of inscribing, naming, and endowing bells with personalities as distinct as the method in which they were cast—bells at the time were still made from intuitively determined recipes that gave each a unique sound and particular vulnerabilities.

When the bell arrived in Philadelphia in 1752, it cracked with the first stroke of the clapper. It was reforged twice by local artisans John Pass and John Stow, and the next year was hoisted into the belfry of the State House, now Independence Hall. From lip to crown, the bell is 3 feet (0.9 m) tall, with a 12 foot (3.6 m) circumference, and weighs 2,080 pounds. It was forged from a mixture of copper, silver, tin, lead, zinc, and arsenic, with trace amounts of gold, magnesium, nickel, and antimony. It hangs from a wooden yoke made of slippery elm.

Every momentous occasion in the life of the new nation was marked by the statehouse bell. Its sound quite literally penetrated the body, making

physical the emotional reverberation of the events for which it rang. It tolled in 1757 when Benjamin Franklin went to England to seek redress of colonial grievances and in 1761 when King George III ascended to the British throne. The bell tolled in 1764 when the Sugar Act was repealed and again the next year when it called Philadelphians to discuss the Stamp Act. It marked the 1775 battle at Lexington and

In an attempt to repair the 1846 crack, the bell was drilled out, creating the widened, now familiar crack, and rivets were inserted to hold the bell together. Also visible is the spider, a structural brace much like a flying buttress that helps the bell support its own weight. Inset photo by Peter Aaron/Esto.

Concord. It did not ring on July 4, 1776, but four days later, on July 8, when the Declaration of Independence was read to the public for the first time.

Legend has it that the bell's fatal crack occurred in 1846 when it was rung for George Washington's birthday. Although ceremonially tapped from time to time, it never pealed again. From that moment, its utility as a bell ceased, and it assumed its new role as a symbol of freedom. The fracture occurred just as the issue of slavery was gaining visibility. The bell was adopted as a symbol in the 1840s by antislavery groups, who first dubbed it the Liberty Bell in "The Anti-Slavery Record," an 1835 abolitionist pamphlet.

By the end of the twentieth century, Independence Mall had become a three-block swath of mixed messages, an urban hodgepodge of the good, the bad, and the ugly. In the words of Laurie Olin, the landscape architect who was hired in 1997, along with the architectural firm of Bohlin Cywinski Jackson, to create a new master plan for the site, the Mall was "a resounding failure, whether judged as a work of art, a social setting,

urban design or architecture." Olin became absorbed by historic Philadelphia's urban yet pastoral character, its *rus in urbs* (a Latin phrase meaning "the country in the city"), and reconfigured the Mall as a green grove with broad lawns for civic assembly. An ensemble of three new buildings—Liberty Bell Center, Independence Visitor Center, and National Constitution Center—would be placed within the park. Key to the plan's success was the assembly of a group

Right Conceptual drawings illuminate the earliest seeds of ideas. A 1998 drawing by Bernard Cywinski shows the Bell Center's plan, including the colonnade structure and floor crossings that correspond to the city's alleyways. A transitional "hinge" off the central axis angles the bell chamber toward Independence Hall.

Visitors approach the Liberty Bell via a corridor of interactive displays placed along an undulating wall that recalls the serpentine walls Thomas Jefferson designed for the University of Virginia. "Fast" and "slow" lanes were created so visitors can enjoy the exhibits at their own pace.

Irreparably Cracked

A.D.

A.D. 1
The codex form, in which parchment sheets are folded and stitched into pages, begins to supplant the scroll in Rome and Greece

A.D. 43
London founded by Romans

THE DECLARATION.—The Declaration of Independence was adopted Thursday, July 4, 1776, by the Second Continental Congress, which met at Philadelphia, with representatives from the thirteen States (or Colonies) then existing. The first resolution for independence was introduced June 7, 1776, by Richard Henry Lee, of Virginia; and on June 11 a committee, consisting of Thomas Jefferson, John Adams, Benjamin Franklin, Roger Sherman and Robert Livingston was appointed to prepare the Declaration. Jefferson wrote the document, which was originally much more lengthy. It was debated over, altered, amended, and finally passed as we now have it by the unanimous vote of the States present; later (August, 1776) it was engrossed on parchment and signed by all of the fifty-six delegates.

THE LIBERTY BELL.—The old bell which hung in the tower of the State House (now Independence Hall) and which was rung to announce the adoption of the Declaration was cast in Whitechapel, London, and weighed 2,080 lbs. It was brought to this country in 1752 and was broken up and recast in 1753, by Pass & Stow of Philadelphia. It was cracked and hopelessly ruined on the morning of July 8, 1835, while being tolled in memory of Chief Justice Marshall. That it should have had the quotation, proclaim liberty, etc., inscribed on it was a peculiar coincidence. The entire inscription reads: Proclaim liberty throughout all the land, to all the inhabitants thereof, Lev. xxv. By order of the Assembly of the Province of Pennsylvania, for the State House in the City of Philadelphia, 1752.

ALL NATIONS LISTENING
THE TONE OF THIS OLD LIBERTY BELL HAS IMPROVED WITH AGE

of designers, preservationists, and engineers, all of whom knew the city and site well and cared deeply about its future.

On October 9, 2003, the Liberty Bell moved to a light-filled 12,000-square-foot (1,115-square m) building designed by architect Bernard J. Cywinski (b. 1940) of Bohlin Cywinski Jackson. Resisting the urge to replicate Philadelphia's eighteenth- and nineteenth-century architectural traditions, he instead designed a glass, steel, and granite building, with some red brick, that relates to the Georgian-style Independence Hall but primarily responds to the larger themes of memory, diversity, and community. The building consists of three components: a covered outdoor interpretive area, a long rectilinear exhibit hall, and a glass and marble chamber, accessible by day and illuminated at night, that houses the bell itself.

Cywinski's team had to develop a progression of spaces that would inform and entertain visitors and culminate in a memorable experience when one first encountered the bell and Independence Hall. They accomplished this with a masterful orchestration of space and architectural features that subtly set the pacing of the experience and integrated it within its broader urban setting. Everything is distilled to its most minimal expression, inverting the usual formula of making monumental structures as ponderous as pos-

sible to convey the weight of history. The Center's transparency is underscored by the generous window views of the streets and gardens outside, which in turn change and grow.

One does not see the bell immediately. Instead, visitors embark on a journey, emphasized by the gently inclined floor plane, which heightens anticipation and the sense that one is moving through time. A rhythmic colonnade with glass infill supports a copper roof. Woven through the exhibits is an undulating wall that regulates the pace and adds to the serenity of the interior. Cut from Chelmsford granite flecked with mica, the wall catches the sun and sparkles. The content of the interpretive material parallels the spatial sequencing, beginning with eighteenth-century printed texts, followed by objects, photography, and finally electronic displays. The exhibition culminates in the dramatic high-ceilinged bell chamber.

Because the Liberty Bell is no taller than a child, it required housing that was proportioned to its actual physical size as well as its outsized reputation. Additionally, the designers wanted visitors to be able to move around the bell and see it from many vantage points, the most powerful one being the view across to Independence Hall and the spire where the bell originally hung. This view is visible from the moment one steps across the chamber's threshold. Thus aligned with the spire, the bell is not merely an object of singular veneration, but directly tied to the place where the ideals of the Constitution took shape.

The chamber also recognizes the bell's significance as a national icon. Two 14-foot- (4.3 m) high walls, cut from lustrous Carrara marble, cup the bell like protective hands and impart a sense of ceremony as well. Practically speaking, the marble walls bring the tall, 28-foot (8.5 m) ceiling down to human scale. There are no texts in the room to distract from the contemplation of the bell. To minimize echoing, the walls are ever so slightly canted back. That tilt naturally directs the view up toward the Independence Hall spire. Panes of crystal-clear low-iron glass are held in place with glass mullions and "spider" clamps to maximize the view and minimize the

Left To celebrate the sesquicentennial of the Declaration of Independence in 1926, broadsides such as this one set the Declaration in the shape of the Liberty Bell. Brief histories of the Declaration and bell are given side by side on the headstock.

Philadelphia's Independence National Historical Park contains twenty buildings that pertain to the birth of America and the years from 1790 to 1800 when the city was the capital of the United States. The National Constitution Center (2003) celebrates the Constitution that was written, amended, and signed on September 17, 1787, in Independence Hall. Designed by architects Pei Cobb Freed & Partners with exhibit design by Ralph Appelbaum Associates, the Center tells the story of the Constitution in a series of dazzling interactive displays. None has more immediacy than Signers Hall, which allows visitors to walk among life-sized bronze figures of the thirty-nine delegates who signed the Constitution as well as the three who dissented. Standing shoulder to shoulder with the delegates makes concrete the fundamental ideal of a nation created by and for the people.

boundary between the bell chamber and the outside world.

Controversy erupted when the public learned that visitors would enter the new building by walking over the unmarked slave quarters of the house at Sixth and Market streets where George Washington had lived while the city was the nation's capital; the president's house was demolished in the 1830s. Little had been said publicly about the nine slaves in Washington's Philadelphia household, and the Park Service, charged with "perpetuating historical amnesia," agreed to expand the Center's displays to include exhibits on the historical relationship and interdependence between slavery and freedom, as well as immigration and the treatment of women. In 2005, plans moved forward to build a slavery memorial.

Underscoring the Center's celebratory exhibits are sober reminders that the bell is a "symbol of liberties gained and a reminder of liberties denied." The bell was exhibited around the country after the Civil War, when the riven nation was hungry for symbols of its hard-won unity. It traveled to New Orleans in 1885, Chicago in 1893, Atlanta in 1895, Charleston in 1902, Boston in 1903, St. Louis in 1904, and San Francisco and San Diego in 1915.

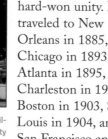

For the Bicentennial, architect Romaldo Giurgola designed a jaunty glass pavilion that housed the bell from 1976 until 2003, when it was made into a security checkpoint. This modernist gem was demolished in March 2006. Parts of it were salvaged and will become part of a new memorial park in Anchorage, Alaska.

After that spate of road trips, the bell did not travel again. Instead, it was replicated. For starters, every state has its own Liberty Bell. In 1950, the U.S. Department of the Treasury cast fifty-five full-sized replicas of the bell which were given as gifts to American states and territories as part of a savings bond drive held that same year; most are displayed at Capitol buildings.

The bell became a symbol of the struggle for suffrage. Katharine Wentworth Ruschenberger, a Philadelphia Main Line dowager, commissioned the "Justice Bell," a replica of the Liberty Bell, that would not ring until women won the right to vote. As she told *The New York Times*, "The original Liberty Bell announced the creation of democracy, the women's Liberty Bell will announce the completion of democracy." Pennsylvanian suffragists crisscrossed their state with the bell, its clapper chained to its side, during the summer of 1915, urging men to vote for women's right to do the same. Once the Nineteenth Amendment was finally adopted on August 26, 1920, the Justice Bell tolled in Independence Square. Shortly afterward, the Justice Bell was abandoned. Restored and rededicated in 1997, it is now displayed in the Washington Memorial National Carillon and Patriots' Tower at Valley Forge.

To commemorate the sixtieth anniversary of the United States landing at Normandy during World War II, a ringable replica of the Liberty Bell was created using laser imaging technology to capture the exact shape and sound structure of the original. Located outside l'Abbaye aux Dames in Caen, France, the Normandy Liberty Bell was rung on June 6, 2004. The bell's E-flat note can be heard online, as Benjamin Franklin once heard it, at ushistory.org/libertybell/more/normandybell.htm.

The Philadelphia icon symbolizes both patriotism and protest, bell but also bellwether of the democratic process. It is not a commemorative marker but the bell itself, the authenticity of which is paralleled in the design of its new home. The Liberty Bell Center possesses a clarity of purpose that reinforces an understanding of the bell's historic function and democratic vision that unites diverse people and opinions.

A.D. 105

Chinese dynastic records attribute paper's invention to Ts'ai Lun, whose process for papermaking remains nearly unchanged until the nineteenth century

C. A.D. 114

Rome celebrates its imperial victories with masterfully inscribed monuments such as Trajan's column that testify to their dictum, "the written word remains"

The bell chamber is sheltered with window louvers and an extended roof that shields it from the sun.

By aligning the bell chamber with Independence Hall, designers were able to show the Liberty Bell against the historic backdrop of its former home. Photographed by Peter Aaron/Esto.

A.D. 121

Marcus Aurelius, Roman emperor, born (Apr. 26; d. A.D. Mar. 17, 180)

A.D. 165

Confucian classics begin to be carved into stone tablets to ensure a permanent record. Because of their weight, copies of their inscriptions are made with ink rubbings

*The grave hath a voice of eloquence, nay,
of superhuman eloquence . . . which addresses
all times, and all ages.*
—Joseph Story, remarks at dedication of Mount Auburn Cemetery, 1831

A.D. 190

Column of Marcus Aurelius, Rome, erected by
Commodus, depicting Marcus Aurelius' northern campaigns

Mount Auburn
Cemetery

LOCATION	DEDICATION	DESIGNER	COMMEMORATION
Watertown and Cambridge, Massachusetts	*1831*	*Henry A. S. Dearborn, Jacob Bigelow, and others*	*Deceased individuals*

Before Mount Auburn Cemetery opened in 1831, America's dead were not so much laid to rest as they were stockpiled, one on top of another, in fetid, unsightly tracts of land. Flat stretches of unadorned real estate were studded with simple stone markers, lacking trees, bushes, or flowers to mitigate either the landscape or mourning itself.

These yards of graves were part of the city proper, embedded in neighborhoods where Bostonians lived, worked, and played. Worse than the odor of rotting corpses, however, was the suspicion that the graveyards were a breeding ground for disease. Medical opinion at the time held that foul smells and gases emanating from graveyards could trigger an epidemic. Timothy Dwight, an early president of Yale College, summed up the situation in his *Travels in New England and New York:* "The memorials of the dead are presented to the mind in circumstances so gross and indicative of so little respect in the living as to eradicate every emotion naturally excited by the remembrance of the deceased."

By the early 1800s, Boston's three original burial grounds were filled to bursting, making it sometimes necessary for gravediggers to shuffle coffins around to make room for new arrivals (if one of these coffins broke open in the process, and its contents tumbled out, that was unfortunate). Adding to the indignities were roaming vandals who stripped

Mount Auburn features more than six thousand foreign and native trees, which together represent six hundred species. The cemetery's lush vegetation make it a popular place for birds and bird-watchers alike. It also includes a crematory, an observatory tower, green-houses, and two chapels that exist in communion with natu-ral features such as wood-lands, ornamental gardens, rocky moraines, and lakes. A nonprofit organization main-tains the cemetery, which is open to the public 365 days a year, and, through its Friends organization, offers educa-tional and cultural programs.

bodies of jewelry, clothes, and gold-filled teeth. The dead didn't get much respect. This attitude is not surprising, given that the Puritans who founded Massachusetts believed death was something to be feared, not memorialized.

A headstone is the closest thing to a personal monument most of us will ever have. It records the common measure of when and where we lived, when we married, what we accomplished. What remains of us is our memory, fragile, malleable, and often forgotten. Like these memories, the markers erected to our lives are a means of transforming grief that soon enough erode and become nothing more or less than a rock. Yet our essential truths that only we know—our secret history—will die with us. Like pharaohs, we take our treasures with us into the earth.

It took five years of dedicated campaigning by Bigelow and other Boston Brahmins, that city's intellectual and financial elite, to make the cemetery a reality. Their effort was rooted in a broader social movement to improve city life, which was beginning to suffer from overcrowding and poor sanitation in the early nineteenth century.

More than 93,000 people are buried at Mount Auburn. They include many remarkable Americans, among them the poet Henry Wadsworth Longfellow (1807–1882); painter and illustrator Winslow Homer (1836–1910); author and reformer Julia Ward Howe (1819–1910); Pulitzer Prize–winning author Bernard Malamud (1914–1986); inventor, designer, and visionary Buckminster Fuller (1895–1983); and escaped slave and author Harriet Jacobs (1813–1897).

In 1822, a frustrated Mayor Josiah Quincy of Boston proposed closing the city's graveyards to new burials. But where would the bodies go? Enter Dr. Jacob Bigelow, a Boston physician and Harvard professor, whom history credits with ushering in a new movement for burying the dead in this country. Influenced by the opening of Paris's now-famous Père Lachaise Cemetery, Bigelow proposed creating a burial ground four miles west of Boston in a wooded tract of rolling farmland that straddled the towns of Watertown and Cambridge. Harvard students, who often strolled and studied there, called it "Sweet Auburn," after the village in "The Deserted Village," a poem by Oliver Goldsmith, and the nickname evolved into "Mount Auburn" by the time the 175-acre cemetery was dedicated in 1831.

Bigelow extolled the virtues of nature during this public relations campaign, tapping into a romanticism that was beginning to sweep the country and which would come to full flower a few decades later during the Victorian Age.

Indeed, nature and its consoling power set Mount Auburn Cemetery apart from the graveyards that preceded it. The idea was to create a setting that would uplift the living as well as honor the dead in a landscape where horticulture, sculpture, and architecture combined with the beauty of God's natural vistas would soothe the grieving. That other Bostonians would also flock to the cemetery for much-needed respite from the grit and congestion of urban life was an added benefit. And flock they did. Upon opening on September 24, 1831, Mount

Auburn Cemetery became a popular destination and one of Boston's major tourist attractions.

"Have you ever been to Mount Auburn?" Emily Dickinson gushed in a letter. "It seems as if Nature had formed the spot with a distinct idea in view of its being a resting place for her children." And later, perhaps her memories of Mount Auburn inspired her to invoke not angels but that most natural of nuisances in one of her great opening lines, "I heard a fly buzz when I died."

To create the cemetery, Bigelow joined forces with Henry A. S. Dearborn, president of the newly formed Massachusetts Horticulture Society. Dearborn designed Mount Auburn using eighteenth-century English gardens for inspiration. The result was a series of winding paths and roads that complemented the site's varied topography. Dearborn planted some trees, but otherwise left the landscape alone. His goal was to delicately embellish nature, not boldly rearrange it.

styles that were popular when the cemetery opened, to Victorian angels, to the simple beauty of a stone bench sheltered under a canopy of trees. New landscape designs are added on occasion, since the cemetery is still active, with more than 650 burials a year. Effort is made to ensure that the new complements the old and that the basic rural and garden feel of the cemetery is maintained.

In another trendsetting development, Mount Auburn's founders insisted that its grounds be nonsectarian and open to all. This was an important and, arguably, progressive requirement in a city whose population became increasingly diverse in the nineteenth century. The movement away from a bleak, religious view of death to one that was more liberal and secular is also apparent in its large neoclassical monuments and sculptures. They celebrated the life of the deceased and, if the person was well known, often served as public monuments as well as private memorials.

Today, there are more than thirty thousand monuments at Mount Auburn, reflecting a range of styles from the Egyptian Revival and neoclassical

Mount Auburn was the first large-scale designed landscape open to the public in the United States. It preserves a "remarkably illustrative chronicle of American landscape design, attitudes toward death and commemoration, aesthetic and spiritual values, material culture and changing technology," as its nomination to the National Register of Historic Places states.

The garden or "rural cemetery" movement, as it is known in the United States, ushered in a new age of respect for the dead and raised awareness of the need for open green spaces and parks for the living.

Once Mount Auburn opened, other cities quickly followed suit. Mount Auburn influenced the creation of such notable cemeteries as Laurel Hill (1836) in Philadelphia, Swan Point (1846) in Providence, and Oak Hill (1848) in Washington, D.C.

C. A.D. 325

Christianity, adopted as the Roman state religion, elevates the importance of books and graphic format as symbols of religious belief

A.D. 337

Constantine the Great dies

The
Alamo

Remember the Alamo!

LOCATION	DEDICATION	DESIGNER	COMMEMORATION
San Antonio, Texas	*1836*	*Unknown;* *Ford, Powell & Carson*	*Battle of the Alamo*

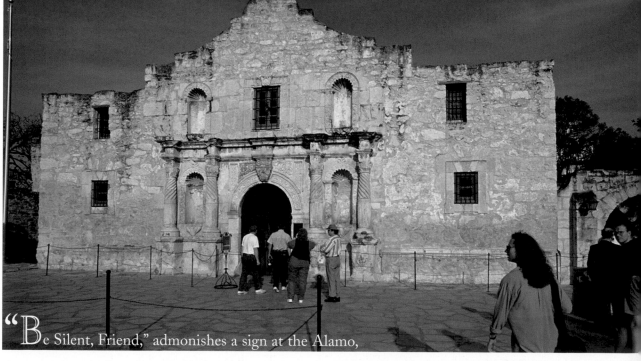

Alice Wingwall, the conceptual artist who took this photograph of the church façade, was not always blind. After losing her sight, the artist continued to shoot photographs, relying on memory, touch, smell, and sound. Her photographs provoke vital questions about what it means to "see" and how, once something has been seen, it is remembered. Is vision tied only to one sense, or is it, like memory, a collection of impressions from all the senses leavened over time? Like memory, vision takes place in the brain and is less tethered to physical sight or a physical object than we might imagine.

"Be Silent, Friend," admonishes a sign at the Alamo, "here heroes died to blaze a trail for other men." Hats must be removed and cameras put away. San Antonio's Alamo, also called the Shrine, Cradle, and Altar of Texas Liberty, is both monument and tourist destination, and the most sacred ground in the Lone Star State. The thirteen-day battle that took place there, its heroes and aftermath, continue to occupy a Texas-sized portion of the American imagination.

Holed up there with a band of ragtag "Texian" defenders on February 24, 1836, William Barret Travis, a young lawyer turned soldier, wrote one of the classic letters of American history, which was carried by a courier past the Mexican troops outside the compound. Addressed to the "People of Texas and all Americans in the world," the letter is reproduced on a bronze plaque at the site:

Fellow citizens & compatriots—I am besieged, by a thousand or more of the Mexicans under Santa Anna—I have sustained a continual Bombardment & cannonade for 24 hours & have not lost a man—The enemy has demanded a surrender at discretion, otherwise, the garrison are to be put to the sword, if the fort is taken—I have answered the demand with a cannon shot, & our flag still waves proudly from the walls—I shall never surrender or retreat. Then, I call on you in the name of Liberty, of patriotism & everything dear to the American character, to come to our aid, with all dispatch—The enemy is receiving reinforcements daily & will no doubt increase to three or four thousand in four or five days. If this call is neglected, I am determined to sustain myself as long as possible & die like a soldier who never forgets what is due to his own honor & that of his country—Victory or Death.

In December 1835, San Antonio, which had been occupied by Mexican troops under General Martín Perfecto de Cós, fell to the Texians, as residents of Texas were called throughout the period of the Texas Republic. However, on January 17, 1836, Texian army commander Sam Houston ordered Jim Bowie and his men to destroy the Alamo and withdraw to a more defendable position. Instead, Bowie fortified the Alamo.

Intent on recapturing it, Gen. Antonio López de Santa Anna arrived with his army on February 23, 1836. Bowie, a seasoned fighter but deathly ill, ceded command to Travis, whose garrison included Davy Crockett, the famed frontiersman. Most place the number of Alamo defenders at 189, a fraction of their enemy's strength. Legend has it that Travis drew a line in the sand and asked those who would fight to step over; all but one did. This is the story's keystone moment when all united as one. True or not, that line is now memorialized as a bronze strip set into the pavement in front of the church.

After thirteen days of siege, Santa Anna's men scaled the walls, blasted open the church's barricaded doors, and slaughtered those inside. Spared were some women and children, including one Susanna Dickinson, who was released with a letter of warning from Santa Anna for Sam Houston.

Word of the massacre electrified the Texian cause. Two months later, shouting "Remember the Alamo!" Houston's army defeated Santa Anna at the Battle of San Jacinto, forcing the Mexican general to relinquish Texas. His life spared, Santa Anna signed the Treaty of Velasco on May 14 and secretly pledged to use his influence to secure Texas independence from Mexico, though Mexico would not recognize that independence until 1848. Houston became president of the new republic and, ten years after applying for statehood, Texas was admitted into the United States in 1845.

Founded by Franciscan brothers, the Mission San Antonio de Valero, today known as the Alamo, was the first of five missions constructed in San Antonio. Much of the Alamo is reconstructed. Only the church and pieces of the *convento* (now the Long Barrack) are original. Most memorable is the limestone church's ornately carved façade with its spiraled columns, arched doorway, and distinctive curved gable, which was added in 1850. The *convento* was the first permanent structure of the mission, built between 1724 and 1727, and had a Spanish colonial design typically built by the Franciscans on the Texas frontier. Living quarters for the missionaries, the enclosed compound also included a two-story arched cloister.

The church was erected in 1744 but never completed. According to Fray Juan Augustín de Morfi in 1777, the original church was being built again with the "solidity and perfection that is required for its beauty and to sustain the vaults." A new church was built on the same spot, but that too was roofless and crumbling when the battle took place. The mission was secularized in 1793

The perimeter of the original mission property was erased long ago by new development, but is marked with stone pavers set into the surrounding sidewalks.

and leased to the U.S. Army for use as a military outpost. The Alamo changed hands many times over the next seven decades. Upon learning that it was to be demolished, a group of preservation-minded women (who would become the Daughters of the Republic of Texas) acquired the Long Barrack in 1905.

Nestled in the heart of downtown San Antonio, the Alamo strikes one initially as being far smaller in actuality than it is in legend. It is difficult to imagine it as a desolate outpost, although the sight of the stone ruins amid the surrounding office buildings reinforces its romance. The area

The property contains extensive gardens lush with botanical specimens, many given as commemorative gifts.

A.D. 400

A.D. 410
Alaric, king of the Visigoths, captures and sacks Rome

around the mission has been developed for over a century, obliterating the original footprint and requiring the re-creation of much of the 4.2-acre site that remains. Only the church and Long Barrack are original, and they have been renovated,

A Moment in Time by Gary Zaboly depicts the Alamo at dawn, under siege and in flames, on March 6, 1836. The church, with its thick walls and spare, vaulted interior, actually saw little action—the battle took place in the sprawling walled compound that abuts it—but "Alamo" has come to refer to that one building.

The *Alamo Cenotaph* (1939) honoring the battle heroes was carved by Pompeo Coppini (1870–1957) and dedicated in 1940 to commemorate the centennial of Texas's independence.

most notably with the U.S. Army's 1850 additions and the 1913 removal of the Long Barrack's second story. The restored convento, where most of the hellish fighting occurred, was rededicated in 1968 as the Long Barrack Museum. In 1985, the architectural firm of Ford, Powell & Carson designed a master plan for the site and supervised its restoration.

Although almost two hundred men died in the conflict, the names of three have lived on: Davy Crockett, Jim Bowie, and William Barret "Buck" Travis. William C. Davis's biography of their lives shows that the trio went to Texas as failures hoping to begin anew: Crockett had lost his bid

for reelection to Congress; Bowie, famed for his handiwork with the eponymous knife and described by Davis as "just over half dishonest," was a forger and land thief; and the vainglorious Travis, although only twenty-six, had managed to rack up impressive losses in law, publishing, and marriage before arriving in San Antonio. Theirs is a redemptive tale of facing unwinnable odds, mirroring the larger myth of America as a place for second chances.

The Alamo mystique was enhanced when Hollywood turned out *Davy Crockett at the Alamo* in 1955, the film that made the coonskin cap a must-have accessory for every child in America, and reprised the story five years later in *The Alamo*, directed by and starring John Wayne as Crockett. Of the Wayne movie, Frank Thompson wrote in *Alamo Movies*, "There isn't an instant in the film that corresponds to the historical event of 1836 in any way, except coincidentally."

The late paleontologist Stephen Jay Gould, an unlikely Alamo aficionado, contended that our favorite stories, especially ones like the Alamo's, help make sense of confused, often tragic events in a complex world. We are irresistibly drawn to stories that proceed logically, although finding order in the universe is sheer luck of the draw, and tend to leave out those parts of a tale that do not fit with the main story line. Monuments order history in similar ways. Had Jim Bowie not been too ill to negotiate with Santa Anna, the story of the Alamo might have ended differently. Instead, the fate of 189 men fell to Travis, whose hotheaded decisions were later reframed as valorous duty in the face of certain death. It makes for a much better story, the one that is now told in San Antonio.

Santa Anna slaughtered most of those hiding in the chapel and its ancillary rooms, indicated on the blueprint.

Freedom Schooner
Amistad

LOCATION	DEDICATION	DESIGNER	COMMEMORATION
New Haven, Connecticut	*1836, replica 2000*	*Unknown; restoration by Mystic Seaport*	*Amistad revolt of 1839 and U.S. Supreme Court decision of 1841*

La Amistad, the small wooden schooner that launched a chain of events from Africa to New Haven and back and changed American history, was last known to be in the Caribbean in 1844 and has never been found. After extensive archival sleuthing to determine the boat's structure and size, Mystic Seaport shipwrights spent two years reconstructing a seaworthy version of the original. The story of the recreated Freedom Schooner *Amistad,* a uniquely interactive monument, as well as one that floats, illuminates how lost pieces of history can be retrieved, redressed, and retold to new generations.

This story begins in April 1839 in West Africa, where fifty-three Africans from Mendi (present-day Sierra Leone) were captured, forced aboard the slave ship *Teçora,* and deplorably treated for two months on open seas.

Amistad's first master, Captain William Pinkney, the only African American to circumnavigate the globe solo by sail via the southern ocean route under Cape Horn, led efforts with Warren Marr to realize the dream of Amistad.

The moment you come to the Declaration of Independence, that every man has a right to life and liberty, an inalienable right, this case is decided.
—John Quincy Adams, argument before the Supreme Court, February 24, 1841

Upon landing in Havana, the Africans were sold and loaded onto *La Amistad*. Spanish plantation owner José Ruiz bought the forty-nine adult males, paying $450 for each, and Pedro Montes, another planter, bought three girls and one boy. Ruiz and Montes had obtained fraudulent passports that indicated the Africans were "ladinos," or legal slaves born in Spanish territory. Within three days of setting sail, the Africans revolted, led by twenty-five-year-old Sengbe Pieh, called Joseph Cinque by his Spanish captors. Killing two, they took control of the boat. Thwarted in efforts to return to Africa, they were eventually seized by the American Navy. The survivors were jailed in New Haven to await trial for murder and piracy.

The prisoners' cause was taken up by New York businessman Lewis Tappan (1788–1863), a leader of the growing, divisive, and sometimes violent movement to abolish slavery. Among many publications, Tappan founded the *Emancipator*, an abolitionist weekly. That paper and others vociferously debated the pros and cons of slavery and kept the issue of abolition at the forefront of the news.

Below The Amistad Memorial Foundation commissioned sculptor Ed Hamilton (b.1947) to create the Amistad Memorial (1992), a bronze sculpture at the site of New Haven's City Hall, to mark the spot where the Africans were jailed awaiting trial. The three-panel work depicts Sengbe Pieh in Africa; a scene from the trial; and Sengbe, portrayed as Joseph Cinque in Western clothing, ready to board a ship back to his homeland.

Above Owned and operated by the non-profit AMISTAD America organization, under the direction of Captain Eliza N. Garfield, the *Amistad* visits ports internationally as an ambassador of goodwill and provides innovative educational programs onboard.

Right Wojtek Wacowski, whose maritime photographs grace these pages, and who lived on the *Amistad* for nearly a year, fully subscribes, like most tall-ship sailors, to the sentiment of Honoré de Balzac in *Old Goriot*: "There is no more beautiful sight than a frigate in full sail, a galloping horse, or a woman dancing." He recalled a group of elderly women who came on board and took off their shoes. They stepped onto the king plank—the widest, central plank in the deck that is made of iroko wood from Sierra Leone—and said that walking on that piece of wood barefoot allowed them to connect to the spirit of Africa, the land of their ancestors.

"MAKE US FREE"

C. A.D. 612

Islam emerges from the teachings of the prophet Muhammad. Followers embrace aniconism, an opposition to the figurative representation of living creatures, thus lifting calligraphy to transcendent levels of sacred expression

The Mende languished in New Haven. Speaking no English, they were powerless to defend themselves and would have been doomed if not for the ingenuity of a professor of ancient languages at Yale. Josiah Willard Gibbs learned to say numbers from one to ten in rudimentary Mende and wandered the docks of New York City reciting them until Mende speaker James Covey overheard him. Covey translated for the Mende, who were overjoyed to be able to tell their story.

On September 19, 1839, the first round of trials began in the U.S. Circuit Court in Hartford to untangle the case's myriad issues of criminal law, property law, admiralty law, and jurisdiction. The courtroom was jammed with those for and against the Mende, including Yale Law and Yale Divinity students who held on to their seats, even during long recesses, so as not to lose their places. The trial lasted until January 13, 1840, when it was ruled that the Africans had been illegally enslaved and they were ordered to be returned to Africa. The proslavery Van Buren administration, keen to stay in the good graces of Southern voters, appealed the decision.

With biting sarcasm and persuasive eloquence, former president John Quincy Adams defended the *Amistad* captives before the Supreme Court, which on March 9, 1841, affirmed the Africans' freedom. The Mende then moved to Farmington, Connecticut, and on November 27, having raised the money to return home, they did so.

Warren Q. Marr II, a leading advocate for the preservation of African American history, spearheaded efforts to rebuild the *Amistad.* While attending Operation Sail 1976, a spectacular Bicentennial gathering of tall ships in New York harbor, Marr saw a replica of *La Amistad,* actually the schooner *Western Union* that had temporarily been renamed for the event. He became determined to tell the Mende's story aboard a craft that would sail from port to port and provide lessons that would promote racial unity.

It took two dozen years of painstaking investigation to recreate the original ship's plans. That boat had been auctioned off to Rhode Islander George Howland, sailed to the Caribbean, sold in 1844, and not heard of again. Beginning in 1998, the *Amistad* was reconstructed over two years at the Mystic Seaport shipyard under the direction of master shipwright Quentin T. Snediker, who also led the exceptional research efforts.

The new *Amistad* was built using construction techniques common to nineteenth-century shipwrights, as well as modern technology. California-based Tri-Coastal Marine created the boat's plans digitally, incorporating twin diesel engines for auxiliary power and state-of-the-art navigational instruments. With a length from bowsprit to end of boom of 129 feet (39.3 m), the *Amistad* is 10 feet longer than the original *La Amistad* to accommodate the engines. Most of the ship's major elements were made of live oak and white oak. Purpleheart, a dense tropical hardwood harvested in Guyana, South America, under sustainable forestry management practices, was used for the hull construction. The two masts are carved from Douglas fir. Some of the deck's framing is made from iroko, a durable hardwood that was a gift from the government of the Republic of Sierra Leone.

Steven Spielberg's 1998 film about the *Amistad* revolt, the Hollywood equivalent of a marble monument, did much to bring the rebuilding efforts to the public's attention. Although Spielberg's interpretation has been questioned, the film realistically portrayed the Middle Passage, the agonizing journey from Africa endured for weeks in grim deprivation without adequate food or water in the holds of slave ships.

On March 26, 2000, the boat's launching ceremony began with the tolling of a bell fifty-three times in honor of the *Amistad* captives. A bottle containing water from Sierra Leone, Cuba, and New Haven was broken across its bow, cannon fire boomed from the nearby tall ship HMS *Rose,* and six white doves were released to freedom before the wooden ship was lowered into the Mystic River. Preceding the Civil War by two decades, the *Amistad* incident was one of the first human rights cases successfully argued at U.S. Supreme Court level on behalf of people of African descent, and it led to the reforms that allow scholars and students today to interpret American history more inclusively.

Amistad at her birthplace, Mystic Seaport, in Connecticut. *Amistad* is not an exact replica but a re-creation of the original vessel, which was built in Cuba in 1836.

A.D. **632**
Muhammad, founder of Islam, dies (b. A.D. 570)

Over the course of the Civil War from 1861 until 1865, 2.9 million soldiers, nearly one in every ten Americans at the time, fought over eighteen states and territories. Some 10,455 military actions took place, from titanic battles to smaller raids and skirmishes, and exacted more than 620,000 lives. The fratricide's many names—the War Between the States, the War Against Northern Aggression, the Second American Revolution, the Cause, the Lost Cause, the War of the Rebellion, the Brothers' War, the Late Unpleasantness, the War of Attempted Secession—testify to its wounding divisiveness and the long pull it has exerted on the nation's civic imagination.

Above Pickett's Charge, shown from the Confederate position, is a wide-open field across which twelve thousand Confederate infantrymen advanced in chaos into a wall of Union fire.

No arena of this conflict is more renowned than Gettysburg, a small Pennsylvania town that witnessed the bloodiest engagement on American soil: There were an estimated fifty thousand casualties, of which eleven thousand were killed, twenty-nine thousand wounded, and ten thousand captured or missing. Five times as many Americans died there as on Normandy's beaches on June 6, 1944. The battlefield's key landmarks, both cultural and natural, were preserved because the significance of what transpired there was apparent almost immediately. Thus christened, its land was staked for posterity—with primitive wooden markers that were replaced with granite monuments, with photographs that captured the landscape and were multiplied a hundredfold, and with words that addressed the "birth of freedom" in a nation that was no longer new but newly mature. Over time these meanings would evolve into what Robert Penn Warren described as the "very ritual of being American," but the essential monument of Gettysburg existed, if not at the precise moment of conflict, within weeks of its ending.

Gettysburg
National Military Park

LOCATION	DEDICATION	DESIGNER	COMMEMORATION
Gettysburg, Pennsylvania	*1863, 1895*	*Various*	*Battle of Gettysburg*

At no other time was the South closer to victory than in June 1863. At the end of that month, Confederate commander Robert E. Lee was at Chambersburg, Pennsylvania, where he learned that the Army of the Potomac was marching northward. Approaching Gettysburg from the Chambersburg Pike on July 1, the Confederates encountered the distinctive black hats of the famed Iron Bridge, a unit of troops from Michigan, Indiana, and Wisconsin. This unexpected skirmish escalated into a full-scale battle. By the afternoon of July 2, the full strength of both armies, an estimated ninety thousand Union and seventy-five thousand Confederate troops, was on the field. Lee was positioned on Seminary Ridge. Less than a mile away, General George Meade's men waited

Left With the reconciliation flowing from the 1913 reunion at Gettysburg, the southern states began to erect single-state memorials. Virginia erected the first, an equestrian portrait sculpted by F. William Sievers of Lee astride Traveller, in 1917.

This Alexander Gardner photograph taken on July 15, 1863, is the only early photograph to show the terrain between Little Round Top and Cemetery Hill. Looking north from the crest of Little Round Top, visible landmarks include the Wheatfield Road between the boulder and large tree to the right; Weikert's farm, on level with the top of the boulder; Ziegler's Grove, left center on the horizon; and the woods near Evergreen Cemetery, right center on the horizon.

on Cemetery Ridge, a fishhook of land that stretched for three miles between Cemetery Hill and Culp's Hill. The violent fighting that ensued carved into history names such as Little Round Top, Devil's Den, Spangler's Spring, the Wheatfield, and the Peach Orchard.

Pickett's Charge, the ultimate confrontation, took place in the heat of the afternoon of July 3. A mile-wide column of twelve thousand Confederate infantrymen met a wall of Union fire. Fewer than two hundred Confederates breached The Angle, the stone wall that marked the Union line. The disastrous charge, less than thirty minutes long, ended the Gettysburg battle and signaled the turning point of the war.

The grisly duty of burying deceased soldiers and horses who had been alternatively baked by the sun and soaked by rain fell first to the Union men, as Lee already had retreated to Virginia with a wagon train of wounded said to be seventeen miles long, and then to the 2,400 residents of Gettysburg. Additional wounded, numbering about 22,000, filled virtually every church, barn, and home in the area for months afterwards. On July 15, 1863, *The New York Times* reported that

the "battlefield is visited daily by thousands of people. . . in quest of those who have fallen in battle, while most of them come through sheer curiosity." Like hungry crows, visitors picked through the corpse-choked fields, taking guns, cannonballs, blankets, and other combat relics. When apprehended, the treasure hunters were made to assist with the burials as well. Union graves were marked with wooden slats on which were scribbled, when known, the names of the dead. No one, however, moved quickly to bury the southerners. Those bodies turned into swollen bags of slippery, fermented death that were hastily covered over with soil and afforded some dignity, at least until the next rain.

From a distance, the battlefield appears pristine, verdant, and still. A closer look reveals that its grounds are inscribed with a profusion of monuments to virtually every Union and Confederate action and unit. Physical markers alone include more than thirteen hundred monuments and commemorative tablets, four hundred cannons, more than one hundred historic structures, eight miles of defense works, and twenty miles of fencing that are spread over nearly six thousand acres. Its monuments are not randomly placed but positioned where officers and regiments fell, whether in fields, in woods, or on rocky outcroppings.

The Confederate in the Attic by Tony Horwitz is a necessary parlando to understanding the obsession with and ongoing embellishment of the meanings of the Civil War, personified most visibly in the persons and habits of war reenactors,

Massive boulders form the landscape of Devil's Den, the sharpshooter position for the Confederates.

A.D. 760
The rock-cut temple of Kailasanatha, Ellora, India, is begun by Krishna I

A.D. 789
In Aachen, King Charlemagne orders that copies of important religious texts be made, emphasizes standardization of letters that lead to the lowercase letters used today

or "living historians" as they call themselves. The reenactors, whose numbers are legion, represent a mere fraction of armchair Civil War strategists who participate in the endless game of "what if" played against the battle's many imponderables, selecting the version that suits them best or inventing new ones spun of fact and fancy. To quote William Faulkner, "History isn't dead, it isn't even past."

Most agree that the battlefield's extraordinary state of preservation is due to the early efforts of local residents. David McConaughy, a Gettysburg lawyer and president of the Evergreen Cemetery around which the battle raged, wrote to Pennsylvania governor Andrew Curtin on July 25, 1863, about securing natural and artificial defenses of the battlefield in the "actual form and condition they were in, during the battles." McConaughy had already arranged by that date to purchase portions of Little Round Top, Culp's Hill, Stevens Knoll, and East Cemetery Hill. Sold at cost to the Gettysburg Battlefield Memorial Association once it formed in September 1863 (it was later chartered in April 1864), McConaughy's acquisitions were crucial to the Association's aims. According to an 1869 *New York Times* article, the Association intended to "perpetuate the history of the battle in its simple truth, and to that end to make the battlefield its own interpreter" and sought "fidelity to the truth of history" by enlisting the aid of both sides. Although McConaughy's "inexhaustible and far-ranging interests pervaded the history of both our present National Cemetery and National Military Park," according to Gettysburg historian Kathleen Georg Harrison, his contribution has been relegated today to virtual anonymity.

In contrast, John Badger Bachelder (1825–1894), an artist from New Hampshire with virtually no military experience but inflamed with the desire to paint the world's greatest battle scene, was considered the battleground's leading historian until his death in 1894. Within days of the campaign's finish, Bachelder arrived in Gettysburg and began to sketch its roads, houses, fields, woods—everything, as he wrote on August 10, 1863, to Curtin, "that could effect [*sic*] the tide of battle or be of interest to the public." During

1863 and 1864, Bachelder doggedly interviewed thousands of officers and soldiers and drew a series of precisely rendered, visually appealing maps and drawings which, when published, exponentially expanded his authority.

Two photographs taken on July 6 by Alexander Gardner and one of his cameramen, most probably Timothy O'Sullivan, depict Devil's Den. Historian William Frassanito argued in 1974 that Gardner's crew came upon the Confederate soldier and, touched by his youth, took four photographs, one of which is shown on the left; a short while later, having found a more picturesque spot that emphasized the Den's advantage to the Southern sharpshooters, they moved the body, repositioned it along with the rifle, and reshot the image, shown below. Richard Pougher, an expert in Confederate uniforms, countered in 1988 that there were significant differences between the two figures. Debates such as this one, under way for almost a century and a half, will no doubt continue.

By the 1880s, when a plethora of monuments were erected, Bachelder's expertise earned him an appointment as the Gettysburg Battlefield Monument Association's Superintendent of Tablets and Legends, a position which gave him authority to determine not only their location but their wording as well. In *These Honored Dead*, Thomas Desjardin's meditation on how history is made, the author observes that Bachelder needed Gettysburg to be the greatest conflict of the war, initially to validate the epic painting he envisioned, but soon to bolster his reputation and income as the battle's "official" historian. He provides a stunning example in Bachelder's realization in 1869 that by anointing one patch of land—the grove of trees at the Union line that was the Confederates' target on July 3, which he baptized the "High Water Mark of the Rebellion"—as the exact spot where the Civil War was lost and won, he could unequivocally establish Gettysburg as the war's key battle. To this end, he designed the eponymous monument at that location, and the High Water Mark entered the pantheon of American folklore. Though Bachelder never got around to painting his opus, he did amass a storehouse of stories upon which the Gettysburg legend rests.

Photographer Mathew Brady (c. 1823–1896) opened the "Dead of Antietam" exhibition at his New York City gallery in October 1862. It was the first time the public had seen the Civil War dead. Alexander Gardner (1821–1882), while working for Brady, took this photograph, one half of a stereographic pair, at the Antietam battlefield between September 19 and 22, 1862. Of the exhibit, The New York Times said, "If he has not brought bodies and laid them in our dooryards and along the streets, he has done something very like it." Despite their incendiary fascination, scenes like this one were rarely recorded; bodies were buried quickly and the photographers simply could not get to the bloodied fields in time.

Returning to July 1863: The bodies of the Union dead had to be rapidly interred, a task taken up by Gettysburg citizens. William Saunders, head gardener at the U.S. Department of Agriculture, designed a cemetery near the center of the Union line. To represent the equality of the Union soldiers, he conceived the Soldiers' National Cemetery as a series of radiating semicircles composed of simple marble markers to be placed equidistantly from an as-yet-undesigned central monument. Soon opulently landscaped and dotted with statuary, the cemetery reflects the "rural cemetery movement" ushered in by the 1831 opening of the genteel Mount Auburn Cemetery.

Graves in the National Cemetery are arranged in a semicircle around the Soldiers' National Monument, the first monument erected at Gettysburg. A female figure of Liberty, atop the column, holds a sheathed sword and laurel wreath, an ancient symbol of victory. More than 7,000 soldiers from all major American conflicts are interred here, 3,500 of whom are from the Civil War.

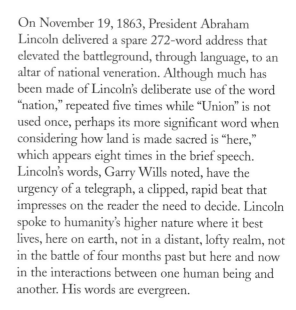

On November 19, 1863, President Abraham Lincoln delivered a spare 272-word address that elevated the battleground, through language, to an altar of national veneration. Although much has been made of Lincoln's deliberate use of the word "nation," repeated five times while "Union" is not used once, perhaps its more significant word when considering how land is made sacred is "here," which appears eight times in the brief speech. Lincoln's words, Garry Wills noted, have the urgency of a telegraph, a clipped, rapid beat that impresses on the reader the need to decide. Lincoln spoke to humanity's higher nature where it best lives, here on earth, not in a distant, lofty realm, not in the battle of four months past but here and now in the interactions between one human being and another. His words are evergreen.

The Soldiers' National Monument (1869) was the first memorial erected at Gettysburg. Long attributed to James Goodwin Batterson, the work was most probably designed, according to art historian Wayne Craven, by his employee George Keller. Randolph Rogers (1825–1892) sculpted the four marble figures representing War, History, Peace, and Plenty that sit at the monument's granite base. Peace is unusual in that it is an American male in contemporary clothing (allegorical peace figures are ordinarily classical, robed females). The figure is depicted as a mechanic holding a mallet and surrounded by the symbols of industry, including a steam engine, ship, and globe, thus extending the peculiarly American equation of peace with the unfettered pursuit of commerce.

Beyond the cemetery, the first battlefield memorial was a small stone placed in 1878 on Little Round Top that marked the spot where Pennsylvanian Col. Strong Vincent fell. It was followed the next year by the first regimental marker placed by the 3rd Massachusetts. The first statue erected was an 1888 bronze by Karl Gerhardt of General Gouverneur K. Warren, Chief Engineer of the Army of the Potomac, which is located at the summit of Little Round Top.

When Gettysburg came under the jurisdiction of the federal government in 1895, an energetic ten-year preservation program, carried out by immigrant laborers and local artisans, was inaugurated.

Renamed the Gettysburg National Military Park, the park was groomed to make the strategies of both sides apparent. Harrison reports the construction of twenty miles of roads; reconstruction of defense works; placement of cast iron and bronze narrative tablets that signaled the positions

and composed, spyglass in hand, is Meade, portrayed by Henry Kirke Bush-Brown. The two generals, their gazes locked for eternity across the broad field that determined their military fortunes, show the park's statuary installation at its most brilliant and dynamic.

Left John Bachelder designed the High Water Mark Memorial (1892) as an open book resting on two pyramidal stacks of cannonballs. The book's bronze pages are inscribed with the names of the Confederate and Union divisions that participated in the July 3 attack.

Below An 1896 portrait of George Gordon Meade, commander of the Army of the Potomac, faces a portrait of his nemesis, Robert E. Lee, less than a mile away.

of each battery, brigade, division, and corps, with separate markers for each U.S. Regular Army battery and regiment; positioning of three hundred original cannon to approximate battery positions; erection of five observation towers to teach the art of war to military students; construction of thirty miles of fencing and stone walls; and planting of thousands of trees. In 1933, the National Park Service assumed management of Gettysburg, as well as most other major Civil War battle sites.

Today, Gettysburg is a veritable outdoor museum representing some of America's most eminent sculptors of the late nineteenth and early twentieth century, including John Quincy Adams Ward, Gutzon Borglum, J. Massey Rhind, Lee Lawrie, and Cyrus Dallin.

The seven equestrian statues at Gettysburg depict infantry commanders and all are elevated on pedestals, with the exception of the 1998 ground-level bronze of General James Longstreet, Lee's much-maligned second in command. The most notable are the tranquil portrait of Lee, astride his charger Traveller, who stares across the fields where Pickett's Charge unfolded toward another equestrian statue, that of his adversary Meade. The Lee, erected in 1917, depicts the general lost in thought and raised above a grouping of seven writhing soldiers, two of them boys, who convey rebel courage and determination. Equally solemn

The Lee has additional significance. Initially, the monuments represented the Union presence on the field exclusively. Fifty years would pass before the Confederate armies received significant battlefield recognition. Lingering animosity toward the South was reinforced by an 1887 GBMA stipulation that markers could only be placed

A.D. 800

Irish monks expand the concept of the book with a trove of exuberantly illuminated manuscripts, including the milestone *Book of Kells*

John Bachelder's early maps of the battlefield were so arrestingly beautiful that he became Gettysburg's leading historian. This widely distributed map of 1863, endorsed by Major General George G. Meade, helped shape the commonly accepted history of the battle. The bird's-eye view shows the battlefield's topography, drainage, vegetation, and myriad man-made structures. It designates the locations of both armies, with the names of commanding officers and the locations where they were killed or wounded.

GETTYSBURG

BATTLE-FIELD.

The massive dome of the Pennsylvania State Memorial (1910) is supported by four archways and topped with a bronze figure representing Victory and Peace. Designed by architect W. Liance Cottrell, the granite monument honors the more than thirty thousand Pennsylvanians who fought in the battle.

We can not dedicate—we can not consecrate—we can not hallow—this ground. The brave men, living and dead, who struggled here, have consecrated it, far above our poor power to add or detract.

—Abraham Lincoln, Gettysburg Address, November 19, 1863

where soldiers entered the battle. Largely on the offensive, Confederate battle lines were far from the places where their men fell. The southern states were understandably reluctant to erect monuments that were hidden away in the back lines. Eventually, with the end of Reconstruction and the spirit of reconciliation flowing from the 1913 reunion, the southern states settled on the idea of creating single memorials that would honor the sacrifice of all soldiers from a given state. Virginia led with the Lee equestrian statue in 1917. Not until 1982, with the completion of the Tennessee memorial, was the South fully represented on the battlegrounds.

As the dust of years began to settle on memory, the significance of Pickett's Charge shifted. If it marked the beginning of the Confederate end, it was also the symbolic high point of Southern courage and honor. Comforting George Edward

Pickett after his crushing defeat on July 3, Lee said, "Come, General Pickett, this has been my fight, and upon my shoulders rests the blame. The men and officers of your command have written the name of Virginia as high today as it has ever been written before."

The Eternal Light Peace Memorial, symbolizing the reconciliation of North and South, was dedicated in 1938 on the battle's seventy-fifth anniversary in the presence of approximately two thousand Blues and Grays and two hundred thousand others. It stands on Oak Hill, ground occupied by both sides during the conflict. It was designed by noted architect Paul Philippe Cret (1875–1945), who was responsible for numerous significant war memorials internationally, with bas-relief ornament by Lee Lawrie (1877–1963), a sculptor best known for the heroic gilded figure of Atlas at the entrance to Manhattan's Rockefeller Center. Inscribed

The battlefield's monuments have been maintained under three successive organizations, the Gettysburg Battlefield Memorial Association (1864–95), War Department (1885–1933), and National Park Service (1933–present).

Gettysburg's monuments are tied directly to the landscape's topographical features, which determined the movements of the armies. The rusticated granite castle honoring New York's 44th Infantry and two companies of the 2nd Infantry was built in 1893 on the summit of Little Round Top.

"Peace Eternal in a Nation United," the monument is capped with an urn that holds an eternal flame.

Although the Soldiers' National, High Water Mark, and Peace Light monuments do not dominate the park, and are not necessarily the most beautiful examples of its statuary, as a group they signal the park's larger meaning as it evolved during the first seventy years after the battle. As geographer Kenneth Foote has noted, Gettysburg is hailed as a rallying site for the war-weary North in the 1869 monument; as a turning point for a conflicted nation in the 1892 monument; and as a symbol of peace, unity, and friendship in the culminating Peace Light memorial of 1938.

The nascent art of photography burst into its first full expression during the Civil War and, from the outset of the battle, played a crucial role in defining the legacy of Gettysburg's topography.

Though photography had been used to document earlier wars, the dates of the Civil War roughly coincided with the development of technologies that permitted photographs to be inexpensively made and distributed. Consequently it was the first war to be extensively documented.

At that time, Americans were caught up in "cartomania," the feverish collection of *cartes de visite*, small photographs on paper of celebrities and exotic vistas. Thousands of soldiers marched to urban photographic studios to have their likeness made, possibly their last, before heading off to war. The war ensured the substantial profits of photographers and photographic studios that turned out tintypes, ambrotypes, *cartes de visite*, and stereographs by the albumful. It is estimated that fifteen hundred professional and amateur photographers made photographs of the war—the bulk of which depicted Union activities and personnel.

Despite the quantity of images made, they provide only fragmentary evidence of the breadth of the conflict. Most are of unidentified soldiers and portraits of officers and war scenes; some document buildings, bridges, and ships, and a handful of battlefields. No clear image of an actual battle exists because the equipment needed for wet-plate field photography was far too heavy to drag to, and rapidly from, gunfire. Most documented the war in the North, where supplies were easily gotten and the market for photographs strong. Early on, the Union blockade of southern ports, and the region's depleted economy, made it difficult for Confederate photographers to obtain supplies and sell their work. As historian Keith Davis notes, the one-sided documentation of the war shaped subsequent memory of the war in curious ways, conferring importance on widely photographed, though historically insignificant, events and locations while marginalizing others, such as Fort Sumter, of which there exists only one photograph prior to its bombardment on April 12, 1861, the day the nation exploded into civil war.

Gettysburg's most important documentarians were Alexander Gardner, Timothy O'Sullivan, and James Gibson, who were first on the scene, by noon on July 5, according to historian William Frassanito. The trio focused on close-up shots of the dead, the commercial value of which had been proven by an 1862 exhibition entitled "The Dead of Antietam," one image of which is illustrated on these pages. Mathew B. Brady, the celebrated photographic impresario, arrived later, by July 15, and, too late to record the human carnage, focused on sweeping views and significant landscape features such as McPherson's Woods, Lee's headquarters at the Thompson house, Culp's Hill, and Little Round Top. These images, invaluable documents of the land in the war's immediate aftermath, also shaped interpretation of Gettysburg.

Gettysburg mythos is evidenced in *The Battle of Gettysburg,* also known as *High Tide of the Confederacy,* a colossal cyclorama painting by the French artist Paul D. Philippoteaux (1846–1923). Cycloramas, or circular panoramas, first appeared in Europe at the end of the eighteenth century and were the epitome of public entertainment. The IMAX theaters of their day, cycloramas recreated epic events in 360 degrees, placing the viewer in the center of the scene. The you-are-there illusion was intensified by light, sound, and landscaped foregrounds dotted with three-dimen-

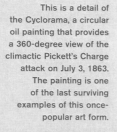

This is a detail of the Cyclorama, a circular oil painting that provides a 360-degree view of the climactic Pickett's Charge attack on July 3, 1863. The painting is one of the last surviving examples of this once-popular art form.

1040
Alchemist Pi Cheng produces first known movable type made of baked clay
blocks

sional objects. Arriving in Gettysburg in 1882, Philippoteaux spent several weeks observing the terrain, interviewing veterans, and hiring a photographer to shoot documentary photos before returning to Paris to paint.

The Gettysburg cyclorama was Philippoteaux's second version of four panoramas of Gettysburg. The painting depicts Pickett's Charge and puts the spectator in the shoes of the Union army looking outward toward the advancing Confederates. The experience was said to be so real that when it opened in Boston in 1884, veterans wept. In its original form, the painting is believed to have been 400 feet (121.9 m) long and 50 feet (15.2 m) high. What remains today is considerably smaller—359 feet (109.4 m) long and 27 feet (8.2 m) high.

Philippoteaux's massive circular painting was housed in the Cyclorama Building, a cylindrical structure (1959–61) designed by the distinguished modernist architect Richard Neutra (1892–1970), his partner, Robert Alexander, and son, Dion Neutra, who acted as project architect. It was a flagship project of Mission 66, a ten-year federal program begun in 1956 to improve the National Park infrastructure. Sited in the southern portion of Ziegler's Grove, a critical portion of the battlefield, the Cyclorama Building consists of a concrete drum on a fieldstone base that is attached to a two-story wing whose roof served as a viewing platform.

The Gettysburg National Battlefield Museum Foundation was established in 1998 to create a new visitor center and Cyclorama gallery, part of a twenty-year program to remove certain features, including the Neutra building, that obstructed views of the park's key terrain attributes as they existed in 1863. In 1999, the Advisory Council on Historic Preservation, a federal agency that advises Congress on historic preservation policy, stated, "There are other Neutra buildings; there is only one Gettysburg Battlefield. . . . The building must yield." Despite numerous appeals, the Cyclorama Center is slated for demolition.

The dilemma is that all three historic entities—the battlefield, which, as a national military park, is automatically listed on the National Register of Historic Places; the Cyclorama painting, designated as a National Historic Object under the Historic Sites Act of 1935; and Neutra's building, a product of the historic Mission 66 program—share literal common ground, a fact that has frustrated efforts to find a metaphoric common ground.

All those for and against the retention of the Neutra building were preservationists—from conflicting centuries. For those who wanted to restore the open field to its 1863 condition, the modernist building was an intrusion that had to be removed as part of a larger "architectural cleansing"; a controversial 300-foot observation tower adjacent to Evergreen Cemetery was dismantled in 2000 for that reason, just one of dozens of properties within the park scheduled for removal over the next two decades. Inexplicably, however, gaudy motels and fast food restaurants, most within view and some on battle sites, will not be removed. Too old to be chic, too young to be revered, as Dion Neutra described it, the Neutra building had the bad fortune to be built where meaning depends on the exquisite, though selective, replication of a century other than its own.

In 2004, ground was broken for a new museum complex that will include a Cyclorama gallery, visitor center, library, shops, and offices. It was designed by the New York firm of Cooper, Robertson & Partners to look like a turn-of-the-century Pennsylvania farm, complete with a grain silo and tin-roofed circular barn.

The Gettysburg restoration illuminates the fundamental debate regarding memory and historic preservation: Is history a series of events to be frozen in time's curio cabinet so that a particular moment can be remembered, or should it acknowledge life's ever-changing continuum as well as the fallibility of human memory and motives?

Mission 66 planners developed the concept of the "visitor center," of which the Neutra building was one of the first, and built approximately one hundred of them before the program ended in 1966.

Gettysburg Address

Fourscore and seven years ago our fathers brought forth on this continent a new nation, conceived in liberty and dedicated to the proposition that all men are created equal.

Now we are engaged in a great civil war, testing whether that nation or any nation so conceived and so dedicated can long endure. We are met on a great battlefield of that war. We have come to dedicate a portion of that field as a final resting-place for those who here gave their lives that that nation might live. It is altogether fitting and proper that we should do this.

1100

1170
Archbishop Thomas à Becket murdered in Canterbury Cathedral

But, in a larger sense, we cannot dedicate, we cannot consecrate, we cannot hallow this ground. The brave men, living and dead who struggled here have consecrated it far above our poor power to add or detract. The world will little note nor long remember what we say here, but it can never forget what they did here. It is for us the living rather to be dedicated here to the unfinished work which they who fought here have thus far so nobly advanced. It is rather for us to be here dedicated to the great task remaining before us—that from these honored dead we take increased devotion to that cause for which they gave the last full measure of devotion—that we here highly resolve that these dead shall not have died in vain, that this nation under God shall have a new birth of freedom, and that government of the people, by the people, for the people shall not perish from the earth.

Abraham Lincoln, Gettysburg Address, November 19, 1863

Pickett's Charge, the engagement that ended the Gettysburg battle, is shown here from the Union position. Fewer than two hundred Confederates breached The Angle, as the stone wall that marked the Union line is called.

1187
Saladin, Kurdish ruler of Egypt and Syria (b. 1138; d. 1193), takes Jerusalem

1200

1227
Genghis Khan, founder of the Mongol empire, dies (b. 1155)

R inged with sandy beaches banked with blue mussel shells, Hart Island is a lush 101-acre patch situated in Long Island Sound. Swooping gulls and butterflies frame the island's spectacular views of the Manhattan skyline and Long Island's Gatsbyesque oceanfront estates. In autumn, expanses of wild grasses and flowers turn into fields of gold. In the middle of this seemingly deserted paradise, inmates from the Rikers Island prison carefully bury the anonymous, unwanted, unclaimed dead.

Hart Island

Hart Island, better known as Potter's Field, is the largest public burial ground in the United States. New York City's sole surviving potter's field, it was established in 1869 after those in Madison Square Park, Washington Square Park, Bryant Park, Randall's Island, and Ward's Island, among others, were redeveloped. A generic term referring to any public cemetery for unknowns and paupers, "potter's field" is biblical in origin, taking its name from Matthew 27:3–10; Judas, ashamed of accepting thirty pieces of silver for Jesus' betrayal, turned them over to the chief priests who "bought with them the potter's field to bury strangers in."

In 1654, Thomas Pell acquired Hart Island from the Siwanoy tribe. The land was acquired in 1869 by the City of New York; since 1895, it has been operated by the city's Department of Correction.

The island has a colorful history, including a spell as a pugilistic hideaway that saw an 1842 "fisticuffins" between Irishman James "Yankee" Sullivan and Englishman Billy Bell. Six thousand "loafers and rowdies" sailed out to witness the slugfest, won by Sullivan in thirty-eight minutes.

During the Civil War, the island served as a Union training ground and later as a prison for rebel soldiers. The isolated island has also been employed as a quarantine for yellow fever victims, a lunatic asylum, an old men's home, a reformatory for delinquent boys, a school for traffic violators, and a testing ground for socially progressive prison reforms.

In 1922, entrepreneur Solomon Riley purchased four acres on its southern tip with the intention of creating a "Coney Island of the Negroes" for African Americans. A month shy of its July 4, 1925, opening—after Riley had constructed a boardwalk, a dance hall, and a bathing house—the City shut it down, saying it would facilitate inmate escape, while denying accusations of racial prejudice.

During World War II, the island was a Navy disciplinary barracks. Brambles now cover the remains of a decommissioned Nike missile battery, built in 1955 during the fevered duck-and-cover days of the cold war. Bleachers salvaged from Ebbets Field after the Brooklyn Dodgers

1271

Marco Polo (b. c. 1254; d. c. 1324) leaves Venice for China; spends seventeen years in court of Kublai Khan; returns to Venice in 1295

1274

Thomas Aquinas dies (b. 1225)

left the city in 1957 were used for baseball games and, collectors note, have since been removed. Hart Island was briefly resurrected as a prison from 1982 until 1991, when the inmates were transferred to Rikers Island.

Some two dozen abandoned buildings line the island's pitted roads. They include a gutted chapel with a shattered rose window; an entertainment pavilion; a doctor's house with Victorian ginger-bread flourishes; a butcher shop and laundry building; and a 1912 power station, called the Dynamo Room. No one lives on the island today and it is off-limits to tourists.

Louisa Van Slyke, an orphaned victim of yellow fever, was interred here in 1869, the first civilian burial after the city acquired Hart Island. Since then, it is estimated that one million people have been interred on the island, although an exact count cannot be made because of lost records. None has been afforded the distinction of an individual gravestone. Mass graves, each holding 150 coffins stacked three high and two abreast, are staked with concrete markers and meticulous-ly organized in a grid system so that disinter-ments can be made.

A handful of memorials dot the landscape. An obelisk, surrounded by an intricate wall made of river stones, was erected in 1877 by the New York City Army Reserve to mark the graves of twenty Union veterans; in 1941, their remains were transferred to Cypress Hills National Cemetery

in Brooklyn. A white tower inscribed with the word "Peace" was erected opposite the under-ground Nike silo in 1948 by prisoners at their own suggestion. A rusticated granite cross marks the area where an estimated eleven thousand babies are buried and is inscribed, "He calleth his own by name."

The majority *are* known by name; less than 20 percent are John and Jane Does. About half of the approximately three thousand burials that take place annually are children. All are unclaimed or those for whom no one is willing or able to afford a private funeral. Four days a week, bodies are collected from morgues in the five boroughs and taken to the island on a Department of Correction ferry, the only link to the island. They are buried from Tuesday through Friday. Disinterments, possible in most cases for ten years after a burial, take place on Mondays.

Dressed in Day-Glo orange jumpsuits and under armed guard, prisoners remove the simple pine coffins, one at a time, from the morgue wagon. A name, if known, and an identification number are written in indelible ink and also gouged into the coffin before it is lowered into a long trench that eventually will accommodate dozens. Although buried without ceremony, the marginalized are interred by the marginalized with dignity. The necropolis is quiet but for the rattle of dirt mixed with mussel shells when it falls on the caskets.

It seems to me that the people that are buried here are the people that people forgot. I for one don't want to die poor or without family, people not knowing who you were or that you ever existed. I would like to be remembered.
—Douglas, inmate on burial duty, 1992, from Hart Island

Little Bighorn Battlefield
National Monument

LOCATION		DEDICATION		DESIGNER		COMMEMORATION
Crow Agency, Montana		*1879, 1946, 2003*		*Various*		*Battle of Little Bighorn*

The rolling hills of southern Montana are cut by a sparkling pebbled stream called the Little Bighorn. The river lends its name to the mythic confrontation that took place on June 25–26, 1876, a decade after the Civil War, another war in which Americans fought Americans. The battle became the high water mark in a four-hundred-year struggle between European Americans, who battled for national expansion, and Native Americans, who fought to preserve their lands and way of life. Although the number of casualties was relatively low, the round defeat of Lt. Col. George Armstrong Custer and his men, on the eve of the country's centennial celebrations, assumed enormous symbolic power that has yet to relinquish its hold on the nation's imagination.

The Battle of the Little Bighorn was fought between the U.S. 7th Cavalry under Custer and his officers Maj. Marcus A. Reno and Capt. Frederick W. Benteen, and the allied tribes of the Lakota Sioux, Cheyenne, and Arapaho, who were led by Tatanka-Iyotanka, the Hunkpapa Lakota better known as Sitting Bull. Custer and all 262 of his men were killed in the space of two hours, having fatally underestimated the strength of American Indian forces, some three thousand of them, encamped in the basin along the river they called the Greasy Grass near what is now the reservation of the Crow nation.

Paradoxically, the name by which the battle is commonly known—Custer's Last Stand—overshadows the fact that the American Indians won the battle. Last Stand Hill is another misnomer—the battle petered out south of that site, at Deep Ravine. In his book *Archaeology, History, and Custer's Last Battle,* archaeologist Richard Fox, who was part of the 1984–85 excavation of the site, says the popular image of Custer's men fighting to the last, which accounted for the battle's subsequent glorification in the popular imagination, ignores the eyewitness reports made by Indians of massive panic and tactical confusion on that field, confirmed by the disposition of bodies and weaponry. The masterful stratagems of Crazy Horse, military genius of the Oglala Sioux, ensured an Indian victory.

The conflict was the last major battle as the nation pursued its manifest destiny across to the American West. It was a watershed battle, in truth a last stand, though not for Custer or the United States government, but for the American Indians, who within years would end up on reservations, thus ending their traditional ways and setting the stage for a century of impoverishment and its attendant plagues.

Little Bighorn's identity as a commemorative site evolved gradually. It was designated a national cemetery in 1879, transferred in 1940 to the care of the National Park Service, and made a national monument on March 22, 1946. The first monument on Last Stand Hill was a stack of logs, 11 feet high, that was filled with horse bones gathered on the field. It was replaced in 1881 by a truncated granite obelisk that was erected over the mass grave of the 7th Cavalry soldiers and their Crow and Arikara allies. In 1890, white marble markers, now 259 in number, were clustered around the 7th Cavalry obelisk. For over a century, these were the site's only memorials.

The battlefield landscape itself played a decisive role. The memorials are sited unobtrusively to allow personal reflection that is uninterrupted by the distractions typical of tourist meccas.

Custer seems to be alive and well and riding in our midst.

—James Welch and Paul Stekler, *Killing Custer,* 1994

Although repeated efforts were made to officially commemorate the Native Americans who died, it took more than a hundred years to dismantle Custer's bragging rights. The battlefield came to represent the struggle for the control of an important collective symbol. The problem, as described by Rebecca Solnit, was that "Native Americans were either cast as adversaries in a manifest-destiny version of events or were seen as outside history altogether, as timeless and infinitely co-optable totemic figures, signifying something large and vague, like 'the spirit of the land.'"

Miniconjou Lakota chief Red Horse made forty-one drawings of the battle in 1881. The images are rendered in colored pencil and ink on manila paper, and constitute a rare, eyewitness account of the conflict. They are superb examples of ledger drawing, a unique Indian art form. Native Americans adapted European materials, including graphite, colored pencils, and paper—often in the form of lined ledger books, which gave the genre its name. These stylized drawings are visual descendants of the images painted to inspire courage on Plains tipis, buffalo robes, and war shirts.

1412
Joan of Arc, Saint, born (d. May 30, 1431)

In 1925, Nellie Beaverheart, whose father, Chief Lame White Man, fell, wrote to the War Department and offered to identify the exact site of his death so that the place might be marked. The superintendent never replied. Lame White Man was remembered with a stone cairn placed in 1916, then a wooden sign, and, in 1999, a red granite marker, the first in a series planned to commemorate Indian warriors.

Vine Deloria's *Custer Died for Your Sins* (1969) addressed the "invisibility" of the American Indian, debunked the romantic image of the Hollywood Indian, all eagle feathers and war whoops, and updated what it meant to be an American Indian in contemporary culture. *Little Big Man*, Thomas Berger's picaresque novel that was made into a popular 1970 movie starring Dustin Hoffman as Jack Crabb, the only white survivor of Little Bighorn, further called attention to the injustice visited on American Indians.

bottom photo Headstones mark the places where U.S. soldiers fell. The dark-faced stone is Custer's, although his remains were exhumed in 1877 and reinterred at the West Point Military Academy Cemetery; at that same time, others were removed for private burials in the east. Shortly after the conflict, the fallen Native Americans were buried according to Plains tradition, most typically on above-ground burial platforms.

In 1976, the centennial of the battle and bicentennial of the nation, the American Indian Movement (AIM) led by Lakota rights activist Russell Means held a protest that was, in the face of bicentennial patriotism, impotent. AIM did not succeed in getting an Indian memorial, although a sign quoting Oglala visionary Black Elk, "Know the power that is peace," was mounted outside the park's visitor center. In 1988, AIM demonstrated again and placed a metal plaque at the base of Custer's memorial that read: "In honor of our Indian Patriots who fought and defeated the U.S. Calvary [sic]. In order to save our women and children from mass-murder. In doing so, preserving rights to our Homelands, Treaties and Sovereignty. 6/25/1988 G. Magpie Cheyenne." That plaque, the first step toward a permanent memorial, is now exhibited at the visitor center.

Changing public perception depended first on changing the name of the Custer Battlefield.

National Park Service historian Robert Utley pointed out to Congress that that name was "deeply repugnant" to Native Americans and suggested that it offended them in the same way the Confederate flag offended African Americans. Through efforts led by Barbara Sutteer, the park's first Native American superintendent, the site was redesignated Little Bighorn Battlefield National Monument in 1991.

At the same time Congress authorized a memorial that would recognize the Indians. The national competition, themed "Peace Through Unity," called for a "living memorial to the Plains Indian women, children, and men who took part in the battle and whose spirit and culture survive." John R. Collins and Alison J. Towers won the competition in 1997. Although the memorial design was flawed in some of the ways it reflected Indian culture, most believed it better to have something rather than nothing built.

The Indian Memorial is made of sandstone. It is a circular berm, a potent form for many cultures, none more so than the American Indian, recalling as it does the earthworks built by ancient indigenous people throughout the Americas. It is sited on axis with the earlier 7th Cavalry Monument, which is framed by an aperture described as a "spirit gate" window that has been cut into the memorial. The interior interpretive panels narrate the battle in the words and images of the tribal combatants. Also inscribed on the interior walls are the names of the fifty-four Lakota and Cheyenne warriors, women, and children who died. The Weeping Wall, a water feature that trickles "tears," represents the suffering of both sides.

The memorial's most prominent feature is *Spirit Warriors*, a two-dimensional cast bronze sculpted by Colleen Cutschall (Oglala and Sicangu, b. 1951). *Spirit Warriors* depicts a trio of figures in a style reminiscent of ledger art, a unique Plains art form. The trio is led by the romantic image of a Plains warrior in full eagle feather headdress. The central figure, protected by the horse's body, embodies the legendary Plains horsemanship and holds a hooked "coup stick," used to touch rather than kill the enemy, the consummate act of courage. The grouping culminates with a woman,

Left Sitting Bull (1831–1890), Hunkpapa medicine man and political chief who fought the encroaching westward expansion, presided over the Little Bighorn encampment, having received a vision of an Indian victory during a Sun Dance.

Right Lt. Colonel George Armstrong Custer (1839–1876), with his shoulder-length red-blond hair and flamboyant style, was known first as the "Boy General," having risen from the bottom of his class at West Point to the rank of brevet major general in the Civil War, and then for his legendary "Custer Luck," after surviving eleven horses shot out from under him. Drained by a fatal combination of arrogance, miscalculation, and miscommunication, that luck ran out at Little Bighorn.

Below The Indian Memorial has earthen embankments that reach to the top of its 8-foot walls and conceal it within the landscape. The competition stipulated that the design could not compete visually with the Custer obelisk or intrude on the landscape.

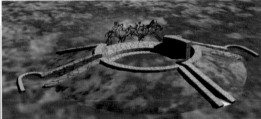

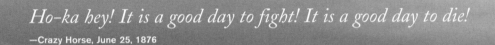

Ho-ka hey! It is a good day to fight! It is a good day to die!
—Crazy Horse, June 25, 1876

representative of the women and children also on the battlefield, who wears a belt of thirteen conches that symbolize her "moon cycles." She hands a shield illustrated with a quartered earth to the man who holds a modern rifle, a technological contrast to the psychological protection implied by the shield.

At the memorial's June 25, 2003, dedication, U.S. senator Ben Nighthorse Campbell, whose Cheyenne great-grandfather fought Custer, encouraged the audience "to come back sometime early in the morning after a rain when the fog is laying in the valleys and things are quiet and the

moon is waning, and perhaps all you can hear is the sounds of nature. If you're here by yourself during that time, I know you'll feel like Indian people feel when they're here."

The battle of Little Bighorn didn't end on June 26; it went on for another hundred years. The century-long battle that ensued gained equal recognition for the Indian perspective of events. By representing both new and native Americans, the amended commemorative landscape expands the democratic ideal of a national identity that is determined by a willingness to recognize the dignity and rights of all who live here.

Colleen Cutschall's bronze *Spirit Warriors*, measuring 35 x 14 foot (10.6 x 4.2 m), was modeled at full size by Christopher Collins and cast by Eagle Bronze Foundry of Wyoming. Colorful bits of fabric flutter on the sculpture. Tying prayer flags, prayer bundles containing tobacco or sage, and other symbolic items to trees is common practice in traditional Native American cultures. This tradition of leaving offerings at sacred sites has been co-opted by mainstream society and is now a staple component of "spontaneous memorials."

1450-1455
Metalsmith Johannes Gutenberg of Mainz, Germany, produces the first printed book, the Gutenberg Bible, and unleashes an information explosion; by 1500, an estimated nine million books are in print

1452
Leonardo da Vinci, artist, born (Apr. 15; d. May 2, 1519)

Washington Monument

LOCATION	DEDICATION	DESIGNER	COMMEMORATION
The Mall, Washington, D.C.	*1885*	*Robert Mills (1845–1854); Thomas L. Casey (1876–1884)*	*President George Washington*

Talk of building a monument to President George Washington—the beloved commander of the Continental Army who led that ragtag band to an impossible victory over Great Britain—began within days of his burial in 1799. The debate continued through the administrations of fifteen presidents, after construction of the memorial began in 1848, and did not cease until its dedication in February 1885. The various missteps that characterized America's quest to commemorate her first president paralleled the fits and starts of the developing country.

In 1783, the Congress of the Confederation resolved to create an equestrian statue honoring Washington. By that time, veneration of Washington had already reached feverish proportions. Congress called for a portrait that would show him "in a Roman dress," to be erected at the location of the yet-to-be-built congressional building, but it was never realized because of lack of funds. After Washington's death, another proposal for a pyramidal mausoleum to be placed in the rotunda of the Capitol came to nothing, again for lack of money. For the 1832 centennial of Washington's birth, a third scheme, for a tomb for both George and his wife Martha, evaporated when Washington's nephew refused to remove their remains from Mount Vernon.

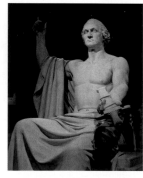

Horatio Greenough portrayed Washington as Zeus as carved by Phidias in about 430 B.C., one of the seven wonders of the ancient world. Despite the storied reference, the toga-clad figure shocked many. His gesture—his right hand pointing to heaven, his left gripping a sword—caused one nineteenth-century wit to imagine Washington saying, "My body is at Mount Vernon, my clothes are in the Patent Office."

Congress then commissioned the American sculptor Horatio Greenough (1805–1852) to execute a seated portrait. Completed in 1840 and carved from Carrara marble, *Lieutenant General George Washington* is considered an important early work of American monumental sculpture. The uproar over Greenough's sculpture of the first president as a Greek god exposed nineteenth-century prudery at its finest. Now clad in a toga, George was dragged all over D.C. until 1963, when the much-maligned statue was placed on the second floor of the Smithsonian's National Museum of History and Technology, where he remains.

Robert Mills won the Washington National Monument Society competition to honor the first president with this 1833 design, which was never realized.

The commemorative logjam was finally broken by the Washington National Monument Society, a group formed in September 1833 by private citizens led by journalist George Watterson. The Society intended to raise $1 million—limited to one-dollar contributions to encourage wide participation—in order to raise a monument that would "harmoniously blend durability, simplicity and grandeur." They sponsored an invitational competition in 1836 that was won by Robert Mills.

Mills (1781–1855), born in Charleston, South Carolina, claimed to be the first native-born professionally trained architect. He was mentored by James Hoban, builder-architect of the White House; Thomas Jefferson, a skilled amateur architect; and Benjamin Henry Latrobe, a leading British architect who worked in the United States. Mills's proactive, influential practice saw the design of houses, churches, bridges, and governmental buildings up and down the East Coast. His elegantly rational, classical style, and recognition of the symbolic importance of that style, would help define American architecture in the nineteenth century.

Two early projects influenced Mills's Washington design: the Washington Monument in Baltimore (1815–25) and the Bunker Hill Monument (1827–43) in Charlestown, Massachusetts. For the Baltimore monument, the first major tribute to the president, Mills conceived of a single, colossal column. Although he wrote in his winning submission entry that he hoped the monument design would not fall "to foreign genius and to foreign hands," in fact, a solitary column had been employed to express a commemorative ideal earlier by Hadrian, Trajan, and Christopher Wren, among others. The Baltimore monument is a 164-foot (50 m) Doric column with a hollow shaft and a spiral interior staircase that is crowned with a statue of the president. Its square two-story base gives some sense of what Mills would propose for the District of Columbia.

Mills was one of four architects who professed authorship of the Bunker Hill Monument. Although Mills could claim the design with some authority, it was never recognized. His 1825 proposal, the drawings for which have disappeared, describes a 220-foot obelisk having the same proportions as the one eventually built. At the time, it was not uncommon to adapt multiple ideas into a composite design; not until 1857, with the founding of the American Institute of Architects, would architects begin to protect their intellectual property rights.

The monument's apex is made of aluminum, an exotic material at the time, to protect the structure from electrical storms. The facts of the monument's long birth are inscribed on the aluminum tip beyond anyone's view. One face reads "Chief Engineer and Architect, Thos. Lincoln Casey, Colonel, Corps of Engineers. Assistants: George W. Davis, Captain, 14th Infantry. Bernard R. Green, Civil Engineer. Master Mechanic, P.H. McLaughlin." The second reads "Corner Stone Laid on Bed of Foundation July 4, 1848. First Stone at Height of 152 feet laid August 7, 1880. Capstone set December 6, 1884." The third says "Joint Commission at Setting of Capstone. Chester A. Arthur. W.W. Corcoran, Chairman. M.E. Bell. Edward Clark. John Newton. Act of August 2, 1876." The last face is inscribed "Laus Deo," a Latin phrase meaning "Praise be to God." Robert Mills's name is not inscribed.

Thomas L. Casey increased the foundation's surface bearings by about three and a half times, taking the original 80-square-foot foundation to 146½ square feet. He lessened the walls' thickness to lighten the masonry load on the foundation. The upper structure was built by hauling stones up through the central core on an elevator that was fitted for passengers after completion.

Another influence was Mills's boyhood fascination with lighthouses and beacons that led, in 1832, to his publishing *The American Pharos, or Light-House Guide,* the first comprehensive book on American navigational aids. Mills's biographer John M. Bryan notes that this early interest, coupled with the architect's preference for buildings that expressed permanence and social purpose, caused these two structural types to naturally and inevitably blend in his mind.

Mills's 1836 design for the Washington Monument was not adopted by the Society until 1845. It consisted of a classical colonnaded temple adorned with statues, including a *quadriga,* a chariot drawn by four horses abreast. This pantheon would be surmounted by a 500-foot (152.4 m) tapering obelisk with carved symbols and inscriptions. Mills's ornate Greco-Egyptian confection was criticized. Those objections, combined with the practical inability to meet its magnificent price tag, caused the Society to jettison the lower pantheon almost immediately and scale back the obelisk to a more manageable height. Obtaining the site, an elevated thirty-acre parcel on the Potomac on axis with both the White House and Capitol, is considered the Society's greatest coup.

The cornerstone, laid on July 4, 1848, included a time capsule holding items typical of those depositories: national newspapers, currency, a Bible, memorabilia of Washington's family, and, ironically, some of Mills's monument proposal drawings. Robert C. Winthrop, Speaker of the House, floridly compared the monument's great eventual height with the first president's singularity, saying, "Exhaust upon it the rules and principles of ancient and modern art; you cannot make it more proportionate than his character." Despite the grand ceremony, a final plan had not yet been agreed upon.

That same year, the Society invited the states to contribute memorial stones that had to be cut of durable material native to the state, with the dimensions of 4 x 2 feet (1.21 x 0.60 m), and a thickness of 18 inches (0.45 m). Stones poured in, ultimately 193 of them, donated by states but also individuals, civic and religious groups, cities, and nations, and were stored in a building called the lapidarium.

1581
Galileo discovers that a pendulum swings at a fixed rate

The temporary restoration cladding designed by Michael Graves actually gave the public two monuments, as a shimmering new external structure replicated the form of the internal monument undergoing repair. In 2000, the obelisk was encased in a blue mesh scrim stretched over an aluminum scaffolding in a way that recalled the ingenuity that raising obelisks has always required. The brief, remarkable transformation allowed the monument to be seen anew.

It may suit the departed George Washington —I don't know. He may think it is pretty. It may be a comfort to him to look at it out of the clouds. He may enjoy perching on it to look around upon the scene of his earthly greatness, but it is not likely. It is not likely that any spirit would be so taken with that lumbering thing as to want to roost there. It is an eyesore to the people. It ought to be either pulled down or built up and finished.

—Mark Twain, Letter to the *Alta California,* February 14, 1868

The stones would figure in a celebrated theft. In 1853, Pope Pius IX donated a marble stone from the Roman Temple of Concord (367 B.C.). This incited the Know-Nothing Party, a fanatical anti-immigrant, anti-Catholic group that, in the four short years after its founding in 1850, counted a million members; they vowed the stone would never be part of the monument. On March 6, 1854, in the dark of night, the papal stone was forcibly taken and dumped into the Potomac River. It was never recovered and the perpetrators never identified, causing Society donations to cease and construction to lag once again. In 1982, the Archdiocese of Spokane, Washington, donated a replacement stone.

Work proceeded until 1852, faltered, and finally stopped in 1854. The obelisk had reached 152 feet (46.32 m). Mills died the following year. The Civil War halted construction for more than two decades. Surrounded by shantytowns, wandering cattle and pigs, and the accompanying stench and debris, the abandoned stump of a monument spoke more than any words could about the country's tenuous union. The finished monument bears witness to those difficult times: When construction resumed, the original marble was no longer available, and a subtle line dividing the obelisk's two distinct eras is still visible.

The construction delays ultimately proved fortuitous. In 1878, Lt. Col. Thomas Lincoln Casey of the United States Army Corps of Engineers took over the construction. He discovered that the existing foundation would not support the full weight of the proposed obelisk. Furthermore, Mills's decorative lower base wasn't affordable, and yet a stark, solitary obelisk was an affront to the growing Victorian taste for lavish and exotic ornament.

The design issue was settled when Casey was introduced to George Perkins Marsh, American ambassador to Italy and an authority on Egyptian obelisks. Marsh's studies of obelisks in Rome, most of them from Egypt, showed that the height of the obelisk should be roughly ten times the width of the base, and that the pyramidion—the pyramidal capstone and apex that terminated the obelisk—should join the lower shaft without a break, ledge, or molding. Because the existing shaft was 55 feet (16.8 m) on each side, the monument would have to rise to 550 feet (167.6 m) (later adjusted to the current height of 555 feet [169.2 m]) to maintain the Egyptians' ten-to-one base-to-height ratio. Casey adapted Perkins's suggestions and then argued for the taller obelisk, point by point, in a letter to Congress. They accepted, thus ending the decades-long debate.

Despite Casey's conscientious management, mistakes and delays occurred. Numerous vendors were dismissed because they were unable to quarry sufficient amounts of marble, make timely deliveries, or produce stone of the correct color. The slow dressing of the marble, an easily damaged material,

1600
Charles I, king of Great Britain, born (Nov. 19; beheaded Jan. 30, 1649)

1630
Boston founded by John Winthrop (Sept.)

created more delays. At its height, the project employed a workforce of 170, the majority of whom were stonecutters making about $2.50 for a ten-hour day, and laborers who made half that.

The new foundation, begun in 1879, was a triumph. Casey's two-part plan widened and deepened the existing foundation so the monument's weight would be distributed over a larger area. This required excavating around and beneath the existing base, a laborious and exacting operation. Seventy percent of the earth below the old foundation was removed and replaced with a concrete slab, 13.5 feet (4.1 m) thick, that also extended 23 feet (7 m) beyond the foundation's edge. The second step involved constructing massive concrete buttresses on all four corners and in between to fuse the new and old foundations. Louis Torres, whose account of the monument's construction remains the standard, wrote that although Casey's plan was not novel, what was "new was his ability to accomplish such a delicate operation on such a large scale."

The public seemed curiously unmoved at the time by the marvel rising before them. One architect, writing anonymously to the *Atlantic Monthly* in 1879, questioned this apathy, given the public's "blazing ardor, not yet spent, to cover the land with monuments" and the enduring affection for Washington whose "statues are in our legislative halls, his head on our money and our postage stamps, his name strewn over all the towns in the country."

The patriarchal monument is an unsurpassed feat of engineering. When built, it was the tallest structure ever erected—more than five times taller than the obelisk at St. John Lateran in Rome which, at just under 106 feet (32.3 m), had been the tallest obelisk. The Washington Monument is the tallest masonry structure in the world, made of some thirty-six thousand stones, and it is unlikely it will ever relinquish that distinction. While it was under construction, technology had already shifted toward metals and would soon find its seminal expression in Gustave Eiffel's tower. To nineteenth-century eyes, the monument must have been an astonishing sight—the highest place on earth, virtually heaven, and reachable by elevator.

The marble capstone and aluminum apex were set into position on December 6, 1884. Casey and assorted engineers, journalists, and dignitaries stood on a narrow platform built at the 500-foot mark. Above them towered the 3,300-pound capstone suspended from a framework of heavy joists that Casey had the honor of moving into place. Several weeks later, President Chester Arthur presided at the dedication on the cold and windy morning of February 21, 1885, the day before Washington's birthday. That night, fireworks lit up the sky.

Most of the commemorative stones date from 1849 to 1855. Cut from materials such as granite, marble, limestone, and jade, today they line the monument's interior and comprise a veritable museum of nineteenth-century inscriptional carving.

In 1997 the National Park Service, in partnership with Target Stores and other large American companies, began an extensive maintenance program on the monument, the most ambitious ever and the first since the 1930s. Reopened for the 2000 millennial celebration, the restoration included patching, repointing, and cleaning the monument's masonry; restoring the commemorative stones that line the shaft's interior; and installing windows in the elevator cabs so the commemorative stones can be viewed.

Raising an obelisk to the height of the Washington Monument required structural and nationalistic hubris that America could not muster until after the divisive Civil War, when the glory days of surging national identity and economy took hold. "First in war, first in peace, and first in the hearts of his countrymen," George Washington established the precedents that would set the young republic on its course. His monument is a barometer of the country's protracted struggle to mature as a nation. It commemorates America's first hard-won battle for independence and successive efforts over the next century to rise to the lofty democratic ideals of her founding and become one nation, tested repeatedly, nearly divided, but still, miraculously, one.

1648

Taj Mahal, Agra, India, completed by Shah Jahan (b. Jan. 5, 1592; d. June 22, 1666), fifth Mogul emperor of India, in memory of his second wife, Mumtaz Mahal (d. 1631)

1656

Dutch mathematician and astronomer Christiaan Huygens invents the first pendulum clock, accurate to five minutes a day, and revolutionizes time-keeping

Statue of Liberty

LOCATION	DEDICATION	DESIGNER	COMMEMORATION
New York Harbor	*1886*	*Frédéric-Auguste Bartholdi, sculptor; Gustave Eiffel, engineer*	*Freedom, democracy, and international friendship*

The Statue of Liberty is the quintessential symbol of America. The colossal copper woman was a gift from France to celebrate a century-long friendship between that country and the United States and the ideals of freedom they share. Originally titled *Liberty Enlightening the World,* she is a universal symbol of freedom and democracy, occupying a sacred altar in the collective imagination of Americans as well as foreigners.

As a monument type, Liberty has few rivals. The statue is one of the largest and certainly the most beautiful of the colossi (oversized statuary based on the human figure). Such colossal statuary is an ancient form of commemoration and yet, paradoxically, Liberty is an ageless beauty. She is, after all, French.

In the summer of 1865, the French jurist Edouard de Laboulaye held a dinner for a distinguished group of politicians, writers, and artists that included the sculptor Frédéric-Auguste Bartholdi (1834–1904). Laboulaye wanted to make a point to the French about liberty and equality, ideals that had been squashed under Napoleon III

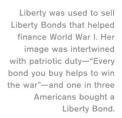

Liberty was used to sell Liberty Bonds that helped finance World War I. Her image was intertwined with patriotic duty—"Every bond you buy helps to win the war"—and one in three Americans bought a Liberty Bond.

1665

A portable camera obscura, a device used since antiquity to create a photographic image by passing light through a pinhole into darkness, is developed

1666

Five-sixths of London is destroyed in the Great Fire, including 87 churches and at least 13,000 dwellings; recounted by famed diarist Samuel Pepys (Sept. 2–6)

Centre of equal daughters, equal sons,
All, all alike endear'd, grown, ungrown, young or old,
Strong, ample, fair, enduring, capable, rich,
Perennial with the Earth, with Freedom,
        Law and Love,
A grand, sane, towering, seated Mother,
Chair'd in the adamant of Time.

—Walt Whitman, "America,"
Leaves of Grass, 1891–92

helped America gain independence a century earlier. He proposed that the two countries build the monument together: France would provide the statue and America the pedestal. The Franco-American Union, headed by Laboulaye, was formed in 1875 to realize the monument.

Bartholdi maintained that the image of Liberty did not crystallize until he sailed into New York Harbor. On that day, June 21, 1871, on board the steamship *Pereire,* Bartholdi saw Bedloe's Island and realized that every boat bound for Manhattan would pass that spot. Now called Liberty Island, the site is a 12.7-acre bit of land left behind when the glaciers retreated. With its neighbors, Ellis and Governor's islands, it is located in New York Harbor just south of the tip of Manhattan at the point where the mighty Hudson River empties into the Atlantic Ocean.

Once Bartholdi settled on a final version of Liberty in 1875, he made a model that

but that flowered under the American constitution. In a not so subtle political ploy, he suggested that a monument dedicated to liberty be erected in America in honor of the friendship the countries had shared since the Marquis de Lafayette

was 4 feet (1.25 m) in height and then made another model, taking measurements with calipers, and then another, four times larger, to yield a 36-foot (11 m) model. That model was divided into three hundred sections that were

---

1672
Peter the Great, Russian czar, born (May 30; d. Jan. 28, 1725)

1675
An obelisk in South Kingston, R.I. commemorates the Great Swamp Fight during King Philip's War between English settlers and the Narragansett Indians (Dec. 19)

Visitors to the museum can touch a full-scale copper replica of Liberty's face.

enlarged four times. The sections were recreated in wood and then covered with copper sheets, 3/32 inch (0.24 cm) thick, about the thickness of a coin, that were hand-hammered over the molds. Utilizing this traditional repoussé technique permitted the copper to be as thin as possible. Bartholdi chose copper over bronze because it was lighter, less costly, and more impervious to the salty Atlantic air. Once the rich brown color of a penny, the copper has acquired a pale green patina over the decades.

Bartholdi intimated, though never confirmed, that Liberty's stern face is that of his mother, and her hands and arms are modeled after Jeanne-Emilie Baheux de Puysieux, whom he would later marry. The seven rays emanating from Liberty's crown symbolize the seven seas and seven continents. The observation platform within the head, now closed, accommodated about thirty people at a time who could see through its windows the tablet held in Liberty's left hand bearing the date July 4, 1776, America's official birthday.

The chains under Liberty's feet, which symbolize the broken shackles of tyranny, cannot be seen by visitors.

Liberty is also an engineering monument: At the time of its completion it was the world's tallest iron structure. As designed by Gustave Eiffel (1832–1923), the internal support system presaged "curtain wall construction"—the breakthrough structural technology that would allow the modern skyscraper to emerge in Chicago in 1885.

The first pieces completed—the torch and arm—were displayed at the 1876 Centennial Exhibition in Philadelphia to encourage pedestal donations. They were then moved to Madison Square Park in Manhattan. Philadelphians, as well as residents of Boston, Baltimore, and San Francisco, among others, lobbied to have the statue erected in their city.

The "Magician in Iron," Eiffel responded to the forces of wind and gravity in hundreds of structures, notably railroad bridges, that possessed a precise logic and revolutionary industrial aesthetic that remain unsurpassed. For the Statue of Liberty, Eiffel devised a sturdy but elastic framework that allowed the outer copper shell to withstand gale-force winds and extreme temperature changes. The central 96-foot (29 m) pylon consists of four iron beams cross-braced with vertical and horizontal iron bars that support a secondary iron framework. Extending from the secondary framework are flat bars that are bolted to a network of iron ribs backing the copper sections that make up the statue. The upraised right arm is supported by a secondary skeletal form attached to the central pylon. Ironically, the most avant-garde structure in Manhattan is hidden under Liberty's voluminous robe.

The work was fabricated in the Parisian atelier of M. M. Gaget, Gauthier and Company in the 17th arrondissement and assembled, because of its height, in the courtyard outside. It was at that spot that she was formally presented to the United States on July 4, 1884, and then shipped to New York on board the frigate *Isere* on May 21, 1885.

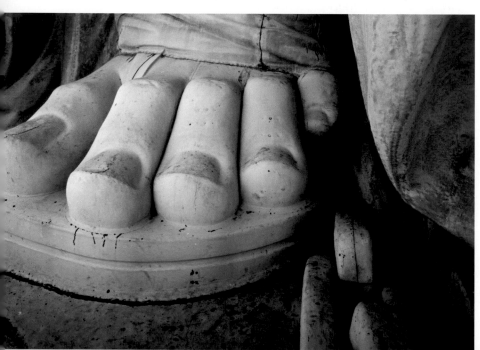

1706
Benjamin Franklin, American statesman, writer and inventor born (Jan. 17; d. Apr. 17, 1790)

1718
Englishman James Puckle patents the machine gun

The *Brooklyn Eagle* reported that the pedestal cornerstone was laid on August 5, 1884. Inside the cornerstone, among many items, were medals struck to commemorate two other cultural and technical marvels—the Egyptian obelisk in Central Park in 1881 and the Brooklyn Bridge two years later—thus securing Liberty's monumental claims. But a cornerstone a pedestal does not make.

Americans were apathetic about funding the pedestal. Some groused that the statue belonged to New York, not the nation, and so New Yorkers should pay for its base. Donations crept upward when the statue was completed in 1884, paid for by the French through lotteries and charity events, but raising the $250,000 needed for the pedestal moved at a snail's pace.

Joseph Pulitzer, a Hungarian émigré and entrepreneurial publisher of the *World,* a daily New York newspaper, got things rolling with a time-tested strategy: guilt. On the front page of the March 16, 1885, edition, he chided the public for ignoring "not a gift from the millionaires of France to the millionaires of America but a gift of the whole people of France" paid for "by the tradesmen, the shopgirls, the artisans—by all, irrespective of class." With a marketing flourish worthy of Barnum, he offered to publish the name of every donor, no matter how modest the sum, in the paper every week.

By August, in less than five months, Pulitzer had collected more than $100,000. The last spate of contributions was probably spurred by the outpouring of patriotism that accompanied the death of President Ulysses S. Grant on July 23, 1885. Pulitzer's contribution is recognized on the pedestal: "This pedestal to Liberty was provided by the voluntary contributions of 120,000 patriotic citizens of the American Union through the *New York World.*"

Architect Richard Morris Hunt (1827–1895), designer of sumptuous palaces for the very rich in Newport, Rhode Island, and elsewhere, was commissioned to design the pedestal in 1882. He designed a tapered base, monumental in its own right but so perfectly proportioned that it seems to disappear, allowing full focus to be on the upper statue. Hunt cleverly integrated into his design Fort Wood, an existing fortress on the island, using it to anchor Eiffel's internal framework. The pedestal, from the ground to its top, is 154 feet (47 m) high. Its concrete core is faced with rusticated granite quarried in Leete's Island, Connecticut.

On October 28, 1886, in rain and fog, surrounded by the colors of France and the United States, before a harbor crammed with yachts, rowboats, tugs, barges, and before the thousands who lined Manhattan's edges and squinted southward, a young boy madly waved a white handkerchief at Bartholdi and two others in the crown who held a cord attached to the veil covering the statue's face and waited for just this signal. One tug, and all bedlam broke loose. Whistles blew, guns boomed, bands played, fireworks exploded, and nearly everyone cheered for Liberty, revealed.

Not joining in the hurrah were two hundred members of the New York State Suffrage Association who, denied a part in the ceremonies on Bedloe's Island, hired a steamer and maneuvered it into a prime position in the harbor. From bullhorns they protested the irony of "erecting a statue of Liberty embodied as a woman in a land where no woman has political liberty."

When Liberty was dedicated in 1886 there were only a few structures in Manhattan that could match her height, which, measured from pedestal to torch, was a hair over 305 feet (93 m). The Brooklyn Bridge, which had opened in 1883, had a center span height of 119 feet (36 m) and the highest point in New York one could reach on foot. Trinity Church in lower Manhattan, at 284 feet (87 m), was the tallest building in the United States when it was completed in 1846. Liberty remains the tallest American colossus; her international rivals include Mother Russia, 270 feet (82 m), in Volgograd, Russia; the wondrous Bamiyan Buddhas, 175 feet (53 m) and 110 feet (34 m), of Afghanistan that were destroyed by the Taliban in March 2001; and the Ushiku Amida Buddha erected in 1995 outside Tokyo, which, at 328 feet (100 m), is the tallest statue in the world. These structures derive from the bronze Colossus

1732
George Washington, first U.S. president, born (Feb. 22; d. Dec. 14, 1799)

The monument was set into Fort Wood, a star-shaped fortress that had been built to defend the Battery and Ellis Island during the War of 1812. Steely-browed with a slight frown, Liberty is nonetheless beautiful, her hips slightly and provocatively akimbo, a goddess swathed in a flowing toga.

at Rhodes (282 B.C.), one of the seven wonders of the world, which was toppled by an earthquake in 226 B.C.

Throughout history, civilizations have erected immense works in honor of their deities. Colossal statuary addresses the innate human drive for power in a none too subtle manner: *I am large, therefore I am powerful.* Bartholdi put it eloquently: "Colossal statuary does not consist simply in making an enormous statue. It ought to produce an emotion in the breast of the spectator, not because of its volume, but because its size is in keeping with the idea that it interprets and with the place which it ought to occupy."

Another reason for Liberty's evergreen appeal can be summed up in three words: location, location, location. She is at the tip of Manhattan, the financial and cultural capital of the United States. She stands at America's metaphoric front door, the mythic portal through which millions of immigrants arrived. She is literally incomparable: Sited on an island, two miles away from New York City's soaring skyline, she cannot be diminished by Manhattan's skyscrapers. Her scale will remain intact.

Like a savvy guest, Liberty made her entrance at just the right moment in America's history, when the nation's population was swelling. According to the Statue of Liberty–Ellis Island Foundation, between 1880 and 1930 more than 27 million people entered the United States, the vast majority of whom sailed past the Statue en route to Castle Garden and then, when it opened in 1892, Ellis Island. With their arrival, Liberty evolved from a symbol of freedom to her mature identity as the avatar of America's promise.

Without much of a leap, one can imagine that Liberty assumed in the minds of the vulnerable Christian immigrants arriving from Europe the cosmic proportions of Mary, the mother of Jesus. For them, this beloved Marian protectoress at the portal of the new world was a giantess of compassion and the "Mother of Exiles" immortalized by the poet Emma Lazarus.

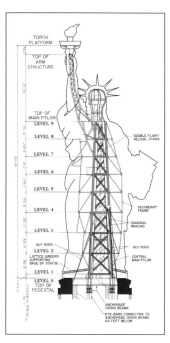

TORCH PLATFORM
TOP OF ARM STRUCTURE
TOP OF MAIN PYLON
LEVEL 9
LEVEL 8   DOUBLE FLIGHT HELICAL STAIRS
LEVEL 7
LEVEL 6
LEVEL 5
LEVEL 4   SECONDARY FRAME
                 DIAGONAL BRACING
LEVEL 3
GUY RODS
LEVEL 2   GUY RODS
LATTICE GIRDERS
SUPPORTING   CENTRAL
BASE OF STATUE   MAIN PYLON
LEVEL 1
LEVEL 0
TOP OF PEDESTAL
                 ANCHORAGE CROSS BEAMS
                 EYE-BARS CONNECTING TO ANCHORAGE CROSS BEAMS 60 FEET BELOW

A sectional drawing shows Eiffel's internal wrought-iron skeleton. The statue is supported by a central pylon constructed around a spiral staircase. Attached to the pylon is a secondary frame to which is attached the exterior copper shell. Liberty's upraised arm and torch is a separate frame attached to the central pylon.

1743
Thomas Jefferson, U.S. president, born (April 13; d. July 4, 1826)

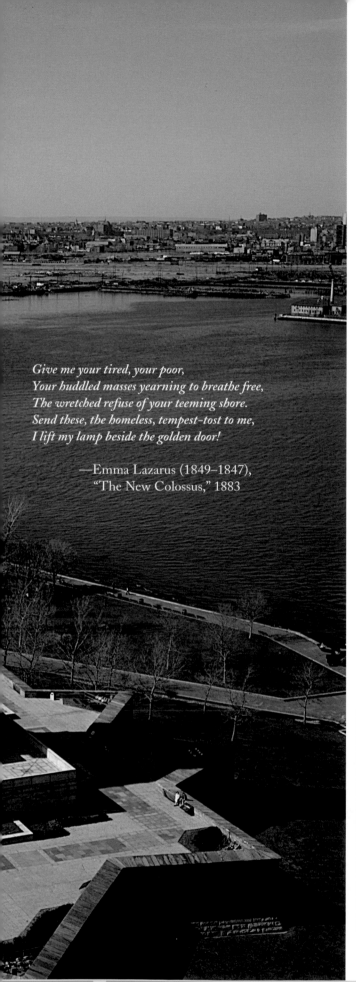

Give me your tired, your poor,
Your huddled masses yearning to breathe free,
The wretched refuse of your teeming shore.
Send these, the homeless, tempest-tost to me,
I lift my lamp beside the golden door!

—Emma Lazarus (1849–1847),
"The New Colossus," 1883

At one time visitors could enter Liberty and climb an endless corkscrew of a staircase, ascending or descending but always claustrophobic, especially in the summer, when humidity and the breath of panting visitors condensed on the interior walls and dripped down in rivulets. Those who circulated inside, patiently inching up and down her narrow arteries, her very blood, became part of her most potent metaphor.

Liberty's message has expanded beyond the original intention of the French. Her significance is not tied to any one meaning but is found within her capacity to express any number of meanings, as diverse as Americans themselves.

Liberty was extensively restored for her hundredth birthday. In 1916, the original copper-clad and gilded torch was replaced with one composed of six hundred pieces of yellow glass designed by Gutzon Borglum of Mount Rushmore fame that was more beautiful than practical. That torch, on view in the museum, was replaced in 1986 with a golden version of the original torch. Because copper and iron contract and expand at different rates, the copper sheathing is not directly attached to the iron ribs that extend from the central pylon, but is affixed instead to copper saddles that slide back and forth to accommodate temperature changes. During the 1986 restoration, the rusted iron ribs were replaced with ribs of stainless steel and ferralium.

Nearly half of all Americans today can trace their ancestry to someone who passed through Ellis Island, a 27.5-acre island near Liberty Island that was used as a federal immigration station between 1892 and 1954. Ellis Island became part of the Statue of Liberty National Monument in 1965.

1756
Wolfgang Amadeus Mozart born (Jan. 27; d. Dec. 5, 1791)

1769
Napoleon I, French emperor, born in Corsica (Aug. 15; d. May 5, 1821, St. Helena Island)

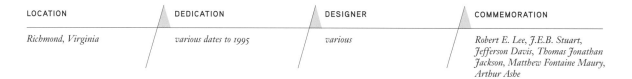

Monument Avenue

LOCATION	DEDICATION	DESIGNER	COMMEMORATION
Richmond, Virginia	*various dates to 1995*	*various*	*Robert E. Lee, J.E.B. Stuart, Jefferson Davis, Thomas Jonathan Jackson, Matthew Fontaine Maury, Arthur Ashe*

Adjustments were made to the Lee statue on the advice of the Lee Monument Association, the general's nephew, Governor Fitzhugh Lee, his daughter, Mary Custis Lee, and a host of others, who came bearing Lee's death mask, sword, spurs, hat, the boots he had worn at Gettysburg, and other items that would ensure an authentic portrait.

Nowhere was the deeply felt allegiance to the short-lived Confederate nation expressed more evidently than in Richmond, Virginia, the former capital of the Confederacy and the symbolic seat of its "Lost Cause." The American South was beaten badly in the Civil War. They had lost their sons, their livelihoods, and, profoundly, their way of life. Although the economy in Richmond, bolstered by tobacco and iron money, survived the war, its strength was a rarity in the postwar South.

For several years, pride ruled and recovery was slow. Many southerners were obsessed with thinking about the Lost Cause in a way that ran along the lines of "We had good reasons to fight this war, and though we may have lost, we demand your respect."

If the Lost Cause had assumed the dimensions of a civic religion, its shrine, still called "Confederate Avenue" by some, is Monument Avenue, largely built between 1890 and the Great Depression. The Avenue, an unusual combination of grand residential boulevard and ceremonial public space, was inspired by the City Beautiful movement that gained momentum after the 1893 Columbian Exposition. According to the authors of *Richmond's Monument Avenue,* a meticulous portrait of the thoroughfare's monuments and historic homes, the avenue "embodies recovery and reconciliation."

1770
Five men are killed by British troops in downtown Boston; the Boston Massacre foreshadows the American Revolution (Mar. 5)

1775
American Revolution begins

It is home to a unique grouping of statuary that speaks to the nation's complex relationship to the Civil War. The first monument, erected in 1890 in a circle along its center axis, commemorates General Robert E. Lee, commander in chief of the Confederate Army. The Lee was followed over the decades by five more monuments that recognized Jefferson Davis, president of the Confederacy; Confederate generals Stonewall Jackson and J.E.B. Stuart; Matthew Fontaine Maury, oceanographer and commander of the Confederate Navy; and, most recently, the African American tennis star Arthur Ashe.

An examination of the Avenue's oldest and newest monuments, those dedicated to Lee and Ashe, sheds light on the pressures exerted by societal change within the confines of a symbolic monumental space.

The first statue erected on Monument Avenue, in honor of Robert E. Lee, is shown shrouded before its May 29, 1890, unveiling. The statue is 21 feet high and sits on a 40-foot-high granite pedestal designed by French architect Paul Pujol.

Simply inscribed LEE, the Robert E. Lee monument faces southward. The bronze equestrian statue was sculpted by Marius-Jean-Antonin Mercié (1845–1916), a French sculptor who enjoyed an international reputation for his public works. Mercié's commission is primarily attributed to his long friendship with the influential American sculptor Augustus Saint-Gaudens, whom he had met at the Ecole des Beaux-Arts in Paris and who served on the Lee competition jury. As has been observed, Saint-Gaudens pulled strings on behalf of Mercié's commission amid some dissent but without much difficulty, as Richmonders believed that engaging a French sculptor would not only bolster the late general's stature, but propel their city into a cultural league on par with New York or Boston.

The Civil War was the last great conflict in which horses played a key role. Lee's close association with his beloved gray steed Traveller came about

in part because horses were more essential to and integrated into the culture of the agrarian South than the urban, industrial North. Mercié worked from photographs of Lee and his horse, although, because Traveller was not proportionately large enough in the opinion of the sculptor, another horse, a dignified thoroughbred, served as the model. Cast by Thubout Brothers in Paris, the bronze statue eventually arrived in Richmond on May 4, 1890, where, as local papers reported, crowds estimated at twenty thousand hauled the heavy work to its destination.

Lee was the central icon of the Lost Cause. Mercié portrayed him, patiently gazing toward a distant horizon, in a way that upheld and protected the ideals of the Old South. Southerners identified with Lee's leadership and dignity in the face of extreme loss, and those ideals were captured in Mercié's depiction.

Two statues were added in 1907; one commemorated the dynamic J.E.B. Stuart on a quarter horse and the other Jefferson Davis, standing before a 60-foot-high Doric column topped by an allegorical figure, "Vindicatrix." Stuart's monument, sculpted by English émigré Frederick

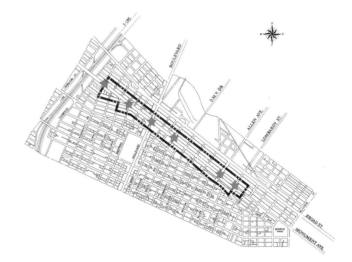

A map shows the boundaries of the Monument Avenue Historic District and is starred with the locations of the monuments.

Moynihan (1843–1910), was unveiled on May 30, 1907. In 1919, an equestrian statue by F. William Sievers (1872–1966) honoring "Stonewall" Jackson, Lee's right-hand man, was erected at the intersection of Monument and Boulevard. Ten years later, another Sievers work was dedicated, this one commemorating the Confederate naval

Off to my left is Stuart Circle Hospital. Inside are my father Stuart and my mother Mary. Dad may be dying.

Dad is an ex-Marine who voted for Nixon three times and I'm an artist who voted for McGovern. But he has always told me that he loved me. Told me he loved me just a few minutes ago when I left the hospital for the night.

The hospital is south of me, out of the frame. My Rollei is set up, pointing toward the monument of J.E.B. Stuart, at the far eastern end of Monument Avenue. I line up the shot, with the flood lit Presbyterian Church on the left, J.E.B. on the right, and the circular traffic in the foreground. People are taking their time going around the circle. Richmond is a southern city. Still wonderfully slow at times.

I cock the shutter and wait. Waiting for the right set of cars to approach. The exposure will be only be for a few seconds. There's a car at the light. I open the shutter. The car slowly rounds the statue and leaves the circle. Then another car, and another. I wait, counting seconds in my head. I close the shutter. I do this for a few more exposures, but soon stop. My heart isn't in it tonight.

I walk to the rental truck, throw my Rollei and tripod into the back seat, and drive around J.E.B. Stuart myself, listening to Emmylou Harris singing about losing love, missing Elvis, and living life even as it fades away.

I really wish Dad wasn't dying. I cry hard without making a sound.

—Stu Jenks's recollection of taking this photograph, 1999, of the J.E.B. Stuart monument

commander Matthew Fontaine Maury, considered the father of modern oceanography. Unlike the earlier honorees, Maury did not achieve fame through the war, having been an internationally recognized deep-water expert before its onset, but lent his considerable skills to the Cause, and initiated, among many duties, the first use of electronically detonated torpedoes.

Every dedication ceremony drew thousands to the Avenue who cheered orations that reaffirmed the ideals of the Lost Cause. With each successive statue, Monument Avenue became more firmly linked to a particularly southern appraisal of the Civil War. In the minds of some residents, however, the Avenue came to represent the marginalization of Richmond's African American population.

Although the abandonment of the Avenue's Confederate theme was repeatedly called for over the decades, its political symbolism did not pivot until the controversial 1996 addition of a heroic bronze of the tennis star and civil rights activist Arthur Ashe (1943–1993), a Richmond native. Ashe, the only black athlete to win Wimbledon as well as the United States and Australian Open tennis championships, dedicated his professional tennis career to fighting discrimination and spent the final days of his life working to raise public awareness about AIDS before he died of AIDS-related pneumonia.

Richmond sculptor Paul DiPasquale (b. 1951) met Ashe in 1992. After securing Ashe's willingness to participate in a monumental portrait, he began working under the auspices of the Ashe Monument Committee and Virginia Heroes organization, who approached the city about placement. Firestorms raged, fed by controversies that ranged from the aesthetic depiction of Ashe to the proposed location on Monument Avenue, which some argued should remain dedicated to the Confederacy heroes while others thought Ashe deserved better company. In July 1995, in a unanimous vote, the Richmond city council approved the statue's placement at the intersection of Monument Avenue and Roseneath Road, the terminus of the historic district. It was dedicated on July 10, 1996, Ashe's birthday.

Left Jefferson Davis, portrayed in bronze with arm outstretched, is encircled by a colonnade of thirteen Doric columns, representing the eleven Confederate states plus Missouri and Kentucky, which were also represented at the Confederate Congress. Above Davis, atop a 60-foot (18.2 m) column, is a bronze female figure representing the South.

Second from left The bronze and granite memorial at Belmont to Matthew Fontaine Maury, who was called "Pathfinder to the Seas," depicts him seated below a globe held aloft by roiling seas from which emerge allegorical figures, shown on this page's background, that recall his oceanographic accomplishments.

Center The first monument on Monument Avenue, an equestrian portrait erected in 1890, honors General Robert E. Lee, who commanded the Confederate Army.

Second from right Thomas Jonathan Jackson, second only to Lee in popular acclaim, is shown on his horse Little Sorrel. He earned the moniker "Stonewall" for "standing like a stone wall" after Bull Run, the first major battle of the Civil War that took place near Manassas, Virginia. After engineering a number of Confederate victories, Jackson died in 1863 at age thirty-nine as a result of friendly fire in the Battle of Chancellorsville.

Right Arthur Ashe, a tennis racket in one hand, books in the other, stands in the presence of four rapt children. The 12-foot (3.65 m) bronze stands on a granite pedestal that is inscribed with a biblical quote: "Since we are surrounded by so great a cloud of witnesses, let us lay aside every weight, and the sin which so easily ensnares us, and let us run with endurance the race that is set before us."

Opposite J.E.B. Stuart, the dashing Confederate cavalry general who was mortally wounded in Richmond on May 11, 1864, begins the east-to-west parade at Stuart Circle.

Erected after years of divisive argument, the Ashe statue faces eternally westward, away from the segregated public tennis courts he could not play on as a child, and away from the pantheon of Confederate generals on horseback.

The contrast between the Avenue's first monument—Lee, uniformed and stoically upright in his saddle—and its most recent one—Ashe, smiling and in a warm-up suit—illustrates how symbols and meanings change over time. As the authors of the Monument Avenue monograph observed, "The stories the statues tell as artistic and cultural creations vary: the sculpture can be read as monuments to martial exploits, as symbols of the Lost Cause, as a parade of Virginia's heroes, or as triumph over adversity." With the erection of the Ashe memorial, the citizens of Richmond had the opportunity to retrace, rethink, and readdress the continuum between Lee and Ashe, more than 130 years long, that defined the southern capital's identity. The shift between old and expanded identities was not easy, nor has it been adopted by all, but its occurrence has been marked, and so it has changed the future.

1790
First U.S. patent issued to William Pollard of Philadelphia for a machine that spins cotton

1799
The Rosetta Stone, an incised black slab that unlocks the mysteries of Egyptian hieroglyphics, is unearthed by Napoleon's troops in Egypt

Adams  Memorial

LOCATION	DEDICATION	DESIGNER	COMMEMORATION
Rock Creek Cemetery, Washington, D.C.	1891	Augustus Saint-Gaudens, sculptor; Stanford White, architect	Marian Hooper (Clover) Adams (1843–1885)

During 1919, a personally tumultuous year for Eleanor Roosevelt, she regularly went to the Rock Creek Cemetery in Washington's Fort Totten neighborhood to sit with a figure hidden in a grove of evergreens. Neither man nor woman, the figure was enigmatic, dispassionate, and, above all, silent about its reasons for being. The bronze statue was made in 1891 to commemorate Clover Adams, a woman who possessed in death a tranquillity that was not hers in life. To Eleanor, as has been noted, Clover seemed to have attained self-mastery, the supreme goal, by continuing to love when she herself was not loved.

Marian Sturgis Hooper (1843–1885), known as Clover since childhood, was born into an affluent, patrician, liberal Boston family. Witty, widely traveled, a photographer and linguist, Clover's translations and research assistance were invaluable to her celebrated husband, Henry Adams (1838–1918)—writer, philosopher, aesthete, and grandson and great-grandson of two American presidents. Aristocratic by virtue of their social pedigree, flawless taste, and generous self-appraisal, the couple were very much at home in society's upper altitudes—indeed, they *were* its upper altitudes. In the capital, they presided over a political and literary salon that, as culturist Lincoln Kirstein observed, "fostered an exchange of ideas and information among the best minds then serving the national destiny."

More intimately, the Adamses traded Washington gossip with President Lincoln's former secretary and future secretary of state John Hay and his wife Clara, and geologist-adventurer Clarence King. Dubbing themselves "The Five of Hearts," this cozy set met regularly to exchange acidic appraisals of local politics while sipping tea from heart-shaped cups.

Clover was also an avid amateur photographer. On December 6, 1885, the day she decided to die, she drank potassium cyanide, a lethal chemical used to develop photographs. Many have speculated as to why she killed herself. Was it depression over her beloved father's death in April of that year, her dissatisfaction with being a brilliant woman without societal permission to express herself or even vote, the absence of children, her lack of beauty and her husband's apparent infatuation with a lovely neighbor, the romantic resignation of a soul ill-suited to a cynical world, a genetic legacy of mental imbalance (several of the Hoopers ended their own lives), or any tangled number of these possibilities?

1814
Treaty of Ghent ends War of 1812

The Ecole des Beaux-Arts in Paris, founded in the study of Greco-Roman antiquity, was the training ground for America's most eminent artists and architects in the nineteenth century.

Could it be that, as her friend Henry James wrote, "Poor Mrs. Adams found, the other day, the solution to the knottiness of existence"? There are only two certainties: Questions that cannot be answered are compelling, and suicide never tells the whole story.

Henry Adams's brilliant and bitter autobiography, *The Education of Henry Adams,* was published in 1918, the year of his death, and written in the third person. The writer's lucid detachment that served so well in the minutely observed *Mont St. Michel and Chartres* (1913) became in *Education* a clear unwillingness to publicly limn his personal anguish, or perhaps humiliation. Clover is never mentioned in the book. The twenty-year gap in the autobiography's narrative begins in 1872, the year Adams married Clover, and ends in 1892. After her death he destroyed their correspondence and his own diaries of that period, consigning to oblivion any further knowledge of their marriage. Together they disappeared into a dark void: Clover to her death and Henry to the commissioning of her memorial, which would illuminate his simultaneous remorse and defiance.

In June 1886, a restless Adams went to Japan with the artist John La Farge (1835–1910). They had met while La Farge was engaged on the murals and stained glass of Boston's Trinity Church (1873–77), a milestone American building by Henry Hobson Richardson, who also designed Adams's Washington home. In addition to La Farge, Richardson's Trinity collaborators included the sculptors Augustus Saint-Gaudens (1848–1907) and Daniel Chester French (1850–1931); the charismatic preacher and Adams cousin Phillips Brooks (1835–1893); budding architect Stanford White (1853–1906), who designed the architectural component of the Adams Memorial; and engineer Orlando Whitney Norcross (1839–1920), who constructed it. All involved with Clover's monument were part of an enormously influential circle of artists who forged a renaissance in American art.

La Farge shared and expanded Adams's knowledge of Eastern art and philosophy, which was in vogue in elegant circles at that time. When he set off for Japan, Adams said, half in jest, that he was a "Pagan searching [for] Nirvana," the Buddhist concept of release from all suffering and desire.

Despite Adams's chronic complaints in letters home about Japanese food, women, and hygiene, he was moved by what he experienced there to the extent that he began to think about a Buddhist-inspired memorial for his wife.

Upon their return, Adams decided to replace Clover's simple headstone with a more elaborate marker that would embody nirvana. La Farge introduced him to Saint-Gaudens. Adams gave the sculptor no clue as to what he wanted the memorial to look like, other than the desire that it symbolize "the acceptance, intellectually, of the inevitable." After discussing a few possible poses, Saint-Gaudens is said to have draped a rough cloth over his young apprentice to show Adams what he envisioned. Satisfied with pose and shroud, Adams told Saint-Gaudens to talk to La Farge about any questions he might have, as he didn't want to see the statue until it was finished. After the meeting, Saint-Gaudens jotted down, "Calm reflection in contrast with violence or force in nature."

The circuitous manner in which Adams's pain was transmuted into art is reflected in the process of creating the memorial. After meeting Adams, Saint-Gaudens appears to have struggled over several years with various possibilities under the guidance of La Farge, who acted as an interme-diary between sculptor and client. Saint-Gaudens, the most eminent sculptor of the era, operated brilliantly in the realm of images but was less sure in that of words. His natural reticence was intensified no doubt by Adams's unassailable and acerbic intellect, as well as his maddening unwillingness to comment directly on the various clay models and sketches that Saint-Gaudens made and then discarded. The sculptor was put repeatedly in the uncomfortable position of having to guess the answers to questions unvoiced by Adams, who, when he was not aiming sardonic darts with stinging precision, deemed silence his next best weapon.

Adams did furnish photographs of Buddhist fig-ures and the sibyls portrayed in Michelangelo's Sistine Chapel ceiling, while La Farge familiar-ized Saint-Gaudens with the white-robed Kwannon, the bodhisattva of compassion, which he and Adams had seen at the imperial shrine in Nikko. Kwannon was female in her Japanese emanation but had originated in India as a male; Saint-Gaudens sought to create an androgynous figure that would combine Eastern and Western ideals. The Western influence, accentuated by White's neoclassical base, is seen in the flowing drapery and pose of the figure, which recalls the seated goddesses sculpted on the Parthenon. Some scholars also believe Saint-Gaudens took the opportunity of the Adams commission to rework ideas he hadn't fully realized in *Silence* (1874), an oversized marble of a woman with closed eyes and a finger to her lips that he had made for the Masons.

The Adams Memorial is Saint-Gaudens's most abstract work, and a harbinger of the trend toward abstract art in the coming decades. Although the sculptor had an unsurpassed knowledge of composition and the nature of materials, the demands of the memorial (for a death resulting from an inexplicable act of suicide), the program (the figure was to be sexless and passionless), and the client pushed him to a psychological realism hitherto unseen in his work. Ultimately, however, art itself superseded the boundaries imposed by both patron and circumstances.

The 70-inch-high (178 cm) seated bronze figure is over-life-sized. It is completely shrouded, with the

The bronze figure sits on a rough chunk of granite from Quincy, Massachusetts, Adams's ancestral home. It is placed on a block of red granite that has been minimally decorated with an egg-and-dart molding at the cornice and a ribbon-bound laurel base.

1827

In France, Joseph Niepce makes the first photograph on a polished pewter plate cov-ered with bitumen of Judea

exception of the face and right arm, in a heavy cloak that was textured with burlap, a symbol of humility. Nearly hidden under a deep cowl, the face is strong and impassive, with full lips and closed eyes. The face is sensuous but not committed to any gender. Most think it is a woman. Adams insisted it wasn't, and imperiously corrected President Theodore Roosevelt after he referred to it as "her." "Should you allude to my bronze figure," Adams wrote, "will you try to do Saint-Gaudens the justice to remark that his expression was a little higher than sex can give. . . . The figure is sexless."

As historian Ernest Scheyer observed, Saint-Gaudens created the first colorful monument in American history. With its malachite-green figure and mottled red granite platform, it was a remarkable exception in a sea of earlier memorials cut from monochromatic stone.

At a time when Americans tended to think of sculpture as apart and isolated from its surroundings, Saint-Gaudens pioneered working in collaboration with architects and landscape designers. As with the sculptor's other ensembles, this statue's beauty is derived in large part from its harmony with the surrounding landscape. In 1892, architect Stanford White designed the neoclassical hexagonal setting. It includes the austere plinth behind the figure; an exedra, or semicircular bench, the ends of which are capped with owl wings representing the night; and a ornamental pebbled floor. Originally, evergreen plantings enclosed the ensemble and heightened its aura of seclusion from the world. The mature plantings were replaced with scraggly yews in a 2002 restoration, obliterating, temporarily at least, this crucial aspect of the setting.

When the work was installed, Adams was in the South Seas on a two-year journey. In June 1891, he relayed to Saint-Gaudens John Hay's observation that the memorial was "full of poetry and suggestion, infinite wisdom, a past without beginning and a future without end, a repose after limitless experience, a peace to which nothing matters—all are embodied in this austere and beautiful face and form." He adds, "If your work approaches Hay's description, you cannot fear criticism from me." Significantly, Adams had in

hand photographs of the completed memorial, but, as he admitted to the artist, chose to rely on Hay's assessment instead. It seems that Adams could not trust his own taste, validated by so many as impeccable, when it came to the emotional matter of his wife's memorial.

From the start, Clover's monument was intended to transcend individual tragedy and commemoration. At Adams's request, reiterated in his last will, there are no names, dates, or inscriptions on the memorial. It is little wonder that Adams wanted to shield his private loss. In the nineteenth century, suicide was still considered by most to be a moral failing, not a violent symptom of certain types of mental illness. The inscrutable figure expresses the unanswerable questions left in suicide's wake and the realization that the most that can be hoped for is acceptance.

The memorial is a testament to taste and status as much as to loss. The figure's understatement would be accessible, so Adams thought, exclusively to those in his rarefied circle who appreciated Asian art. What he didn't count on was the pull the figure would exert almost immediately on people from all classes. Ironically, the memorial's hermetic persona fanned public interest, first by word of mouth and then through newspaper and magazine articles. Rock Creek became a spot of pilgrimage. Adams's solitary contemplation at the grave was disrupted by the crowds, and his sensibility appalled by their wonderings aloud about whether the figure was a man or a woman and, less superficially, what the statue meant. The masses' search for meaning annoyed Adams most, and he wrote in *Education* that they "were vacant-minded in the absence of a personal guide. None felt what would have been a nursery-instinct to a Hindu baby or a Japanese rinricksha-runner."

The memorial's myriad names indicate its oracular impenetrability. Mark Twain is said to have coined the name Grief, as the figure is commonly known, saying that it embodied all of human grief. St. Gaudens called it *The Peace of God That Passeth Understanding* and also *The Mystery of the Hereafter;* still others called it *Nirvana* or *The Muse of Life and Death*. Ultimately, the mysterious figure puzzled even Adams, who wrote to Saint-Gaudens in 1902, "I see or think I see, an expression almost answering to defiance in the mouth and nostrils. You did not put it there nor did I." Adams could not bear the possibility, as Kirstein has remarked, "that there was indeed a mystery past his potential reckoning." He was buried there with Clover when he died in 1918.

The Adams Memorial does not attempt to engage the visitor, convey a specific message, or relinquish even the names of the deceased. Much has been read into its haunting silence. What Saint-Gaudens knew, and what Henry Adams came to accept, was that the meaning of any transcendent work of art varies from individual to individual. Indeed, the measure of its transcendence rests on its ability to provoke questions and compel multiple readings. Like the independent-minded woman it commemorates, the memorial requires that one think for oneself.

Augustus Saint-Gaudens, the foremost American sculptor of the nineteenth century, was born in Dublin in 1848 during the potato famine and came to New York City as an infant. After apprenticing as a cameo cutter in New York, he went to Paris and studied at the fabled Ecole des Beaux-Arts. This was followed by five years immersed in the study of the classical antiquities of Rome. A sculptor whose work fused technical mastery with heroic realism and expressive feeling, Saint-Gaudens created monuments that defined American public sculpture during the later nineteenth century, when the country broke away from the restraints of European cultural traditions. His civic works include monuments to Admiral David Farragut, Peter Cooper, and William Tecumseh Sherman in Manhattan; the Shaw Memorial in Boston; and the standing Abraham Lincoln in Chicago. In addition to his public monuments, which are his greatest legacy, his prolific output includes portraits executed in bas-relief, cameos, medals, and coins, including the twenty-dollar Liberty gold piece that is considered the most exquisite coin ever minted in the United States. He was artistic adviser to the 1893 Columbian Exposition and a member of the influential McMillan Commission, which reconfigured the National Mall. Saint-Gaudens spent his first summer in Cornish, New Hampshire, in 1885 and eventually built a house and studio there. Dozens of well-known artists—Herbert Adams, Lucia Fuller, Frederick MacMonnies, Paul Manship, William Zorach, and Maxfield Parrish among them—followed him and established the Cornish Colony, a generative force in American art. He died in 1907 at age fifty-nine after a long battle with cancer. An image of the Adams Memorial adorned the cover of the program handed out at his memorial service held in New York City on February 29, 1908. He is buried at Aspet, his home in Cornish, which is open to the public and maintained by the National Park Service.

1836
Samuel Colt patents the revolver

1836
Battle of the Alamo; Texas becomes an independent republic

General Grant National Memorial, popularly known as Grant's Tomb, was once Manhattan's most popular gathering place. On any given Sunday, carriages holding thousands of visitors beneath brim and parasol would travel uptown to Riverside Park to visit the luminous granite temple set high above the Hudson and take in the sweeping vistas and river breezes. By the 1970s, Grant's Tomb was marred by graffiti and littered with the detritus of the addicted and abandoned. In the early 1990s, a student whose passion for the old general led him to volunteer at the memorial made his case before Congress to have the tomb restored. The changing fortunes of this largely forgotten relic, tucked away in a park far from tourism's usual paths, illuminate how the vagaries of memory and geography can eclipse even the most significant monument's importance in the public's consciousness.

Identical mahogany-red granite sarcophagi on the lower level, reminiscent of Napoleon's tomb, contain Grant's body and that of his wife, Julia, who died in 1902. The niches hold bronze portrait busts of Grant's five key generals—William Tecumseh Sherman and Philip Henry Sheridan, sculpted by A. W. Mues, and George H. Thomas, James Birdseye McPherson, and Edward O. C. Ord by Jeno Juszko—that were made in 1938 under the WPA's Federal Art Project.

General Grant

National Memorial

LOCATION	DEDICATION	DESIGNER	COMMEMORATION
New York City	1897	John H. Duncan	Ulysses S. Grant

With bulldog persistence and brilliantly unorthodox stratagem, Ulysses S. Grant (1822–1885) led the North to a victory that would settle the Civil War and, at least nominally, the issue of slavery. After accepting at Appomattox the surrender of his equally, some would say more, talented and complex rival, Robert E. Lee, Grant returned home to a hero's welcome. He won the eighteenth presidency of the United States in 1868, elected on his record as a soldier, and faced the daunting task of peace. His two-term administration was stained with corruption, although he himself was beyond reproach—as his secretary of state Hamilton Fish said, it would have been impossible for Grant to tell a lie "even if he had composed it and written it down." After losing a third term, Grant and his wife, Julia Dent Grant, traveled the world to enthusiastic reception and settled in New York City. Plagued throughout life by drink and, later, bad investments, he was encouraged by Mark Twain to write his memoirs. A plainspoken tanner's son from Ohio with an unexpected genius for horses and war, Grant finished *Personal Memoirs* four days before his death from throat cancer. Edited and marketed to best-sellerdom by the savvy Twain, the book proved Julia's financial salvation.

Grant's adopted home treated him better in death, it seems, than in life. His demise on July 23, 1885, would inspire the most visible outpouring of grief in New York City's history. On August 8, a seven-mile-long column of sixty thousand mourners that included three presidents, Confederate and Union pallbearers, a phalanx of militia, and political dignitaries moved north under clouds of black bunting and past an estimated one million spectators in a funeral procession that began at City Hall in lower Manhattan and ended at Riverside Park. The event was without precedent. As *Harper's Weekly* reported, "the mere interring of his bones brought the continent to his feet." In a temporary brick-vaulted tomb erected near the present memorial, Grant was entombed for twelve years.

Within five days of his death, the first meeting was held of what would become the Grant Monument Association (GMA), whose purpose was to raise funds for a memorial; $600,000 contributed by 90,000 subscribers was eventually collected. After holding a competition that yielded sixty-five entries, none of them deemed satisfactory, a second, secret competition was held by invitation only. On September 11, 1890, the GMA announced the winning plan, that of architect John H. Duncan (1855–1929), who had distinguished himself with his earlier Soldiers' and Sailors' Memorial Arch (1889–91) in Brooklyn's Prospect Park.

c. 1839

English scientist William Fox Talbot invents the positive/negative process still used today to develop photographs

1839

French artist and chemist Louis J. M. Daguerre (1787–1851) discovers a method to permanently record and affix an image, which becomes the first commercially used photographic process. After acquiring Daguerre's patent, the French government declares the invention a gift, "free to the world"

Duncan's eclectic design—in his words, "unmistakably a monumental tomb from every point of view"—represents a stylistic departure from the more somber and modest funereal monuments of

The rectangular granite building is 150 feet (45.7 m) high and 90 feet (27.4 m) square, and occupies a one-acre site. The entrance portico is supported by two rows of fluted Doric columns. The square lower portion of the monument is surmounted by a drum colonnade surrounded with freestanding Ionic columns and terminates in a conical, stepped roof.

the past and reflects the period's taste for the extravagantly restated forms of antiquity. To emphasize Grant's exalted place in history, Duncan derived his design from paeans to earlier rulers. A primary influence was the tomb of King Mausolus at Halicarnassus (350 B.C.) in what is now Turkey, one of the seven wonders of the ancient world. That celebrated tomb, long since destroyed, gave us the term "mausoleum." The lower, open crypt that holds the twin sarcophagi of Grant and his wife was directly influenced by Napoleon's tomb at the Dôme des Invalides in Paris. The emperor Hadrian's tomb in Rome and the Garfield Memorial in Cleveland are subtly referenced as well. The cornerstone was laid by President Benjamin Harrison on April 27, 1892. The dedication of Grant's Tomb took place exactly five years later, on a chilly spring day that had been declared a state holiday and in the presence of immense crowds whose numbers rivaled those that attended his funeral cortège.

On the mausoleum's façade is Grant's epitaph, "Let Us Have Peace," a line taken from his 1868 letter accepting the Republican presidential nomination and the keynote of the reconciliatory aims

of his political career. Bookending the motto are two allegorical figures, said to represent Victory and Peace, sculpted by John Massey Rhind (1868–1936). Although Duncan had proposed a larger monument as well as an elaborate exterior sculptural program, insufficient funds prevented both. An innovative staircase leading to a Hudson

1840
Auguste Rodin, French sculptor, born (Nov. 12; d. Nov. 17, 1917)

1840
English scientist William Fox Talbot patents the calotype or talbotype, the first photographic process that produces negatives from which identical prints can be made

The dome rises 150 feet (45.7 m). The four vault pendentives are adorned with allegorical figures designed by John Massey Rhind, and cast in plaster and cement, that represent Grant's birth, military and civilian careers, and death. Finished in Carrara and Lee marbles, the interior focuses on a circular central opening that looks down upon the tombs on the lower level.

River dock for visitors arriving by boat was jettisoned for the same reason. Nonetheless, attendance averaged half a million visitors a year.

Modifications and additions were made to the tomb on numerous occasions after its dedication. Most radical was a 1928 plan by architect John

Russell Pope that profoundly changed Duncan's conception of the site and belied the reasoning behind its selection decades earlier. After Grant's death, a number of sites were offered to his family, including Central Park and Union Square, but they settled on the more remote Riverside Park location because its unobstructed views would

1841

Scottish clockmaker Alexander Bain patents the first electric clock allow the tomb, like the man, to stand alone. Pope's plan, which called for a plaza and trees in front of the monument, as well as the encroachment of new building in the neighborhood, all but guaranteed the tomb would be overshadowed, but this work came to an abrupt halt after the market crash of 1929. Paradoxically, as has been noted, the tomb benefited from New Deal employment relief programs overseen by the Works Progress Administration (WPA), which provided the labor and skills to implement Pope's plans, make repairs, and expand the informational exhibits—now needed to explain to visitors the tomb's significance. New art was created, including murals on the main level and bronze busts on the lower level, and outdoors, two heroic eagles were installed that had once graced the main New York City post office. A small Art Deco gem, an unrealized maquette of an equestrian statue of Grant by Paul Manship (1885–1966), graces the interior.

In 1959, the GMA transferred the tomb's care to the National Park Service. Before that, and since its inception, the site was known as Grant's Tomb or, more formally, as the Grant Monument. Officials of the Department of the Interior, which maintains the national park system, proposed the name be changed to the General Grant National Memorial in the belief that what the site primarily honored was Grant's military career. Others, who believe the current name disparages what Grant accomplished in his highest rank, have lobbied, as yet unsuccessfully, to have the site redesignated as the Grant's Tomb National Monument, thus acknowledging its most familiar name as well as the monument designation that was part of its formal, original name.

Seven years after the National Park Service took over, three mosaic murals depicting Grant at Vicksburg, Chattanooga, and Appomattox were installed in the lunettes, crescent-shaped recesses, high on the interior walls. Made by the Venetian Art Mosaics studio of the Bronx after paintings by New York artist Allyn Cox, the scenes are those specified by Duncan decades previously.

However, the sixties and the seventies marked the tomb's decline. In an effort to make it more appealing to visitors, and following a general national trend to modernize by stripping away architectural details and brightening colors, the Park Service made changes that would not be tolerated today; at that time, architectural preservation in the United States had yet to be championed by more than a handful. Consequently, the renovation saw the destruction of two ornate flag cases designed by the architect and the loss of archival materials, including original memorial competition drawings. Murals in the east and west flag rooms that depicted Grant's battles, painted by Dean Fausett (1913–1998) during the Depression, were obliterated with raspberry-pink and blue paint. Water discolored and damaged the rotunda, and the exterior paving stones were cracked.

With patriotism at a low ebb at the end of the sixties, the number of visitors decreased. The tomb was covered with graffiti and its grounds were littered. To counteract the graffiti epidemic and increasing vandalism, neighbor volunteers worked with Chilean artist Pedro Silva to create the serpentine mosaic benches that wander around the site's perimeter, which, while they detract from the tomb's formal character, mark an era in its history.

Change would come again in the person of Frank J. Scaturro, a Columbia University undergraduate who began working at the site as a volunteer tour guide in 1991. His repeated attempts to call the Park Service's attention to the tomb's compromised physical plant were ignored. After two years of unsuccessful lobbying, he went public in 1993 with a 325-page report to President Bill Clinton and Congress that documented the tomb's deplorable condition. The media howled. Scaturro resurrected the defunct GMA in 1993 and sued the government in 1994. He was joined in the suit by Grant's descendants, who threatened to remove the Grants' remains and bury them elsewhere if the monument was not restored. Scaturro's efforts were answered in 1997, the monument's centennial, with a $1.8 million face-lift that included repair and cleaning; restoration of the rotunda, murals, and plaza; new ceilings and roof; reconstruction of the octagonal cast-iron flag cases; and an upgrade of the wiring and lighting.

1843
Charles Goodyear patents his process for "vulcanizing" rubber

1844
Samuel F. B. Morse patents the telegraph and sends the first message, "What hath God wrought?"

Right Almost lost at the northern edge of the acre commanded by the tomb is a small fenced plot that contains a modest stone urn "Erected to the Memory of an Amiable Child, St. Claire Pollock." Pollock was a five-year-old who fell from the park's cliffs to his death on July 15, 1797. When his family sold the property, they asked that his grave be kept "always enclosed and sacred." The request has been honored, and this remains one of the few private graves on public land in the City of New York.

Below Completed in 1973 and modeled after Antonio Gaudí's Güell Park mosaics in Barcelona, Pedro Silva's playful mosaic benches—which include a portrait of Grant, an elephant ambling through a jungle, a stalled taxicab, and bouquets of flowers—provide an unexpected respite from the tomb's formality.

For the first three decades of its existence, while the Civil War was fresh in memory and her veterans alive, Grant's Tomb was New York's most frequently visited attraction. As those who promised "never to forget" faded away, they took with them the life of this monument and left future generations with only a vague notion of its location and a diminished sense of the significance of Grant and his worthy company on the battlefields. From points west, the tomb's pyramidal dome pokes through the treetops, elevated upon a high bluff along with the distinctive neo-Gothic belltower of the Riverside Church. The pair form an unlikely urban vista: a holy city on a hill, distant and apart from the busy streets below.

1846

Mexican War begins (ends 1848 with Treaty of Guadalupe Hidalgo; Mexico cedes California, Arizona, Nevada, Utah, and parts of New Mexico, Colorado, and Wyoming to U.S.)

Shaw
Memorial

LOCATION	DEDICATION	DESIGNER	COMMEMORATION
Boston, Massachusetts	*1897*	*Augustus Saint-Gaudens, sculptor; Charles F. McKim, architect*	*Robert Gould Shaw and the 54th Massachusetts Regiment*

On a warm May day in 1863, the 54th Massachusetts Volunteer Infantry, the first African American regiment raised by the Union to fight in the war that would end slavery, marched through Boston's winding lanes, turned onto Beacon Street, and strode one thousand strong past the reviewing stand that stood between the trees before the golden-domed State House. At their head was Robert Gould Shaw (1837–1863), a blue-eyed child of fortune and veteran of the battles at Antietam and Cedar Mountain, who was chosen to lead the regiment because of his antislavery principles. By July, he and nearly a third of his men would be dead and buried in a trench in South Carolina. Their monument, which occupies the space where the reviewing stand once stood, is the first major civic monument to commemorate the heroism of African American soldiers.

1847

Paul von Hindenburg, German president, born (Oct. 2; president of Germany, 1925–1934; d. Aug. 2, 1934)

On July 18, 1863, Shaw's troops attacked Fort Wagner, which, along with Forts Sumter and Gregg, protected the strategic port of Charleston, South Carolina, the cradle of Confederate secession. Within moments, Shaw was shot through the heart. Left for some reason without cover, the 54th was driven out, with 281 men killed, wounded, or missing; that number was increased by summary executions of the captured and desultory medical care for the wounded. A semi-fictionalized account of the tragic clash was told in the 1989 movie *Glory.*

The battle captivated the Northern mind for several reasons. Foremost were the sobering sense of the worth and weight of the Civil War's toll, a sentiment that would only grow stronger in the war's wake; the gallant death of Shaw, twenty-six years old, from a patrician Boston family, and now a symbolic martyr of the abolitionist movement; and the realization that the black troops, though inadequately trained and less well armed than their white counterparts, had fought bravely to the death nonetheless. Sympathy extended as well to Shaw's family, who were actively involved in the worldwide abolitionist movement. Upon learning that their only son had been unceremoniously stripped and thrown into a trench with the other anonymous dead instead of receiving the honorable burial normally accorded officers, the family rejected efforts to exhume the body and said there was "no holier place" for him than "surrounded by his brave and devoted soldiers."

However, the fundamental impetus for the canonization of Shaw and his regiment was summed up in words attributed to Horace Greeley that appeared in Boston's *Sunday Herald* on May 30, 1897: "It is not too much to say that if this Massachusetts 54th had faltered when its trial came, 200,000 colored troops for whom it was a pioneer, would never have been put in for another year, which would have been equivalent to protracting the war into 1866." As has been noted, black enlistment and emancipation advanced together and inseparably.

Immediately after the battle, funds to construct a monument to Shaw in the vicinity of Fort Wagner were raised by survivors of the 54th and freed slaves of Beaufort, South Carolina. Unstable ground conditions at the site, coupled with the resentment of the local white population, scuttled those plans; the funds were later used to found the first free black school in Charleston. Joshua B. Smith, a former slave, raised several thousand dollars to erect an equestrian monument to Shaw, but efforts to commemorate the officer would not succeed until the project was taken up by a group of influential Boston Brahmins over a decade later. In 1881, the architect H. H. Richardson spoke about the Shaw commission to Augustus Saint-Gaudens (1848–1907), the dean of American sculpture, who was, more than anyone else at the time, and many would argue since, America's finest interpreter of historical subjects. Commemorative works proliferated after the Civil War, and six of the finest came from his hands.

Saint-Gaudens initially suggested an equestrian statue, never having sculpted one before, but the idea was rejected by Shaw's family as being too pretentious; their son, after all, was a young colonel, not a general, and had led the charge on foot. The artist recalled that "in casting about for some manner of reconciling my desire [to have a horse] with their idea, I fell upon a plan of associating him directly with his troops in a bas-relief, and thereby reducing his importance." Subsequently, he invented a hybrid work that draws on the long equestrian tradition in Western art, most notably the Roman *Marcus Aurelius* and the *Colleoni* statue in Venice, and fuses it with a subtly modeled bas-relief. The memorial also presages Saint-Gaudens's majestic 1903 portrait of William Tecumseh Sherman that anchors the southeastern corner of New York's Central Park. Saint-Gaudens's monumental relief in Boston is stylistically unprecedented in the nineteenth century, one earlier exception being François Rude's sculptural group on the façade of the Arc de Triomphe in Paris.

The twenty-three soldiers are organized in six rows up to four deep and led by two drummer boys. Shaw, on horseback, dominates the composition and is sculpted in deep, nearly three-dimensional, relief. The men in the foreground are sculpted in high relief that recedes to low relief to create the impression of limitless numbers. Overhead, an angelic figure beckons the regiment onward with one hand and in the other holds an olive branch and poppies, symbolizing

1849 — Sir David Brewster, who invented the kaleidoscope in 1816, invents a viewer for stereoscopes, paired photographs that create the illusion of three dimensions; by the 1850s, viewing stereographs, especially of famous faces and places, is an international obsession

1850 — Compromise of 1850 which allows free and slave states, passed by Congress

1855

Roger Fenton produces 360 photographs of the Crimean War, one of the earliest systematic attempts to document war through photography

Richard Benson's photographs were first published in *Lay This Laurel* (1973) by Lincoln Kirstein. In order to show the memorial as Saint-Gaudens intended—he designed it to be viewed at eye level—Benson built a wooden platform, reassembled onsite each day, so his camera lens was pointed at midsculpture. His photographs allow us to scrutinize the sculpture in a way not ordinarily possible. Since they were taken, the memorial's patina and stonework have been restored. These images, however, provide unique testimony to the power of the printed works that laud them: Leslie George Katz, who published *Lay This Laurel,* always wanted the names of the men of the 54th Regiment carved on the memorial; the officers' names were inscribed on the memorial, but the soldiers' names, though originally intended to be included, never were. In order to call attention to the missing names, he published the book, which lists everyone who died. In 1982, the soldiers' names—designed by John Everett Benson of the John Stevens Shop and cut by Brooke Roberts—were finally included on the monument.

1858

Abraham Lincoln and Stephen Douglas (b. Apr. 13, 1813; d. June 3, 1861) debate seven times on slavery during Illinois senatorial race

1860

James Clerk Maxwell (1831–1879), a Scottish physicist, discovers while investigating color blindness that color photographs can be made using red, green, and blue filters

peace and death. The figures of the angel and Shaw overlap and so intimate his immortality. Saint-Gaudens unifies and animates the whole by contrasting the rhythmic patterns of the soldiers' and horse's legs, which move forward to the right, with the raised bayonets that slant back to the left. The composition's controlled formality, which evokes the soldiers' solidarity as well as the inevitability of their march, is balanced by the material expressiveness of their rumpled uniforms and assorted rifles, packs, and canteens. We feel

anecdotes, lampoons, and caricatures pervaded the popular press of the era, prejudices that Saint-Gaudens himself perpetuated in word if not deed, as Albert Boime has observed in *The Art of Exclusion,* a study of the codified portrayal of African Americans in nineteenth-century art. Boime maintains that Saint-Gaudens's depiction of Shaw's regiment—who, by virtue of the composition, are on the same level as the horse and below the elevated white officer—perpetuates the racial hierarchy the memorial was intended to

By every consideration which binds you to your enslaved fellow countrymen, and the peace and welfare of your country; by every aspiration which you cherish for the freedom and equality of yourself and your children; by all the ties of blood and identity which make us one with the brave black men now fighting our battles in Louisiana, in South Carolina, I urge you to fly to arms, and smite with death the power that would bury the Government and your liberty in the same hopeless grave.

—Frederick Douglass, "Men of Color, To Arms!" March 2, 1863

the weight they carry. Though the erect figure of Shaw contrasts with the forward thrust of the troops, he is not separate from them—they move forward as one.

The portraits affirm beauty, nobility, and technical mastery. Each face, whether showing dogged determination, grim acceptance, or youthful anticipation, has been closely observed and lucidly modeled to convey their individual humanity. The cause was political, but the bravery was individual. The artist shows the full range of the soldiers' physiognomies; their occupations, which ranged from laborer to dentist; and ages—some of the 54th were as young as sixteen, others were fathers who had enlisted with their sons. Saint-Gaudens walked Manhattan's streets, looking into dozens of faces, until he found the models he wanted. He offered them merely "a job," having quickly found that asking them if they'd like their picture made scared them away.

Their suspicion was understandable. Racial discrimination against all ethnic groups in the form of

dispel. It is indisputable, however, that the memorial's subject matter had few if any precedents. Before 1860 there are no known images of African Americans, slave or free, in marble or bronze, according to historian Kirk Savage. Moreover, the widely recognized standard of male beauty was that of classical antiquity—white males as sculpted by the Greeks and reissued by the Romans. Savage writes in *Standing Soldiers, Kneeling Slaves* that the medium's "obsession with ideal human form made the whole subject of slavery extremely difficult for sculptors to represent" because "racism, like sculpture, centered on the analysis and representation of the human body." Saint-Gaudens's achievement was creating the first portrait of black soldiers who marched—not crept, crouched, or knelt—toward their destiny.

With the death of Richardson in 1886, Charles Follen McKim (1847–1909), a partner in the leading firm of McKim, Mead and White and a great friend of the sculptor's, was selected to design the memorial's architectural elements. He set the bronze relief, which measures 11 x 14 feet (33 x 42 m), within an arched stone tablet with a seat. The whole is bookended with eagles that perch on balls. The tablet sits on a quadrangular terrace bordered on three sides by

After the 1897 installation of the Shaw Memorial, Saint-Gaudens continued to make changes to plaster models of the work that were exhibited in the Paris salon of 1900 and at the Pan American Exhibition in Buffalo in 1901. A plaster version was displayed at Aspet, Saint-Gaudens's home in Cornish, New Hampshire, until 1996, when funds were raised to have it cast in bronze. That bronze is at the Saint-Gaudens National Historic Site in Cornish, and the original plaster is on loan to the National Gallery of Art in Washington, D.C.

a carved granite balustrade. McKim deliberately positioned the memorial between two standing elms that frame and emphasize the central bronze relief. On the Common side are various inscriptions, along with three life-size lion heads whose mouths cascade water into a lower basin.

Saint-Gaudens, who had once apprenticed to a cameo cutter, was painstaking. He reconsidered and reworked the piece, slowly coaxing it into being over a period of fourteen years, despite the increasingly vocal impatience of the memorial committee. But his slowness was not merely the consequence of a compulsion for detail. The evolution of the artist's conception of the work paralleled the nation's collective pause as people tried to make sense of the divisive conflict. The phalanx of soldier monuments that sprung up after the war typically celebrated the age-old urges to kill and to defend one's turf; soldiers, black and white alike, were depicted as undifferentiated warriors. Rarely expressed was the larger ideal of civic valor, that "more lonely courage," as orator William James would later describe it at the Shaw memorial's dedication. At the same time that America was erecting monuments that would confirm the "new birth of freedom" proclaimed by Lincoln at Gettysburg and an expanded nationality that now included four million ex-slaves, the meaning of that new identity continued to change, then as now, in dramatic and unpredictable ways. The sculptor's difficult commission was to give permanent voice to the multiple and often opposing stories in the national collective memory after the Civil War. His work portrays far more than a specific battle; it attempts to justify the war itself.

The memorial was dedicated on Memorial Day, May 31, 1897. Under gray skies and in a fine mist, members of the 54th, many with empty sleeves and crippled gaits, marched along Beacon Street once more. For Saint-Gaudens, the sight blurred the lines so frequently drawn between past and present. To him, the soldiers "seemed as if returning from the war, the troops of bronze marching in the opposite direction— the direction in which they left for the front, the young men in the bas-relief showing these veterans the hope and vigor of youth. . . . It was a consecration."

Inscribed on the right side of the relief is the motto of the Society of the Cincinnati, an organization whose members were descendants of Revolutionary War officers and to which Shaw belonged: OMNIA.RELINQVIT / SERVARE. REMPVBLICAM "He forsook all to preserve the public weal"

Charles W. Eliot, then president of Harvard University, composed three tributes on the rear of the memorial:

The White Officers
Taking life and honor in their hands cast in their lot with men of a despised race unproved in war and risked death as inciters of servile insurrection if taken prisoners besides encountering all the common perils of camp march and battle

The Black Rank and File
Volunteered when disaster clouded the Union cause served without pay for eighteen months till given that of white troops faced threatened enslavement if captured were brave in action patient under heavy and dangerous labors and cheerful amid hardships and privations

Together
They gave to the nation and the world undying proof that Americans of African descent possess the pride courage and devotion of the patriot soldier one hundred and eighty thousand such Americans enlisted under the Union flag in MDCCCLXII–MDCCCLXV

In 1982, as part of an overall restoration by the Boston firm of Ann Beha Architects, the sixty-two names of the black soldiers who died at Fort Wagner were inscribed on the monument:

HENRY ALBERT ◆ THOMAS R. AMPEY ◆ THOMAS BOWMAN ◆ WILLIAM BRADY ◆ ABRAHAM BROWN ◆ JAMES H. BUCHANAN ◆ HENRY F. BURGHARDT ◆ ELISHA BURKETT ◆ JASON CHAMPLIN ◆ ANDREW CLARK ◆ LEWIS CLARK ◆ HENRY CRAIG ◆ JOSEPHUS CURRY ◆ EDWARD DARKS ◆ HENRY DENNIS ◆ WILLIAM EDGERLY ◆ ALBERT EVANS ◆ WILLIAM S. EVERSON ◆ SAMUEL FORD ◆ RICHARD M. FOSTER ◆ CHARLES S. GAMRELL ◆ LEWIS C. GREEN ◆ JOHN HALL ◆ WILLIAM HENRY HARRISON, 2ND ◆ EDWARD HINES ◆ BENJAMIN HOGAN ◆ CHARLES M. HOLLOWAY ◆ GEORGE JACKSON ◆ JAMES P. JOHNS ◆ JOHN H. JOHNSON ◆ DANIEL A. KELLEY ◆ HENRY KING ◆ CYRUS KRUNKLETON ◆ AUGUSTUS LEWIS ◆ THOMAS LLOYD ◆ WILLIAM LLOYD ◆ LEWIS J. LOCARD ◆ FRANCIS LOWE ◆ ROBERT MCJOHNSON ◆ JOHN MILLER ◆ JAMES M. MILLS ◆ WILLIAM H. MORRIS ◆ CHARLES E. NELSON ◆ STEPHEN NEWTON ◆ HARRISON PIERCE ◆ CORNELIUS PRICE ◆ THOMAS PETER RIGGS ◆ DAVID R. ROPER ◆ ANTHONY SCHENCK ◆ THOMAS SHELDON ◆ WILLIAM J. SMITH ◆ SAMUEL SUFSHAY ◆ JOHN TANNER ◆ WILLIAM THOMAS ◆ CHARLES VAN ALLEN ◆ GEORGE VANDERPOOL ◆ CORNELIUS WATSON ◆ EDWARD WILLIAMS ◆ FRANKLIN WILLIS ◆ JOSEPH D. WILSON ◆ WILLIAM WILSON ◆ JOHN W. WINSLOW

1861
Confederate States of America is formed; Jefferson Davis elected president of CSA

Lincoln Memorial

LOCATION	DEDICATION	DESIGNER	COMMEMORATION
The Mall, Washington, D.C.	*1922*	*Henry Bacon, architect; Daniel Chester French, sculptor*	*President Abraham Lincoln*

Bacon's design differs from the Parthenon with the addition of a raised attic parapet and an entrance and façade on the temple's long side. The exterior is constructed in gleaming white Colorado-Yule marble. The shrine is surrounded by a peristyle porch with thirty-six Doric columns that represent the states in the Union at the time of Lincoln's death in 1865. Above that, a frieze of forty-eight inscriptions and festoons represents the number of states at the time of the memorial's dedication.

The World's Columbian Exposition held in Chicago in 1893, attended by millions, molded a fundamentally new American identity—visitor Frank Baum based his vision of Oz on it, Walt Disney's father, Elias, helped build it, and icons no less than the Pledge of Allegiance, the Ferris wheel, the hamburger, Juicy Fruit gum, Aunt Jemima syrup, and Cracker Jack were introduced there. But it was more than a launching pad for new products. The Chicago exposition spawned a revolution in American urban design that would influence the appearance of the Lincoln Memorial and National Mall, and of cities across the country.

Visitors to the 1893 World's Columbian Exposition saw exotic pavilions from Asia, Europe, and Africa, and entertainment such as Little Egypt twitching her hips in the hootchie-cootchie, and brought home their enthusiasm. The exposition inspired the design of the National Mall and hundreds of neoclassical buildings and urban parks.

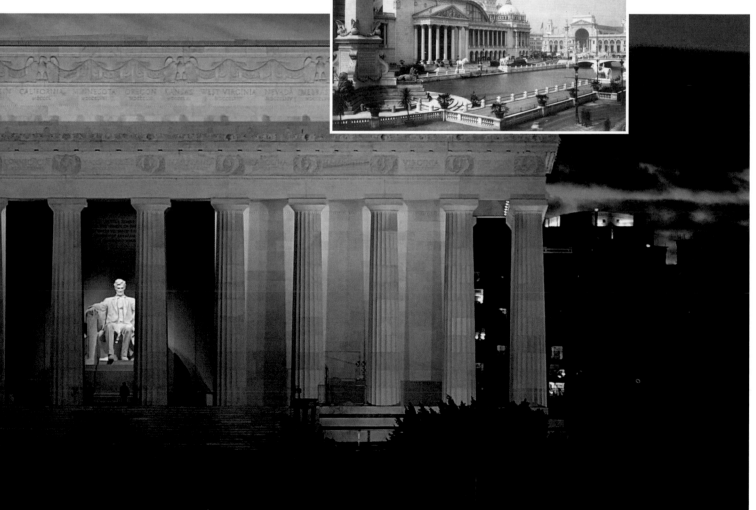

1863

Lincoln issues Emancipation Proclamation—all slaves held in rebelling states declared free (Jan. 1)

1863

Confederates led by General Robert E. Lee defeated at Gettysburg, Pa., by Union forces under General George G. Meade (July 1–4)

Its neoclassical exhibit buildings described a modern Athens, a vision, albeit a temporary one, of urban order and reason, with a whitewashed elegance that satisfied the gilded tastes of the wealthy in the late nineteenth century. The fair opened the national psyche to the power of architecture. People began to realize that cities could be more than meanly piled commercial sprawls—they could be beautiful.

Nicknamed the White City, the six-month fair was orchestrated by architect Daniel H. Burnham (1846–1912). Spread out over 633 acres, the exposition was set in a landscape of lakes and long vistas designed by Frederick Law Olmsted, Jr. (1822–1903). In 1901, Michigan senator James McMillan recruited Burnham and Olmsted, together with architect Charles Follen McKim and sculptor Augustus Saint-Gaudens, to form the McMillan Commission for the purpose of

revising Pierre L'Enfant's 1791 plan for Washington, D.C. The four devised an eternal Columbian Exposition set in the heart of the capital. The McMillan Plan, as their project was called, transformed the way Washington looked.

Key to the plan was the Lincoln Memorial's design and placement at the western end of the Mall's major axis. The McMillan Commission specified the site as a place for "a great portico of Doric columns," whose design would provide a counterpoint to two other national icons on that same axis, the Capitol and the Washington Monument. With the Reflecting Pool, the plan articulated a perfected, symbolic universe with a long view of the nation's aspirations.

On February 9, 1911, Congress legislated a bipartisan Lincoln Memorial Commission, which was chaired by President William Howard Taft. The Memorial Commission, in consultation with the U.S. Commission of Fine Arts, considered other sites and designs for the memorial, notably plans submitted by John Russell Pope. Sculptor Gutzon Borglum lobbied furiously for a memorial with realistic figures that spoke to an American rather than European sensibility, but had to wait to realize his heroic vision at Mount Rushmore. Ultimately, the memorial's site and design were those recommended a decade earlier by the McMillan Commission.

The memorial design by architect Henry Bacon (1866–1924), who also worked on the Columbian Exposition, reaches back to the vocabulary of the Parthenon (432 B.C.) in Athens, Greece. Like every Greek temple, the Parthenon enshrined a deity, in this case a statue of the goddess Athena, and had an altar outside to the east for public sacrifice and ritual. Similarly, Bacon proposed an eastern-facing temple that would house a heroic portrait of Lincoln, and placed it in a setting conducive to public ritual.

The colossal figure of Lincoln was carved in the Bronx by the legendary Piccirilli brothers, who translated French's model into the 19-foot-high (0.30 m) memorial sculpture. The Piccirillis carved nearly everything designed by French, as well as works by most major American sculptors. Ernest C. Bairstow, with Evelyn Beatrice Longman, carved the decorative friezes and inscriptions.

In 1913, when the Memorial Commission recommended Bacon's design to Congress, it was vehemently debated. Defending Bacon's classical scheme, Representative Samuel McCall of the Memorial Commission told Congress, "The Greek column speaks. It illustrates dignity, beauty,

The McMillan Commission recommended a pool be built in front of the proposed memorial to Lincoln. The Reflecting Pool is 2,029 feet (618.4 m) long and approximately 30 inches (76 cm) deep.

simplicity, and strength. And, however the soul of Lincoln might have been chiseled in its making, as he came finally to be, every one of those elements was represented in his character."

Other memorial proposals included one for a highway lined with commemorative statuary to be built between Washington and Gettysburg. The Gettysburg Road plan, supported by advocates of

columns create the sense that one is in a vast forest, a sacred chamber, protected from and yet still a part of the outer world. Around the columns' 6-foot mark, the limestone is discolored from hair oils where people have leaned their heads to look up at the central godlike figure of Lincoln. It is nearly impossible for the caretakers of this austere temple to erase these marks of human presence.

Each Jules Guérin mural is 12 feet (3.65 m) high and 60 feet (18.3 m) wide. The artist painted them in Manhattan and delivered them to Washington, D.C., where they were glued directly to the walls. Lincoln's accomplishments are depicted allegorically with classically dressed figures that nonetheless conjure the jazzy flamboyance of the era.

Lincoln had the dual virtue of his humble origins and his rise to prodigious power, learning, and morality, a combination that made him a useful model of ideal Americanism to an elite that was wedded to the rhetoric but not the substance of democracy.

—Christopher A. Thomas, *The Lincoln Memorial and American Life*, 2002

the good roads movement—remember, Ford began mass-producing his Model T in 1908—envisioned not just a road leading to the very spot where Lincoln delivered his immortal address but, as they wrote to 275,000 potential backers, "a transcontinental highway that will become the nucleus of a great national system of public roads." But even congressmen who had been impressed with the plan began to shudder at the inroads it would make upon the Treasury. Bacon's design prevailed in a 153–31 vote. "Idle sentimentalism," cried the defeated joyriders.

The memorial's interior is deliberately stark to focus attention on the Lincoln statue. It is divided into three sections by 50-foot columns. The

If he had done nothing else, Lincoln would be remembered still for the imperishable beauty and power of his language. The Gettysburg Address, a gem of literary genius and exquisite economy, is inscribed in its entirety—272 words—on the south wall. Opposite is his equally magnificent Second Inaugural Address. Royal Cortissoz, an art critic for the *New York Herald Tribune* and a friend of Henry Bacon, wrote the dedicatory inscription that appears over the Lincoln statue:

IN THIS TEMPLE
AS IN THE HEARTS OF THE PEOPLE
FOR WHOM HE SAVED THE UNION
THE MEMORY OF ABRAHAM LINCOLN
IS ENSHRINED FOREVER.

High above the address inscriptions are two wall paintings by the architectural illustrator Jules Guérin (1866–1946), who had also executed Bacon's memorial proposal illustrations. The exotically hued murals sidestepped issues of race, and, as historian Christopher Thomas has observed, kept "the whole matter of African-American servitude ethereal and unnamed."

1864
Union army under General William Tecumseh Sherman (Feb. 8, 1829–Feb. 14, 1891) captures and burns Atlanta (Nov. 12–15) then "Marches to the Sea" (Nov.–Dec) and occupies Savannah (Dec. 21)

1864
Abraham Lincoln re-elected president of the U.S.

The memorial's most compelling aspect is the person of Lincoln. Lincoln was not easily captured. Of his effervescent features, his secretary John Nicolay wrote, "Graphic art was powerless before a face that moved through a thousand delicate gradations of line and contour, light and shade, sparkle of the eye and curve of the lip, in the long gamut of expression from grave to gay,

them both with his myth, which grew exponentially after his assassination five days after Lee's surrender at Appomattox. As has been observed, the image of Lincoln emerged as the national icon of emancipation.

There was discussion of adapting the standing bronze Lincoln (1909–12) that French and Bacon

Emancipation of a Race, the mural above the Gettysburg Address, shows the Angel of Truth freeing slaves. *Unification,* located above the Second Inaugural Address and shown on opposite page, depicts the reconciliation of the North and South.

and back again from the rollicking jollity of laughter to that serious, far-away look that with prophetic intuitions beheld the awful panorama of war, and heard the cry of oppression and suffering. There are many pictures of Lincoln; there is no portrait of him."

Lincoln was the first American president to be widely photographed. He appears cold and petrified in most photographs, due to the lengthy exposure times required to make them. In any case, it is difficult to imagine the sorrowful Lincoln holding a smile for that long. Only his hair, different in every picture, implies his mercurial features. Lincoln quipped that his "wild republican hair" had "a way of getting up as far as possible in the world."

The formidable task before Daniel Chester French (1850–1931), the leading American sculptor at the time, was to express Lincoln's myriad personas—country lawyer, rail splitter, prophet, martyr, hero, Great Emancipator—and his gangly person, all height and nose and hair, and reconcile

had designed for the Nebraska capital. A replica of the seated Lincoln (1906) in Chicago's Grant Park by Saint-Gaudens, the canonical Lincoln portrayer until French, was also considered. However, Bacon was set on French, with whom he had collaborated on numerous projects. It was decided the figure should be seated because a standing figure would be lost among the façade columns. That made sense from an iconic standpoint as well, since a seated figure was a time-hallowed way in Western art of representing a dead statesman or king.

Bacon and French worked together to determine the statue's size and pose. After the proposed 10-foot statue was approved in 1916, it became apparent that it would be dwarfed in the cavernous interior space. The sculpture was nearly doubled in size, to 19 feet (5.8 m), and the floor was reinforced with steel to accommodate its weight. Because no single, unblemished piece of marble of sufficient size could be found, the statue was realized by Piccirilli Brothers, then the nation's foremost stone-carvers, from twenty-eight blocks of white Georgia marble and seamlessly assembled inside the memorial.

Existing small-scale models indicate that French spent considerable time repositioning Lincoln's

Civil rights leaders, including Martin Luther King, Jr., in the front row, left of center, march on Washington on August 28, 1963.

Coretta Scott King, flanked by her children, at the celebration of the fortieth anniversary of Martin Luther King, Jr.'s "I Have a Dream" speech. That address was given on August 28, 1963, to about a quarter of a million people. The concise, unadorned inscription is located on the granite landing between the memorial's two staircases. By matching historical photos and film footage of the speech with the features of the exterior stone, park rangers were able to pinpoint the precise spot where King stood.

confidence in his ability to carry the thing to a successful finish. If any of this 'gets over,' I think it is probably as much due to the whole pose of the figure and particularly to the action of the hands as to the expression of the face," wrote French in a 1922 letter to Charles Moore of the Commission of Fine Arts.

French's portrait balances authority with accessibility. As one faces the sculpture, Lincoln appears to be an august head of state—grave and immovable. From the side, however, his features are softened and transform the myth into the man. Details such as the unbuttoned coat, square-toed shoes, and rough hair and beard underscore this approachability. Most powerful is Lincoln's inscrutable gaze. He peers eastward in deep concentration toward a distant point, beyond the memorials to Washington and Grant and into the future. Ultimately, the sculpture has the inevitability of nature. Langston Hughes wrote of Lincoln's monumental portrait that he is "Quiet—/And yet a voice forever/Against the / Timeless walls / Of time— / Old Abe."

He sits alone.

hands and legs to express his mental and physical determination. His right hand appears to be impatiently tapping the edge of the chair, while his left is clenched resolutely in a fist. His legs are asymmetrically arranged in a relaxed pose, but both feet are solidly planted on the plinth above the pedestal.

"What I wanted to convey was the mental and physical strength of the great president and his

1865
Confederate States of America under General Robert E. Lee formally surrender to General Ulysses S. Grant at Appomattox, VA, ending the Civil War (Apr. 9)

1865
Abraham Lincoln, American president, assassinated by John Wilkes Booth and other conspirators (Apr. 14; born Feb. 12, 1809)

At the memorial's May 30, 1922, dedication, President Warren G. Harding reiterated Lincoln's belief that emancipation was the means to the greater end of maintaining the Union, that this "was the great purpose, the towering hope, the supreme faith." Other speakers included Dr. Robert R. Moton, president of the Tuskegee Industrial Institute in Alabama, whose comments about the continuing struggle between liberty and bondage were largely ignored by the press. With the exception of Moton's speech, the day was given to exalted rhetoric delivered to an audience whose strict segregation more accurately mirrored the historical reality of life for African Americans at the time of the dedication.

Embedded as Lincoln was in the nation's moral consciousness, and given the memorial's pivotal location, it was inevitable that his shrine would serve as the setting for social protest and change. In 1939, the Daughters of the American Revolution, owners of Constitution Hall in Washington, denied African American Marian Anderson a concert there because of her race. First Lady Eleanor Roosevelt, who resigned from the

a great American, in whose symbolic shadow we stand today, signed the Emancipation Proclamation"), delivered an oration that has been called the Second Emancipation Proclamation, and crescendoed with his memorable "I have a dream" conclusion. That speech, as has been noted, "legitimized the ongoing black revolution in the eyes of most Americans and came to symbolize a historical national turning point."

Since then, the Lincoln Memorial has evolved into the nation's preeminent place of assembly to advocate Lincoln's humanitarian goals. Built to sanctify his preservation of the Union, the memorial's meaning since has shifted to an examination of how the constitutional ideals of equality and justice can serve future generations. It does not define the Civil War's legacy as much as it encourages the expectation that the unanswered questions of the aftermath of that war will be addressed as long as need be. An icon of American commemorative design, it is a singular monument, a timeless and ceaseless meditation on the unresolved issues of the disenfranchised in a free nation.

In giving freedom to the slave, we assure freedom to the free—honorable alike in what we give, and what we preserve. We shall nobly save, or meanly lose, the last best hope of earth.

—Abraham Lincoln, Congressional Address, December 1, 1862

DAR during the controversy, made arrangements for the renowned contralto to sing instead at the Lincoln Memorial. Anderson wrote in her autobiography, "I had become, whether I liked it or not, a symbol, representing my people." On Easter Sunday, April 9, 1939, before seventy-five thousand people, she sang a program that included the national anthem and the Ave Maria, and closed with "Nobody Knows the Troubles I've Seen." With her appearance, Lincoln's idealized temple became irrevocably associated with the goals of the civil rights movement.

An even larger crowd gathered in August 1963 during the March on Washington for Jobs and Freedom. Martin Luther King, Jr., used the memorial as more than a patriotic backdrop. He began by invoking Lincoln ("Fivescore years ago,

Partitioning the space with columns gave the flanking inscription panels their own significance. The ceiling is of Alabama marble saturated with paraffin for translucency.

1868

General John A. Logan declares that Decoration Day, or Memorial Day, as it comes to be called, will be observed by placing flowers on graves at Arlington National Cemetery on May 30

1868

Ulysses S. Grant elected president of the U.S.

Fellow countrymen: At this second appearing to take the oath of the presidential office, there is less occasion for an extended address than there was at the first. Then a statement, somewhat in detail, of a course to be pursued, seemed fitting and proper. Now, at the expiration of four years, during which public declarations have been constantly called forth on every point and phase of the great contest which still absorbs the attention, and engrosses the energies of the nation, little that is new could be presented. The progress of our arms, upon which all else chiefly depends, is as well known to the public as to myself; and it is, I trust, reasonably satisfactory and encouraging to all. With high hope for the future, no prediction in regard to it is ventured.

Second Inaugural Address

On the occasion corresponding to this four years ago, all thoughts were anxiously directed to an impending civil war. All dreaded it—all sought to avert it. While the inaugural address was being delivered from this place, devoted altogether to saving the Union without war, insurgent agents were in the city seeking to destroy it without war—seeking to dissolve the Union, and divide effects, by negotiation. Both parties deprecated war; but one of them would make war rather than let the nation survive; and the other would accept war rather than let it perish. And the war came.

One eighth of the whole population were colored slaves, not distributed generally over the Union, but localized in the Southern part of it. These slaves constituted a peculiar and powerful interest. All knew that this interest was, somehow, the cause of the war. To strengthen, perpetuate, and extend this interest was the object for which the insurgents would rend the Union, even by war; while the government claimed no right to do more than to restrict the territorial enlargement of it. Neither party expected for the war, the magnitude, or the duration, which it has already attained. Neither anticipated that the cause of the conflict might cease with, or even before, the conflict itself should cease. Each looked for an easier triumph, and a result less fundamental and astounding. Both read the same Bible, and pray to the same God; and each invokes His aid against the other. It may seem strange that any men should dare to ask a just God's assistance in wringing their bread from the sweat of other men's faces; but let us judge not, that we be not judged. The prayers of both could not be answered; that of neither has been answered fully. The Almighty has his own purposes. "Woe unto the world because of offenses! for it must needs be that offenses come; but woe to that man by whom the offense cometh."

If we shall suppose that American Slavery is one of those offenses which, in the providence of God, must needs come, but which, having continued through His appointed time, He now wills to remove, and that He gives to both North and South, this terrible war, as the woe due to those by whom the offense came, shall we discern therein any departure from those divine attributes which the believers in a living God always ascribe to him? Fondly do we hope—fervently do we pray—that this mighty scourge of war may speedily pass away. Yet, if God wills that it continue, until all the wealth piled by the bond-man's two hundred and fifty years of unrequited toil shall be sunk, and until every drop of blood drawn by the lash, shall be paid by another drawn with the sword, as was said three thousand years ago, so still it must be said, "the judgments of the Lord, are true and righteous altogether."

With malice toward none; with charity for all; with firmness in the right, as God gives us to see the right, let us strive on to finish the work we are in; to bind up the nation's wounds; to care for him who shall have borne the battle, and for his widow, and his orphan—to do all which may achieve and cherish a just and lasting peace, among ourselves, and with all nations.

—Abraham Lincoln, Second Inaugural Address, March 4, 1865

This is traditionally considered the last portrait made of Linclon from life, taken in spring 1865 by Alexander Gardner. An albumen print was made from the cracked glass negative that was soon discarded. Master printer Richard Benson was able to recover much of the original lost detail in this and other Lincoln photographs in The Face of Lincoln *(1979)*

Balto

Balto, the charismatic canine of Central Park and the only statue in New York City that commemorates a dog, enjoys unrivaled popularity among the fifty-one other sculptures, monuments, and ornamental fountains spread out over Central Park's 843

I gave Balto, my lead dog,
his head and trusted to him.
He never once faltered.
It was Balto who led the way
—the credit is his.
—Gunnar Kasson, February 2, 1925

acres. A green oasis in midtown Manhattan, Central Park was codesigned by Frederick Law Olmsted and Calvert Vaux (rhymes with "rocks") after they won a competition with their 1858 Greensward Plan. Although the park is entirely man-made— Olmsted said the "undignified tricks of disguise" were necessary to achieve its rustic simplicity—the designers were not in favor of

placing sculpture in the park, which they preferred to be free of "incident." Incidents happen, however. Inundated with gifts of sculpture, the park's commissioners limited memorials to those subjects who had been dead for at least five years.

1869

A monument marks the place in Promontory Point, UT, where the Union Pacific and Central Pacific railroads met and made possible transcontinental travel (May 10)

That five-year rule has been overturned only once—for a half-wolf, half-Malamute sled dog. Balto, very much alive at the time of his commemoration, led eight other dogs 674 miles over Alaska's frozen tundra to save the 1,429 residents of Nome from a raging diphtheria epidemic. Dr. Curtis Welch, Nome's sole doctor, telegraphed an appeal for antitoxin serum to the "outside," as the rest of the country was called, on January 21, 1925. The only available serum was in Anchorage. Using an airplane—there were two in the state—wasn't possible because of low visibility and high winds. Instead, the serum was sent by rail to Nenana. The last 674-mile leg between Nenana and Nome was made by dogsled over the Iditarod Trail, a two-thousand-mile network of trails that was the primary means of navigating the north country.

Twenty teams of mushers and 150 dogs ran in relays in high winds and blinding snow in temperatures that hovered at 50° below zero. The entire world was riveted by the "race against death," and knew by heart the names of the lead dogs—the brains and steering wheel of the mushing operation. The distance to Nome was covered in the record-breaking time of five and a half days; the trip normally took three weeks or more. The longest leg of the trip, some 260 miles, was made by veteran musher Leonhard Seppala and his lead dog, Togo. However, it was Balto who covered the last 53-mile lap and delivered the frozen solid serum to Nome on February 2, 1925. (Seppala, although he owned Balto, always felt that Togo didn't receive enough recognition for his efforts. Shortly before Togo's death in 1929, he was honored at Madison Square Garden in New York City before twenty thousand well-wishers.) The next morning, Balto was featured on the front pages of newspapers around the world, and within days Parks Commissioner Francis D. Gallatin suggested the dog's heroism be commemorated with a statue in Central Park.

Balto was sculpted by Frederick G. R. Roth (1872–1944), chief sculptor of the New York City Parks Department. Roth used Chinook, a malamute from New Hampshire, as a model for Balto. The bronze stands on a natural rock outcropping located west of the park entrance at Fifth Avenue and Sixty-seventh Street. The inscription set into the rock pedestal reads, "Dedicated to the indomitable spirit of the sled dogs that relayed antitoxin 600 miles over rough ice, across treacherous waters, through Arctic blizzards, from Nenana to the relief of stricken Nome, in the Winter of 1925. Endurance Fidelity Intelligence." A bas-relief depicts the dogs mushing toward Nome. The piece was dedicated on December 15, 1925, ten months after the journey's conclusion. Balto himself was present but unmoved by the fanfare.

Now international celebrities, Balto and his team toured the United States. But their fame was fleeting. After the dogs arrived in Los Angeles for a scuttled movie deal, they were sold to vaudevillians and became an act in a sideshow. The dogs were discovered in 1927 by George Kimble, a Cleveland businessman who persuaded his hometown to raise the $2,000 needed to buy Balto and his six companions (Tillie, Fox, Skye, Billie, Old Moctoc, and Alaska Slim). After a few peaceful years at the Cleveland Zoo, Balto died in 1933. His body was subsequently stuffed and mounted by the Cleveland Museum of Natural History, where he is on periodic display.

The historic serum run and the role of sled teams in the settlement of Alaska are also commemorated by the Iditarod Trail Sled Dog Race. Called the "Last Great Race on Earth," the Iditarod is an annual competition held since 1973 that starts in Anchorage in south central Alaska on the first Saturday in March and concludes in Nome on the coast of the western Bering Sea ten to seventeen days later. A portion of the 1,150-mile (1,850 km) race follows the old Iditarod Trail used by Balto.

The serum delivery quashed the 1925 epidemic in Nome, and the diphtheria vaccine came into widespread use shortly afterward. The dogsled was made obsolete with the advent of popular air travel and, later, snowmobiles. The reasons for blazing the trail that was covered by Balto and his intrepid companions no longer exist either, except in the imaginations of those Iditarodders who annually seek to resurrect their death-defying spirit.

1870
Vladimir Lenin, Russian Communist leader, born (Apr. 10; U.S.S.R. leader 1917–1924; d. Jan. 21, 1924)

Château-Thierry
Monument

LOCATION	DEDICATION	DESIGNER	COMMEMORATION
Château-Thierry, France	*1928*	*Paul P. Cret*	*World War I American and French armed forces who fought in the Château-Thierry region*

The Allied and German forces, who sustained fatalities in the Great War of 1914–18 that were exponentially greater than those of the United States—eight million died in the war, 84,000 of whom were Americans—established massive cemeteries on the war's battlegrounds to deal with the sheer number of bodies and the tens of thousands of names for which bodies could not be found. For myriad reasons, not the least of them national

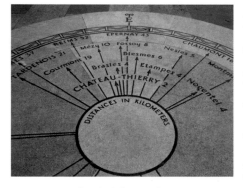

An orientation map to significant battle sites relative to Château-Thierry is set into the floor of the eastern terrace.

pride, the United States government sought to build memorials with a strong architectural presence that would focus attention on key American battles and coalesce the sacrifice of many into a handful of monumental ideological statements. To this end, they commissioned eleven prominent architects to build eleven World War I memorials and eight chapels under the auspices of the American Battle Monuments Commission (ABMC), authorized by Congress in 1923, chaired by General John J. Pershing, and guided by the architect Paul Philippe Cret (1876–1945).

Although all important American war operations were commemorated, the three most ambitious World War I projects—those at Château-Thierry, Mont Sec, and Montfaucon—were built in France. The focus of this essay is Château-Thierry, designed by Paul Cret.

The name of Verdun evokes impressions of death and motionlessness and frozen land under gray skies. The place is associated with a sense of being overwhelmed by a destiny marked by a colossal tragedy no one can recover from. Diversion is just impossible. As a child, I remember visiting my widowed grandmother and her sisters, eternally dressed in black. One had lost a fiancé and the other two sons in the war, and life had stopped for them. I do not remember ever hearing them laugh. Deep sadness was imprinted forever in their eyes. World War I caused one million and a half deaths. For four years, battles were fought to gain a few yards one day, which were often lost the day after.

My grandfather was the mayor of the village at the core of the Fleury-devant-Douaumont battlefield. All houses were destroyed, and a simple monument was erected out of the rubble. A pledge was made never to rebuild the land so that memory would endure. As children, we were not allowed to wander in the woods, because bombs were still buried in the landscape, sometimes killing those innocently taking a stroll, decades later.

Soon the city, deserted by industry, made a profit out of death. I lived across from a church and every Sunday or so, bells rang to mark veterans' celebrations and yet there was silence. They came from all over France and from neighboring countries, and I would watch them with their berets, carrying their medals and their flags. Then banquets would bring the veterans together, and little chocolate bombs would explode, filled with colorful treats and candies for the children.

When I became a teenager and started dating boys, it was not unusual to wander along the Ossuary of Douaumont, a massive grim monument of concrete, filled with skulls, which could be seen through the basement windows. Lists of boys' names killed at war and engraved on the walls revealed that in the same family, brothers as young as 16, 17, 18 had been killed one year after the other. The ossuary faced miles and miles of land spotted with white crosses, most of which had never been visited by loved ones. Another walk led to the Trench of Bayonets where young men had been buried alive after bombs drove them deep into the earth. Their bayonets facing the sky slowly emerged from the soil after a few years. We were both horrified and fascinated by the gruesome tales reported from that period and circulated within families, although the survivors themselves were too traumatized to ever talk about the war.

What is it like to grow up in Verdun? At a certain point you decide to leave. You leave as soon as you can. You go as far away as you can. I left Verdun and my family before I was seventeen, and so did a lot of my schoolmates. Now and then, we bump into one another in Paris and ask, "Have you ever gone back to Verdun?" No one has. Verdun remains a wounded, dying city. But we have carried our lives and our dreams elsewhere. —Sophie Body-Gendrot

A 1927 *Washington Post* article reported plans to build three monuments dedicated to the Allied cause in Château-Thierry, St. Mihiel, and the Meuse-Argonne region, and that the French government would preserve the ruins at Montfaucon as an "everlasting memory." The three memorials were located on the sites of the conflicts they commemorate, and reflect in their colonnaded and sparely elegant forms the vocabulary of the ancient Greeks, typical of the neoclassical style popular at the time they were built. By making direct reference to the ancients' revolutionary understanding of the relationship of the citizen to the state, such neoclassically styled architecture affirmed what the American culture once viewed as unchanging democratic values. Historian Jay Winter believes this nineteenth-century commemorative style offered the public a more reassuring response to the "universality of bereavement" than did the ironic stance and austere forms of the modernist style that would follow it.

Cret served as a foot soldier in the French Army and as liaison to the American Expeditionary Force in Europe during the war, after which he immigrated to the United States. Trained at the Ecole des Beaux-Arts, he was affiliated with the University of Pennsylvania for most of his career, which was dominated by civic buildings and memorial designs. In addition to domestic monuments for the Pennsylvania Battle Monuments Commission and other organizations, he designed American memorials abroad at Varennes and Bellicourt, the Quentin Roosevelt Memorial in Chamery, and the Pennsylvania 28th Division Memorial Bridge in Fismes, all in France, and for the Flanders Fields Cemetery at Waregem, Belgium. With Achille-Henri Chauquet, he designed the American memorial church of Château-Thierry (1924). The Folger Shakespeare Library and Federal Reserve Building in Washington, D.C., are two noteworthy examples of his numerous institutional designs.

The Château-Thierry Monument, located fifty miles east of Paris just west of the town for which it is named, sits atop Hill 204, as it was referred to on the battle maps, and commands a wide view of the Marne Valley. To cobble together the twenty-five-acre site, the ABMC, aided by Cret, had to negotiate the purchase of numerous small parcels of land on which the monument stands.

The limestone memorial stands in a quiet forest of chestnut trees. It commemorates the achievements of the American and French forces that fought in this region during the Great War. Architectural historian Elizabeth Grossman has observed that the memorial's pyramidal design, which builds upward in a series of rectangular setbacks, formally reiterates the hill on which it was built, as well as the stoic commitment to what was achieved by the armies that battled there. It consists of a narrow double-colonnade structure that rises above a long terrace. The east face, situated before the expansive countryside where the battle took place, features a massive carved eagle and shield, as well as a map showing American military operations in the region.

The interior walls are inscribed with a brief résumé of the action in the area that is given in French and English:

"In Flanders Fields," an elegiac poem written by the Canadian poet and army surgeon John McCrae in 1915, is a touchstone of the Great War. Its central image is the poppies that "blow between the crosses, row on row," that mark graves of those who "short days ago . . . felt dawn, saw sunset glow, loved and were loved." The blood-red poppy, the Flower of Forgetfulness, grew wild on the European battle-fields and became a symbol of the war.

In late May 1918 the German army made a surprise attack along the Aisne River and advanced rapidly toward the Marne. Allied reinforcements were hurriedly brought up, including the 2nd and 3rd American divisions which went into position directly across the German line of advance toward Paris. After severe fighting these divisions definitely stopped the progress of the attack on their front and the lines stabilized, the German forces having driven a deep salient roughly defined by Reims, Château-Thierry, and Soissons into Allied territory.

The last German offensive of the war, on 15 July, included an attack in the eastern part of this salient and there the 3rd American Division and elements of the 28th were important factors in the successful defense of the Allied positions.

On July 18 the Allied troops began a general counteroffensive against the whole salient in which the 1st, 2nd, 3rd, 4th, 26th, 28th, 32nd and 42nd American Divisions, most of which served under the I and III Corps, took a brilliant part. This offensive was a complete success, and by August 6 the enemy had been driven beyond the Vesle River. Later the 4th, 28th, 32nd and 77th American Divisions and elements of the 3rd and 93rd played a prominent role in the desperate fighting on the north of the Vesle. Of the 310,000 American soldiers who fought in these operations, 67,000 were casualties.

The entablature above the incised columns is inscribed with the names of the places where important battles were fought: Grimpettes Wood, Vaux, Missy-aux-Bois, Belleau Wood, Juvigny, Mézy, Noroy-sur-Ourcq-Sergy, Seringes-et-Nesles, Vierzy, Le Charmel, Bazoches, Fismette, Berzy-le-Sec, Trugny, La Croix-Rouge Farm, and Torcy.

It is worth recalling that the Château-Thierry Monument and ten others of its kind, joined by at least seven hundred smaller commemorative markers, monuments, and plaques, hold an important piece of American history that is far removed, much as the soldiers were, from home.

The American Battle Monuments Commission (ABMC) is the guardian of almost fifty overseas cemeteries and memorials that honor the service of United States Armed Forces. Congress established the ABMC in 1923. President Warren G. Harding named General of the Armies John J. Pershing, commander in chief of the American Expeditionary Forces in World War I, as the commission's first chairman, a position he held until his death in 1948. He was succeeded by General George C. Marshall. General Frederick M. Franks, Jr., ABMC's current chairman, continues the commemorative mission of his predecessors, all of whom have been four- or five-star generals.

The commission's work in fifteen countries includes the design, construction, and maintenance of twenty-four overseas military cemeteries that serve as resting places for 124,917 American war dead from the First and Second World Wars and the Mexican-American War; Tablets of the Missing that memorialize 94,135 U.S. service men and women from the world wars and the Korean and Vietnam wars; and twenty-five overseas memorials, monuments, and markers. One ABMC site, the Meuse-Argonne American Cemetery in France, pictured above, is the largest American burial ground in Europe. In Washington, D.C., the ABMC established the World War II Memorial, Korean War Veterans Memorial, and American Expeditionary Forces Memorial, which are now maintained by the National Park Service.

Two allegorical figures carved in deep relief on the west façade honor the friendship between France and the United States. They were designed by the French sculptor Alfred Bottiau (1889–1951).

The wall overlooking the terrace is carved with the numerical designations and insignia of the U.S. Corps and divisions commemorated there. From left to right, these are: the 1st, 2nd, and 3rd Divisions; I and III Corps; and the 28th, 32nd, 42nd, 77th, and 83rd Divisions.

Time Will Not Dim the Glory of Their Deeds

—General of the Armies John J. Pershing, inscription on the Château-Thierry Monument

1877

Thomas Alva Edison perfects the phonograph

1879

Joseph Stalin, Soviet Union ruler, born (Dec. 21; d. Mar. 5, 1953)

Entombed in a marble sarcophagus at Arlington National Cemetery is the body of a soldier who died during World War I. One of 1,543 unidentified dead of that conflict, it is not known whether he came from Idaho, Kentucky, or Manhattan, whether he fell in the Argonne Forest, on the banks of the Marne, or in the bloody valley of the Somme.

Tomb of the Unknowns

LOCATION	DEDICATION	DESIGNER	COMMEMORATION
Arlington National Cemetery, Virginia	1932	Lorimer Rich, Thomas H. Jones	Unidentified American soldiers who died in World War I, World War II, and the Korean War

The power of the Tomb of the Unknowns (also known as the Tomb of the Unknown Soldier) is found in its anonymity. It is not the first such tomb at Arlington—an unknown soldier from the Civil War was buried here on May 15, 1864—nor the only such tomb in the United States or abroad, but the one that holds a special place of honor.

Following the example of France and Britain, General John J. "Black Jack" Pershing, commander of the U.S. Army during the Great War, recommended that Americans show their appreciation of the two million doughboys who fought for their liberties. On October 24, 1921, four earth-stained caskets that had been exhumed from each of the American military cemeteries at Belleau, Bony, Thiaucourt, and Romagne were assembled in the city hall in Châlons-sur-Marne, France. Corporal Edward Younger of the 59th Infantry, recognized for his outstanding service, walked back and forth in front of the coffins before placing a bouquet of white roses on the one that henceforth would garner the honors for all unidentified soldiers.

The three remaining coffins were reinterred at Romagne, while the selected casket traveled on the ship *Olympia* across the Atlantic and up the Potomac, along with a box of earth from the American cemetery at Suresnes, with which it would be buried at Arlington. After arriving in Washington on November 9, the body lay in state in the Rotunda of the Capitol on the catafalque that once bore the body of Abraham Lincoln. The bier was covered with flowers by national and international delegations of dignitaries and tens of thousands of private citizens. On Armistice Day 1921, with somber pomp, the remains were interred under a simple marble slab. The elaborate tomb that stands today would not be constructed for another eleven years.

Architect Lorimer Rich (1891–1978) and sculptor Thomas Hudson Jones (1892–1969) designed the tomb as well as its siting and approaches. The pair also reconfigured the site and various roadways so that the adjacent Memorial Amphitheater of 1920 was brought into relationship with the rest of the cemetery. Completed in 1932, the tomb rests on top of the original marble base of 1921. It sits on a stepped plaza that overlooks Washington and is situated before the colonnaded amphitheater, itself a general memorial to the soldiers and sailors of all American wars, and the site of annual Memorial Day and Veterans Day services.

Historian James M. Goode, in his classic guide, *The Outdoor Sculpture of Washington, D.C.*, describes the three stylized and classically draped figures that adorn the tomb's east face as symbols of "Allied spirit" during the First World War.

The tomb was cut from white marble from the Yule Marble Quarry in Marble, Colorado, where the marble used in the Lincoln Memorial was also quarried. On Memorial Day 1958, the bodies of unknown combatants who perished in World War II and the Korean War were interred in crypts on the plaza in front of the tomb.

Let us now sing the praises of famous men,

our ancestors in their generations . . .

Some of them have left behind a name,

so that others declare their praise.

But of others there is no memory;

they have perished as though they had never existed;

they have become as though they had never been born,

they and their children after them.

But these also were godly men,

whose righteous deeds have not been forgotten . . .

their offspring will continue forever,

and their glory will never be blotted out.

Their bodies are buried in peace,

but their name lives on generation after generation.

—Ecclesiasticus 44:1, 8–10, 13–14.

1883
Benito Mussolini, Italian dictator, born (July 29; d. by firing squad Apr. 28, 1945)

1884
The World Time Conference establishes Greenwich Observatory in England as the prime meridian from which world time is calculated

A central female figure of Victory is flanked by and holds hands with two male figures representing Peace and Valor. The north and south faces are ornamented with Doric pilasters and inverted laurel wreaths. The tomb's west face is inscribed, "Here Rests In Honored Glory An American Soldier Known But To God" in lettering designed by August Reuling.

Tombs honoring unidentified warriors have been built throughout recorded history. Monuments, as *Washington Post* culture critic Philip Kennicott characterized them, are an "attempt to place some fact, or some understanding of history, beyond dispute: This man was heroic; this war was good; these people should be remembered. They demand our assent to some basic proposition, which we can give or we can withhold." One of the most famous Western war monuments, now lost, was erected to the memory of the three hundred Spartans who in 480 B.C. fought to the last defending the pass at Thermopylae against two hundred thousand invading Persians. Their dedication to duty was described with a starkly unequivocal inscription that read, according to Herodotus, "Go and tell the Spartans, stranger passing by, / That here, obedient to their laws, we lie."

The unknown military Everyman has lost not only his life but his identity as well, a transformative loss that bestows upon him immortality. His tomb embodies the hope that awful sacrifices of war have some redeeming value. This is not a new idea. Pericles, delivering in 431 B.C. what is considered the most influential funerary oration, said,

For this offering of their lives made in common by them all, they each of them individually received that renown which never grows old, and for a sepulcher, not so much that in which their bones have been deposited, but that noblest of shrines wherein their glory is laid up to be eternally remembered. . . . For heroes have the whole earth for their tomb; and in lands far from their own, where the column with its epitaph declares it, there is enshrined in every breast a record unwritten with no tablet to preserve it, except that of the heart.

Lincoln echoed these sentiments at Gettysburg when he urged those assembled to be "dedicated here to the unfinished work which they who fought here have thus far so nobly advanced." More than simply a remembrance, the tomb asks us to preserve the ideals for which the unknowns have died. In other words, *Earn this.*

Science has rendered the Tomb of the Unknowns an anachronism. With the availability of DNA testing, it is possible to conclusively identify remains, something that was not possible before the end of the twentieth century. DNA testing revealed that the remains of the Vietnam War serviceman placed in the Tomb in 1984 were those of Air Force pilot 1st Lt. Michael J. Blassie, who was shot down over An Loc, South Vietnam, in May 1972; through the efforts of his family, Blassie was exhumed, identified, and reinterred in 1998 in his hometown of Saint Louis, Missouri. Even though advances in forensic genetics have diminished some of the mystery shrouding the Tomb of the Unknowns, the memorial remains a viable cultural entity. It joins together the population in contemplation of the contribution and sacrifice of those who fight for the larger citizenry. Although technically speaking there will be no more unknowns, the tomb that commemorates them will continue to make visible the noble sacrifice of a few for the many.

Since 1937, the tomb has been guarded by a hand-selected group of rigorously trained members of the 3rd Infantry Regiment. In a formal ceremony that is repeated on the half hour in summer and hourly during the rest of the year, twenty-four hours a day, the guards pace back and forth in front of the tomb, marching twenty-one steps, pausing for twenty-one seconds, and then making a crisp turn; twenty-one refers to the twenty-one-gun salute, the highest military honor.

Mount Rushmore
National Memorial

1886

In the *New York Tribune* offices, Ottmar Mergenthaler demonstrates his invention—Linotype, a high-speed, mechanical means of setting type—which will open a new era in mass communications

It would be easy to label Mount Rushmore, a beloved yet controversial American icon,

as the product of one man's obsession, the triumph of a relentless ego over a stubborn

mountain of stone. Critics of the celebrated national monument, located in South Dakota's

Black Hills, decry its invasiveness, cut into a place of unspoiled natural beauty; others

dislike the sculptures' realism; and many call attention to the fact that the Black Hills are

sacred land to the Lakota Sioux Indians. For them, the blasting away of tons of granite

to carve the faces of four American presidents was an act of desecration.

LOCATION	DEDICATION	DESIGNER	COMMEMORATION
Black Hills, South Dakota	1925–1941	Gutzon Borglum	U.S. presidents George Washington, Thomas Jefferson, Abraham Lincoln, Theodore Roosevelt

1887
Queen Victoria celebrates her Golden Jubilee

Washington Head
Work began on Mount Rushmore in 1927 with George Washington's head, which was dedicated on July 4, 1934.

Jefferson Head
"I had seen the photographs, I had seen the drawings, and I had talked with those who are responsible for this great work, and yet I had no conception, until about ten minutes ago, not only of its magnitude, but also its permanent beauty and importance," President Franklin Roosevelt said at the unveiling of the Jefferson head on August 30, 1936.

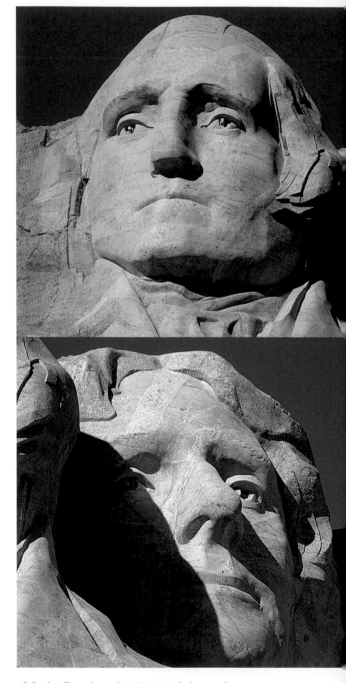

But the truth is Mount Rushmore has never been easy to pigeonhole. It is too big (in that respect, quintessentially American), and a phenomenon so multifaceted and contested that it has come to represent the history of the United States better than anyone dreamed when the idea for the colossal mountain carving was first born in the 1920s.

At that time, South Dakota was a sparsely populated state, and memories of the Indian wars that had erupted when gold was discovered in the Black Hills in the 1870s were still fresh in memory. It was only forty-seven years earlier that Crazy Horse and his Sioux warriors had dispatched Col. George Armstrong Custer and his 7th Cavalry at the battle of Little Bighorn. Grandparents were still alive who could recall those days.

In the end, as everyone knows, Crazy Horse lost the war against the white man for control of the Plains, and the Black Hills became part of the new state of South Dakota. It was a remote and wildly beautiful region, featuring geological wonders such as a series of tall jagged rocks that looked like sand drippings. Locals called them the Needles. Could the Needles be used in a way that would draw tourists to South Dakota? Doane Robinson, South Dakota's state historian in 1923, thought they could.

Robinson proposed carving the Needles into a lineup of men and women who helped forge the West. To Robinson's credit, Native Americans were included in this mix. The sculptures would serve as a "Gateway to the West" and, in Robinson's mind at least, attract tourists—who by that time were taking to the road in record numbers.

But who knew how to carve mountains? The American sculptor born John Gutzon de la

Mothe Borglum (1867–1941), better known as Gutzon Borglum, did. By the time Robinson needed him, Borglum had begun to carve Georgia's Stone Mountain into a memorial to the defeated Confederacy. That project was aborted, but did whet Borglum's appetite for making the grand statement in stone. At Robinson's invitation, Borglum toured the Black Hills on horseback in 1924. The Needles' cragged beauty inspired him to propose carving the spires into

1888
Kaiser Wilhelm II succeeds to German throne (d. 1918)

1888
With the slogan "You press the button, we do the rest," George Eastman puts the first simple, handheld camera into consumers' hands

Roosevelt Head
Borglum adapted the heads to the existing stone formation in ingenious ways, seen in his placement of Roosevelt. This slowed down the carving, as each new head determined the placement of the next, but gave the work an organic inevitability and a natural place on the mountain.

Lincoln Head
Borglum dreamed of including something he called the Entablature, a condensed history of the United States that would be carved in the spot where Lincoln's head is located. Eventually, the Entablature plan was scrapped, for various reasons, including the practical impossibility of reading type from a great distance.

"A monument's dimensions should be determined by the importance to civilization of the events commemorated," he declared. In other words, western heroes were well and good for a smaller project, but not for the face of a mountain. Always one to swing for the fences, Borglum envisioned a work that would rival the monuments of Egypt, Greece, and Rome.

The monument Borglum had in mind would depict four presidents who historians agreed were seminal to the nation's rapid rise. The inclusion of Washington, Jefferson, and Lincoln for their roles in founding, expanding, and preserving the Union, respectively, was obvious. Theodore Roosevelt, preferred by Borglum for his dedication to the conservation of America's natural resources, was a prescient choice, if unpopular at the time. Others considered for the coveted fourth spot were President Woodrow Wilson and suffragette Susan B. Anthony. Roosevelt prevailed. A 1999 campaign to have Ronald Reagan added was cut off at the pass by the National Park Service, which, after studying the mountain's stability, concluded it could not handle any more carving or drilling.

America will march along that skyline.
—Gutzon Borglum, 1924, upon seeing Mount Rushmore for the first time

full-figured heroes but ultimately proved too controversial a site for a colossal monument.

Instead, Borglum chose Mount Rushmore, 5,725 feet high (17.37 m), because it had an expansive granite wall that faced southeast, enabling the sun to shine on it for most of the day. Borglum persuaded Robinson to discard his idea for a celebration of the West in favor of a tribute to the history of the American Republic.

Borglum was a perfect match for Mount Rushmore. Born in Idaho on the heels of the Civil War, he reached maturity just as the United States began to understand itself as a player on the international stage, and sought to assemble epic symbols of its identity. Brilliant and contentious, a self-proclaimed American Phidias, Borglum had a will as formidable as the mountain. A country as big as America needed a big

1889
Adolf Hitler, German dictator, born in Braunau am Inn, Austria (Apr. 20)

Borglum's first foray into mountain carving came at Stone Mountain, a granite monolith outside Atlanta. In 1923, he began carving the Confederate memorial first envisioned by the formidable United Daughters of the Confederacy, later commissioned by the Stone Mountain Confederate Monumental Association, and supported wholeheartedly by the Ku Klux Klan. The sculpture was to depict an army of thousands led by the greats of the Lost Cause, specifically Robert E. Lee, T. J. "Stonewall" Jackson, and Jefferson Davis. Borglum did complete Lee's head in time for the anniversary of Lee's birth on January 19, 1924. Following a clash of the titanic egos involved, Borglum defied the sponsors by destroying his models and drawings in 1925, and left for South Dakota. Lee, the only figure at the time, was blasted off so that the new Stone Mountain, designed by Augustus Lukeman (1871–1935), would be visually harmonious. Lukeman's extravagant plan, never fully realized, added a reflecting pool, memorial hall, and tomb of an unknown soldier to the three figures on horseback that Borglum had envisioned. Occupying three acres (12,000 square m), it is the largest bas-relief in the world. Lukeman could not complete the work by the 1928 deadline imposed by the Commission; the work languished until 1958 when the state of Georgia took control of the site. Using Lukeman's plans, Walker Kirtland Hancock (1901–1998) took over as chief sculptor in 1963, and his chief carver, Roy Faulkner, completed the monument in 1972.

monument, Borglum said time and again, rebuffing concerns of conservationists who disliked Robinson's scheme from the start.

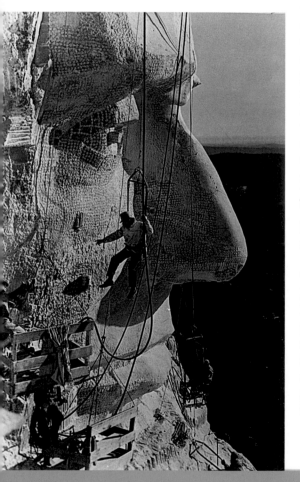

Sculptor Gutzon Borglum can be seen in the bosun's chair in front of Lincoln's cheek.

Nothing daunted Borglum, not marshaling a workforce of four hundred men and training them how to use dynamite and other treacherous tools while they hung by ropes hundreds of feet in the air; not working year in and year out in the quixotic climate of the Black Hills, where lightning and thunderclaps can come on suddenly, bringing work to an unexpected halt for the day; not even having to relocate Jefferson's head from the left of Washington's to the right because there wasn't enough rock in the first location.

"Life is a kind of campaign," Borglum told his daughter Mary in a letter. "It means plans, purpose, resolution and maybe fight; and people have no idea what strength comes to one's soul and spirit through a good fight." An insurgent's insurgent, the sculptor regularly claimed real estate in national newspapers headed by incendiary lines, such as this 1915 gem from *The New York Times:* "New York a Sieve for Art Junk."

On October 4, 1927, the carving of the mountain began with Washington. At first, Borglum wasn't going to use dynamite, but after confronting the stubbornness of the granite rock face, he changed his mind. The sculptor did not drill the actual stone; he designed the piece and directed the crew—mostly unemployed miners, glad for a job during the Depression. Soon, the men became skilled in precision blasting, a delicate and dangerous art, that was followed by drilling that smoothed the stone's surface. They used plaster casts of the heads to guide them, but even more important was a device called a "pointing machine" that enabled Borglum to translate measurements from the model to the monument—one inch on the monument model equaled one foot on the mountain—and thus reproduce his model on the mountainside on a vastly larger scale.

"The longer we were there, the more we began to sense that we were building a truly great thing, and after a while all of us old hands became truly dedicated to it and determined to stick to it," Otto "Red" Anderson, one of the monument's carvers, told Rex Alan Smith, the author of *The Carving of Mount Rushmore,* a 1985 account of the monument's creation.

1894

Nicholas II becomes last czar of Russia

One by one, the faces of the presidents emerged from the rock. Massive, placid, and beautifully articulated, each face measures some sixty feet from chin to forehead. President Calvin Coolidge, wearing new cowboy boots, had extolled the monument as an example of American can-do spirit during a dedication ceremony in August 1927: "The fact that this enterprise is being begun in one of our new states not yet great in population, not largely developed in its resources, discloses that the old American spirit still goes where our people go," Coolidge told a gathering of three hundred people.

Ultimately, it took fourteen years to create Mount Rushmore, over a time span that included the Great Depression. Lacking funding, the work proceeded in fits and starts and gained a reputation for being perpetually unfinished. But Borglum, paradoxically the cause of some of the delays as well as the reason Mount Rushmore exists at all, never gave up. He lobbied lawmakers in Washington, D.C., telling them that Mount Rushmore was a national monument that needed national support. Ultimately, Mount Rushmore cost $989,992.32, and the federal government pitched in $836,000 of the total.

But whose America does Mount Rushmore celebrate? This question has dogged the monument even as it has become one of the nation's most popular tourist attractions. Certainly, Crazy Horse's people don't consider it their monument.

After defeating the Sioux in 1877 and killing Crazy Horse, the United States purportedly purchased the Black Hills. But one hundred years later, in 1980, the U.S. Supreme Court ruled that the taking was illegal and ordered the government to pay the tribe more than $1 million. There's just one problem: The Lakota Sioux don't want the money—they want the Black Hills, which are considered sacred land by the Lakota.

Crazy Horse (c. 1840–1877) was an Oglala Sioux chief, who banded together with Sitting Bull (c. 1831–1890), a chief of the Hunkpapa Sioux, during the last, tragic battles for the Plains. He became a legend for putting an end to Custer's last stand and resisting the white man's invasion; he would not be confined to a reservation. Crazy Horse refused to have his photograph taken. The enigmatic warrior was described by Larry McMurtry as "one of the great Resisters, men who do not compromise, do not negotiate . . . who exist in a realm beyond the give-and-take of conventional politics and who stumble and are defeated only when hard circumstances force them to live in that realm."

To commemorate his legend, another colossal mountain sculpture is under way in the Black Hills. Seventeen miles from Mount Rushmore, the Crazy Horse portrait was begun in the 1940s by American sculptor Korczak Ziolkowski (1908–1982). The passion of Ziolkowski and his family, who continue to carve the enormous statue of Crazy Horse, is unquestioned, as is the fascination the piece wields on the imaginations of the thousands annually who visit its emergent form, one with a kitsch factor that ranks with other nostalgic paeans to the unsullied warrior.

Though it has generated controversy, impossible to avoid in Indian country, Ian Frazier captures the general sentiment when he says, in *Great Plains*, "The Crazy Horse monument is the one place on the plains where I saw lots of Indians smiling." The Crazy Horse monument is even bigger than Mount Rushmore; his face is 87 feet high compared to a mere 60 feet for the presidents. In scale, at least, it evens the historical score.

Less than one hundred miles away from the Crazy Horse monument stands a simple marker surrounded by a chain link fence in Wounded Knee, eight miles east of Pine Ridge, South Dakota. The fence encloses the mass grave of the more than three hundred Lakota who were massacred there by the United States government on December 29, 1890, a battle that marks the last military encounter of the Indian wars period of the nineteenth century. In 1995, Congress introduced a bill to establish a national memorial there, but it failed to pass.

A model of Korczak Ziolkowski's Crazy Horse memorial shows how the mountain will be transformed once the monument is completed.

Jefferson Memorial

LOCATION	DEDICATION	DESIGNER	COMMEMORATION
The National Mall, Washington, D.C.	*1943*	*John Russell Pope; Otto R. Eggers and Daniel P. Higgins*	*President Thomas Jefferson*

The trials that accompany the creation of most civic monuments are an inevitable rite of passage. Invariably, the high-stakes battles cease within days of the dedication. The Jefferson Memorial is no exception. In a country where the arts and government rarely mix comfortably, its construction required moving the American public beyond its Puritanical distrust of extravagant stone paeans—misgivings deepened by the Great Depression and Second World War—and weathering bitter criticism from groups ranging from architects to garden clubs.

Thomas Jefferson (1743–1826) asserted the individual's right to freedom and equality. Merrill Peterson, a leading Jefferson biographer, claims that his appeal lay in capturing the cherished ideal, if not the practical realities, of American democracy. His visionary appeal resurged in the 1930s, when the liberties he advocated were challenged on the world stage of war.

The circular temple and portico are surrounded by eighty Ionic columns and rise 25 feet above grade on reinforced concrete foundations. Cascading steps and two concentric terraces spill down to the water. The dome is a double shell construction with a self-supporting interior dome. The weight of the roof and exterior dome, rising nearly 120 feet (36.6 m), is carried by the columns and massive masonry walls.

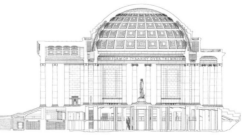

1899–1902

The Boer War, South Africa, between Great Britain and the two Boer republics, the South African Republic (Transvaal) and the Orange Free State; British win; Peace Treaty of Vereeniging signed at Melrose House, Pretoria (May 31, 1902)

1900

1900

Boxer Rebellion in China

Adopted in the 1920s as the patron saint of the Democratic Party, Jefferson hovered like a guardian spirit over Franklin Delano Roosevelt's rallying administration. Roosevelt deftly aligned Jefferson's expansive vision, conjured first for the nation with the words of the Declaration of Independence and later through the Louisiana Purchase, which doubled the size of the United States, with the objectives of his 1933 New Deal

patriot and idealist with a common touch. Not surprisingly, he supported building a monument to Jefferson in the capital.

After advocating for years for a Jefferson monument, Representative John J. Boylan, a Tammany Hall Democrat of New York, formed and chaired the twelve-member Thomas Jefferson Memorial Commission that was authorized by Congress in

program and eventually with the country's engagement in World War II. Jefferson's stock soared in the decade leading up to the bicentennial of his birth: In 1934 Congress authorized a stupendous Jefferson memorial on the Saint Louis waterfront, and two years later, his visage, writ large, was dedicated at Mount Rushmore. Wrapping himself in Jeffersonian symbolism, Roosevelt strengthened his own public image as a

1934. The Commission invited architect John Russell Pope (1874–1937), whose neoclassical buildings earned him the sobriquet "the last of the Romans," to submit a memorial plan. They also selected the Tidal Basin site, the last available of the five cardinal points of the Mall. The McMillan Commission had proposed that a domed building honoring the Founding Fathers be constructed on that site.

1900

The Kodak Brownie camera debuts in February at the price of one U.S. dollar, making photography an affordable hobby. The word "snapshot," a nineteenth-century hunting term for shooting from the hip without careful aim, quickly comes to describe Brownie photographs.

The 19-foot (5.8 m) figure of Jefferson was executed in plaster and painted a faux bronze for the 1943 dedication; the current bronze was cast in 1947 after World War II restrictions on metal were lifted. Jefferson holds the Declaration of Independence in one hand. His key role in summoning the justifying language for the country's independence is reiterated on the triangular exterior pediment.

Pope submitted a design in 1936 for a shallow-domed temple encircled by an Ionic colonnade. Both Pope and Jefferson drew inspiration from the transcendent Pantheon (A.D. 118–28) in Rome, one of three domical structures from which all Western dome structures have descended, and arguably the most perfect architectural space on earth. That building, along with Andrea Palladio's Villa Rotunda in Vicenza, Italy, had influenced the domed buildings designed by Jefferson himself, specifically Monticello, his home, and the Rotunda at the University of Virginia. And, as noted by historian Hugh Howard, "Thanks largely to Jefferson, classical architecture became America's de facto governmental mode of building." In defending his scheme, Pope was assisted by Fiske Kimball (1888–1955), the only architect on the Jefferson Commission, an expert on Jefferson's buildings, and a passionate defender of neoclassicism as the only appropriate monumental vocabulary.

Pope had studied abroad at the Ecole des Beaux-Arts, which emphasized the traditions of Greco-Roman antiquity and the Renaissance. Pope retained this classical bent for his entire life, bringing to his designs an elegant formality and a subdued use of materials that made his work ideal for institutional structures. He was a Washington insider, having served on the Commission of Fine

1901
Queen Victoria dies; succeeded by son Edward VII

We hold these truths to be self-evident: that all men are created equal, that they are endowed by their creator with certain inalienable rights, among these are life, liberty, and the pursuit of happiness. That to secure these rights governments are instituted among men. We solemnly publish and declare, that these colonies are and of right ought to be free and independent states. And for the support of this declaration, with a firm reliance on the protection of divine Providence, we mutually pledge our lives, our fortunes and our sacred honour.

—Excerpt from the Declaration of Independence
as inscribed at the Jefferson Memorial

Above Executed by Adolph A. Weinman, the marble relief shows Jefferson flanked by Benjamin Franklin and John Adams, who collaborated in the writing and editing of the document, and Roger Sherman and Robert Livingston, who approved the draft submitted to the Continental Congress.

Arts, and designed numerous capital buildings, including, most memorably, the National Gallery of Art, the National Archives Building, and the Temple of the Scottish Rite. He had also designed a memorial to Lincoln, losing that commission in 1911 to Henry Bacon, but in the process captivating the civic imagination of the era. Pope spurned the International Style, the modernist movement that had gained full momentum in America by the time of his Jefferson plan, and that incited the memorial controversy. Excoriated in influential publications, Pope became the poster boy for everything that was deemed wrong with classicism. Only in recent years has Pope's work been reevaluated.

Assaults on Pope's design were acrimonious. Arguments pro and con were made based on

1902

French mathematician Henri Poincaré publishes *Science and Hypothesis,* in which he declares, "There is no absolute time"

1902

In Germany, Arthur Korn reduces photographic images to data bits that can be transmitted by wire; wire-photos are in wide use in Europe by 1910 and transmitted internationally by 1922

attempts to get inside Jefferson's psyche: What would the president, a skilled amateur architect himself, a champion of both progressive thought and the architecture of ancient Rome, want his monument to look like, if he desired such a commemoration at all? Pope's design was judged either the epitome of Jeffersonian philosophy or a counterfeit imitation scavenged from the dustbins of history that had no relevance for the twentieth century, especially at a time when most of the country was inadequately housed and fed. What seemed to goad most architects, who continued to struggle with the fallout of the Depression, was the secrecy surrounding Pope's selection. It was undemocratic, against everything Jefferson stood for, not to hold an open competition to select a designer, especially for a project that would be paid for by the government. The $3 million price tag was also criticized, most trenchantly by Frank Lloyd Wright, who deemed the enterprise a "total confession of impotence that no ignorance whatever can excuse to the young American that will be taxed to pay the bills."

Perhaps the 1938 issue of the new nickel depicting Jefferson's home, Monticello, with its distinctive dome and portico, finally turned the tide in favor of John Russell Pope's Monticello-inspired design.

The site itself was a problem. Proponents, including two great-great-grandsons of Jefferson who sat on the Jefferson Commission, agreed with the McMillan Commission's location choice. Opponents, including landscape architect Frederick Law Olmsted, the sole surviving member of the McMillan Commission, said that L'Enfant intended the entire south side of the Mall to be structure-free and that a more suitable site should be found.

Related to the site issue was that of the Japanese cherry trees, a gift from Japan in 1912 and the definition of springtime in Washington. Some flowering trees would have to be removed to accommodate the reconfiguration of the site and traffic patterns. This "landscape butchery" became a cause célèbre and incited a "cherry tree rebellion." Overnight, conversations and tabloid pages were laced with botanical analyses of the cherry trees—their lack of actual fruit and fragrance, brief blossoming, and life span, which, depending on the source, was anywhere from twenty to three hundred years. Some feared that destroying the

trees would endanger diplomatic relations with Japan, while organizations like the Chamber of Commerce and the Automobile Association of America worried about losing tourism dollars. The "Chop Down a Cherry Tree Club," who took George Washington as their honorary president and a hatchet as their logo, launched a counter-protest in hopes of restoring some peace to the capital. The majority of the trees were spared by moving the site some 450 feet to the southwest, and the brouhaha ended altogether with Japan's entry into the war.

The memorial was the first challenge to the Commission of Fine Arts' authority over designs built on federal property in Washington. The Commission condemned the pantheon scheme as antithetical to their interpretation of the McMillan Plan. In deference to these objections, Pope submitted two alternative designs. The first was an open colonnade with a statue of Jefferson in the center; the second consisted of two quarter-circle colonnades, open in the center, with a fountain and statuary on axis. The latter plan, similar to a 1925 Pope design for a Theodore Roosevelt memorial for the same site that was never realized, was favored by the Commission of Fine Arts.

Criticism of the memorial reached fever pitch. In August 1937, Congress withdrew funding, and Pope's firm was ordered to stop work on the twenty-third of that month. Four days later, Pope died from cancer. Pope's widow insisted on the pantheon scheme in a series of letters to the president, a distant cousin of hers. Pope's surviving partners, Otto R. Eggers and Daniel P. Higgins, ultimately saw the memorial to completion.

At the groundbreaking in December 1938, Roosevelt took pains to reiterate the goals of the McMillan Commission and settle the site issue forever. That same month—as Washington continued to disagree about the proposed memorial design—Jefferson's face, now pocket-sized, appeared on the new nickel. Though debate about the memorial's final form continued after the groundbreaking, the Memorial Commission's congressional connections and Roosevelt's personal support eventually ensured that the pantheon design was built. According to architectural

1903

In France, brothers Augustus and Louis Lumière patent the Autochrome Lumière color photography process, the only color processing available until 1935

1903

Orville and Wilbur Wright make the first powered, sustained, and controlled airplane flight lasting twelve seconds at Kitty Hawk, NC (Dec. 17)

historian Steven Bedford, the final structure, modified and reduced in size by a third, was a "weak shadow of the normally forceful and austere monumentality that was Pope's trademark."

After winning a national competition in 1938 and scrutinizing all known portraits of Jefferson, sculptor Rudulph Evans (1878–1960) created a composite likeness of the president that is the memorial centerpiece. Jefferson is shown in knee breeches and a fur-collared coat. Sculpted corn, tobacco, and

books indicate Jefferson's agrarian and intellectual pursuits, though the dignified, not to say leaden, portrait reveals nothing of the enormous mental vitality of the gentleman farmer who it was said had mastered all knowledge of his day.

Applied bronze letters on the interior walls excerpt four of Jefferson's best-known writings; a fifth encircles the lower lip of the dome. The first quotation is from the Declaration of Independence.

Given the reverence for that document, which was principally authored by Jefferson, and that it is present in his place of homage, it is notable that some words on the monument panel are misspelled or deliberately omitted because of space limitations; that quote is reproduced on these pages. The second panel text, also by Jefferson, quotes the Act for Religious Freedom, while the third consists of six quotes taken from Jefferson's writings. The fourth panel encompasses Jefferson's vision for the evolution of the Constitution as written in a letter to Samuel Kercheval in 1816. Jefferson wrote the domical quote—"I have sworn upon the altar of God eternal hostility against every form of tyranny over the mind of man"—to Benjamin Rush in 1800. Paralleling these texts is Jefferson's self-assessment, which appears on his tombstone at Monticello: "Author of the Declaration of American Independence, of the Statute of Virginia for religious freedom, and Father of the University of Virginia."

The marble memorial's sublime setting is its most important identity. It is a gleaming city on a hill, whether bathed in the pink light of early morning or a luminous nighttime presence. For all of Jefferson's malleable persona as the American Everyman, paradoxically and by most accounts, his was an impenetrable character. The memorial's expansive natural setting reflects this elusive distance. The stretch of open water mirrors its radiant image and elevates it beyond the fray of the Mall and greater city.

The memorial was dedicated on April 13, 1943, the two hundredth anniversary of Jefferson's birth. "In the midst of a great war for freedom," Roosevelt drew parallels at the dedication between Jefferson's administration and his own, saying that the "seeming eclipse of liberty can well become the dawn of more liberty" and that the world's "would-be masters have taught this generation what its liberties can mean." The Jefferson Memorial, the nation's last great Beaux-Arts memorial, has become an icon of monumental Washington.

Left The French sculptor Jean-Antoine Houdon executed this marble bust of Jefferson in Paris in 1789. Considered to be a superb likeness, it has served as the model for many portraits of the president, including that on the modern United States nickel.

1904
In America's most deadly peacetime maritime disaster, the *General Slocum* steamboat, out on a church excursion, catches fire and sinks in Manhattan's East River, taking more than 1,000 lives (June 15)

1904
Russo-Japanese war begins (ends 1905)

1905

Albert Einstein publishes his theory of relativity, which abolishes the concept of absolute time

1906

San Francisco earthquake and fire (Apr. 19–21); 500 people dead; 28,188 buildings destroyed on 497 city blocks; $1 billion in property damage

Remembering
World War II

The most memorable presence at the May 2004 dedication of the long-awaited World War II Memorial in Washington, D.C., was that of the war's veterans. Stalwart children of the Depression, who had learned then what counted most, the veterans served with a legendary dedication to duty. They represented the sixteen million Americans who served in World War II, more than four hundred thousand of whom died in the war; the nearly seven hundred thousand soldiers, sailors, airmen, and marines who returned home wounded or disabled; and the ten million veterans who had died during the intervening years.

World War II, the last morally unambiguous war, has been remembered with thousands of monuments, plaques, parks, and statues. Federal agencies such as the American Battle Monuments Commission, which maintains American memorials overseas, and the National Park Service, which maintains domestic sites, are responsible for most of the largest monuments and historic locations, but hundreds of smaller commemorations have been erected by veterans associations, states and municipalities, and private organizations and individuals. Indeed, one would be hard pressed to find a city that lacks some form of World War II commemoration. This overview examines key commemorations at Pearl Harbor, Iwo Jima, and Normandy; two monuments honoring the home front effort; and a visual sampling of World War II markers internationally.

Omaha Beach was one of five beaches where Allied forces landed on D-Day. In Normandy, there are thirty-six monuments of notable size erected by the Allies, and hundreds of smaller markers along the roads, in village squares, and in churches. There are two dozen museums devoted to the war, and almost as many cemeteries.

1908

Henry Ford (b. July 30, 1863; d. Apr. 7, 1947) produces first mass-produced automobile, the Model T, at the Ford Motor Company assembly line (Oct.)

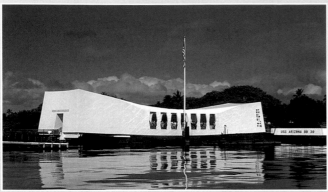

The memorial of the USS *Arizona*, the first casualty of World War II and a National Historic Landmark, has been administered since 1980 by the National Park Service. It is funded in part by the *Arizona* Memorial Museum Association, a group of Pearl Harbor survivors and others interested in preserving its legacy.

PEARL HARBOR

1909

Robert E. Peary (b. May 6, 1856; d. Feb. 20, 1920), American explorer, reaches the North Pole (Apr. 6)

A display case at the Franklin D. Roosevelt Presidential Library and Museum in Hyde Park, New York, contains a typed draft of the speech the president gave to Congress the day after the Japanese bombed Pearl Harbor. "Yesterday, December 7, 1941," it opens, "a date which will live in world history . . ." The last two words of the phrase are crossed out and in FDR's angular hand is substituted "infamy," one small word that shoved the nation from its neutral position into war.

The USS *Arizona*, a steel-hulled battleship with an overall length of 608 feet, was sunk by bombing and possibly torpedoes as she stood moored in Oahu's Pearl Harbor.

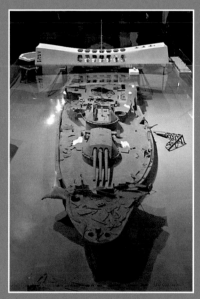

A scale model shows the relationship of the Pearl Harbor memorial to the submerged ruins of the USS *Arizona*.

When the Japanese air attack began, at 7:53 A.M. on that December morning, most of the U.S. Navy's fleet in the Pacific, some 130 naval vessels, was in Pearl Harbor on the island of Oahu. It ended two hours later, with 2,388 men, women, and children dead and 1,261 wounded. More than half of those killed—1,177 sailors and marines—were on the battleship USS *Arizona*. Twenty-one ships were damaged or destroyed, along with hundreds of planes. The rallying cry "Remember Pearl Harbor!" quickly came into conversational currency and was repeated throughout the war that lasted, officially, until September 2, 1945, when the Japanese formally surrendered aboard the battleship USS *Missouri* anchored in Tokyo Bay.

An underwater view taken through a porthole of the *Arizona* shows the Admiral's Cabin with a conference table and hanging light fixture. To the left of the table is an armchair with exposed springs that has tipped over. The ship is entered only with an ROV (remotely operated vehicle), never with divers, out of respect for the 1,177 men still entombed.

Wide openings in the observation room flood the interior with sunlight and allow visitors to see the rusting pieces of the *Arizona* 8 feet below Pearl Harbor's blue-green waters.

1910
Edward VII, king of Great Britain, dies; succeeded by George V (d. 1936)

The Honolulu Memorial is located within the National Memorial Cemetery of the Pacific in the Puowaina Crater, an extinct volcano referred to locally as the Punchbowl because of its shape. On either side of the grand stairs leading to the memorial's chapel and galleries are ten Courts of the Missing on which are inscribed the names of American armed forces missing from the Pacific (excluding those from the southwest Pacific) in World War II, and from the Korean and Vietnam wars. Nearly thirteen thousand war dead are buried in the adjacent cemetery, brought from the battlefields at Guadalcanal, China, Burma, Saipan, Guam, and Iwo Jima, and from the prisoner of war camps in Japan. Also interred are the unidentified remains of eight hundred American servicemen who died fighting in the Korean and Vietnam wars.

The *Arizona* was the only ship lost during World War II whose wreckage was accessible; all the others went down in deep water. In addition to being a war memorial, the vessel is a gravesite: Her 1,177 crew members remain entombed in the ship, which sank in 38 feet of water. Attempts to memorialize the *Arizona* were made as early as 1943, but solid plans did not materialize until 1949, when the territory of Hawaii established the Pacific War Memorial Commission. Although Congress would not authorize construction of a memorial until 1958, the American flag was raised over her wreckage daily beginning in 1950.

Visitors to Pearl Harbor take a short boat ride to the memorial. It was designed by architect Alfred Preis (1911–1994), an Austrian émigré who was arrested after the bombing of Pearl Harbor and interned for three months, along with other Germans and Europeans from countries annexed by Germany, on Sand Island, in the harbor where he would eventually build his war tribute.

Dedicated on Memorial Day 1962, the gleaming white memorial spans, but for symbolic reasons does not touch, the submerged remains beneath it. The 184-foot (56 m) memorial consists of three sections: an entrance area, an observation room from which the *Arizona* can be seen, and a Shrine Room with a marble wall inscribed with the names of the dead. The memorial is supported by two 250-ton steel girders and 36 concrete pilings driven deep into the bed of the harbor.

Of its concave design, Preis said, "The structure sags in the center but stands strong and vigorous at the ends," to express "initial defeat and ultimate victory."

At low tide, when the sun shines on the sunken ruins, in the words of the designer, "the barnacles which encrust it shimmer like golden jewels . . . a beautiful sarcophagus." When the memorial opened, its minimalist design invited comparisons to a squashed milk carton, but that criticism was silenced by the reverence it commands.

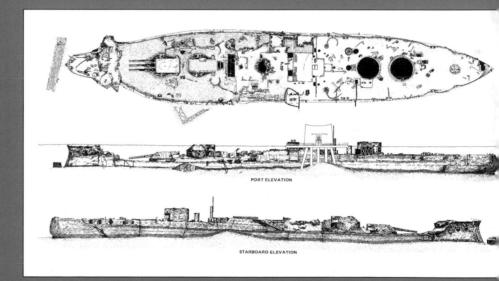

PORT ELEVATION

STARBOARD ELEVATION

The *Arizona* presents a unique stewardship challenge to the Submerged Resources Center (SRC) of the National Park Service. The *Arizona*'s steel ruins, submerged in salt water, are vulnerable to corrosion and other natural deterioration. Its preservation is made more complex by several hundred thousand gallons of fuel oil that have been slowly bleeding from the corroding hull since its sinking. The SBC's ongoing task is to preserve the historically significant hull while minimizing the possibility of a catastrophic oil spill.

In 1984 and 1986, the submerged ruins of the USS *Arizona* were measured and drawn to scale by the Submerged Cultural Resources Unit of the National Park Service. The drawings provide a bird's-eye view of the ship's deck, an elevation of its starboard profile, and the location of the memorial.

1910
Japan annexes Korea

NORMANDY

On June 6, 1944, war photographer Robert Capa shot the moment of the D-Day landing, only eight prints of which survive, that would become iconic images of the morning. Later he explained in *Images of War,* "The excited darkroom assistant, while drying the negatives, had turned on too much heat and the emulsions had melted and run down before the eyes of the London office. Out of one hundred and six pictures in all, only eight were salvaged." Capa's brilliant career ended abruptly in 1954 when he stepped on a land mine in an Indochina battlefield, still clutching his camera.

To the German commander: Nuts!

—General Anthony McAuliffe's response to the German demand for surrender during the Battle of the Bulge, December 22, 1944

1911

A discreet bronze plaque in New York City marks the site of the Triangle Shirtwaist Fire that takes the lives of 146 young women and leads to the establishment of the International Ladies' Garment Workers' Union (Mar. 25)

1911

Roald Amundsen (b. July 16, 1872; disappeared off Norway, Sept. 1928), Norwegian explorer, reaches the South Pole (Dec. 14)

Normandy is a dissonantly beautiful province in northwest France of green pastures that hug the rocky cliffs overlooking the English Channel and miles of sandy beaches. Embellished by meadows, winding roads, tall hedgerows, well-kept Norman households in the energetic tradition of the good French wife, stone churches, and a variety of other structures, Normandy was the stage of the greatest invasion in history. Despite its beauty, the mind can never truly escape Robert Capa's grainy photographs of the D-Day invasion, later brought brutally to life by Steven Spielberg, mental images that are stronger than the sight of the actual beaches at Omaha and Utah, and that threaten like clouds no matter how sunny the day.

Months of preparation preceded the D-Day operation, given the code name Overlord, in which the land, air, and sea forces of the Allied armies led by General Dwight D. Eisenhower, supreme commander of Allied Expeditionary Force, took the northern coast of France. The assault began in the early morning hours of June 6, 1944. An armada of seven thousand vessels manned by more than 195,000 naval personnel from eight countries assembled in the English Channel to cover the landing craft tanks that were crammed with soldiers, most mere youngsters, and poised to make land.

At 0630 hours, under cover of intense naval and air bombardment, six American, British, and Canadian divisions began landing on Utah, Omaha, Gold, Juno, and Sword beaches. The U.S. 4th Division pushed rapidly inward at Utah, a relatively flat and open beach, while the U.S. 1st and 29th had to run a 250-foot gauntlet in the direct line of fire from the German forces gathered on the steep hills rising from Omaha Beach. Casualties were heavy at Omaha. East of the Americans, the British and Canadians forged ahead on Gold, Juno, and Sword beaches.

Within a week, under cover of continuous naval gunfire and air support, the individual beachheads had been linked together. Ghostly remains of concrete caissons and derelict ships that were scuttled in shallow water to form breakwaters and facilitate the movement of troops and cargo are still visible. By the end of June, more than

Outside the Musée du Débarquement at Utah Beach, constructed in a German blockhouse, is a landing craft tank and several American memorials. Tanks, planes, and munitions, some whole, others in pieces, are a common sight throughout the area.

A new visitors center at the American Cemetery opens to views of the English Channel and historic landing beaches. It was dedicated on June 6, 2007.

Pointe du Hoc is still pitted with bomb and shell craters, and retains the vestiges of German pillboxes, bunkers, and gun emplacements.

850,000 men, 148,000 vehicles, and 570,000 tons of supplies had arrived in Normandy.

Daily headlines back home reflected the gains made by the Allies. Cherbourg was freed on June 26, British and Canadians fought their way into Caen on July 9, and nine days later the United States took Saint-Lô. On July 25, following a paralyzing bombardment by the U.S. and Royal air forces, a gap opened in the enemy line, a move that was quickly exploited by the infantry and armored divisions that freed Coutances on July 28. After their initial success, however, the Allied forces were stymied in the beachhead area. In August, General George S. Patton aggressively led the Third Army, code name Lucky Forward, who finally broke through enemy lines and advanced on a broad front. The Lucky Forward lived up to its moniker in a fierce August campaign across Europe that covered six hundred miles in France, Belgium, Luxembourg, Germany, Austria, and Czechoslovakia. On August 25, 1944, Paris was liberated.

The Spirit of American Youth Rising from the Waves, a bronze by Donald De Lue (1897–1988), is the centerpiece of the colonnaded memorial at the American Cemetery in Normandy. The cemetery's architects were Harbeson, Hough, Livingston and Larson, with landscape design by Markley Stevenson, both Philadelphia firms.

Eleven months after the decisive effort in Normandy, Eisenhower accepted Germany's unconditional surrender in Rheims, France, on May 7, 1945. President Franklin Delano Roosevelt, who had died a month earlier, was succeeded by Harry S. Truman, who authorized the bombing of Hiroshima and Nagasaki on August 6 and August 9, 1945, respectively. "Little Boy," the first atomic bomb, was dropped from the *Enola Gay*, a B-29 bomber that has become a monument of sorts and parts of which are on permanent display at the Smithsonian National Air and Space Museum in Washington, D.C.

Temporary cemeteries were established immediately after D-Day. After the war, the families of the deceased could elect to have them interred permanently at one of fourteen World War II military cemeteries maintained by the ABMC on foreign soil. The fabled American Cemetery, focal point of the United States' commemorations in Normandy, consists of 172.5 meticulously manicured acres on the cliffs overlooking Omaha Beach. It was dedicated in 1956.

The memorial consists of a semicircular colonnade with a loggia at either end that encircles a large bronze in its center. The colonnade and loggias are cut from Vaurion, a French limestone, with Brittany granite plinths and steps. Pebbles taken from the invasion beaches are embedded into the floor, as are bronze letters that read, "Mine Eyes Have Seen the Glory of the Coming of the Lord." The Garden of the

1914
The Panama Canal is completed after thirty-six years' labor and the deaths of 25,000 men

Missing contains stone tablets that are engraved with the names of 1,557 who gave their lives but whose remains are unrecovered or unidentifiable. Their date of death was established by the War Department as being a year and a day from the date on which the individual was reported missing in action.

On the interior walls of the loggias, four orientation maps engraved in stone and detailed with enamel depict the June 6 landings and the establishment of a beachhead; the air operations over Normandy from March until August 1944; and the amphibious assault of the Navy, also on June 6. A separate map in the north loggia records the progress of military operations in northwest Europe from June 6, 1944, through May 8, 1945.

Most compelling is the graveyard with its identical white marble tombstones that mark the interments of 9,387 service men and women. The long rows are formed of crosses and stars, incised with Italian, French, German, Jewish, Polish, Irish, and English names. The uniformity of the stones, their placement in row upon identical row, bone white against the emerald green lawn, makes an unforgettable visual impression.

The markers at the American Cemetery in Normandy are nearly uniform, either Latin crosses or Stars of David for Jewish soldiers. Each provides the same brief story of a life: the soldier's full name, rank, date of death, unit, and date of entry into military service.

Our deaths are not ours:
They are yours:
They will mean what you make them.
—Archibald MacLeish, "The Young Dead Soldiers," 1948

1914
Archduke Ferdinand, heir to the Austrian throne, and wife, assassinated in Sarajevo by Serbian nationalist Gavrilo Princip (June 28)

IWO JIMA

Nothing prepares you for the size of the Marine Corps War Memorial, the monolithic bronze in Arlington, Virginia, that replicates the 1945 flag raising on Iwo Jima. The sculpture is one of those rare celebrities—it is one of the most recognizable of American memorials—that actually look larger rather than smaller in person.

Photographer Joseph Rosenthal, whose poor eyesight kept him from serving in the military, shot the triumphant flag raising on Iwo Jima, the most famous photograph of the Second World War, using a Speed Graphic camera and 4 x 5-inch black-and-white film. In addition to the Marine Corps monument, his image inspired Treasury Department posters, a commemorative 3-cent stamp, and a 2006 Clint Eastwood movie.

The memorial is the only major American monument that was inspired by a photograph. The image was snapped on February 23, 1945, by Associated Press photographer Joseph Rosenthal (1911–2006), who received a Pulitzer Prize for his valorous portrait of five marines and a Navy corpsman raising the flag on Mount Suribachi during the Battle of Iwo Jima.

Having recaptured much of the territory taken by the Japanese, and seeking to conclude the Pacific campaign, U.S. troops staked out Iwo Jima, "Sulphur Island" in English, a strategically located island 660 miles south of Tokyo and dominated by Mount Suribachi, an extinct volcano. The battle, one of the most savage of the war, raged for thirty-six days. Finally, on the morning of February 23, 1945, in full view of troops all over the island and offshore, forty men from Company

E, Second Battalion, 28th Marines under the command of Lieutenant Harold G. Schrier gained control of the summit. Rejoicing, they raised a small American flag attached to a pipe found on the mountain. Three hours later, a larger flag was procured and raised by the six men now immortalized in Rosenthal's photograph: Sergeant Michael Strank, Pharmacist's Mate 2/c John H. Bradley, Corporal Harlon H. Block, and Privates First Class Ira H. Hayes, Franklin R. Sousley, and Rene A. Gagnon.

We have been described as a nation of weaklings, playboys. . . . Let them tell that to General MacArthur and his men. Let them tell that to the sailors who today are hitting hard in the far waters of the Pacific. Let them tell that to the boys in the Flying Fortresses. Let them tell that to the Marines!
—President Franklin D. Roosevelt, radio address, February 23, 1942

Afterward, reprised in a 1991 book by Karal Ann Marling and John Wetenhall, Rosenthal was accused of staging the photograph. He denied this in an interview with Benis Frank of the Marine Corps oral history program: "Had I posed that shot, I would, of course, have ruined it . . . I'd have picked fewer men. . . . I would have also made them turn their heads so that they could be identified for [Associated Press] members throughout the country, and nothing like the existing picture would have resulted."

Soon after the photograph was released, sculptor Felix W. deWeldon (1907–2003), then on duty with the U.S. Navy, and the sculptor of some twelve hundred public memorials worldwide, was moved to copy it in plaster. Later, he made a life-sized model in clay for which Gagnon, Hayes, and Bradley, who had survived the flag raising (the other three had been killed in action) posed, assuming the same positions as in the famous photograph. Casting the mammoth piece in bronze took three years. It was dedicated by President Dwight D. Eisenhower on November 10, 1954, the 179th anniversary of the U.S. Marine Corps.

1914

World War I begins (July 28)

1914

First Battle of the Marne (Sept. 5–9). It was a French-British victory against the German army under General von Moltke. Over 2 million troops fought in the battle and 100,000 were killed or wounded

Over-life-sized bronzes commemorate General Douglas MacArthur's famous return to Leyte Island on October 20, 1944. MacArthur is shown with Philippine president Sergio Osmeña and five others.

I shall return.

—General Douglas MacArthur, on leaving the Philippines, 1942

The 78-foot (24-m) tall Marine Corps War Memorial depicts the historic flag raising at Iwo Jima. The figures, six times larger than life, are based on a photograph taken by Joe Rosenthal, and were sculpted by Felix deWeldon.

Two months later, Ira Hayes, thirty-two, was found dead on his Pima Indian reservation, a victim of acute alcoholism. In the 1964 "Ballad of Ira Hayes," Johnny Cash sang that the loner "was wined and speeched and honored, everybody shook his hand," but "at home nobody cared what Ira'd done." James Bradley, the son of the only flag bearer who lived until old age, found a letter upon John Bradley's death in 1994 and learned for the first time what his father had done. In 2000, he published *Flags of Our Fathers*, an account of the lives of the flag raisers and the battle at Iwo Jima.

Although the 32-foot (9.8 m) figures are rendered with high realism and specific detail, the overall impression is of the sextet's determination to put up the flag. Their faces are not easily discernible. One is most aware of the strength and rhythm of their legs, and the totem of hands that clasps the flagpole and holds it upright. A unique feature that animates the entire composition is an actual cloth flag which flies twenty-four hours a day by presidential decree. The base was cut from black Swedish granite, intended to simulate the volcanic rock of Mount Suribachi, and is inscribed with the names and dates of every principal Marine Corps engagement since 1775. It is also inscribed with Felix deWeldon's name, as is usual, but also, appropriately, with Rosenthal's name.

THE HOME FRONT

"This was a people's war, and everyone was in it." The words of Colonel Oveta Culp Hobby, the pioneering director of the Women's Army Corps, sum up the wartime service of ordinary citizens. A 1942 photograph shows women assembling the tail fuselage of a B-17 bomber at the Douglas Aircraft plant in Long Beach, California.

A unique war memorial is tucked away at the New York Buddhist Church on Manhattan's Riverside Drive at 105th Street. The bronze statue of Shinran Shonin, founder of the Jodo Shinshu school of Buddhism, somehow survived when the *Enola Gay* dropped the first atomic bomb on Hiroshima on August 6, 1945. Japanese businessman Seiichi Hirose gave it as a peace gesture to the United States, where it was dedicated on September 11, 1955.

The Liberty Ship Memorial, designed by Woodworth Associates and Richard Renner Architects, is a 35-foot-tall steel same-size replica of the ship's bow. Interpretative panels inside tell the Liberty Ship story. The memorial's situation on busy Portland Harbor makes it easy to imagine the ships once launched there.

American women powered the nation's economy during the war, filling the jobs traditionally held by men who had gone off to fight. Nearly three million women, many of them entering the workforce for the first time, worked to provide the airplanes and munitions needed by the military. Only recently have monuments been built that recognize women's heroic contributions to the war effort.

"Th' hell this ain't th' most important hole in th' world. I'm in it."

Willie and Joe, two unshaven, cynical dogfaces, became enduring symbols of the American infantry. They were created by Bill Mauldin (1921–2003), himself an Army sergeant, who eventually won two Pulitzers for his editorial lampoons, the first in 1945 for his Willie and Joe cartoons, which appeared in *Stars and Stripes*, the *45th Division News*, and other military publications. Drawn with biting realism and humor, Willie and Joe were the ordinary guys who won the war, the ones who did most of the fighting and the dying. They were also the ones who got sentry duty when it rained, caught shrapnel in their backsides when they left their foxholes, contended with lice, grumbled constantly about K rations, and flirted, always, whether with insubordination or foreign cuties.

1915

In Manhattan, an evocative waterwork is dedicated to Isidor Straus and his wife, Ida, who chose to perish with him instead of leaving his side when the *Titanic* sank (Apr. 15)

The war was a time of unprecedented national unity. Millions tended the home front so that the American military, ranked seventeenth in the world at the start of the war, could muscle its way to victory. At home, 144 million Americans supported the troops by making munitions, planting victory gardens, buying war bonds, sewing uniforms and parachutes, rationing food and gas, and saving twine, bacon fat, and tinfoil. Their work in the defense industries was crucial.

Two monuments on either coast honor the ships that moved urgently needed supplies, munitions, and soldiers across the globe. The Liberty Ship Memorial (2003) at Bug Light Park in South Portland, Maine, is a minimally designed but effective reminder of Maine's contribution to the war effort. Between 1942 and 1945, the New England Shipbuilding Corporation of South Portland constructed 266 of the 2,751 "Liberty Ships" that were built for the U.S. Emergency Shipbuilding Program.

These square-hulled ships were the workhorses of World War II, and ranked with the B-24 Liberator bomber and the jeep as the most important tools in the United States arsenal. Prefabricated and welded together at locations around the country, the ships revolutionized the ancient art of shipbuilding. The Liberty was 441 feet (134.4 m) long and had a three-cylinder steam engine that could reach a speed of eleven knots. According to the U.S. Merchant Marine, she was capable of holding over nine thousand tons of cargo—the equivalent of 2,840 jeeps, 440 tanks, or 230 million rounds of rifle ammunition. Some thirty thousand Mainers built and sailed the ships. The welders worked twenty-four hours a day at blistering speed—ship construction took 40 days instead of the usual 110 days.

Brad Woodworth and Richard Renner, who designed the Maine memorial, traveled to San Francisco to measure one of the two remaining Liberty Ships. Now berthed at Pier 45 at Fisherman's Wharf, the SS *Jeremiah O'Brien*, the only active Liberty Ship in original configuration, was launched from the Portland, Maine, shipyard on June 19, 1943. The ship, now a floating memorial, is the sole survivor of the Allied armada that stormed Normandy on D-Day.

On the West Coast, the Rosie the Riveter Memorial (2000), a waterfront park designed by landscape architect Cheryl Barton and artist Susan Schwartzenberg, inspired the construction of a new national park at the four Kaiser shipyards in Richmond, California, where 747 ships were built during World War II. The memorial tells the story of the Richmond Rosies with historical facts and photographs, personal recollections, landscaping, and abstract sculptures reminiscent of the prefabricated parts assembled by shipyard workers. The memorial is placed along a 441-foot (134.4-m) granite walkway— the length of a Liberty Ship—that is lined with roses and extends out over the water. That memorial, together with the Ford assembly plant and the Red Oak Victory Ship, an ammunition ship in the South Pacific during the war, are the three key components of the 145-acre park. The Rosie the Riveter World War II Home Front National Historical Park is maintained by the National Park Service in cooperation with other federal agencies and private owners.

A plaque in Paris honors the signing of the Marshall Plan.

The war wrought profound societal changes. When the veterans returned home, they shaped enduring postwar military, political, and diplomatic alliances—NATO, the Marshall Plan, the World Bank, and the United Nations among them—that were living monuments to what they accomplished abroad. The 1944 G.I. Bill, which permitted 7.8 million veterans to obtain educations and job training, transformed the country's intellectual and economic climate. Although women's participation in the armed forces was resisted violently at first, they eventually served in every service branch and combat theater of the war with valor. Their service and that of millions of Rosies presaged the expansion of women's rights in the 1960s, a victory still not won nor assured.

World War II
Memorial

LOCATION	DEDICATION	DESIGNER	COMMEMORATION
The National Mall, Washington, D.C.	*2004*	*Friedrich St. Florian*	*World War II veterans and supporters*

The columns of the World War II Memorial in Washington, D.C., were pierced and spaced 6 feet apart to preserve the Mall's sightlines. A sculpted bronze rope binds the columns together to illustrate national unity. Two styles of bronze wreaths on the columns represent the two facets of the home-front effort, as during the war, America was the arsenal of the world as well as its breadbasket. One, the oak wreath, is an ancient symbol of industrial prowess. The other, formed of wheat sheaves, represents the agricultural efforts that fed much of Europe.

Above WWII veteteran J. M. Burke.

It was a just war. That estimation of the Second World War, a global conflict in which fifty-three million souls were lost, finds its architectural expression in the unambiguous lines and exalted situation of the World War II Memorial on the National Mall.

Without question, the 7.4-acre memorial's most important aspect is its location on the Mall at the eastern end of the Reflecting Pool. The design frames the axis between the Washington Monument to the east and the Lincoln Memorial to the west. Most significantly, the memorial provides an open gathering space that reinforces the Mall's venerable role as a place where people can freely express their beliefs—a place, in other words, where democracy is alive and well. Like the soldiers who served in the war it commemorates, the memorial accomplishes what was asked of it, and does so admirably.

1915
First German Zeppelin bomb attack on London

1915
First transcontinental telephone call between Alexander Graham Bell in New York City and Dr. Thomas A. Watson in San Francisco

Illuminated water jets in the Rainbow Pool animate the otherwise formal memorial. According to the architect, the waterworks represent the "joy of living, the joy of being free, which is the legacy of World War II."

1916
Battle of Verdun, the greatest and lengthiest in world history (Feb. 21–Dec. 19), caused over an estimated 700,000 casualties (dead, wounded, and missing)

1916
Battle of the Somme (July–Nov.); Britain loses over 400,000 men; France loses 200,000; Germany loses 350,000

Until the World War II Memorial opened in 2004, the Marine Corps Memorial, which depicts the flag raising at Mount Suribachi, across the Potomac in Arlington, stood in as the commemoration of "the greatest generation." Unlike the memorial to the Vietnam veterans, which finally made public acknowledgment of their sacrifice, World War II veterans returned home to the nation's admiration, and to a less ambiguous time

Entertaining the dedication day throngs were swing dancers jumping to the big band music of Benny Goodman, Count Basie, Glenn Miller, and other war-era favorites. They weren't the only ones hopping at the celebration—cicadas, literally millions of them, dive-bombed the masses and caused them too to jump sky-high. Curiously, the big bugs—periodical cicadas of the Brood X type, according to entomologists—had last emerged

The Announcement Stone reads:

Here in the presence of Washington and Lincoln, one the eighteenth century father and the other the nineteenth century preserver of our nation, we honor those twentieth century Americans who took up the struggle during the Second World War and made the sacrifices to perpetuate the gift our forefathers entrusted to us: a nation conceived in liberty and justice.

in its history. The memorial reflects that clarity in its situation and its open design, which preserves views in all directions. When asked about the memorial, John Lennon of the Third Army, 386th Anti-Aircraft Artillery Battery D, echoed the sentiments of many when he said, "It's nice having a memorial, of course, but we didn't need one. We knew we were great."

Tens of thousands of aging World War II veterans, many of them frail, some in wheelchairs, nearly all wearing ribbons, medals, original uniforms, and other encoded symbols of their sacrifice and service, gathered for the memorial's May 29, 2004, dedication. They represented a handful of the sixteen million Americans who served in World War II. For many, it was a last-of-a-lifetime hurrah. Toward the end of the dedication ceremony, President George W. Bush said, "I ask every man and woman who saw and lived World War II—every member of that generation—to please rise as you are able, and receive the thanks of our great nation." A wave of veterans rose to their feet and collected a thunderous and overdue, though rarely sought, ovation.

seventeen years earlier, in 1987, the same year that Ohio congresswoman Marcy Kaptur introduced legislation to build the memorial after one of her constituents, the late Roger Durbin, who fought in the Battle of the Bulge, asked why there was no monument to the World War II veterans on the Mall.

The struggle to construct the memorial lasted four times as long as it took America to fight the war itself. The controversy might have been anticipated by reviewing the once-passionate opposition to the tributes to Washington, Lincoln, Jefferson, FDR, and the Korean and Vietnam war veterans. Nonetheless, seventeen years of legislative, legal, and artistic entanglements ensued.

The 1996 competition guidelines specified the site's size; the necessity of maintaining the Mall views; the provision of an underground museum; and that the Rainbow Pool, which was on the National Register of Historic Places, could not be altered. Essentially, competitors were given a site and then told they couldn't build on it. Two juries, headed by the New York architects David

M. Childs and Hugh Hardy, unanimously selected architect Friedrich St. Florian's entry, according to St. Florian himself, for one reason: His was the only proposal that sank the Rainbow Pool into the ground.

St. Florian immersed himself in the Mall's many incarnations, from Pierre L'Enfant's earliest template in 1791 to the 1901 McMillan Plan to the

My God, what a great opportunity was given to me, an immigrant. Not only an immigrant, but one from an enemy country because I'm Austrian-born. What country other than America would allow such a thing? I was given the American dream.

—Friedrich St. Florian, November 6, 2003

The Atlantic and Pacific pavilions each contain a bronze baldachino—a traditional architectural canopy supported by columns that marks and encloses a specific spot, most often an altar or a tomb.

improvements made in the 1960s, in order to discover why, among other things, the Rainbow Pool had landmark status. He learned that the Reflecting Pool needed a terminus at its eastern end, which was provided by the otherwise insignificant Rainbow Pool. In his design, the oval pool is lowered by 6 feet in order to create a new space for the memorial without disturbing the views. He also read what McMillan commissioner Charles Follen McKim wrote after a summer tour of Europe's great capital cities: that the framing of the view is just as important as the view itself. This framing is the foundation of St. Florian's design. McKim also observed, after marveling at Rome's many fountains and returning to the hot capital, that the monument of Washington should not be a man on a horse, but a fountain. Not surprisingly, exuberant waterworks are the core of St. Florian's scheme.

While few if any opposed the idea of a memorial dedicated to the Second World War heroes, the discussions about the site and design were vituperative. The primary debate concerned locating the monument on the Mall's axis, where it could

potentially block views of the great monuments and visually rend the Mall in half. Dissenters howled that the location was sacred ground—precisely why the memorial's proponents favored the spot.

Congress authorized the memorial's creation in 1993 and gave authority for its realization to the American Battle Monuments Commission (ABMC). Working with the National Park Service, the National Capital Planning Commission (NCPC), and the Commission of Fine Arts— all of which had to approve the memorial's location and design—the ABMC settled on a site in Constitution Gardens, a leafy quadrant north of the Reflecting Pool. However, J. Carter Brown (1934–2002), formidable chairman of the Commission of Fine Arts from 1971 until his death, pushed for a site on the Mall's main axis.

The populist instincts of the patrician Brown determined the final form and situation of the World War II Memorial, as well as three other additions to the Mall: the Vietnam Veterans Memorial, the Korean War Memorial, and the Franklin Delano Roosevelt Memorial. Early on, Brown deemed St. Florian's design "inevitable" and pushed for its momentous location and molded its design to a form that would meet public approval and—more important, one suspects— his own.

An early, reckless, and provocative media soundbite compared the proposed memorial to the

1917
In Geneva, a haven for Protestant refugees during the Reformation, a 328-foot-long (100 m) wall adorned with statues of Reform movement leaders is erected

1917
U.S. declares war on Germany (Apr. 6) and General Pershing arrives in Paris to head American forces

Thousands of vets jammed the Mall for the May 29, 2004, dedication ceremony. Attendees, from left to right, included WWII veterans John Lennon, Reuben Franz, Fred Miccio, Irving Schneider, Senator John Warner, Doris Wilson, and Vietnam veterans Larry Black Wolf and Raymond Benkosky.

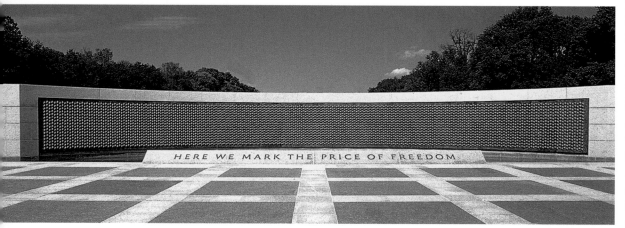

What we dedicate today is not a memorial to war. Rather, it is a tribute to the physical and moral courage that makes heroes out of farm and city boys and that inspired Americans in every generation to lay down their lives for people they will never meet, for ideals that make life itself worth living.

—Army veteran and former U.S. senator Bob Dole, World War II Memorial dedication, May 29, 2004

The Freedom Wall, an 84-foot, 8-inch-wide curved parapet covered with four thousand gold stars, one for every hundred lives lost, commemorates more than four hundred thousand Americans who died during the war. The star motif was inspired by the blue stars that hung in the windows of American households, one for each family member who was serving in World War II; the blue star was replaced by a gold star if they lost their lives. The stars have seven different shapes, each subtly different, to represent the diversity of the armed forces.

HERE WE MARK THE PRICE OF FREEDOM

who lost their lives in the Atlantic Ocean during World War II and features eight two-story-high pylons isolated on a concrete plaza—proves, the understated D.C. memorial has slim claim to the bombast associated with the Third Reich.

Under the leadership of retired U.S. Marine Corps commandant P. X. Kelley, the chairman of the ABMC, and through the fund-raising efforts of veteran and former senator Bob Dole and FedEx founder and president Frederick W. Smith, donations poured in. A flood of popular books and films in the late 1990s, including Stephen Ambrose's *Citizen Soldiers*, Tom Brokaw's *The Greatest Generation*, Steven Spielberg's *Saving Private Ryan*, and the Spielberg and Tom Hanks television miniseries *Band of Brothers*, kept the war veterans and their memorial in the forefront of the public imagination.

imperial designs of Albert Speer, Hitler's architect. Reiterated by many national architecture critics, that criticism did much to obscure St. Florian's willingness to sacrifice his artistic ego, an anomaly these days, for the sake of a larger unity. St. Florian's is a conservative monument but one appropriate to Washington's neoclassical context. Its size, carefully calibrated to human scale, is welcoming and bears little relationship to the dictatorial scale associated with fascism. Indeed, as the 1963 East Coast Memorial in Manhattan's Battery Park—which honors those

Critics continued to pillory the project. The only point everyone agreed on was that with World War II veterans dying at a rate of more than eleven hundred a day, it was important to build something soon. The legal battles did not stop until May 2001, when Congress legislated the memorial's construction, which began in September 2001.

The agony that accompanied the memorial's gestation improved its design. It was pared down to its essence: an elegant frame for the history of

1918

Second Battle of the Marne (July 15–18), near the River Marne. Ends in a French-British-American victory under French General Ferdinand Foch against the German army under General Ludendorff. Allied casualties: French, 95,000; British, 13,000; United States, 12,000; Germany, 168,000.

democracy as expressed by the Mall. It is fundamentally a landscape solution: More than two-thirds of the memorial is either plantings or water. The axial view is embraced by two semicircular colonnades that surround the Rainbow Pool and are punctuated on the north-south axis by arched pavilions.

St. Florian's choice of a seemingly retrograde classical tongue appalled many modernists. Why the brouhaha? After all, George Washington is commemorated with an Egyptian obelisk, Lincoln with a copy of the Greek Pantheon, and Jefferson with a Roman temple. Most of the capital's architecture is classically styled. Additional carping about why this memorial could not have the presence of the Lincoln Memorial ignores history: When the Lincoln was built, the Mall's eastern end was a literal swamp, a tabula rasa just waiting for the grand, dominant terminus that Henry Bacon designed. St. Florian's task was far different from, and more difficult than, Bacon's.

Ultimately, it was the memorial's columns—oddly square, pierced, and truncated—that set off design grumblings. Originally planned as fluted columns without capitals, the columns were modified at the insistence of the Commission of Fine Arts, who wanted to differentiate them from the capital's vast forest of columns. The fifty-six columns are inscribed with the names of forty-eight states, seven territories, and the District of Columbia. The columns also give visitors a special place—at the column inscribed with the name of their home state—within the larger memorial space where they can pose for photographs and leave mementoes. The role may seem a small one,

but it is how the individual relates to the monument. In fact, in 2005, Floridians erected a replica of their state column in Tallahassee as the centerpiece of a new World War II memorial.

Two arched pavilions serve as symbolic gatehouses to the larger Mall and mark the Atlantic and Pacific theaters of war. Rising 43 feet (13.1 m), the structures are largely hidden by the allées of elms that line the perimeter of the central Mall. Each pavilion contains a bronze baldachino in which four eagles perch on four columns representing the four branches of the armed forces—Army, Navy, Air Force, Marines. In their beaks, the eagles hold a suspended laurel wreath, a traditional symbol of victory. The pavilion floors are inlaid with bronze victory medals around which are inscribed, "1941–1945," "Victory on Land," "Victory at Sea," and "Victory in the Air." Gently curving ramps descend from the pavilion to the lower plaza.

Two quotations incised into the memorial's granite surfaces also remember the home-front contribution. The one by President Franklin D. Roosevelt reads: "They have given their sons to the military services. They have stoked the furnaces and hurried the factory wheels. They have made the planes and welded the tanks, riveted the ships and rolled the shells." During the war, ordinary citizens sacrificed in a way that is rare these days, although, as the events of September 11 proved, the nation, if asked, will still rally together. St. Florian worked in collaboration with Leo A. Daly, the architect of record; James A. van Sweden of Oehme, van Sweden & Associates, the landscape architect; sculptor Raymond J. Kaskey;

1918

The Armistice ending World War I signed in a railway carriage in the forest of Compiègne, France (Nov. 11, at 11 a.m., "The eleventh hour of the eleventh day of the eleventh month")

Twenty-four bronze bas-relief sculptures by Raymond Kaskey that line the entrance balustrades depict the mobilization of America's resources. The panels depict vignettes of service at home and overseas. Kaskey worked from World War II–era photographs and models who posed in full military uniform in his studio.

and stone-carver Nicholas Benson, among others. Kaskey (b. 1943), an architect who sculpts, created the two hundred cast bronze elements in the memorial and was responsible for much of its humanizing narrative detail. Van Sweden finessed the memorial's parklike setting and softened its hard edges with canopies of shade trees, flowering plants with white blooms, and expanses of lawn.

Cut into the South Carolina Kershaw granite are the names of the war's two theaters, campaigns, and key battles. Also included are

The waterworks copings are inscribed with the names of key campaigns and battles. Inscriptions on the Atlantic pavilion copings: North Africa, Southern Europe, Western Europe, Central Europe; and Battle of the Atlantic, Murmansk Run, Tunisia, Sicily, Salerno, Anzio, Rome, Po Valley, Normandy, St. Lô, Air War in Europe, Alsace, Rhineland, Huertgen Forest, Battle of the Bulge, Remagen Bridge, and Germany. Inscriptions on the Pacific pavilion copings: China, Burma, India, Southwest Pacific, Central Pacific, North Pacific; and Pearl Harbor, Wake Island, Bataan, Corregidor, Coral Sea, Midway, Guadalcanal, New Guinea, Buna, Tarawa, Kwajalein, Attu, Saipan, Tinian, Guam, Philippine Sea, Peleliu, Leyte Gulf, Luzon, Manila, Iwo Jima, Okinawa, and Japan.

ten memorable quotations by various Allied leaders that mark the war's beginning and end, and D-Day, its turning point. The inscriptions represented another minefield: On the one hand it was crucial that they be historically correct; on the other, political alliances, such as that between the United States and Japan, had changed over time. A low, square tablet, called the Announcement Stone, placed at the entrance clarifies the link between the twentieth-century memorial and its eighteenth- and nineteenth-century neighbors.

A monument's journey from object of anguished controversy to treasured icon is always uncertain. The World War II Memorial's sublime location makes clear the judgment that the Second World War had as formative an influence on the national character as the Revolutionary and Civil wars. Its enthusiastic embrace by the public suggests that the memorial's location will come to seem as ineffably right as the Mall's other tumultuous additions.

Interview with
Nick Benson, stone-carver

A third-generation stone-carver and calligrapher born in 1964, Nicholas Benson creates tombstones and architectural lettering for public buildings, memorials, and monuments. He owns and operates the John Stevens Shop, a historic stone-carving business in Newport, Rhode Island. The shop was run by eight generations of Stevenses until 1927, when it was purchased by Benson's grandfather, John Howard Benson (1901–1956), a distinguished calligrapher, author, and teacher, who was at the forefront of the renaissance in American stone carving between the wars. Benson learned his craft from his father, John Everett Benson (b. 1939), a renowned letter carver who has incised such national treasures as the John F. Kennedy Memorial, the Franklin Delano Roosevelt Memorial, and the National Gallery of Art. Nicholas Benson has done inscriptional work at the National Gallery of Art, the Mellon Auditorium, and the National Cathedral in Washington. In 2000, he was commissioned to design and carve the inscriptions for the National World War II Memorial in Washington, D.C.

Above **A detail of a 1998 headstone in Wakefield, Rhode Island, commissioned by Robert Loffredo in honor of his late wife, Elaine.**

Right **Nick Benson carving the World War II Memorial in Washington, D.C.**

JD: How much stone cutting did the World War II Memorial involve?

NB: There are 4,682 letters in total—a lot of lettering—in twenty-two inscription locations. The letters vary in size from three-quarters of an inch tall to more than nineteen inches.

JD: What kind of granite was used?

NB: It's a South Carolina granite called Kershaw. One of the reasons [memorial designer] Friedrich St. Florian chose it is because it has a large grain. Even from a distance, you can see the character of the granite. Finer granite, especially with such large architectural forms, would get lost. We asked the memorial committees to come up with succinct, evocative inscriptions that could have a large physical letter size so they would carry well. As the letters get smaller, they become more difficult to read because the forms compete with the grain of the granite. It's important not to turn this three-dimensional sculptural form into typography. You want the inscriptions to be sculptural elements that will partake of the architecture scale of the monument, so you can't think of the lettering graphically—black on white.

In 1995, students from Fox Middle School in Hartford, Connecticut, began to research the African American slaves who were interred in unmarked graves in that city's oldest burial ground. They looked at "God's Little Acre," a section in Newport's Common Burying Ground where African American slaves were buried in colonial times. It contains the stone of Pompey Brenton, whose face is the only African American visage ever carved on a colonial gravestone. After coincidentally discovering during that same visit the John Stevens Shop, where the Brenton stone was originally carved by John Stevens III, they raised funds to have Nick Benson adapt the stone to commemorate the Hartford slaves. The African American Monument was unveiled in 1998.

JD: Do people read inscribed letters as they would text in a book?

NB: They do. The key thing about carved letters in stone, what's called the "lapidary letter," is its sculptural quality. The interior of the letter is left somewhat rough so that the interior, abraded surface over time will catch debris and give the letter a dimensional patina. Raking light—light that passes across the surface of the stone so shadows go in and bounce off the interior of the carved letter—really shows off the carved letter.

JD: Was the memorial carving done in situ?

NB: All the carving was done in situ. There's one man in particular who was an absolute godsend, Joe Moss. He is one of the best pneumatic carvers you'll find, probably the country's leading pneumatic carver.

JD: Was it carved only with pneumatic tools?

NB: Only pneumatically. It's a two-step process. Initially, we sandblast it. Sandblasting is a method of etching into the stone. You take a rubber mat in which lettering has been cut like a stencil, and place it on the stone. The stone is exposed where the lettering is. As you blast sand at high pressure at the stencil, it etches the letter into the stone. The inscription work was initially blasted to a depth of about three-sixteenths to a quarter of an inch. Then we go in with our chisels and make the pretty U-cut. Some of the colored pieces in the granite are hard, some are soft, some are in between. When you blast at it, the sand etches into the softer part and leaves the harder parts. You are left with a pebbly surface in the interior of the letter. Later, we go in with our pneumatic chisels and make it uniform.

JD: How do you move forward in a situation where a single mistake can be irreversible?

NB: You're taking out such small amounts of stone at any given time that it's not as if you're going to misstroke and blow out the center of an O. It doesn't work that way. The strike of the piston and hammer against the chisel is fairly light, and you're taking off small bits at a time.

JD: Do you invent a new typeface for each project?

NB: I invented one for this project. In my monument work, I generally draw every letter by hand. Every letter is different. My brushwork is consistent, but in the very subtle inconsistencies are the beauty. It's like an oriental rug. Some of what makes it so beautiful is the human error, subtle things, in the design.

JD: Tell me about the typeface for this memorial.

NB: I call it the World War Two font. I had to make it a very heavy weight to carry the material. The memorial design makes nods to the classical, and there are Romanesque arches. Friedrich, in particular, wanted a letter that was connected to the classical form in some way. When I say the classical form, I mean the Roman capital letter. The Trajan Inscription is considered the archetypal Roman capital letter. That letter was developed with the use of the broad-edge brush and through the repetitive movements of the hand. The Trajan Inscription is mind-bogglingly beautiful, yet it is incredibly idiosyncratic.

When you look at my lettering, I have a sweep that's typical of the brush-drawn Roman. The broad-edge brush has flat bristles on the top like a calligraphic pen; when you move one way, it's thin, when you move the other, it's thick. It's held at a forty-five-degree angle, just like a pen. You come down, you put a little more weight at the top as you begin, you draw the weight up a little bit, then you bring pressure down at the bottom. It draws the eye beautifully.

JD: Do you work with a brush when you're in the conceptual phase of the design?

NB: Yes. Water-based black poster paint on paper drawn to scale, full size. One to one. Years of experience tell me what the letter will look like carved in stone regardless of its graphic representation on the page. When I started painting out the World War Two inscriptions, I did several different versions, knowing what I needed to do in order to make it work well with the stone. If you looked at what I painted graphically, you'd think, "Those letters are awfully heavy, the weights are very strong, they are very thick strokes, I don't know, it looks too thick." No. It was all in my

1927

Aviator Charles A. Lindbergh (b. Feb. 4, 1902; d. Aug. 26, 1974) makes first nonstop solo flight across the Atlantic from New York to France, a 3,600-mile, 33½-hour flight, in the *Spirit of St. Louis* (May 20–21)

mind, knowing this is what I am going to need in order to make letters carry.

JD: How long have you been cutting stone?

NB: Twenty years. My dad taught me. He got me into the shop more than twenty years ago. I was fifteen and needed a summer job. My father was hard on me and got me moving quickly, making finished work for him, and carving at the shop level, which is a particularly high level of craftsmanship. He has the highest standards of anybody you're going to find, bar none. I cut his designs from 1979 until 1993. I took over the business in 1993.

JD: When you look at a block of text are you conscious of individual letters or the entire composition?

NB: Both. The entire composition is key, but the proportion of the letter, the design of the particular letter form itself, is extremely important too. Equally important is the cadence of the text, how the negative space is used, word spacing, line spacing—all of that is crucial to good inscriptional carving. And very complicated and subtle. That's the type of thing that people don't see. The inscription will be easy to read, the letters will look pretty, and they won't give it a second thought. The inscription work on this monument was made to be highly legible, easily read, with no strange idiosyncrasies that would have people scratching their heads and wondering.

JD: To obtain "perfect" lettering, you'd think the letters would be of uniform weight, but they're not.

NB: Not even close. There's a subtle shift from thick to thin in every letter. When you go back to the history of monument making in this country in particular—for instance, when you go to the Common Burying Ground in Newport, which is a very old cemetery, and so many of the stones in there are John Stevens Shop stones— all of the interesting colonial tombstones were one-offs. That is, there was one version of a design, one man's thought process from concept to product, all the way through.

JD: Customized for each client?

NB: Pretty much. They put everything they could into developing it, and the styles were constantly progressing. The most interesting thing is that they didn't have typographic standards to look at, so they were developing letter forms from memory.

JD: Weren't they influenced by books and broadsides?

NB: In the early 1700s, in colonial America, there were not a lot of printed pieces, and the examples they had were extremely rough. It wasn't until [John] Baskerville and some of the other English typographers in the eighteenth and early nineteenth century that those faces become popular in America. In early colonial stones, they developed both lettering and the ornamental work at the same time, the two were linked.

They were strong, unified pieces of work. When the typographic standard came in, people began to request specific typefaces. That is when the split occurred between calligraphy and monument work. They were no longer letterers anymore, they were just making facsimiles of typefaces. The ornamental carving was quite good all the way up to the Victorian era, but the lettering fell off. It became odd, stylized, flat-footed. There was no longer that brilliant, lively calligraphic form.

JD: Do you use a graphics program?

NB: I use Fontographer, which takes the scanned, brush-drawn letters and translates that into a typeface. For this project, I drew each letter by hand, scanned it into the computer and made a typeface from which I could type, and then set, in the computer, all the type that we see on the memorial. We spent hours using complicated things like bézier curves, making outlines of the brush-drawn letters, making hair-splitting assessments. It's delicate work, making an outline that will be somewhat of a representation of your brush-drawn letter. Mainly, I brush letters by hand, transfer them onto stone, and then carve. I cut with mallet and chisel 99 percent of the time.

JD: Do you have a favorite letter?

NB: *R* is one of my favorite letters because it incorporates all of the strokes of the alphabet. You have the vertical, the horizontal, the curved form, and the diagonal. That's what we use often as a sample, test letter. It's a good letter.

JD: My son, who is studying Chinese, told me that in China if a woman has a choice between a handsome man and one who writes beautifully, she will always choose the man with the beautiful handwriting.

NB: I'm not surprised. They've got such a reverence for calligraphy in Asia, and everyone has some skill with the brush. People here appreciate calligraphy, but it doesn't receive the same reverence that it does in the East.

JD: Do you judge people based on their handwriting?

NB: Not at all. When I was a kid, my handwriting was nearly illegible.

JD: What happened?

NB: Study, study, study, and perseverance. Hermann Zapf, the great type designer, said, "My friends would go out and drink and dance while I stayed at home and bravely drew letterform." You've got to put in the time.

In 1997 Benson carved a French limestone tablet that was commissioned by Henry Sharpe Lynn to commemorate the renovation of the Anglican Cathedral refectory in Birmingham, Alabama.

1929

Quartz crystal clocks that are accurate to one second in ten years are introduced

1929

New York Stock Exchange collapses on "Black Friday" and the Great Depression begins, lasting until 1939; it is the longest and most severe depression in the industrialized world (Oct. 28)

Civil rights legend Dr. Martin Luther King, Jr., devoted his brief lifetime to the vision and promise of the Declaration of Independence, that all men and women are created equal. He accepted his 1964 Nobel Peace Prize for the "civil rights movement, which is moving with determination and a majestic scorn for risk and danger to establish a reign of freedom and a rule of justice."

Of the dozens of sites dedicated to the bloody history of the American civil rights movement, few have had a greater impact than the quiet Sweet Auburn neighborhood in Atlanta, where Dr. Martin Luther King, Jr. (1929–1968), a self-described drum major for the Lord, was born and raised and, before he was too soon laid to rest there, preached a transformative message of love, nonviolence, equality, and dignity for all persons.

The Martin Luther King, Jr., National Historic Site consists of an ensemble of buildings, parks, plazas, and walkways that teach, each in its own way, about the life of Martin Luther King, Jr. The places where King lived, worked, played, and prayed are strung together like pearls along Auburn Avenue. They allow the visitor to engage with the spirit of his life by providing occasions for recollection and an impetus for storytelling, which is the basis of memory.

The twenty-three-acre Martin Luther King, Jr., Historic Site, a National Historic Landmark established in 1980 and maintained by the National Park Service, consists of four key structures: the King Center, Ebenezer Baptist Church, King's birthplace, and a visitor center. The larger district includes the New Horizon Sanctuary and a variety of structures and places that were important to King's life.

1932
Amelia Earhart, American aviatrix (b. July 24, 1897; disappeared July 2, 1937, near Howland Island, Pacific Ocean), is the first woman to fly solo across the Atlantic from Newfoundland to Ireland; takes 14 hr. 56 min. and covers 2,026 miles (May 20–21)

1933
Hitler appointed chancellor of Germany (Jan. 30)

Martin Luther King, Jr., National Historic Site

LOCATION	DEDICATION	DESIGNER	COMMEMORATION
Atlanta, Georgia	*1980; various*	*J. Max Bond; various*	*The Reverend Dr. Martin Luther King, Jr.*

I have a dream.
—Dr. Martin Luther King, Jr., August 28, 1963

The Ebenezer Baptist Church, where King worshipped as a child, where his father and grandfather preached, and where he himself would preach, was the locus of the civil rights movement in Atlanta. Construction of the three-story red-brick building began in 1914 and was completed in 1922 under the leadership of the church's pastor, Dr. Adam D. Williams. A two-story educational building was added in 1956. Dr. Williams's son-in-law, Martin Luther King, Sr., became pastor in 1932; his wife, Alberta Williams King, played the church organ and, in 1974, was shot and killed as she sat at the organ. Martin Jr. was baptized in the church, gave his first sermon there at the age of eighteen, and served as co-pastor from 1960 until his assassination; his funeral was held there in 1968.

As the Ebenezer congregation swelled, plans were made to build a larger church. To accommodate senior members who still lived in Sweet Auburn and had not, like many, moved to the suburbs, the congregation wanted to build close to the original church. Building was an eleven-year odyssey that ultimately required a literal Act of Congress. The results would be worth the struggle.

The New Horizon Sanctuary (1999) was designed by African American architects William Stanley

The fountain at Atlanta's Olympic Park recalls Dr. King's memorable line, "We will not be satisfied until justice rolls down like waters and righteousness like a mighty stream."

1933
Dachau prison camp built in Germany (Mar.)

(b. 1948) and Ivenue Love-Stanley (b. 1951), who looked to Africa for the symbols incorporated into the eighteen-hundred-seat church. At the entrance stands a bell tower, a neighborhood landmark, designed after the Stele at Axum of East Africa, one of the obelisks erected by the Queen of Sheba. The expansive, light-filled interior also reflects the palette and motifs of African art. New Horizon is the third point on a historic triangle: It sits across the street from Ebenezer Baptist and is angled toward King's crypt to make evident its visual and emotional relationship to the civil rights leader.

The district is anchored by several other churches with vibrant congregations, including the Big Bethel A.M.E., founded in 1840 and Atlanta's first African American church, and the First Congregational Church, founded in 1847.

Coretta Scott King established the King Center, originally called the Martin Luther King Jr. Center for Nonviolent Social Change, which opened in 1981. As designed by architect J. Max Bond, Jr. (b. 1935), the Center is an ensemble of red-brick and concrete structures built around an arcaded plaza

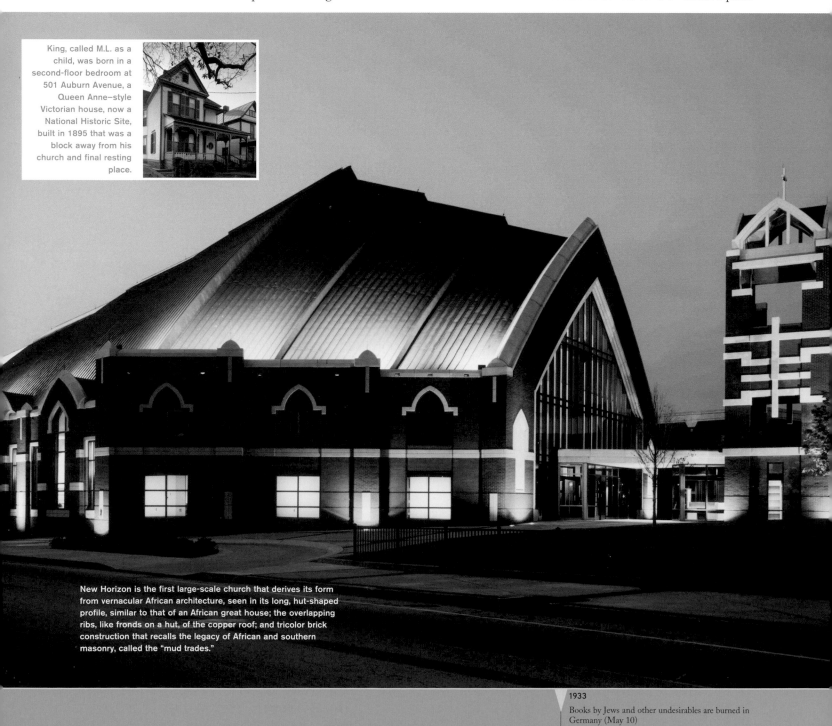

King, called M.L. as a child, was born in a second-floor bedroom at 501 Auburn Avenue, a Queen Anne–style Victorian house, now a National Historic Site, built in 1895 that was a block away from his church and final resting place.

New Horizon is the first large-scale church that derives its form from vernacular African architecture, seen in its long, hut-shaped profile, similar to that of an African great house; the overlapping ribs, like fronds on a hut, of the copper roof; and tricolor brick construction that recalls the legacy of African and southern masonry, called the "mud trades."

1933
Books by Jews and other undesirables are burned in Germany (May 10)

whose centerpiece is King's crypt. The crypt is carved from Georgia marble and placed on a circular brick pad in the center of a reflecting pool. The Africanist aesthetic that infuses Bond's modernism can be seen in his use of columns and barrel-vaulted roofs that were inspired, according to the architect, by the vernacular architecture found in Tunisia, while the curved walls echo those Thomas Jefferson employed in his architectural designs. The pool terminates in an intimate open-air chapel.

Coretta Scott King (1927–2006) founded the Martin Luther King, Jr., Center for Nonviolent Social Change in 1969 to preserve her husband's legacy. It features exhibits on King, Mrs. King, and Mahatma Gandhi, whose pacifist teachings King ardently espoused. The Center once housed the largest repository of primary source materials on King and the American civil rights movement; in 2006, the collection was purchased by King's alma mater, Morehouse College. The sale of the priceless documents, pulled off Sotheby's auction block just a week before private philanthropists rallied to save them intact, fueled the ongoing criticism of the King siblings' administration of the site and care of the tomb. The National Park Service, which is responsible for maintaining most of the landmarks in the popular district, is a likely future steward of the property. On November 12, 2006, ground was broken on the Martin Luther King, Jr., National Memorial, which will be built on a four-acre plot in the northeast corner of the National Mall at the edge of the Tidal Basin near the Lincoln, Jefferson, and FDR memorials.

Mrs. King carried on her husband's message for nearly forty years after his death while also raising their four children. Mrs. King is interred in a crypt near her husband's tomb; between the two burns an eternal flame that was placed there in 2003.

The Visitor Center's exhibits, one geared to children, the other to adults, is chockablock with video, text, photographs, and quotations that trace King's role in the civil rights movement. The centerpiece is Freedom Road, an exhibit peopled with life-sized civil rights marchers and marked with the locations of places of major civil rights protests. The Peace Plaza, with a rose garden and waterfalls, is located in front of the Visitor Center, as is *Behold* (1990), an

oversized bronze sculpted by Patrick Morelli (b. 1945) that depicts a man holding up an infant, a composition the artist said was inspired by the ancient African ritual of lifting a newborn child to

the heavens and saying, "Behold the only thing greater than yourself." Connecting the Visitor Center to the rear parking areas is the International Civil Rights Walk of Fame, a promenade imprinted with the footprints of noted civil rights leaders. Nearby is a life-sized bronze portrait of Mahatma Gandhi (1869–1948) sculpted by Ram Sutar (b. 1925) of New Delhi and donated in 1998 by the Indian Council for Cultural Relations.

These interrelated places, coupled with the neighborhood's strong cultural identity, form the basis of the larger monument that is Sweet Auburn. The avenue is hospitable to life's rhythms and invites quiet contemplation, strolling rather than driving, and conversations with one's neighbor as well as with God. Despite its outsized influence, the Sweet Auburn neighborhood occupies just a short mile and a half along Auburn Avenue. Restrictive Jim Crow laws in the southern states that enforced

More than ninety works of art sprang up in Atlanta for the 1996 Olympics. One of them, *Through His Eyes* (1996), honors the orator and civil rights activist John Wesley Dobbs, who coined "Sweet Auburn" to describe the neighborhood where he lived. Located on Dobbs Plaza on Auburn Avenue, the 7-foot (2.1 m) tall portrait head by Ralph Helmick (b. 1952) was inspired by traditional African ceremonial masks. One can walk into the mask and literally look through Dobbs's eyes down Auburn Avenue.

The boarded-up storefronts of the Herndon Building (1924) at 201–245 Auburn Avenue have been painted temporarily with murals depicting businesses that once operated there while the building awaits renovation. Although designated a National Historic Landmark in 1976, Sweet Auburn fell victim to a lack of investment, crime, and abandonment, compounded by highway construction that split it in two. In 1992, starting with houses surrounding Dr. King's birth home, the Historic District Development Corporation began to turn the area around.

1934
Forced sterilization by the Nazis of Gypsies, African-Germans, and the mentally and physically disabled begins in Germany (Jan.)

1935
Kodachrome film, the first amateur color film, is introduced in 16mm format for motion pictures; 35mm slides and 8mm home movies follow in 1936

segregation brought neighborhoods like Sweet Auburn, with its high concentration of African American religious and social organizations, businesses, and residences, into being.

How do we connect a memorial to its place as well as to residents and visitors and, more cosmically speaking, to history—what has come before the memorial and what will follow it? One answer is found in the organic design of the King district, which frames what already exists, weaving the best features of the past with the sensibility that one's life and work must arise from what one believes. The power of the entire ensemble of ideas, not the solitary gesture, mirrors the life of Martin Luther King, Jr., one person whose influence rippled out like a wave to change the lives of many.

Three generations of Kings served as pastors at Atlanta's historic Ebenezer Baptist Church, founded in 1886. Vital, tightly woven church communities like Ebenezer Baptist's were the cauldrons in which the fundamental principles of civil rights were born, nurtured, and defended.

The tomb of Martin Luther King, Jr., is positioned on axis with the Ebenezer Baptist and New Horizon churches, a placement that intertwines the message of the memorial with those offered by both the historic church and the new one.

1938
Kristallnacht ("Night of Broken Glass")—gangs of Nazi youths in Berlin destroy 101 synagogues, 7,500 Jewish businesses; 91 Jews die and 26,000 are arrested and sent to concentration camps (Nov. 9–10)

Civil Rights Monuments

By 1965, Jim Crow was legally dead, but the modern civil rights movement, a period framed by the *Brown v. Board of Education* decision in 1954 and the assassination of Dr. Martin Luther King, Jr., in 1968, is only now, as the past is being reexamined and key anniversaries approach, being recognized with memorials.

Dozens of civil rights memorials exist or are planned. Many adapt the churches, lunch counters, schools, and bus terminals where key events unfolded, enabling visitors to reimagine in situ what took place. The handful of sites listed give a sense of the wide range of civil rights commemorations.

On December 1, 1955, Rosa Parks refused to give up her seat on a Montgomery City Lines bus. The orange and white 1948 coach, rusting in an Alabama field and ignored for decades, was put up for sale on eBay in 2001. Not sold, it was purchased, after its true identity was verified, by a curator at the Henry Ford Museum in Dearborn, Michigan, where it is now fully restored and on permanent display.

The Sixteenth Street Baptist Church in Birmingham, Alabama, was bombed on Sunday morning, September 15, 1963, by the Ku Klux Klan, killing four young girls. The church contains a memorial nook with photographs and mementos of the blast; it was designated a National Historic Landmark in February 2006.

More than three thousand people of many races and nationalities began a monumental trek on Sunday, March 21, 1965, to demonstrate for the right to vote. That march, and two earlier attempts to march to Montgomery, led to President Lyndon Johnson signing the Voting Rights Act on August 6, 1965. The fifty-four-mile Selma-to-Montgomery National Historic Trail begins at the Brown Chapel A.M.E Church in Selma, Alabama, follows the protesters' march

along U.S. Highway 80, and culminates in Montgomery. The trail is an "All American Road," the highest honor given to a road, indicating that it has national significance, cannot be replicated, and is a destination unto itself.

The Lorraine Motel in downtown Memphis, where Dr. King was assassinated on April 4, 1968, in Room 306, was gutted and transformed in 1991 into the National Civil Rights Museum, the nation's first civil rights museum; the boarding house across the street where James Earl Ray rented a room was acquired and opened with additional exhibits in 2002.

The Daytona City Island Ballpark where Jackie Robinson, the first African American player in the major leagues, played in the first racially integrated baseball game, on March 17, 1946, was renamed in Robinson's honor and is a national historic site.

Maya Lin's design for the Civil Rights Memorial (1989), adjacent to the Southern Poverty Law Center in Montgomery, Alabama, consists of a circular granite table inscribed with a timeline of civil rights milestones over which water flows. It is encircled by a curved Wall of Remembrance. The memorial is near Court Square, where Rosa Parks took her historic bus ride, and the Dexter Avenue King Memorial Baptist Church, where Dr. Martin Luther King, Jr., pastor from 1954 to 1960, began his quest for civil rights.

More memorials are under way. The Woolworth store in Greensboro, North Carolina, where Ezell Blair, Jr., David Richmond, Joseph McNeil, and Franklin McCain sat in the "whites only" section of the lunch counter in 1960—the first "sit-in"—is being made into a museum memorial. In 1999, the National Capital Planning Commission and the Commission of Fine Arts approved a four-acre site for a memorial honoring Dr. King on the National Mall. The contemplative space, consisting largely of landscaped elements with waterfalls, will be located on the axis between the Lincoln and Jefferson memorials. Construction of the first memorial on the Mall to be dedicated to a non-president and an African American began on November 13, 2006.

The most significant civil rights memorial of the nineteenth century is the Underground Railroad, a term referring not to a train but to the efforts to help slaves escape bondage. This network of safe havens provided by black and white citizens consists of private homes, secret passageways, and hidden rooms throughout the eastern and central United States. While the vast majority of the sites cannot be verified, dozens of them have been identified and are preserved as memorials.

Left Participants in the civil rights marches from Selma to Montgomery, Alabama, in March 1965 brought about the Voting Rights Act later that year.

1939
New York World's Fair features the Trylon and Perisphere; attracts 45 million visitors
(opens Apr. 30; closes Oct. 27, 1940)

1939
Hitler invades Poland and World War II begins (Sept. 1)

Vietnam Veterans
Memorial

LOCATION	DEDICATION	DESIGNER	COMMEMORATION
The Mall, Washington, D.C.	*1982*	*Maya Lin*	*Vietnam War veterans*

Maya Lin's competition entry consisted of soft pastel drawings glued to two 30 x 40-inch (76.2 x 101.6-cm) boards, accompanied by a text proposal.

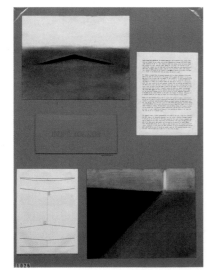

The Vietnam Veterans Memorial transformed all previous notions of what a monument should be. It possesses no laurel wreaths, rearing stallions, aspirant columns, or any other symbols of America's moral and military invincibility. The Wall, as it is popularly known, silently refuses to make any point about the war—its causes or purposes, its heroes or enemies. It affirms only that those who once lived are dead, now mourned, and invites us, in and through reflection, to consider our eventual participation in that same fate. Although its minimalist design met bitter opposition when it was announced, today it remains the standard against which all contemporary memorials are measured.

The brilliance of the memorial design is threefold: the literal descent from the green lawns of the Mall into the submerged realm of the dead; the axial relationship with those symbolic anchors of American ideology, the Lincoln Memorial and the Washington Monument; and, ultimately, the cathartic engagement of the individual with the roll call of the slain.

Each name is preceded by a symbol that tells the fate of its bearer. A diamond indicates a confirmed death, while a cross indicates a person still missing. If a death is confirmed, the cross will be changed to a diamond; if a missing person returns, a circle will be inscribed around the cross. To date, none of the symbols has been changed.

1940

Auschwitz, Poland, designated a Nazi death camp (Jan. 25); beginning in 1942 it becomes the largest extermination camp for the "Final Solution" of killing Jews in Europe; estimated 1.1 to 1.5 million people killed, most in the Birkenau gas chambers; liberated by Red Army soldiers on Jan. 27, 1945; site added to the UNESCO World Heritage List in 1979

1940

Germany invades Denmark, Norway, the Netherlands, France, Belgium, and Luxembourg (Apr.–May)

The memorial is not so much an object as an unfolding event. Visitors gradually descend along the wall, confront the veterans' names, and then ascend. This experience—death, transformation, rebirth—is rooted in the ancient rituals of most cultures. A literal and figurative journey, the Wall asks of its visitors life's fundamental questions: What is the meaning of my life—of any individual's life—and what do we make of war?

The idea for a memorial came to Jan C. Scruggs, a twenty-nine-year-old former rifleman with the U.S. Army 199th Light Infantry Brigade, in 1979 after watching *The Deer Hunter,* Michael Cimino's inspired filmic re-creation of the post-Vietnam era in a blue-collar Pennsylvania town. Scruggs's imagination was engulfed in names, an endless sea of them, of those who had served and died in Vietnam.

Obsessed with the idea of building a memorial that would incorporate the name of every man and woman who served in Southeast Asia but did not return, Scruggs, who had never attended a press conference, called one on May 28, 1979, at the National Press Club in Washington, D.C. "The only thing we're worried about is raising too much money," he assured the dozen reporters who attended. A month later, all he had received was $144.50—that, and notes scribbled from across the country with a plea that their loved ones not be forgotten.

I seek to create an intimate dialogue with the viewer, to allow a place of contemplation, sometimes an incorporation of history, always a reliance on time, memory, a passage or journey.

—Maya Lin, *Boundaries,* 2000

Scruggs had the support of Bob Doubek, an attorney and former Air Force officer who had served in Danang in 1969, and Jack Wheeler, a graduate of West Point, Yale Law School, and Harvard Business School, also a Vietnam vet. With Doubek, Scruggs formed the nonprofit Vietnam Veterans Memorial Fund (VVMF) in April 1979. The trio put together an impossible timetable: 1980, obtain land; 1981, finish raising money; 1982, construct memorial; Veterans Day 1982, dedicate memorial. Scruggs converted Maryland senator Charles McC. Mathias, an outspoken critic of America's involvement in Vietnam, to his cause. He explained that he didn't want money from Congress, just an appropriation of land.

The first location suggested by the Commission of Fine Arts was on a nondescript road leading to Arlington National Cemetery. Mathias advised the VVMF to bypass the federal bureaucracies and have Congress authorize a specific parcel of land. It is said that Mathias picked the monument's future location by randomly planting his thumb on a map of the Mall, and it landed on the sacrosanct Constitution Gardens between the great memorials to Lincoln and Washington.

On October 24, 1979, Doubek explained to the National Capital Memorial Advisory Committee the symbolic appropriateness of the location—where better to commemorate a war that divided the country almost as bitterly as the Civil War?

> *The Vietnam War has been the collective experience of the generation of Americans born during and after World War II. . . . The Vietnam Veterans Memorial is conceived as a means to promote the healing and reconciliation of the country after the divisions caused by the war.*

Twenty-six senators, led by Barry Goldwater, a Republican who supported the conflict, and George McGovern, a Democrat who opposed it, announced on November 8, 1979, that they would cosponsor a bill that granted the vets two acres next to the Lincoln Memorial. The bill was pushed through the Senate, and then struggled to gain acceptance in the House. On July 1, 1980, President Jimmy Carter signed a bill giving the vets their land, with the stipulation that the memorial design would have to be approved by the Secretary of the Interior, the Commission of Fine Arts, and the National Capital Planning Commission.

The VVMF hired Washington architect Paul D. Spreiregen to organize the design competition. At that point, it was unclear what kind of memorial was wanted, and who would decide on the designer, and argument ensued. In September a jury, composed of prominent design professionals who had demonstrated during a lengthy interview process that they were sensitive to what the veterans' service had meant, was chosen. Pietro Belluschi, Harry M. Weese, Garrett Eckbo, Hideo Sasaki, Richard H. Hunt, Constantino Nivola, James Rosati, and Grady Clay—architects, landscape architects, sculptors, and survivors of war and hostile regimes among them—were the jurors, with Clay serving as chairman. The point, well taken in light of the criticism that was to attend the jury's ultimate selection, has been made that the venerable jurors, average age sixty-five, represented respectable, mainstream taste in American art; none engendered a radical aesthetic. The fund specifically chose not to include a veteran on the jury so that the other jurors would not feel obliged to defer to his or her opinion.

Fundraising continued. Donations came in, a flurry of small bills, the ticker tape parade the vets had never had. According to marketing consultants, the problem was that Vietnam just wasn't a hot enough issue to inspire interest. Veterans themselves thought money would be better spent on job programs, education, and counseling. Then businessman and future presidential hopeful Ross Perot contributed $160,000 to underwrite the competition. Eventually, the VVMF raised nearly $9 million. The project received no federal funding.

On January 20, 1981, the day of Ronald Reagan's first inauguration, Iran released fifty-two hostages whose joyous homecoming was covered extensively by the press. The Vietnam vets, who had not received a fraction of the same recognition, were young—the average age in the Vietnam war zone was nineteen—and angry that their sacrifice had been ignored. The hostages' overwhelming reception slowly woke up the media and the public to the near invisibility of millions of Vietnam veterans.

Four points were stressed in the VVMF competition rules: The design must include the 57,661 names of those missing or killed (more names have been added since), and it must harmonize with the site, facilitate a healing process, and make no political statement. It was not to be a war memorial, but one that honored service. The 1981 design competition attracted 1,421 entries—the largest ever held in the United States until the World Trade Center competition in 2003. The proposals were identified only by number, in order that the entrants would remain anonymous. Number 1026 was chosen unanimously as the winner—the one, according to Clay and Spreiregen, that "most clearly meets the spirit and formal requirements of the program."

The winning proposal described a chevron-shaped black granite wall inscribed with the names of those missing and dead. Set below the expansive lawns of Constitution Gardens, it was a work of extreme understatement, devoid of embellishment and adamantly horizontal, piercing the earth rather than the sky. It was nothing more nor less than a wall—the first element of architecture. As the war divided Americans and unleashed a crisis of national identity, the memorial cut the earth in two.

The unlikely winner was Maya Ying Lin (b. 1959), a twenty-one-year-old Yale undergraduate who had entered the competition to fulfill a requirement for a class in funereal architecture. Lin has said her design was influenced by the names etched into the walls of Yale's Woolsey Hall and on Edwin Lutyens's World War I memorial in Thiepval, France. She could not have been unaware of the long history of subterranean funerary monuments that evoke the protective power of Mother Earth. Almost certainly, too, she was aware of earthworks—large-scale contemporary sculptures that were carved into the earth—that were rooted in the "get back to the garden" sensibility of the late sixties.

Paul Goldberger, writing for *The New York Times*, was one of many who hailed the sophistication of Lin's design when it was announced on May 6, 1981, and noted that its "special gift to us will be its capacity for being interpreted in many ways." Despite this and other complimentary reviews, furor ensued.

The controversy centered on what the memorial should be and what it should look like, and how to reach a middle ground with those who didn't want it to be below grade, somber, and abstract. Lin's design was decried as a "black gash of shame," "Orwellian glop," and "unheroic." James H. Webb, Jr., a Vietnam veteran on the VVMF's National Sponsoring Committee, called it "a wailing wall for future anti-draft, anti-nuclear demonstrators." *The New Republic* attacked the design's lack of context, saying it treated the dead like anonymous "victims of some monstrous traffic accident." Tom Wolfe went after the elite "Mullahs of Modernism" who inflicted their minimalist aesthetic on the public. Some didn't understand the choice of black granite or why the monument was sunk into the earth; still others preferred a more traditional, representational work that depicted actual soldiers. Many Vietnam vets thought Lin's design was too abstract to sufficiently convey the war's emotional and political complexities and were angered by its unobtrusive scale and lack of heroic symbols. And Lin herself was attacked for being a woman and an Asian American.

Lin had created the antithesis of the shining city on a hill. For some, the anti-monumental nature of her design embodied the truth of Vietnam. For others, it said something about America and its involvement in the war that many could not bear to hear. The debate propelled people to think about the nature and purpose of a memorial, what it could and should be, in a way they hadn't since the debacle in the 1960s over the Franklin Delano Roosevelt Memorial and wouldn't again until the events of September 11, 2001.

Based on feedback from veterans and a cadre of influentials against the design, including Perot, who eventually withdrew his original seed money, VVMF suggested that a 60-foot flagpole be placed on the lawn above the apex of the wall and a representational bronze of three servicemen by Frederick Hart (1943–1999) be set in front of the wall's central intersection. Lin protested the changes as treating her work as an architectural backdrop, and wrote to the VVMF on the day the Hart model was unveiled, "as each person enters the memorial, seeing his face reflected amongst the names, can the human element escape him? Surely seeing himself and the surroundings reflected within the memorial is a more moving and personal experience than any one artist's figurative or allegorical interpretation could engender." She added that the "visual axis connecting the sculpture and flag splits the memorial at its focal point, the point

Three Servicemen, a figurative bronze by sculptor Frederick Hart, was unveiled on November 11, 1984. The men emerge from a copse of trees and appear to contemplate the wall in the distance. Hart, formerly an apprentice to Felix deWeldon, the sculptor of the Iwo Jima memorial, placed third in the competition won by Lin. Subsequently, Hart and his supporters lobbied for the inclusion of the larger-than-life soldiers.

where it joins in concept . . . and destroys the meaning of the design."

In October 1982, the Commission of Fine Arts heard four hours of emotional testimony from those who asserted that the symbols of the flag and soldiers would demonstrate that the war was fought for freedom, and from those who questioned a literal interpretation of the United States' involvement. Speaking on behalf of the latter, Janice Connally held up as evidence the three iconic photographs of the war: a Vietcong being executed at gunpoint during the Tet offensive; a little girl scorched by napalm running screaming down a village road; and a young woman's anguish over the body of a student killed at Kent State. Opponents of the design found their trump card in the person of Interior Secretary James Watt, who refused to issue a

building permit until the flag and sculpture were added. The Commission approved the two controversial additions but rejected their proposed location; ultimately, the flagpole and Hart's sculpture were placed three hundred feet from the Wall.

It was decided too that a Prologue and an Epilogue would be added to the memorial. The Prologue and Epilogue mirror each other at the Wall's apex:

> Prologue
> *In honor of the men and women of the Armed Forces of the United States who served in the Vietnam War. The names of those who gave their lives and of those who remain missing are inscribed in the order they were taken from us.*
>
> Epilogue
> *Our nation honors the courage, sacrifice and devotion to duty and country of its Vietnam veterans. This memorial was built with private contributions from the American people. November 11, 1982.*

On November 10, 1982, tens of thousands of Vietnam veterans arrived in Washington on foot and in wheelchairs for five days of dedication ceremonies presided over by President Ronald Reagan. The 1960s echoed bittersweetly throughout what may have been the most emotional week ever in the buttoned-up capital. Vets in suits, fatigues, and full combat gear wept, partied, sang hymns, and repeatedly touched and kissed the names on the Wall. Grief held in silent abeyance for years poured forth in a public catharsis. The occasion marked the first time that bereaved family members and surviving veterans could mourn in full view of the nation. The memorial legitimized their loss and the sacrifice of Vietnam veterans. Any uncertainty about the form of the memorial essentially ceased on the day of its dedication. Overnight it became a place of remembrance, reconciliation, and vindication.

The Wall is a splayed V shape, recalling Churchill's and Nixon's V-for-victory gesture but also the protesters' V-for-peace sign. Located at the center of the country's collective memory, the memorial's twin arms point to the two great symbols of American democracy, the Washington Monument and the Lincoln Memorial. One is forced to consider the Vietnam Veterans Memorial in their context, and the metaphoric distance that exists between the bright shrines dedicated to liberty and equality and the contradictory realities of war. Its scale, for all the room it occupies in the imagination, is quite modest.

Of critical moment is the place where the halves of the Wall intersect. As one descends, the top of the wall becomes increasingly higher; at its apex, the panels rise literally "over one's head," as many assessed America's involvement in that war. The panels are fine-grained black granite quarried in

half of the wall is 246.75 feet (75.2 m) long. The wall's tapered arms reach a height of 10.1 feet (3.1 m) at their intersection before slowly decreasing to a height of 8 inches (20.3 cm) at either end. Thus organized, the panels chart the progression of time and the increasing toll exacted by the war.

At close range there is nothing but the names, a remorseless litany of thousands, as specific, eloquent, and quirky as real names are. They are organized chronologically—each name a line in a longer chapter of the year of death—with the names justified right, ragged left, on a panel. It is an elegiac list stretching across a long vista that rises, wanes, and marks the totality of the war's human cost. No military ranks are given; all are equal before the leveling force of mortality.

On the right side of the intersection, at the top, the date of the first death is carved, followed by a

Another controversial addition was made to the Vietnam complex in 1993, when a memorial to the women who served in the military, the first such acknowledgment, was added. The Vietnam Women's Memorial honors the estimated eleven thousand women who served in Vietnam. Sculpted by Glenna Goodacre (b. 1939), the 6.66 foot (13.5 m) high bronze depicts four figures: three nurses and a wounded male soldier. While all four figures wear fatigues, Goodacre deliberately left off any identifying insignia to symbolically include military, medical, and volunteer women.

Bangalore, India, that was chosen for its superbly reflective surface. Three and a half inches (8.9 cm) thick, the slabs were polished to a mirrorlike finish in Barre, Vermont, and then shipped to Memphis, Tennessee, where the names were grit-blasted onto the panels.

One hundred forty panels—seventy to a side—radiate from the center crease of the vertex. Each

chronological listing of names that continues to the wall's end. The incantation resumes on the left wall, where the date of the last death is carved at the bottom of the final panel. In her proposal, Lin wrote, "Thus the war's beginning and end meet; the war is 'complete,' coming full circle, yet broken by the earth that bounds the angle's open side, and contained within the earth itself."

A true war story is never moral.
It does not instruct, nor encourage virtue,
nor suggest models of proper human behavior,
nor restrain men from doing the things
men have always done.
—Tim O'Brien,
The Things They Carried, 1990

Non-organic tributes are gathered and eventually archived at the National Park Service's Museum Archeological Regional Storage Facility in Lanham, Maryland.

1945
Soviet troops liberate Auschwitz (Jan. 27)

Lin had to fight to retain the names' chronological listing. Those in charge assumed an alphabetical arrangement, as is usually done. Lin pulled the list of the war casualties and showed them that more than six hundred Smiths died in Vietnam, and convinced them of the insensitivity of an alphabetical list. She argued, "People don't die in alphabetical order, so why would you possibly want to list them that way?" Ordered by the moment of death, the names point to the loss exacted by war and not its corporate enterprise. The chronological listing summons up Vietnam in real time, and allows veterans to find the time they served and the friends who were lost. It is not difficult to locate an individual's name. Locator books at the monument contain an alphabetized list of names with wall locations pinpointed by panel and line number. Finding a name in the book is part of the ritual of the Wall and heightens the sense that one is participating in a search—for a name, for some larger meaning.

The names are organized chronologically from 1959 through 1975. Less than an inch high, the names appear flat gray against the gleaming black field. They are densely listed, five names to a line. The largest panels have 137 lines; the smallest, one. They are cut in Optima, the widely admired sans serif typeface designed by master typographer Hermann Zapf. Visitors trace their fingertips over the names in a simple, ancient form of remembrance. Many make rubbings.

As of May 2005, the wall bears the names of 58,249 men and women who were killed in Vietnam, remain missing in action, or died because of war-related injury. Since the memorial's dedication in 1982, 296 names have been added. The names of the tens of thousands of veterans who have died of causes unrelated to their Vietnam service cannot be inscribed on the wall; eligibility is determined by the Defense Department.

Since its dedication, the Wall has invited communal storytelling in the form of the offerings left

Because Maya Lin won the competition before she was a registered architect, the memorial was detailed by a local firm, the Cooper-Lecky Partnership, who became the architects of record.

there. Visitors regularly leave souvenirs, a confounding assortment of talismans that have ranged from a Harley-Davidson motorcycle to a can of sardines. Countless messages have been left. Nonverbal offerings imply stories as well. On one occasion, a bereft middle-aged woman left a framed photograph of herself as a beaming high school student. Her choice of photograph reflects the nonlinear nature of time with regard to memory. All that can be surmised from the woman's offering is that it was important to leave an image of herself as she once had been, presumably as someone honored on the Wall had remembered her while in the crucible of the battlefield.

Lin was inspired by the Memorial to the Missing of the Somme (1915–18), Sir Edwin Lutyens's World War I monument inscribed with 73,077 names in Thiepval, France. As architectural historian Vincent Scully, one of Lin's Yale professors, noted, "We see that it is in fact an enormous monster. The right circles of its tondi become demonic eyes; its high arch screams. It is the open mouth of death that will consume us all." It is a triumphal arch, four of them actually, and yet it is earthbound, heavily so, its loyalties clearly with those mortals interred below.

Within the sunken memorial space, a new, virtual reality is constructed via the complex optical properties of the inscribed and highly reflective black granite. The Wall compels personal interaction. It is a mirror and yet a window to the past, present, and future. Visitors must engage, if not with the

1945
Anne Frank, diarist, dies at Bergen-Belsen (Mar.; b. June 12, 1929)

memories of the dead, then with the presence of death. Most powerful is the slightly blurred, hypnotic reflection of one's own face in the mirrored granite, which ensures a unique, supremely subjective experience of the Wall. Like the proper names that can only hint at the lives lived by those who possessed them, the Wall makes shadows of its visitors. The faces of the living hover on its surface like ghosts, disconcertingly sliding forward, slipping back, joining for a brief moment the living and the dead. It is impossible to read the names without seeing one's face in the stone.

While the memorial has human scale—most of the names are within arm's reach—the panorama of death is incomprehensibly enormous. There seems to be no choice but to refocus on the individual names. The dueling images captured in the Wall address the duality of a war that was waged in remote Southeast Asia but also fought in

America, in her streets and conscience. The ghostly reflections are also reminders that Vietnam was the first television war, the first to be broadcast into living rooms on black-and-white television sets, the first to press its grainy, spectral face upon the American public.

The Wall is a symbol of loss, not a symbol of war. Its sole assertion is the sacrifice demanded by war and shared mourning afterward. As much as has been written about Vietnam and its memorial, much more remains unspoken. While the private wars of the soul cannot be measured, Lin's memorial afforded veterans a long-awaited public acknowledgment. This particular memorial, by insisting on reflection and participation, lifted America out of its collective amnesia, diminished some of the cynicism left in the conflict's wake, and restored dignity to those disenfranchised and disillusioned by the Vietnam War.

1945
Franklin D. Roosevelt, U.S. president, dies (Apr. 12; b. Jan. 20, 1882)

1945
Adolf Hitler, German dictator, commits suicide (Apr. 30)

One Soldier's Story is about my childhood neighbor, Rickey Caruolo, who was one of the first to die in the Vietnam War. This is a memorial to one soldier who stands in for all the great guys like him who were killed in Vietnam. It is a snapshot too of a more innocent time in America and a way of life that was lost in the cynicism that followed the Vietnam War. Those who visit the Vietnam Veterans Memorial go because they had a Rick, Joe, or Steve whom they loved and lost. They go because the most precious thing they own is a letter like the one Wayne Burwell wrote to the Caruolo family after their son died in his arms. Not all monuments are made of stone.

One Soldier's Story

On summer nights, my next-door neighbor Rickey Caruolo would play the guitar on his front steps. He always drew a crowd—women mesmerized by his movie-star good looks, his football buddies, old-timers, and lots of children. Fifty-two children lived on Lennon Street, and the undisputed god of that street was Rickey.

Lennon was a street of families, each contributing four, five, six boomers to the tumble, the backbone of the American dream, fifties style. Everyone had two parents then. We saw endless days of four-square, Red Rover, and hide-and-go-seek. We swam in the summer, burned leaves in the fall, starred in Mr. Nickerson's Halloween movies, sang carols in the long night before the annual Christmas party at the Dionnes' house—all of us, every season, every year. Even the dogs played together.

We moved in a bubble of innocence in Providence, in Little Rhody, the smallest state, isolated by size and inclination. It would be easy to dismiss our harmony as typical of any neighborhood with shared small-town values. But it was more than that. There was infinite grace. Almost four decades later, when I added up the number of children on Lennon and arrived at the staggering total of fifty-two, I called Mrs. Dionne, one of our many mothers, just to make sure. "You've got the number exactly right," she said. "We raised the best kids on the planet on Lennon Street." Each head was counted, we counted.

Rickey held court on his front steps. When he wasn't playing guitar, he played hi-lo-jack, his favorite card game. Or he'd unfold the newspaper and read *Peanuts* to us little ones, explaining the comic strip frame by frame. "Do you get it now?" he'd ask. He would tell us what happened on *The Jack Paar Show* because he was the only one old enough to stay up that late. He'd break up the occasional fight, and afterward you'd see him, arm around the beaten kid, coaching and consoling. He was our paperboy. He knew everyone.

There's a reason why the American flag is always flying at my home. It's flying for Rickey, for giving up his life for everything that flag represents. For me, he was the definition and sum of all our losses in Vietnam.

—Michael Dionne, 2003

His peers called him Elvis, because he was cool, cooler than the King, cooler even than James Dean. He was magnetic, smooth, and, by temperament and opportunity, a ladies' man.

He left behind many stories.

"Have Curt tell you the one about the broken-down '34 sedan." Rickey and fifteen guys with names like Big Daddy Lynch chipped in to buy the car and then scribbled their names along with their financial stake on the backseat.

"Get Michael to tell you about the night Rickey showed up at his house, pleading—everything was urgent with Rickey—with his mother to let him take Michael downtown to Loew's Theater to watch a Floyd Patterson heavyweight fight. How Rickey narrated the fuzzy black and white newsreel, blow-by-blow, to his ten-year-old buddy."

"Do you remember him swinging the jump rope for us? The way he made up funny songs as we jumped?"

"How about the time he bought the candy-apple-red Chubby Checker twisting shoes, the ones with the plastic insets in the soles so he could really put the twist into overdrive?"

"Ask your dad about that 1956 Chevy of his, the one that would never start." Used to charming everyone and everything, Rickey would talk aloud to the car, hands flying. "Aw, why are you doing this to me now? Don't you know where I have to be?" He'd kick the car, stomp off, and return a few moments later. "Okay, I am going to give you one more chance." No start, another kick, and he'd be back, swearing to the car that this was absolutely its last chance. He was generous with second chances, whether for cars or people.

Rickey's first tour with the Marines, in 1963–64, took him to the Pacific, where he trained in Okinawa and the Philippines. He was in Tokyo when President Kennedy was shot. In 1965, he received orders to Vietnam.

Rickey died on March 23, 1966, near Quang Ngai in central Vietnam, two weeks short of his return to the United States and three short of his twenty-second birthday. Wayne Burwell, a close friend of his since boot camp, later wrote to his family and described his last hours.

On the day he died, their company had been chasing Vietcong for two days; many were killed. It was their final day out. Eight companies were poised to sweep a village that morning. Rickey, with ten other men, crept ahead, seeing no action until they were thirty feet from the village. Heavily armed Vietcong suddenly opened fire. Rickey's group rushed a trench ten feet away, losing two men as

Rickey with children in Okinawa, Japan, where he first trained with the Marines.

A priest and a Marine officer came to Lennon Street. Marine Lance Cpl. Richard Anthony Caruolo, Kilo Company, 3rd Battalion, 7th Marine Regiment, had been killed in action. He was one of the first of the 224 Rhode Islanders who fell in Vietnam. A stream of people, days long, quietly slipped in and out of the Caruolos' house. For the first time, there were reporters on the street. The realization came for many that there was another world out there, a dangerous world not like Lennon Street.

they did so. Rickey, the team leader, covered until everyone was in the trench and could cover him. Once there, they realized that three Marines, one wounded, were caught between them and the village. Rickey and another soldier left the trench and crawled out to the wounded man.

As he dragged him back, Rickey was hit. When Burwell crawled out to help, Rickey insisted that he first get the other soldier to safety. Only then did he allow Burwell to pull him back. They were still cut off, there was nothing to do. As they waited, Rickey told Burwell he knew he was dying and asked him to write to his family. He told his family he loved them, how much he missed his little sister Joy, and gave his savings to his godson Jim to spend on college or just on fun.

Finally, at nightfall, Burwell and Lenny Byrd, another friend, dragged Rickey on their stomachs four hundred yards before the Vietcong cut them off again. Rickey begged Burwell to abandon him, but he wouldn't. Burwell held him in his arms until he died.

Rickey loved his Marine dress blues. He wore them in his casket, which had been filled with hydrogen and sealed in Plexiglas to survive the long trip back from South Vietnam. A floral wreath placed on top read "Good night, sweet prince." After the funeral at St. Augustine's, his cortège moved slowly down Lennon Street. His beloved dog, Rex, howled as his master's body was borne by.

Outside the cemetery chapel, Rickey was saluted with rifle shots, the loud blasts reverberating inside. Each time, his mother pressed her hand to her heart, a heart that would break and stop a year later almost to the day.

After Rickey's death, the street's shouts turned to whispers, Rex grew white around the snout, and so many Rhode Island soldiers died in Vietnam that it was hard to find military pallbearers. Rickey was posthumously awarded the Silver Star for heroism in combat, and eventually took his place on the Wall on Panel 6E, Line 41. Almost forty years later, the memories of a guy who loved life, loved people, loved his country, are evergreen. We count him among us.

AIDS Memorial Quilt

LOCATION	DEDICATION	DESIGNER	COMMEMORATION
Displayed regularly in various locations; housed in Atlanta, Georgia	*1987 to present*	*Various*	*Lives lost to AIDS*

The AIDS Memorial Quilt, which commemorates a fraction of the tens of millions of people around the world who have died of the AIDS virus, is an atypical monument. It is the quintessential anti-monument, not heroically ascendant, but laid low on the ground. It is soft, domestic, intimate yet epic. It expands constantly, and is exhibited sporadically, though rarely in its entirety. Made of acres of fabric, sequins, ribbons, and other materials more vulnerable than stone or steel, it is a democratic monument—literally made by the people for the people. As such, the Quilt was an early harbinger of the revolution in memorial design in the latter part of the twentieth century.

Until recently, memorials celebrated heroes, not victims and survivors. That changed with the Vietnam Veterans Memorial, the first of what have been called therapeutic monuments. Devoid of the usual trappings of heroism, the primary function of monuments of this type is to offer solace and healing to survivors through interaction and involvement. At both Wall and Quilt, catharsis comes from the experience of finding names among the rows of the dead. The power of these memorials emanates from individual names as well as the ritualistic act of getting "lost" in their endless litany. While the Wall's blank slate invites the living to leave offerings, the Quilt takes the therapeutic a step further by permitting them to create the monument itself.

Family, friends, celebrities, and politicians read the names of those remembered on the panels, a tradition that has been kept at nearly every Quilt display. It has been shown fully only five times, each time on the National Mall in Washington, D.C.

I imagine what it would be like if, each time a lover, friend or stranger died of this disease, their friends, lovers or neighbors would take their dead body and drive with it in a car a hundred miles an hour...

...to Washington D.C. and blast through the gates of the White House and come to a screeching halt before the entrance and then dump their lifeless form on the front steps.

—David Wojnarowicz, "Postcards from America: X-Rays from Hell," 1989

1946

John Eckert and John Mauchly build ENIAC (Electronic Numerical Integrator and Calculator), the first successful all-purpose computer, at the University of Pennsylvania

Horace, the ancient poet, began his famous Ode 3.30 *Exegi monumentum aere perennius,* "I have built a monument more lasting than bronze," referring to his poem, the very intangibility of which guaranteed its immortality. Like Horace, those who conceived of the Quilt understood that the fundamental paradox of any physical monument is its impermanence. Nothing lasts. Even the mightiest stone edifice will, like Shelley's Ozymandias, be reduced over time to rubble. Made of ephemeral materials and temporarily exhibited, the Quilt causes us to consider how the

The keeper of the Quilt is seamstress Gert McMullin, whose creativity has thrived in the improbable environment of grievous loss. In her flamboyant workshop, a shrine with swagger, she stitches together individual panels to form the large display blocks, and maintains and repairs them.

truth of a fleeting life is reflected in those larger truths of existence that time cannot tarnish or erode.

San Francisco gay rights activist Cleve Jones (b. 1954) conceived of the Quilt on November 27, 1985, during a candlelight march held annually since the 1978 assassinations of San Francisco supervisor Harvey Milk, the nation's first openly gay person elected to public office, and Mayor George Moscone. Jones asked his fellow marchers to write on placards the names of the thousand

San Franciscans who had been lost to AIDS. When the march concluded, the cardboard signs were taped like a giant patchwork quilt on the walls of the San Francisco Federal Building. Inspired by this vision, Jones and Joseph Durant created the first two panels for the Quilt a year later in memory of Marvin Feldman and Ed Mock. With Mike Smith, Jones formally established the NAMES Project in 1987 to provide a creative means of remembrance and make visible the enormity of the AIDS pandemic. In June 1987, forty panels were hung from the mayor's balcony at San Francisco City Hall. In October, during the National March on Washington for Lesbian and Gay Rights, the Quilt was displayed on the National Mall for the first time. At that point, it consisted of 1,920 panels.

Jones realized that a quilt could become a powerful political tool because of its "comfortable, middle-class associations." The popular perception of quilts—although quilting has been documented in the ancient world and in Europe since the Middle Ages—is that they are as American as apple pie and, because of the patchwork method of their manufacture, symbolic of the country's mythic "melting pot."

Quilts are powerful instruments of cultural transmission that are literally and metaphorically connected with life, memory, and transformation. As an art, quilting is universal, and distinctly female, practiced without regard to race, class, or geography. The medium itself invites infinite variations within a theme, and gives new form and significance to the fabrics used, whether salvaged scraps or new. Cultural rites of passage historically are accompanied by quilts, such as the Friendship Medley Quilt given to a woman upon her engagement, or the Freedom Quilt presented on the occasion of a man's twenty-first birthday. The period during and after the Civil War was characterized by the creation of memory or mourning quilts, done in somber colors and stitched in the image of a weeping willow tree, a Victorian image of bereavement. The tradition continues in contemporary Plains Indian culture, to give one example, in which infants, newlyweds, and coffins are wrapped in colorful, much-treasured star quilts.

1947
Anne Frank's diary published in Amsterdam (June 25)

1947
Jack R. ("Jackie") Robinson becomes first Negro major-league baseball player when he steps onto the field with the Brooklyn Dodgers (Apr. 15)

As Patricia Mainardi observed in her classic 1973 essay, "Quilts: The Great American Art," quilts were a way for women to express personal convictions at a time when they were not allowed to vote. Quilts addressed in codified, hermetic language opinions about slavery, politics, women's suffrage, and the temperance movement, as well as other, less charged issues. Designs such as the Radical Rose, made during the Civil War, featured roses with black centers to show sympathy with the enslaved, while politically inspired quilts had names such as Lincoln's Platform, Clay's Choice, or Union Star. Mainardi maintains that the quilt has never been seen as high art "because the 'wrong' people were making it, and because these people, for sexist and racist reasons, have not been allowed to represent or define American culture."

This idea of the quilt as "non-art" is essential to the AIDS Memorial Quilt's meaning. Made most often by women for the home, the craft of quilts fell well under the radar of the elite art marketplace with its associations of social position, prestige, and power. The craft of quilting found no place in art history until the end of the twentieth century, when feminists challenged the notion of what constitutes "high" art in works that made use of techniques traditionally associated with the domestic arts. Judy Chicago's seminal *The Dinner Party* (1974–79), a heroically scaled work executed with the participation of hundreds of volunteers, honors thirty-nine women who are represented by oversized plates placed on a banquet table covered with intricately sewn runners and set on a floor inscribed with the names of 999 other women. Jones has said that this work, as well as Christo's *Running Fence* (1976), a twenty-five-mile wall of opalescent fabric that zigzagged over the hills of California's Sonoma and Marin counties for a brief two weeks, also provided inspiration for the Quilt.

The genius of the Quilt's originators lay in recognizing the quilted form as a way to tap into a homely yet subversive tradition that has existed for centuries in the shadows of the dominant white culture. They called a marginalized art into the service of the marginalized.

As the course of the virus changed, the Quilt changed too. The thousands of panels made for men of all races who had died of what was initially called the "gay plague" were joined by panels for hemophiliacs, children, and women. The virus shows no favoritism: Dozens of celebrity names are stitched into the Quilt: Arthur Ashe, tennis player; Tina Chow, clothing designer; Roy Cohn, attorney; Michel Foucault, philosopher; Liberace, performer; Arnold Lobel, children's book author; Robert Mapplethorpe, photographer; Rudolf Nureyev, ballet dancer; Dr. Tom Waddell, Olympic athlete; and Ryan White, the outspoken teenager whose plight shamed the nation into paying for AIDS care. It was nominated for a Nobel Peace Prize in 1989.

Coffin-sized, the 3 x 6-foot panels are laid out in rows. Like a cemetery, it is a landscape of loss, a space of collective grief, where individual loss is amplified by the context of the greater whole. But the individual panels are far from solemn. Spectacularly idiosyncratic in style, sentiment, and construction, they present snapshots of the deceased in ways that relieve the sobriety ordinarily associated with mourning. "The Quilt is cemetery as All Fools' Day, a carnival of the sacred, the homely, the joyous, and the downright tacky, resisting, even *in extremis,* the solemnity of mourning," Elinor Fuchs observed.

Some criticized the Quilt as being passively ineffective, and a literal cover-up of a raging epidemic that was neither beautiful nor comforting. Protest groups such as ACT UP lobbied against homophobia, indifference, and governmental red tape through political and cultural provocation. True beauty, they maintained, could only come out of actively bearing witness to the struggle in ways that acknowledged just how large and sorrowful a price AIDS exacted. Dissent was expressed in vehement public demonstrations in which participants carried mock tombstones, splattered red paint to represent HIV-positive blood, and lay down in massive "die-ins." By the early 1990s, these symbolic actions became real. Political funerals, in which the bodies of deceased victims were carried through the streets, broke the silence around AIDS by turning the ordinarily private and polished rituals of death into gut-wrenching public performances that substantiated its horrific toll.

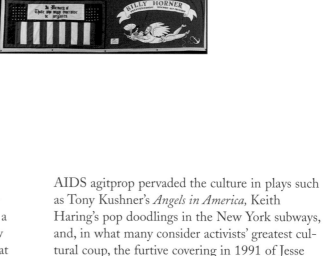

No sewing experience is required to make a tribute panel. Designs can be vertical or horizontal, and appliquéd, painted, stenciled, or decorated with iron-on photo transfers. The finished, hemmed panel must be 3 x 6 feet (90 x 180 cm). Because the Quilt is repeatedly folded and unfolded, durability is crucial. Collected panels are organized in groups of eight, which are sewn into blocks measuring 12 feet (3.65 m) square and assigned a unique tracking number. Submitting letters of remembrance, stories, and photographs for the NAMES Project archives is encouraged.

Many other works of art have been made to explain, defy, and commemorate the AIDS epidemic. As has been noted, AIDS struck first at a sophisticated group—gay men—who knew how to create and distribute images and language that would spotlight sexual prejudice and push medical bureaucracy to provide safe-sex information, lower drug prices, and more research. In the 1970s, activists adapted the inverted pink triangle used by the Nazis to label homosexuals during the Second World War as a symbol of gay solidarity and later a call to action against the AIDS crisis. Stark posters featuring the pink triangle and the slogan "Silence = Death" began appearing on streets in Manhattan in February 1987 and became the unofficial logo of AIDS advocacy and ACT UP.

AIDS agitprop pervaded the culture in plays such as Tony Kushner's *Angels in America,* Keith Haring's pop doodlings in the New York subways, and, in what many consider activists' greatest cultural coup, the furtive covering in 1991 of Jesse Helms's Virginia home in a giant condom.

Visual AIDS, an organization founded in 1988 to increase AIDS awareness through the arts, inaugurated in 1989 the Day With(Out) Art, during which cultural institutions covered up artworks on December 1, and Night Without Light, during which the same institutions blacked their lights on the eve of December 1, World AIDS Day. They also devised the looped red ribbon, a symbol of AIDS awareness that received widespread

1948

American inventor and physicist Edwin Land sells the first Polaroid camera in November after inventing a one-step developing and printing process that permits instant photography

1949

Chinese Communist People's Republic proclaimed under Mao Zedong

The quilt blocks on these two pages celebrate the lives of (top row, left to right): Marvin Feldman/Block 6; Bill Miller/Block 194; Bert Rodney Rebeaud/Block 2605; Tim Kivel/Block 3002; Edward V. Curran, John Leiendecker, Michael Zahratka/Block 2160; Dr. Clark Thompson/Block 1548; (lower row, left to right): Leonce Chabernaud/Block 3945; Billy Horner/Block 514: Lowell/Block 700; Richard DeLong/Block 581; J. Burt Annin/Block 4388; and others.

It is a weapon. It is a fifty-ton fabric weapon made of love to fight against the epidemic.
—Cleve Jones, AIDS Memorial Quilt founder, 2001

exposure when it was first worn by Jeremy Irons at the 1991 Tony Awards. Some condemned the ribbons, and the Quilt, as a way of appearing politically correct without making any real commitment to change.

As of 2006, the Quilt consisted of approximately 46,000 panels dedicated to nearly 83,000 individuals. Although portions of the Quilt are regularly exhibited, displaying it in its entirety is costly, over $2 million, and limited by its sheer size. Since 2001, the Quilt has been housed in a climate-controlled warehouse on Atlanta's Krog Street near the Centers for Disease Control and Prevention. The Atlanta location was chosen for its long history of civil and human rights leader-

ship, and the growing incidence of HIV/AIDS among African Americans in the South.

Unlike Granny's coverlet that has been lovingly mothballed, the Quilt does not have the luxury of timelessness. Despite the development of antiretroviral drugs, it has been estimated that another 68 million will die of AIDS by 2020. That its message is conveyed in brightly colored fabrics appliquéd with teddy bears, rainbows, and hearts heightens the sense of vulnerability it evokes and its aggressive assertion of what has yet to be overcome. Indeed, the fundamental and implicit message of this vast elegiac shroud is the possibility of endless expansion.

1949
First atomic clock is created

1950
North Korean forces invade South Korea; Korean War begins (June 25)

Manzanar

National Historic Site

LOCATION	DEDICATION	DESIGNER	COMMEMORATION
Independence, California	*1992*	*U.S. Army Corps of Engineers, National Park Service*	*Persons of Japanese ancestry incarcerated 1942–45*

Perhaps the fact that the Japanese were held against their will in American detention camps during World War II at the same time that millions were incarcerated in Nazi Europe is best understood in the context of a more recent event. After the September 11, 2001, terrorist attacks, American citizens of Mideastern heritage, Muslims and non-Muslims alike, many easily recognizable by virtue of their dress, met the worst suspicions of their neighbors. Some were killed, businesses were boycotted, and nearly all suffered blatant racist profiling. It was not the first time in American history that fear overtook civil liberty.

On December 8, 1941, the day after Pearl Harbor was bombed, America declared war on Japan. In the weeks that followed, the West Coast, where most Japanese Americans lived, was awash in racial hysteria. "No Japs" signs countered those on the storefronts owned by those of Japanese ancestry that read "I am an American."

A solitary obelisk, erected by the Japanese in 1943, marks Manzanar's cemetery.

President Franklin D. Roosevelt issued Executive Order 9066 on February 19, 1942, which authorized the removal of "any or all persons" from designated areas. Within a month, those of Japanese ancestry who lived in California, Oregon, and Washington, most of whom were American citizens, were forced from their homes and ordered to report to "assembly centers." It was the largest forced migration in American history. Ultimately, 120,313 Japanese were removed to ten war relocation centers in seven western states for fear they would sabotage the United States and help Japan win the Second World War. Evacuees had to leave behind everything that could not be physically carried, and, although it was possible to place certain large items such as pianos in storage, most were forced to sell their homes and businesses in haste and at heavy discounts if not outright loss.

The largest camp was the Manzanar War Relocation Center that opened on March 21, 1942. Manzanar, a Spanish word meaning "apple orchard," was an ersatz city of schools, factories, and living quarters constructed in six weeks using building plans drawn up by the U.S. Army Corps of Engineers. Hundreds of Japanese men and women, eager to prove their loyalty to the American government, arrived early to help build the very camp that would imprison them. The camp was situated on an arid square mile of mesquite and sage located 212 miles (341 km) north of Los Angeles. Although equipped with the amenities typical of a town of its size— about ten thousand people were interned there— Manzanar was ringed with barbed wire and armed military police. Its newspaper, the *Manzanar Free Press,* was censored and thus given to cheery reports such as this one in its first issue of April 11, 1942: "The evacuees now located at Manzanar are greatly satisfied with the excellent comforts the general and his staff have provided for them. 'Can't be better,' is the general feeling of the Manzanar citizen. 'Thank you, General!'"

In fact, the prisoners suffered terrible privations. In *Farewell to Manzanar,* Jeanne Wakatsuki Houston's fine memoir of her incarceration there as a child, she notes the high premium placed on personal privacy, inherited from the generations who had learned to live in a small, crowded country like Japan, and the loss of which—a hundred times a day in sleeping quarters separated by cotton sheets, communal mess halls, and open baths—was nearly unbearable.

The prisoners created the semblance of normal life. Within two months of their arrival, there were already eight baseball teams in fierce competition, according to advocate Steve Kluger, who is lobbying to restore Manzanar's baseball diamond. Perhaps this is a good place to note the thirty-three thousand Japanese Americans who served in World War II, and the celebrated 100th Battalion, 442nd Infantry that became the most decorated unit in United States military history, collecting 9,486 Purple Hearts. These soldiers, along with those interned during the war, are honored by the Japanese American Memorial, featuring two exquisite cranes carved by Nina A. Akamu, that was dedicated on November 9, 2000, in Washington, D.C.

Photographer Ansel Adams (1902–1984) documented Manzanar in 1943 at the suggestion of its director and designer, Ralph P. Merritt. Adams photographed a bleak period of American history, of which there are few physical remains. Other Manzanar photographers included Clem Albers, Dorothea Lange, and Toyo Miyatake. Lange's unflinching photos, taken in 1942, capture the internees' fear and isolation. Commissioned by the War Relocation Authority, approximately 760 of Lange's photos were impounded without explanation and stored at the National Archives; many of her previously unpublished images were reproduced in *Impounded,* a 2006 book by Linda Gordon and Gary Y. Okihiro. Miyatake, a Manzanar intern and professional photographer, made richly detailed photographs of the imprisoned that showed the guard towers and barbed wire that Adams cropped out of his poetic images.

Today Manzanar is virtually bare, its thirty-six blocks of wooden buildings having been hauled away in trucks once the camp closed on November 25, 1945. For $333.13, returning veterans could buy the 20 x 100-foot (6 x 30.5 m) tar-papered barracks, whose former inhabitants had given them names like Dusty Inn, Manzanar Mansion, and, confoundingly, Chicken Pox.

Ansel Adams photographed Corporal Jimmie Shohara's service ribbons and citation medal while he was interned at Manzanar, one of ten camps where Japanese Americans were held with no due process of law during the Second World War.

1953
First ascent of Mount Everest by Sir Edmund Hillary (b. July 20, 1919), New Zealand explorer, and Tenzing Norgay (b. May 15, 1914; d. May 9, 1986), Nepalese guide (May 29)

1953
Korean armistice signed at Panmunjom in the Korean Demilitarized Zone established after the Korean War, 3 miles (5 km) south of the 38th parallel (July 27)

In the early part of World War II, 110,000 persons of Japanese ancestry were interned in relocation centers by Executive Order No. 9066 issued on February 19, 1942. Manzanar, the first of ten such concentration camps, was bounded by barbed wire and guard towers, confining 10,000 persons, the majority being American citizens. May the injustices and humiliation suffered here as a result of hysteria, racism, and economic exploitation never emerge again. California Registered Historical Landmark No. 660.

—Plaque placed by the State Department of Parks and Recreation in cooperation with the Manzanar Committee and the Japanese American Citizens League, April 14, 1973

Visitors can take a 3.2-mile self-guided auto tour of the camp; online visitors can take a virtual tour at the National Park Service's official website. The park includes the area occupied by the internees, cemetery, and camp administration and support facilities such as the hospital and camouflage factory. It occupies approximately 550 acres, a fraction of the original six thousand acres.

There is not much to see. Signs stuck in the sand indicate what once stood in a given block. All but four of the original eight hundred structures were dismantled, leaving behind an evocative ghost town of abandoned concrete foundations, a barely discernible outline of the street grid, and the ruins of once-beautiful rock gardens planted by the residents. The barbed wire fences that once defined the camp's periphery have been replaced with a decorative fence made of bent wood on which visitors have tied bright ribbons and origami cranes. Four surviving structures include two pagoda-like stone sentry posts at the entrance, a wood frame auditorium that was adaptively restored and reopened in 2004 as the site's interpretive center, and a stone obelisk described below. In January 2004, a wooden mess hall that had been moved after the war and variously used over the past fifty years as an infirmary, a golf course clubhouse, and a storage space was moved to the site.

The most striking structure is a concrete monument in the cemetery, where six of the eighty-six original interments are still buried, that was cast by internee Ryozo Kado. Its Japanese inscription describes it as a "Soul Consoling Tower." On the back, the white obelisk reads, "Erected by the Manzanar Japanese, August 1943."

Though little remains of Manzanar, it is the best preserved of the ten relocation camps. The Park Service also maintains facilities at the Minidoka Internment National Monument in Idaho. The other camps, also located in desolate places of extreme geography and possessing varying degrees of monumentation, are Gila River and Poston in Arizona; Granada in Colorado; Heart Mountain in Wyoming; Topaz in Utah; Jerome and Rohwer in Arkansas; and Tule Lake in California.

The U.S. Supreme Court ruled in the case of *Ex parte Endo* on December 18, 1944, that military claims did not justify holding American

1954
Dr. Jonas Salk (b. Oct. 28, 1914; d. June 23, 1995), American virologist, develops a polio vaccine from a killed virus

1955
The *Nautilus*, the world's first nuclear submarine, launched (Jan. 17); developed by scientists at the U.S. Naval Reactors Branch of the U.S. Atomic Energy Commission; constructed at Groton Naval Base, CT, 1951–1954; christened by First Lady Mamie Eisenhower (Jan. 21, 1954)

citizens against their will. Manzanar closed on November 21, 1945; the last relocation center, Tule Lake, closed on March 28, 1946. Upon their release, internees were given twenty-five dollars with which to begin a new life. *The Wall Street Journal* reported that the Federal Reserve Board estimated their losses in 1947 at $400 million but they were paid $38.5 million in subsequent property claims.

In 1978, Manzanar was declared a historic landmark by the State of California, and a simple plaque was erected and subsequently vandalized. Ten years later, the Civil Liberties Act of 1988 apologized for the "grave injustice" done to persons of Japanese ancestry. Saying the internments had been "motivated largely by racial prejudice, wartime hysteria, and a failure of political leadership," it authorized reparations of $20,000 to each internee; in October 1993, President Bill Clinton reiterated the apology. Congress established the Manzanar National Historic Site on March 3, 1992, and in December 2006 passed a bill to pay for restoration and research at ten internment camps. These efforts are checked and challenged, however, by the 2001 U.S.A. Patriot Act, which justifies government surveillance to "intercept and obstruct terrorism."

Manzanar is a spare monument that is re-creating itself slowly and with controversy as the full spectrum of the country's diversity and history is acknowledged. It seeks to remember and mourn a past that many, including those who were once imprisoned there, would rather forget.

*Father's the one who said,
"On Halloween you must say
'treat or trick' not 'trick or treat'—if
you say that, you have to entertain
them." So naturally we said, "trick
or treat" so we must have sang
something like "God Bless America."*

—June Otani, Japanese American internee,
recalling Halloween, 1942

Comparing Manzanar to other "sites of shame" in the United States, including Shiloh and Wounded Knee, historian Robin W. Winks made the point that places that present opposing views of America's past were "neither about shame nor about pride; they were about the lessons of history learned and unlearned" and, further, by virtue of their existence, illuminate the maturity of the nation.

In 1943, Manzanar director Ralph P. Merritt invited eminent American photographer Ansel Adams to photograph the camp. Four images from Adams's 242 original negatives and 209 photographic prints held at the Library of Congress include, from left to right: overview of camp and snowcapped Sierra Nevada, girls' calisthenics class, internees repairing a tractor, and portrait of intern Tom Kobayashi.

Adams's Manzanar photographs were widely exhibited. In 1944, they were shown at the camp and the Museum of Modern Art in New York City; at the end of that year, they were published in a book, *Born Free and Equal: Photographs of the Loyal Japanese-Americans at Manzanar Relocation Center, Inyo County, California.*

In 1965, when Adams gave his Manzanar photos to the Library of Congress, he wrote, "The purpose of my work was to show how these people, suffering under a great injustice, and loss of property, businesses and professions, had overcome the sense of defeat and despair by building for themselves a vital community in an arid (but magnificent) environment."

Korean War Veterans
Memorial

LOCATION	DEDICATION	DESIGNER	COMMEMORATION
The National Mall, Washington, D.C.	*1995*	*Cooper-Lecky Partnership, Frank C. Gaylord, Louis Nelson*	*Korean War veterans*

A memorial honoring veterans of the Korean War (1950–53)—called the "Forgotten War," but one that was fought by one and a half million Americans, more than fifty-four thousand of whom died in the conflict—was dedicated on July 27, 1995. Located on 2.2 acres, the memorial sits at one point of the triangle that includes the Lincoln Memorial and the Vietnam Veterans Memorial. It captures the ancient adrenaline-driven rush to war in a series of figures climbing a commemorative hill.

Cooper-Lecky Architects of Washington, D.C., refashioned the original design submitted by a team from State College, Pennsylvania (Don Alvaro Leon, John Paul Lucas, Veronica Burns Lucas, and Eliza Pennypacker Oberholtzer), who had won the national memorial competition in 1989. That plan called for, among other elements, a design that addressed the site's context by framing views from the memorial to those honoring Lincoln, Washington, and the Vietnam veterans.

President Bill Clinton and President Kim Young Sam of South Korea dedicated the memorial on July 27, 1995, on the forty-second anniversary of the armistice ending the war.

KOREAN WAR VETERANS MEMORIAL / 171

It is a memorial of multiple parts, three of which comprise the essential remembrance. The primary component, and the one having the most visual impact, consists of nineteen oversized figures sculpted by Frank C. Gaylord (b. 1925) that represent a military and ethnic cross section of soldiers. The second component is a granite photo-mural, and the third is the Pool of Remembrance that honors the soldiers who were killed, captured, or wounded.

Gaylord, himself a World War II veteran, sculpted the nineteen stainless steel figures in full battle dress, which are heroically sized at just over 7 feet (2 m). Since the Korean War was the first time U.S. armed forces combat units were fully integrated, the statues are ethnically diverse and include one Air Force, one Navy, three Marine, and fourteen Army soldiers of Caucasian, African American, Asian, Hispanic, and Native American ancestry.

The soldiers are wrapped in flowing rain ponchos, and they march, bent into the wind, across a stepped field planted with dwarf juniper bushes and styled after a Korean rice paddy. Masterfully carved, cast in stainless steel, and choreographed by Gaylord, they are thrillingly realistic, with the square jaws and taut expressions that mirror the heroics of American war movies. The nineteen figures, reflected in the polished granite wall, double to thirty-eight, a symbolic number representing the thirty-eighth parallel dividing North and South Korea.

Gaylord's daring, in a post–Maya Lin era, consisted of depicting the soldiers with utter realism. The risk paid off. Veterans and nonveterans alike are drawn into an empathetic relationship with the troops, gray and vigilant, fatigued but determined, as they approach the implied but unseen enemy. *We are not individuals, but a continuum,* the soldiers imply in their number, placement, and multiplication in the reflective surface of the adjacent wall.

Cooper-Lecky, hoping to trade on the immense popularity of the Vietnam memorial, shamelessly quoted its fundamental element—the wall itself. This component, easily the Korean memorial's weakest aspect, is a highly polished granite wall

164 feet (50 m) in length that was designed by Louis Nelson Associates. Cut from black stone fabricated in Minnesota, the wall was photo-etched with variously sized representations of support troops—drivers, medics, nurses, chaplains—and equipment including rocket launchers, tanks, and ambulances, as well as a range of wartime activities such as bridge building and radio communications. The twenty-four hundred images were based on Korean War photographs held at the National Archives that were digitally etched into the wall's surface. The decorative photographs are intended to blend in with the figures of visitors and the soldier statuary, both of which are reflected back in the wall's polished granite face.

Other design elements amplify the story. Inscribed into the granite curb running along the north side of the statues are the names of the twenty-two nations that helped defend South Korea. A kiosk holds the Korean War Honor Roll, which contains data about the identities, military service, and lives of all those who died in the war. A Dedication Stone located at the tip of the triangle reads, "Our nation honors her sons and daughters who answered the call to defend a country they never knew and a people they never met." Extending into the reflecting pool is a representation of the Korean peninsula that is inscribed, "Freedom is not free."

With the inclusion of warriors taking a metaphoric hill as well as a meditative reflecting pool, the memorial illustrates the dynamic tension that exists between violence and peace, encapsulating the yin and yang of monuments. Considered in its highest light, the memorial mediates the violence and tragedy of warfare with benign and beautiful works of art and landscape. It seems to suggest that our innate nobility seeks to compensate for an equally inherent aggression.

Taken as a whole, the monument, which tries hard to be all things to all people, is an unsatisfying pastiche. Certainly, most visitors are moved by the memorial's inclusive narrative, and its prominent setting ensures that it will be maintained as part of the national canon and memory for as long as the American democracy endures.

1958

In response to the Sputnik program, U.S. government forms the Advanced Research Projects Agency which, in collaboration with others, creates the technologies that form the basis of the Internet

The memorial's plan consists of the triangular Field of Service with nineteen soldiers that is bordered on its south side by a granite photomural and intersects the circular Pool of Remembrance.

They set a standard of courage that may be equaled but never surpassed in the annals of American combat.

—President William Jefferson Clinton, dedication comments, July 27, 1995

Despite the war's relatively short duration, from June 25, 1950, to July 27, 1953, it claimed the lives of 54,246 Americans, 8,200 of whom are listed as missing in action, lost, or buried at sea. An additional 103,284 persons were wounded.

The memorial that commemorates the life and times of Franklin Delano Roosevelt (1882–1945) is organized as a chronological narrative told in four parts. Much like a skillfully crafted novel, albeit one that is life-sized, walk-through, and interactive, the memorial's final chapter could not be predicted. In 2001, four years after its opening, the memorial was revised to include a portrait of FDR in a wheelchair, the first time a major political leader had been shown with a disability. With the illumination of the adversity that revealed FDR's exceptional destiny—to himself and to the nation—his monument was complete.

Franklin Delano Roosevelt
Memorial

LOCATION	DEDICATION	DESIGNER	COMMEMORATION
The National Mall, Washington, D.C.	*1997 and 2001*	*Lawrence Halprin; various artists*	*President Franklin Delano Roosevelt*

Meandering over 7.5 acres (3 hectares) in a secluded location on the Mall's Tidal Basin, the memorial consists of a precisely choreographed sequence of "rooms," or outdoor courtyards, designed by Lawrence Halprin (b. 1916). A leading exponent of participatory landscape architecture, Halprin's pioneering urban designs invite the public to become actively involved in the experience of nature. According to Halprin, archetypal sites such as the Ise Shrine in Japan, Delphi in Greece, and the Western Wall in Jerusalem, which "unfolded like voyages," inspired him to create a metaphoric pilgrimage route. There are five interconnected spaces, with four rooms, each of which is dedicated to one of FDR's eventful four terms.

The rusticated red granite memorial breaks with Washington's traditional white marble monuments. Cut in a variety of sizes and textures to emphasize its strength and permanence, the red Carnelian granite is used to evocative metaphoric effect. The stones symbolize FDR's abiding faith in the exceptional potential of ordinary people. They also make literal reference to the building programs initiated during his tenure that saw the construction of epic public works such as the Golden Gate Bridge, Hoover Dam, Grand Coulee Dam, and others that would jump-start the nation's economy. Moving through Rooms One to Four, the stone becomes progressively rougher and more assertive, to suggest the accelerating tumult and productivity of Roosevelt's administration. In Room Three, the stones are scattered over the pavers, as though blasted by a bomb, to simulate the devastation of war.

Water, another unifying memorial motif, figured prominently in Roosevelt's life. He was born on the Hudson River, loved swimming and sailing, served a seven-year term as assistant secretary of the Navy, and eventually pursued water treatments for polio. His stewardship of water resources was most evident in the Tennessee Valley Authority, an innovative planning and development program of 1933 that saw the construction of dams, reservoirs, and power plants over a vast multistate region that revitalized rural America. Halprin has compared the layered fountain in the second room with the character of the dams built by the TVA.

The memorial's abundant plantings grew out of Roosevelt's love of trees—had he lived to retire, he planned to grow them—and lifelong interest in forestry. Halprin selected maples, pines, elms, dogwoods, and cherries, along with some three thousand shrubs, to soften the granite structure. Nighttime lighting transforms the park into a romantic setting.

Robert Graham's sculpture in the Prologue Room shows President Roosevelt sitting in a wheelchair that he designed and used daily. It was dedicated on January 10, 2001.

1961
Cuban exiles attempt unsuccessful Bay of Pigs invasion of Cuba

1961
Russia puts first man in space

The only thing we have to fear is fear itself.
—FDR's First Inaugural Address, March 4, 1933

Laid out as a history lesson, the memorial has been criticized as having too much architectural "furniture" and leaving too little to the imagination. Because it covers the well-documented emergence of America as a superpower, however, it is appropriate that the memorial is crammed with words and images that re-create that narrative.

Roosevelt's interests extended to the cultural arena as well. About ten thousand artists were

The Breadline, one of three works George Segal made for Room Two, depicts the scarcity of the Depression. Having grown up during that era, Segal himself modeled for one of the downcast figures.

employed under the Federal Art Project (FAP), established in 1935 as a division of the Works Progress Administration. The relatively large number and stylistic diversity of the artists who collaborated on the FDR memorial recall in microcosm FAP programming. Halprin brought in five distinguished American artists to create the sculptural program: Leonard Baskin (1922–2000), Robert Graham (b. 1938), Neil Estern (b. 1926), Tom Hardy (b. 1921), and George Segal (1924–2000). Master stone-carver John Benson (b. 1939) designed and cut the extensive inscriptional program.

Room One celebrates Roosevelt's first term and the optimism expressed in the most famous sentence of his presidency: "The only thing we have to fear is fear itself." Visitors encounter a presidential seal by Tom Hardy, unique among the memorial's sculptures in that it is welded, not cast, bronze. Robert Graham's *First Inaugural,* a 3 x 9-foot bas-relief inspired by a newsreel of that event, captures the new commander in chief's popular appeal.

Room Two is subdivided into two chambers. The first is dedicated to the economic and psychological privations of the Depression, ushered in with the 1929 crash of the stock market and continuing through the next decade, during which one in three people was unemployed. The second chamber is dedicated to FDR's New Deal programs, unveiled in the first hundred days after he entered the White House in 1933, which marshaled federal resources to alleviate crushing unemployment. The room's most powerful quotation sounds radical in the context of today's rapacious fortune building: "I see one-third of a nation ill-housed, ill-clad, and ill-nourished. The test of our progress is not whether we add more to the abundance of those who have much; it is whether we provide enough for those who have little." FDR made the government an agent of social change, a role that was much criticized at the time but one that endures today in public housing, welfare, educational loans, large public works, and protections for the jobs and safety of workers.

Social Programs, a series of bas-reliefs in Room Two by Robert Graham, consists of five 6 x 6-foot (1.82 x 1.82 m) panels and five 6-foot (1.82 m) columns that contain symbolic icons of fifty-four New Deal programs and "alphabet" agencies, with acronyms such as the CCC, REA, FSA, and WPA, the names of which are also provided in Braille. The bas-reliefs, illustrated in *Monuments*'s opening pages, depict hands, faces, and other body parts that speak of the diversity of individuals employed by the New Deal. The surfaces of the corresponding columns are impressed with the same images in reverse,

The inclusion of Fala, FDR's beloved Scotch Terrier, in Neil Estern's portrait emphasizes the predident's approachability.

negative form, and shed light on the casting process. Graham upends the traditional columnar form by endowing the columns with figurative imagery that is more closely associated with the totemic portraits found in Native American ceremonial poles.

Presiding over Room Three is a monumental portrait of FDR sculpted by Neil Estern. The 8.75-foot (2.6 m) portrait shows FDR swathed in a flowing cape that covers one leg. His face is haggard, but his chin is characteristically raised; his hands are aristocratically folded over the arm of the chair carved with the Roosevelt family crest, and his eyes look to a far horizon. Close observation yields subtle clues to his paralysis: His trousers flop slightly over the one visible leg,

Estern studied dozens of images of FDR before deciding to work from a photograph taken of him in January 1945 at the Yalta conference. In order not to draw attention to FDR's handicap at the memorial, the Roosevelt Memorial Commission decided to exhibit a reproduction of FDR's wheelchair at the visitor center.

THEY (WHO) SEEK TO ESTABLISH SYSTEMS OF GOVERNMENT BASED ON THE REGIMENTATION OF ALL HUMAN BEINGS BY A HANDFUL OF INDIVIDUAL RULERS... CALL THIS A NEW ORDER. IT IS NOT NEW AND IT IS NOT ORDER.

1962

James Meredith (b. June 25, 1933), American civil rights activist, begins classes at University of Mississippi escorted by U.S. marshals and three thousand soldiers

1962

The London Sunday Times issues its first color supplement

Closely observed details in Estern's FDR portrait, such as his signet ring, the frog cape clasp, and the ornately carved chair back, punctuate the statue's broad, flowing lines.

and a caster on the rear chair leg reveals that he is seated on a wheelchair, although this detail is virtually hidden at the back of the stone alcove in which the figure sits.

Missing is any reference to FDR's ever-present cigarette holder, which was quietly omitted from this and the rest of the presidential portraits. Similarly, because of potential protests by animal rights lobbyists, Eleanor's portrayal shows her in a simple cloth suit, without her trademark fox boa.

Less successful is Estern's stiff portrait of Eleanor Roosevelt (1884–1962) in Room Four that honors her work as a United Nations delegate and chair of the Commission on Human Rights. Though it is the first time a First Lady has been honored in a presidential memorial, it does not convey Eleanor's far-reaching contributions to her husband's administration. She traveled the world, FDR's de facto eyes and ears, going to those places he could not go in order to tell him how things actually were. Estern's sculpture conveys some of her dignity but little of her drive, idealism, fearless commitment to social justice, or personal warmth. Far better is the 1996 bronze portrait of Eleanor by Penelope Jencks at Seventy-second Street and Riverside Drive in Manhattan that depicts her leaning comfortably against a rock and possessing the sweeping authority that was hers in life.

The last room commemorates FDR's death in 1945 with a 30-foot-long (9.14 m) bas-relief entitled *Funeral Cortege* by Leonard Baskin that depicts the horse-drawn catafalque and mourners who processed up Pennsylvania Avenue to the Capitol. The work is positioned over a still reflecting pool. A timeline of fourteen milestone events in FDR's life that are incised on the risers of the amphitheater steps provides additional eulogistic summary.

Appropriately for a work honoring a powerful orator, FDR's words appear throughout the memorial. John Benson designed and cut the

1963

Civil rights demonstrations in Birmingham, AL, culminate in the arrest of Martin Luther King, Jr., and in President Kennedy's calling out 3,000 troops

1963

John F. Kennedy, U.S. president, assassinated (Nov. 22; b. May 29, 1917)

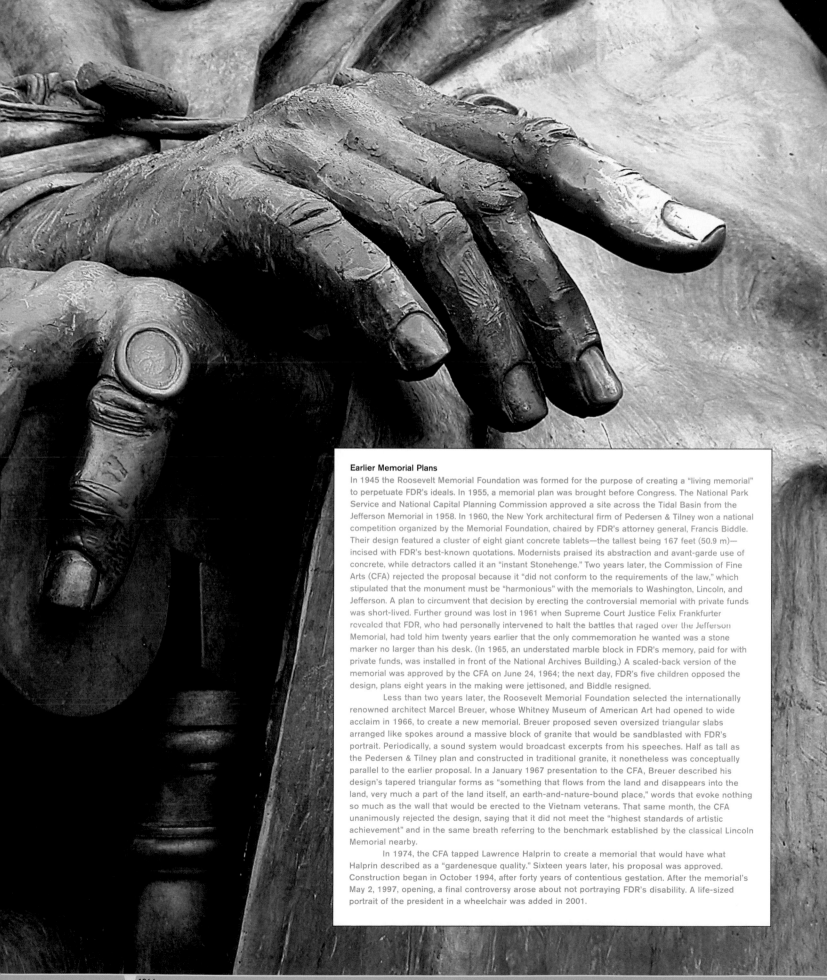

Earlier Memorial Plans

In 1945 the Roosevelt Memorial Foundation was formed for the purpose of creating a "living memorial" to perpetuate FDR's ideals. In 1955, a memorial plan was brought before Congress. The National Park Service and National Capital Planning Commission approved a site across the Tidal Basin from the Jefferson Memorial in 1958. In 1960, the New York architectural firm of Pedersen & Tilney won a national competition organized by the Memorial Foundation, chaired by FDR's attorney general, Francis Biddle. Their design featured a cluster of eight giant concrete tablets—the tallest being 167 feet (50.9 m)— incised with FDR's best-known quotations. Modernists praised its abstraction and avant-garde use of concrete, while detractors called it an "instant Stonehenge." Two years later, the Commission of Fine Arts (CFA) rejected the proposal because it "did not conform to the requirements of the law," which stipulated that the monument must be "harmonious" with the memorials to Washington, Lincoln, and Jefferson. A plan to circumvent that decision by erecting the controversial memorial with private funds was short-lived. Further ground was lost in 1961 when Supreme Court Justice Felix Frankfurter revealed that FDR, who had personally intervened to halt the battles that raged over the Jefferson Memorial, had told him twenty years earlier that the only commemoration he wanted was a stone marker no larger than his desk. (In 1965, an understated marble block in FDR's memory, paid for with private funds, was installed in front of the National Archives Building.) A scaled-back version of the memorial was approved by the CFA on June 24, 1964; the next day, FDR's five children opposed the design, plans eight years in the making were jettisoned, and Biddle resigned.

Less than two years later, the Roosevelt Memorial Foundation selected the internationally renowned architect Marcel Breuer, whose Whitney Museum of American Art had opened to wide acclaim in 1966, to create a new memorial. Breuer proposed seven oversized triangular slabs arranged like spokes around a massive block of granite that would be sandblasted with FDR's portrait. Periodically, a sound system would broadcast excerpts from his speeches. Half as tall as the Pedersen & Tilney plan and constructed in traditional granite, it nonetheless was conceptually parallel to the earlier proposal. In a January 1967 presentation to the CFA, Breuer described his design's tapered triangular forms as "something that flows from the land and disappears into the land, very much a part of the land itself, an earth-and-nature-bound place," words that evoke nothing so much as the wall that would be erected to the Vietnam veterans. That same month, the CFA unanimously rejected the design, saying that it did not meet the "highest standards of artistic achievement" and in the same breath referring to the benchmark established by the classical Lincoln Memorial nearby.

In 1974, the CFA tapped Lawrence Halprin to create a memorial that would have what Halprin described as a "gardenesque quality." Sixteen years later, his proposal was approved. Construction began in October 1994, after forty years of contentious gestation. After the memorial's May 2, 1997, opening, a final controversy arose about not portraying FDR's disability. A life-sized portrait of the president in a wheelchair was added in 2001.

1964

World's Fair in New York City (Apr. 22–Oct. 18 and Apr. 21–Oct. 17, 1965); held in conjunction with the city's 300th anniversary of British forces under the command of the Duke of York gaining control of the Dutch city of New Amsterdam in 1664

It has been said that the memorial suggests one grand public works project. The splashing fountains also serve a practical purpose: Their ambient sound masks some of the air traffic noise from nearby Reagan National Airport.

Although the memorial appears to be solid stone, it is actually constructed of a stone veneer attached to an 800-foot-long concrete wall faced with granite. The stand-alone walls and stepping stones in the fountain are solid granite, however, with the heaviest stone weighing 39 tons and the largest measuring 21 feet long. The structure's massive weight is supported by nine hundred steel pilings sunk into the swampy location.

twenty-one wall inscriptions. They are supplemented by a staircase timeline, four floor inscriptions, and a technically superb title piece at the site's southern end. Fragments of an address Roosevelt made in 1936 are incised on the granite blocks scattered in Room Three: "I have seen war. I have seen war on land and sea. I have seen blood running from the wounded, I have seen the dead in the mud. I have seen cities destroyed. I have seen children starving. I have seen the agony of mothers and wives. I hate war."

Roosevelt was virtually never photographed in his wheelchair. In maintaining what Hugh Gallagher termed his "splendid deception," he was aided by the press, who honored his wish to keep his disability private, despite his spending the last twenty-four years of his life and his entire presidency

1965

Martin Luther King, Jr., leads civil rights march from Selma to Montgomery, AL; Ku Klux Klan shootings in Selma

1965

North Vietnamese MIG aircraft shoot down U.S. jets; students demonstrate in Washington against U.S. bombing of North Vietnam

in heavy leg braces, crutches, and a wheelchair. According to his family, this position was "probably a result of his personal and political judgment of the time that a clear perception of a fully confident and strong leader was needed in order to inspire a country and a world struggling to overcome the debilitation of the Depression and to respond to the challenges of fascism, totalitarianism, and World War II." In 1945, upon his return from Yalta and six weeks before his death, Roosevelt made his first and only comment on his paralysis when he apologized for speaking from a seat: "I know that you will realize that it makes it a lot easier for me in not having to carry about ten pounds of steel around on the bottom of my legs."

Many believe that FDR could not have become who he became without the adversity of polio. Eleanor said the disease "softened his heart. It gave him compassion for others. It toughened his resolve. It added to his courage. It made him a stronger human being." FDR supported the physically disabled more than any other previous president, founding the March of Dimes, the Polio Foundation, and the Warm Springs Foundation. He championed a young doctor, Jonas Salk, who would develop the vaccine that vanquished polio, the discovery of which was announced on April 12, 1955, the tenth anniversary of FDR's death.

Originally, the memorial did not depict Roosevelt's disability. The National Organization on Disability (NOD), which seeks to change the perception of disability and increase the participation of America's fifty-four million disabled, wanted to change that. Demonstrators in wheelchairs protested the oversight at the memorial's 1997 dedication. NOD enlisted the support of FDR's descendants and biographers, the media, and the American public—73 percent of whom, according to a 1995 Harris Poll, endorsed the depiction of the president's disability. Ultimately, it took an act of Congress to mandate the statue's inclusion. NOD commissioned sculptor Robert Graham to create the life-sized bronze statue that forms the centerpiece of a "Prologue Room," from which visitors proceed to the remainder of the site.

FDR's memorial was perfected by the public's demand that it mark his personal trial. The spare, wheelchair-bound figure in the Prologue Room is transformed in the fullness of the Third Room into a triumphant, larger-than-life portrait of a world leader, his disability still subtly visible but the smallest measure of the man.

A plaque affixed to the Prologue Room sculpture shows FDR's drawing for his wheelchair, a homemade contraption consisting of a wooden kitchen chair with bicycle tires.

Of the thousands of photographs of Roosevelt, this is one of only two known to show him in a wheelchair. FDR, Fala, and Ruthie Bie, the caretaker's daughter, were photographed at Top Cottage, his retreat in Hyde Park, New York. Halprin designed the memorial in 1974 to be fully accessible, long before the Americans with Disabilities Act (1990) required such design.

The *New York Times*
Capsule

LOCATION	DEDICATION	DESIGNER	COMMEMORATION
New York City	*2001*	*Santiago Calatrava;* The New York Times Magazine	*Life at the end of the* *twentieth century*

The very act of recording everyday life confers humility: It tells us that we are not first, last, or best, and that there will be others after us. It is to those strangers of the future that we offer the quotidian details of our days and civilization—stories that occasionally take the form of a time capsule—and so acknowledge those seemingly inconsequential actions that have catapulted us down one road and not another, those small things that have, in other words, created our history.

The laws of science do not distinguish between the past and the future.
—Stephen W. Hawking, *A Brief History of Time*, 1988

Communicating that history to the future is an irresistible gesture. A time capsule—most often hidden, buried in the ground, or permanently cemented inside a building's cornerstone—is an anti-monument. Nonetheless, its brief appearance and Persephonean disappearance capture the imagination. Like an attic or a basement, a time capsule conjures the expectation that the things stored inside will someday have use and value. There is a sense that something of import—a message to the future, a benchmark, a cultural explanation—has been established by the container and its contents that will be recognized as such by those who will recover it.

1966
New York *Herald Tribune* ceases publication

1966
A landslide in the mining village of Aberfan, Wales, takes the souls of 116 children and 28 adults who are honored in the country's best-known memorial (Oct. 21)

Over time, after those who buried the capsule are buried themselves, its abstraction increases. The awareness of the existence of a time capsule permits the living to live, if not more fully in the present, into a future time that they themselves will not see. Or perhaps the capsule represents the hope that with a little perspective some larger meaning can be gleaned from the thousands of forgettable details that make up the bulk of our lives.

unearthed—the label "time capsule" was only recently coined, in 1939, as an alternative to "time bomb," which is how Westinghouse described the torpedo-like container it planted in the grounds of the World's Fair in Flushing, Queens.

Two problems have plagued time capsules. Most contain dull ephemera that say little about the people who lived then, other than that they took trains, printed newspapers, and used stamps and

Unlike a traditional monument, whose significance relies directly on the relevance of the values it commemorates, a time capsule from the moment of its burial presumes irrelevance: Its sole message is that a message exists. It contains information that marks a point in time, so that when it is opened our descendants will be able to compare what once was to the present. Much like a child who collects "treasures" in a tin and buries them in the backyard, a time capsule promises that something once of importance has been saved from time, but the very removal renders it meaningless. Some essential part of the past, untethered from its historical period, remains untouched. The same sense of irretrievability permeates monuments too.

A monument typically has a shelf life of a time capsule—about one hundred years. That's enough time for the generation that witnessed the event to die, another generation that retains firsthand though youthful memories to die, a third generation to recall firsthand accounts, and a fourth to retain some vague sense, if any, of who or what is commemorated.

Although the idea of time capsules is not new—in the seventh century B.C., King Esarhaddon of Assyria preserved tales of his military victories on clay tablets that were buried and subsequently

coins. Second, a surprising number, given the ceremony that usually accompanies their interment, are lost. A well-publicized misplacement occurred in Oregon in 2003: Ten days before Theodore Roosevelt IV was due to arrive in Portland to open the copper box his presidential namesake had buried in the cornerstone of a granite monument to Lewis and Clark a century earlier, the capsule could not be found. After exploring the possibility of using gamma radiography, sonograms, and radar technology to examine the earth beneath the brick plaza on which the granite obelisk stands, the Oregon Historical Society, which organized the event, decided to call off the search. In 1793, George Washington buried a container in a corner of the U.S. Capitol in an elaborate time-capsule burial ritual replete with corn and sacred oils, for which his brother Freemasons were known; it met the same fate. The Century Safe, filled with commemorative items during the Philadelphia Centennial Exhibition by Civil War widow Mrs. Charles Diehm, was the first time capsule known to be opened according to plan, with the honors done by President Gerald Ford in 1976.

The New York Times decided to circumvent both problems with the creation of a capsule that would

Calatrava compared his design to the unfolding of a flower, made evident in this sequence of photographs that shows a maquette of the capsule unfolding like a piece of origami. The final steel model contains 50 cubic feet of space, weighs two tons, and was fabricated at A.R.T. Research Enterprises in Lancaster, Pennsylvania.

be placed aboveground and contain an inventory of items that would tell those who opened it something more revealing than our train schedules. Millennial hubris, perhaps, also dictated that the capsule would be opened not in one hundred years, but in one thousand years, which presumed that its caretaker, the American Museum of Natural History (AMNH), another New York City institution, would be around to protect the thing for ten centuries.

The beauty of the situation, of course, is that none of us, and none of our great-great-great-great-grandchildren, will be around to confirm that the object and its contents survived or had meaning. Leaving the entire matter in the hands of the distant future is one way to ensure that the whole process, on the one hand, is taken as a very serious matter of extreme importance, and, on the other, acknowledges that without witnesses, its lack of meaning borders on the hilarious.

By establishing these two conditions, the time capsule creators ensured that its importance will be evident to the living, for at least one hundred years, but beyond that will be anyone's guess.

Despite these risks, *The New York Times* invited forty-eight architects and designers from around the world to submit proposals for a container to hold key cultural artifacts for a millennium. From an inventive range of solutions, an elegantly simple design by Santiago Calatrava (b. 1951) was selected.

Architect, artist, and engineer, Calatrava established his reputation as a brilliant innovator with a series of remarkable bridges in his native Spain. He has been a presence on the New York architectural scene since 1991, when he won a competition to complete the Cathedral of St. John the Divine. The *Times* Capsule, his first realized work in the United States, appropriately took the shape of a

On April 26, 2001, the *New York Times* Capsule was installed outside Manhattan's American Museum of Natural History atop a black granite base. It is to remain on display until the year 3000.

budding flower; 2001 saw the opening of Calatrava's acclaimed expansion of the Milwaukee Art Museum, the first of many American commissions. Calatrava designs structures that are characterized by light and lightness, a deft handling of steel and glass, and a preference for soaring, transcendent spaces that evoke birds, vertebrae, and other natural forms.

The paper's time-capsule team wanted to include artifacts that fell outside the usual inventories. According to Jack Hitt, the journalist hired by the *Times* to report on the enterprise, the goal was to identify those "items or ideas, practices or habits, that won't survive the cultural winnowing of the next thousand years and yet would offer some idea of who we were and how we lived."

The items selected were mostly from Fountain, Colorado, according to the *Times* an archetypal suburban American town, as well as some from overseas. They included a Purple Heart medal from the Vietnam War, a unicorn Beanie Baby, barbed wire, an Atlético Paraná soccer jersey from Brazil, a vial of penicillin from France, and a pack of cigarettes from Zimbabwe. Editors from the *Times* put in archival copies of the six special millennium issues of *The New York Times Magazine;* the *New York Times* newspaper of January 1, 2000; a New York Yankees baseball; a child's tooth; a video rental card; a David Letterman top ten list; worldwide recordings of sounds made on January 1, 2000; a *Weight Watchers* magazine; and twenty-eight hair samples taken from Dolly, the cloned sheep, as well as from a former asbestos worker and United Nations representatives from around the world. Books that were interred included a Betty Crocker cookbook, a 1995 HarperCollins *Dictionary of American Slang, For Colored Girls Who Have Considered Suicide When the Rainbow Is Enuf* by Ntozake Shange, and Primo Levi's *Survival in Auschwitz.* Calatrava submitted his original capsule design proposal. Martin Luther King, Jr.'s "I Have a Dream" speech, Alcoholics Anonymous pamphlets, an Internal Revenue Service federal income tax Form 1040, Post-it notes, and a Garry Trudeau cartoon are representative of the many other items that were sent into the future. Because digital formats such as laser disks and computer chips are not permanent, documents were printed on good old-fashioned acid-free paper. According to Stephen Mihm, project manager for the *Times* Capsule, copyright laws precluded the addition of music or movies, with the exception of a recording of "YMCA" sung by the Village People.

These contents were placed in the 5-foot-high (1.52 m) stainless steel capsule designed by Calatrava. That container opens to reveal eight compartments containing about 50 cubic feet (1.41 cubic m) of storage space that were ultimately sealed with argon gas and suspended in protective vacuum insulation panels.

Located outside the AMNH, the capsule will stay on exhibit, presumably until it is opened in the year 3000. Steps were taken to ensure its safekeeping over the uncertain course of the next thousand years. The AMNH and *The New York Times* appointed Daniel J. Boorstin, historian, Pulitzer Prize–winning author, and Librarian of Congress emeritus as the first ceremonial capsule keeper; Boorstin will pass stewardship of the capsule to a successor. A sign embedded in the plaza reads, "This is the *Times* Capsule, designed by Santiago Calatrava, created by *The New York Times* and placed at the American Museum of Natural History in 2001. The contents are intended to offer insight into daily life today. We ask that it remain sealed until January 1, 3000." The design itself is intended to increase its chances of survival: The idea that "beauty might be its own best defense" surfaced early in the *Times*'s planning sessions and inspired the aesthetic criteria and aboveground location.

Every monument is written in the language of its own time. This one was woven with the silken grace of a structural poet and grounded in the bravura and wit of the greatest of cities at the close of the second millennium. Less than five months after the *Times* Capsule was dedicated on April 26, 2001, its host city took a blow that revealed its vulnerability as well as the capsule's. As that event and the thousand years that preceded it prove, what survives are those spirited and spiritual objects that confirm, quite simply, that it's good to be alive.

Oklahoma City
National Memorial

LOCATION	DEDICATION	DESIGNER	COMMEMORATION
Oklahoma City, Oklahoma	*2000*	*Butzer Design Partnership*	*1995 Oklahoma City federal building bombing*

1968

U.S. Navy intelligence ship *Pueblo* captured by North Korea; crew released in December

The gates conjure the heroic forms at Karnak and other Egyptian funerary complexes. Hans Butzer's father, an Egyptologist, believes his son's design may have been influenced by childhood memories of these places. Made of a lightly oxidized bronze, the gates capture fingerprints and make visible the passage of time.

Within days after a two-ton truck bomb ripped apart the Alfred P. Murrah Federal Building on April 19, 1995, taking 168 lives, officials and ordinary citizens in the Sooner capital were inundated with suggestions for a memorial. It was quickly apparent that obtaining consensus on the memorial design would be a Sisyphean task. Oklahomans struggled to create a blueprint that would transform raw grief into an acknowledgment of individual and national loss. The way in which they negotiated the myriad obstacles of the memorial process and integrated them into the final design has made Oklahoma City a model for other communities.

Early deliberations were swathed in emotion and set in a complex, often unspoken, hierarchy of loss: the overwhelming grief and anger of the victims' relatives, the guilt of the survivors who felt they didn't "deserve" a voice, the hurt of those whose loss of longtime colleagues or friends somehow didn't count as much as those who lost a relative, and the suspicion of the "suits and ties" appointed to lead them.

"A memorial process of integrity in Oklahoma City had to struggle with the sensibilities and conditions of so many different people with intimate connections to the bombing. It had to find a way to forthrightly acknowledge these clashing sensibilities and convictions and incorporate them in a larger vision of the purposes of memorialization," historian Edward T. Linenthal wrote in his comprehensive study of events leading to the current memorial. "It wasn't what was built, it was how we got there," according to memorial executive director Kari F. Watkins.

1968
President Lyndon Johnson announces that he will not seek another term

We wanted to provide textures that are attractive to the individual—the stones, the bronze of the gates, the bronze of the chairs, the reflecting pool, the chalk in the Children's Area— these are avenues that allow people to transport themselves more deeply into the history of the site.

—Hans Butzer, convesation with the author, 2003

The terrain's natural slope, and the need for an ADA-compliant entrance, inspired the site's two different approaches. Through the eastern gate, one descends down into the site. Through the opposite gate, one ascends upward on ramps. The two approaches provide different threshold experiences and underscore the theme, amplified throughout the site, of the passage between life and death.

Ultimately, the 350-member memorial task force headed by local attorney Robert M. Johnson decided to focus not on what the memorial would look like, but on developing in 1996 a mission statement from which the design would flow:

> *We come here to remember*
> *those who were killed,*
> *Those who survived*
> *and those changed forever.*
> *May all who leave here*
> *know the impact of violence.*
> *May this memorial offer comfort,*
> *strength, peace, hope and serenity.*

Architects Torrey and Hans Butzer, in collaboration with Sven Berg, won the international design competition in 1997 with a plan for an outdoor urban room that would evoke the lives of the victims, survivors, and rescuers and call forth new stories from those who would eventually stand in witness. The memorial narrative unfolds in a series of distinct areas for public gathering and private contemplation, with individual sculptural forms functioning as charac-

ters in the larger story. Navigating the 3.3-acre site conveys a sense of journey that is more critical than any one element. Photographs do not convey the serenity that pervades the memorial during the day, the dramatic shift in its persona that occurs at night, nor its masterful integration with the colors and forms of the city beyond its borders.

The idea of the "gap," the passage between life and death, underpins the design. Gaps appear everywhere: in the slots of the gates and the backs of the chairs; between the pool and the walkways, the chairs, and the lawn; and between the panels that form the gate façades. Driving past the site's perimeter yields a filmic experience: As the gaps reveal and obscure the memorial, its ever-shifting persona is reinforced.

To the east and west, twin monumental gates frame the destruction. The East Gate is inscribed 9:01 A.M., the moment before the blast, and the West Gate, 9:03 A.M., the moment after. Physical and psychological portals, the gates mediate between the outer streets and the memorial's interior. Constructed of cast-in-place reinforced concrete and clad in bronze, each gate is made of two freestanding panels, the outer walls of which are inscribed with the Mission Statement.

Stretching between the gates, slightly below street level, is a shallow, 318-foot-long (97 m) reflective pool lined with black granite shot with feldspar crystals. In a gesture typical of many visitors, President Bill Clinton dipped his hand into the pool at the dedication ceremony, held on the fifth anniversary of the explosion, and compared the site to Valley Forge, Gettysburg, and Selma, landscapes that had been "scarred by freedom's sacrifice."

The memorial's focal point is the Field of Empty Chairs, a grouping of 168 chairs, one for each victim, whose remains are interred elsewhere. The chairs' moving gestalt arises paradoxically from the democratic utility of the chair—so familiar and unexpectedly resonant in that ubiquity. It came to Torrey Butzer, as she tried to find a way to put the tremendous sense of absence to form, that there was an "American tradition of leaving a chair empty at the dining room table to honor a family member who has passed away. That gesture says so much about the loss of a person and the place he or she still has in the minds of the living."

The chairs are arranged in nine rows, referring to the nine floors of the Murrah Building. Five chairs representing those who died outside the building stand slightly apart from the main grouping. Toward the middle, at the epicenter of the bomb's impact, the chairs are clustered more tightly. They are in two sizes, small and large, with the miniature versions representing the nineteen children, age five and under, who were lost. Each glass base is etched with a victim's name.

At night, when illuminated from below, the bases of the chairs are reflected in the pool like a string of gently bobbing Japanese lanterns.

The American-born Butzers, who worked in Berlin for most of their professional careers before winning the competition and relocating to Oklahoma City, sought to uphold the European tradition of craftsmanship and the belief that how something is built is a key part of the memorializing process. The glass, bronze, and granite chairs were fabricated individually to ensure that no two were alike, and each has unique anomalies. The glass bases were cast in forms lined

Memorial chairs occupy the footprint of the destroyed building. Within each of the nine rows, the chairs are grouped by the agencies for whom the victims worked. Friends are with friends.

Bud Welch, the father of victim Julie Welch, is credited with naming the Survivor Tree when he said, "This is the only living thing left. It's a real survivor."

The museum's Gallery of Honor features 168 individual displays of the deceased containing objects selected by their families. The mementos are personal, and most hold meanings that are not decipherable by a stranger.

with leather book bindings to achieve the pebbled surface and amplify the idea that each one has a story to tell. The biggest challenge was finding a glass that would accommodate the area's diurnal temperature swings. After two years of testing, the original Pyrex glass was scrapped in favor of soda-lime glass.

Within months, the rye grass that had been planted around the chairs, considered from the start a temporary solution, turned to mud. Although it was replaced by a hardier Cavalier-Zoysia grass, turf specialists agreed that no lawn could withstand the stress induced by the huge number of visitors. To maintain its pristine appearance, the Memorial Trust decided to enclose the field with a low, bordering fence. Different entry points along that border are opened daily to vary foot traffic patterns on the grass while allowing full access to the Field of Empty Chairs.

Tucked behind the chairs on the site's eastern side is the Survivor Chapel, where the names of survivors are inscribed on granite panels salvaged from the rubble of the Murrah Building. They are hung on that building's two remaining walls, the crumbling, broken nature of which disturbs the order imposed by the remainder of the site. Along with the scarred shell of the *Journal Record* building, the panels enshrine the evidence of the violence that occurred.

The centerpiece of the northern half of the site is the Survivor Tree, a resilient American elm tree that, long ignored as it grew in the Murrah parking lot, became a national treasure after it survived the scorching blast. The original tree enjoys protection in perpetuity. That it will live forever has also been guaranteed: Arborists have obtained cuttings so that when this elm dies, a genetically identical clone will take its place. Raised on a natural promontory overlooking the chairs, the tree is surrounded by a circular stone platform and retaining wall carved with quotations honoring the rescue efforts.

A section of the chain-link fence that was erected initially around the site's perimeter to preserve the crime scene, and became covered with a spontaneous flood of stuffed animals, flowers, and poems, has also been incorporated into the

design. Just before the memorial's groundbreaking, there was a cry to keep the fence because, for many, it *was* the memorial. The Butzers came up with a compromise, which was to include half of the fence, on the 9:03 side (or healing side as it is commonly called). Of the fence's compelling attraction, landscape architect Katherine A. Melcher said, "It has no unity or plan or order. It is not an elegant single red rose on a perfect chair. It is cheap and tacky. It is real."

Current thinking contends that catharsis, though crucial, is only one part of a memorial solution. Consequently, the tripartite Oklahoma memorial has a "never again" educational mandate expressed in its Memorial Institute for the Prevention of Terrorism, which sponsors programs that raise awareness of terrorism, and the National Memorial Museum which tells the story of April 19, 1995, in ten "chapters" that are housed in the former *Journal Record* building.

Museum visitors encounter video presentations, oversized photographs, and artifacts that commemorate the bombing, rescue effort, and memorial design. It is not for the faint-hearted. Early on, visitors enter a reconstructed hearing room once located in the building adjacent to the Murrah Building and listen to the recorded drone of a female voice speaking at an Oklahoma Water Resources Board deposition. Two minutes into it,

a recording of the blast explodes the silence and is followed by the sounds of the chaos after 9:02 A.M. The room goes dark, and then the 168 faces of the victims are briefly illuminated. From there, visitors enter an emotionally wrought sequence of rooms that recreate the bombing's aftermath with a you-are-there realism. One area, a men's restroom that has been left exactly as it was after the blast, contains the collapsed ceiling, blown-in windows, and exposed pipes. Kiosks hold unclaimed possessions such as shoes and briefcases. From computer terminals, visitors can access stories told by survivors, rescuers, and volunteers. Prominently displayed in the area narrating the sixteen days of recovery and rescue are two flags, the larger of which was flying on the GSA plaza at the time of the explosion, and a smaller one, the first flag taken from the destroyed building, that was flown from a crane removing site debris. Relief is provided by sweeping window views of the outdoor memorial and, in a room called Hope, a calming waterfall that flows over a dark stone wall.

One year after the memorial's unveiling, Manhattan was devastated by an even deadlier act of terrorism. New York faces many of the same issues that Oklahoma City did: What form of commemoration most fully honors the spectrum of loss, and how can one structure address a phalanx of constituencies with conflicting priorities, mourning traditions, and aesthetic sensibilities? Those charged with creating the memorial at Ground Zero visited Oklahoma City in October 2002 and observed what might be the most enduring legacy of its commemorative complex: A meaningful and coherent memorial can arise from the voices of many.

Left Non-organic materials left on the fence are collected monthly and used in the museum's innovative educational outreach program. Sent to schools nationally, the artifacts provide a hands-on lesson in nonviolent resolution of conflict in a way that texts alone could not. The collection is replenished with new items left on the fence.

Right The thousands of teddy bears and other stuffed animals that are left at the fence become part of the museum's Hope Bear program. Once cleaned up and labeled with this tag, Hope Bears are sent out to American communities that have been traumatized by violence.

Robert F. Kennedy (b. Nov. 25, 1925), American senator, assassinated during presidential campaign, in Los Angeles (June 4); Sirhan Sirhan (b. Mar. 19, 1944) arrested and later convicted

U.S. Congress passes a law to observe Memorial Day on the last Monday in May; in 1971 it is declared a national holiday

Empty Sky

I woke up this morning
I could barely breathe
Just an empty impression
In the bed where you used to be

I want a kiss from your lips
I want an eye for an eye
I woke up this morning to the empty sky

Empty sky, empty sky
I woke up this morning to an empty sky
Empty sky, empty sky
I woke up this morning to an empty sky

Blood on the streets
Yeah blood flowin' down
I hear the blood of my blood
Cryin' from the ground

Empty sky, empty sky
I woke up this morning to an empty sky
Empty sky, empty sky
I woke up this morning to an empty sky

On the plains of Jordan
I cut my bow from the wood
Of this tree of evil
Of this tree of good
I want a kiss from your lips
I want an eye for an eye
I woke up this morning to an empty sky

Empty sky, empty sky
I woke up this morning to an empty sky
Empty sky, empty sky
I woke up this morning to an empty sky
Empty sky, empty sky
I woke up this morning to an empty sky

—Bruce Springsteen, from *The Rising,* 2002

1968
Chicago Democratic Convention marked by riots and police brutality

The Temporary Memorials of

9/11

On the final day, their 110 stories stood against a cloudless blue sky with the lapidary clarity that airline pilots call "severe clear." Once the tallest buildings in the world, the World Trade Towers were works of outsized ego and imagination. Body surrogates writ large, they were monuments to ourselves, to our ingenuity and economic might. And then these giants, and our fragile illusions, were gone.

Let's roll!

—Todd Beamer, Flight 93, September 11, 2001

Temporary shrines proliferated throughout the city, especially at firehouses. Internationally, flowers and mementos were left at almost any landmark with an American connection.

The Tribute in Light's ethereality, juxtaposed with the massive hardware needed for its creation, parallels Manhattan's fragility yet strength of purpose after 9/11. The project was conceived by artists Julian LaVerdiere and Paul Myoda, architects John Bennett and Gustavo Bonevardi, and lighting designer Paul Marantz; produced by the Municipal Art Society and Creative Time, in collaboration with the Battery Park City Authority; and photographed by Charlie Samuels.

1968

Richard M. Nixon elected U.S. president promising to end Vietnam War

Commemoration of September 11, 2001, began at once with candlelight vigils, posters of the missing, spontaneous shrines, and musical tributes. Less tangible was the event's immediate impact on vocabulary, newspaper design, and Internet use. Other temporary memorials—posters, Ground Zero displays, and a nocturnal light sculpture—all shaped attempts to come to terms with what happened and how it should be remembered.

The initial emphasis was on measurements, first of time—8:46, 9:03, 9:38, 9:59, 10:06, 10:28—then of numbers: flights 11, 175, 77, and 93; 2 towers; 92 countries; 19 hijackers—as though exactitude could ease the day's final accounting, which was instinctively known to be, as Mayor Rudolph Giuliani put it, "more than any of us can bear." Six years later, the total casualties in the war in Iraq far exceed the estimated 2,976 people who died on September 11, 2001, as a result of the terrorist attacks on the World Trade Center in New York City, the Pentagon, and United Airlines Flight 93 that crashed in Shanksville, Pennsylvania, and no major 9/11 memorial has been built.

The current lack of consensus regarding the memorial at Ground Zero raises the question whether a work of artistic genius with the staying power to inspire today and in the future can be selected by stakeholders with widely varying agendas and degrees of design expertise. The answer might be found by looking back to works such as *Moby-Dick* or Beethoven's Ninth Symphony, prescient works of transformative power that were unrecognized as such at the time of their creation.

The question of scale also influences what is preserved. Just as the Trade Towers rendered insignificant the physical presence of a person on the plaza, their gargantuan shards of steel garnered more respect as artifacts by virtue of sheer size than a hastily copied flyer of a missing individual. Similarly, the image of the initial impact, more compelling than anything scripted in Hollywood, wrests greater attention than stories of individual loss and perception. But which, ultimately, is more meaningful? That which speaks to the communal memory of the day, or the infinitesimal number of personal memories that form life's larger mosaic?

1969

Hundreds of thousands protest against Vietnam War in several U.S. cities

How do we recognize a face? First, there's the eye's natural inability to see everything in focus. . . . The eye

An accounting of the temporary memorials of 9/11 before memory blurs, as it always does, is itself a memorial of sorts. Although these expressions do not have equal weight, taken together they provide the foundation of what will eventually be built. Even permanent memorials are not a last step, but rather one more stage in the commemorative process.

September 11 was a television event. But even the smooth polish of the press vanished in a haphazard collage of images and eyewitness accounts, strung together like beads on a larger string that was punctuated, over and over again, with the glittering image of the exploding towers. The global audience, glued to television screens, could not stop watching the orange fireball that blossomed with sensuous inevitability before the twin collapses, felt in the gut, slid down, down, down, dropping on themselves in ten seconds before rising again as a mushroom cloud of ash. A child, watching the endlessly televised detonations, asked "When will they stop blowing up all the buildings?" as though every structure on earth were being destroyed. The experience was comparable to watching the loop of Jackie Kennedy scrambling over the back of the limo in Dallas, footage still so raw as to seem newly shot, and yet as familiar as an often-told family story with its codified details and sequencing.

Stories, hundreds of thousands of them, were told, recounted, repeated, in small knots on the street, over the phone, via e-mail, in traditional letters that flowed out from New York, Virginia, and Pennsylvania and circled back. Business memos, reports, analyses, and other urgent messages from the towers were briefly airborne, then descended to carpet the streets below. Elaborate explanations of the apocalypse were available to passersby, as though posting these thoughts—one writer's version of the story that no one could explain—would provide insight. Ornately printed, carefully typeset, boldly spray-painted, or fingered on ashen surfaces were pleas for pacifism,

1969

Mylai Massacre, Vietnam; Lt. William L. Calley, Jr., stands trial for murder (found guilty, 1971)

vanders through a face, scanning for familiarity. It goes from point to point, making every face a narrative.

rivers of volcanic rage, and rebukes of God, Bush, and bin Laden. And these too were papered over, blacked out, edited, amended, until the city itself, bound with layers upon layers of stories, became a book of the dead.

Tens of thousands of missing persons notices were posted in New York beginning on the afternoon of the attack. The genial image of Mark Rasweiler, according to Marshall Sella in an October 2001 *New York Times* reportorial gem, was the first poster made in response to the initial belief, soon dispelled, that thousands of victims were unidentified in hospital beds or walking around in an amnesiac state. With mad hope, survivors scanned, copied, and pasted the faces and particulars of loved ones on bus shelters, telephone booths, subway walls, store windows, and every other conceivable surface.

The missing posters were remarkably consistent in design—8½ x 11 inches in size, centered on a family snapshot, with minimal identification and contact information—an invention of mourning and remembrance at its most compelling. It was easy to identify with those faces with their dazzling smiles and goofy grins, in tuxedos, shorts, and suits, poised over grills, at weddings, on vacation—because glued in our photo albums are variations of those same pictures. A second wave of posters, an acknowledgment of the diminishing chance of life, gave additional data about birthmarks, scars, earrings, shoes, and tattoos to aid forensic identification—intimate details that further increased their familiarity. The images evolved a third time, now marked "remember me," "pray for," or other words of release, into posthumous Everyman memorials that were both germ and zenith of the vast photographic collage that would emerge from the event.

The catastrophe launched the Internet's most expressive hour. It allowed people to do what they most needed: to talk together. After a brief shock-induced lull, in-boxes were inundated with messages that bore tentative subject lines—

Every face is a story. —Vik Muniz, interview with Danilo Eccher, August 2003

Margaret Morton shot *Wall of the Missing* (2001) at the massive wall of missing persons posters mounted at St. Vincent's Hospital in Greenwich Village. Morton used a medium format camera, overlapping each frame, and then digitally stitched together a composite image that is nearly 15 feet long; a detail is reproduced here. The posters exemplify what Roland Barthes described in *Camera Lucida* as the retrospective irony of looking at photographs—knowing what the subjects depicted in the image will never know.

September 17, the first such postponement since World War I, and resumed in New York with a Mets-Braves matchup at Shea Stadium on September 21.

That same evening, Bruce Springsteen opened *America: A Tribute to Heroes,* a star-spangled benefit concert, with "My City of Ruins," an unreleased song that he had written several years earlier about Asbury Park, New Jersey, that was eerily adaptable to 9/11. That song, and others he wrote specifically about that day, would later be released in *The Rising,* the first significant album of popular music to respond to the attacks. Springsteen's home, Monmouth County, lost 158 people in the towers, more than any other county in New Jersey. Inspired to help, the musician called survivors who had lost family members who had loved his music, and the intimacies shared in those conversations were critical to *The Rising*'s blend of deeply personal and collective feeling. In "Empty Sky," he describes the battle between certainty and doubt, anger and love, lamentation and revenge—*I want a kiss from your lips / I want an eye for an eye*—that captured the long emotional axis of that autumn.

U OK?—and expressions of concern. Millions gathered on the "virtual commons"—chat rooms, bulletin boards, and commemorative sites—to express grief, prayers, and political opinions. The online response mirrored the larger picture: According to an October 2001 Pew Charitable Trusts report, 94 percent of all Americans took at least one step to respond personally to the assaults, whether displaying an American flag, contributing money or donating blood, or attending a memorial service.

Patriotic songs and musical tributes washed over the nation. Radio waves were jammed with country musicians vowing to kick al-Qaeda butt. The emotional touchstones of earlier wars, standards such as Rosemary Clooney's "For All We Know," were revived and captured the pervasive uncertainty of those first weeks. "Take Me Out to the Ball Game," traditionally sung during baseball's seventh-inning stretch, was replaced by "God Bless America," its lyrics now less a litany of America's natural beauty than a mournful plea for solace. Baseball itself was suspended until

Just as a building can come to represent an entire culture, a single object can summon an event in its entirety. Yoshito Matsushige's 1945 photograph of a person's shadow burned into the stairs of the Sumitomo Bank conveyed with terrible specificity the horror of Hiroshima. Efforts to interpret September 11 through its artifacts focused on discerning which objects would best describe the event to future generations for whom 9/11 will be an historical abstraction.

For some, incorporating the disaster's artifacts into a memorial is as necessary as the addition of the two figurative sculptures to the Vietnam Veterans Memorial. The documentary value of the recognizable, the language that everyone

1969
Apollo 11 astronauts Neil Armstrong and Edwin "Buzz" Aldrin land on the Moon while a third, Michael Collins, remains in orbit

1969
About 400,000 people jam Max Yasgur's farm near Bethel, NY, for Woodstock, a three-day rock concert with performances by Joan Baez, Jimi Hendrix, Jefferson Airplane, and others (Aug. 15–17)

understands, is confirmation of what was survived, and of those who did not survive, that can be more emotionally resonant than an abstract memorial, no matter how transcendent its concept.

What was stunning, after the collapse of the largest human-made structures ever destroyed, was how relatively little was left. The relics of the first martyred skyscrapers number about seven hundred pieces that are stored at Hangar 17, a cavernous space at Kennedy International Airport. Within two weeks of the attack, the Port Authority of New York and New Jersey began to scour the rubble for objects that might be appropriately included in an interpretive museum planned for the site before the debris and steel were hauled away to Fresh Kills in Staten Island, a 2,200-acre landfill that was reopened to accommodate them.

Soon after the attacks, architect Michael Arad (b. 1969) created a temporary work on his East Village apartment rooftop to express the emptiness he felt which was transmuted in his 2004 design for the World Trade Center memorial in Manhattan.

They collected sections of the North Tower broadcast mast, crumpled red slices from Alexander Calder's *World Trade Center Stabile*, twenty mangled vehicles, and PATH station turnstiles. One of the most precious objects was the 58-ton, 36½-foot-long Column 1001-B from the South Tower, etched with inscriptions from firefighters and ironworkers and the last load to be removed, on May 30, 2002.

At 6:55 P.M. on the six-month anniversary of September 11, Valerie Webb, the twelve-year-old daughter of a Port Authority police officer who died in the attack, switched on *Tribute in Light*, the first official memorial at Ground Zero. A beacon of hope that on some nights was visible for miles, the display consisted of twin beams of azure light sent heavenward. The columns of light are actually produced by two banks of eighty-eight searchlight beams that merge when seen at a distance. When one looks straight up, the multiple light strands converge overhead in a single point somewhere amid the stars. Lit daily from dusk until 11 P.M. between March 11 and April 13, 2002, this temporary memorial was so well received that it has been reprised on subsequent anniversaries.

Tribute in Light's essential idea was that the most fitting response to the loss of so many souls and the skyline itself would be luminous absence, not presence, a void, not a solid. It conjures many things: ghost limbs that can be felt although they are no longer there, the glow from candles lit at spontaneous shrines, an ethereal etching of the towers themselves. An immediate parallel can be made to the eternal flames that burn at memorial sites around the globe. Was this fitting response made too early in the mourning process to be considered as a permanent memorial, or was its form too ethereal to comfort those left behind?

Located in the heart of the financial district, the World Trade Center occupied an extraordinarily valuable piece of real estate, but the fact that the disaster occurred in this densely populated area—forty thousand people worked at the towers—demands that its commemoration be made in situ. Some, especially those who lost loved ones whose remains were never recovered, felt the site should be preserved in its entirety as a parklike cemetery. Others, equally adamant, believed that aggressive rebuilding was the best monument.

At Listening to the City, a public forum held on July 20, 2002, the citizens of New York roundly rejected six unimaginative plans for the WTC site's rebuilding. Later that year, the LMDC

1970
Student protests against Vietnam War result in killing of four by National Guardsmen at Kent State University, OH (May 4)

(Lower Manhattan Development Corporation) held a second invitational competition among the world's most formidable architects and designers; their proposals were released in December 2002 in a glossy public spectacle of models, renderings, and video walk-throughs that was, for architecture, unprecedented. On February 27, 2003, Studio Daniel Libeskind's master plan, "Memory Foundations," was selected. It called for, among its many parts, a 1,776-foot (541.3 m) Freedom Tower and permanent memorial.

The World Trade Center Memorial Competition of April 2003 was based on guidelines developed by family members, residents, survivors, first responders, arts professionals, and community leaders, and additionally shaped by comments generated at public meetings in the five boroughs, Long Island, Connecticut, and New Jersey, and those submitted from around the world. The largest design competition in history, it generated 5,201 submissions from 63 nations and 49 states, most from nonprofessionals who, despite the low odds of winning, were moved to express their feelings. These were winnowed by a distinguished thirteen-member jury. The winning proposal, "Reflecting Absence," designed by architect Michael Arad, eventually joined by landscape architect Peter Walker and architect

The 25-foot (7.6 m) steel and bronze *Sphere* (1971), conceived by the artist Fritz Koenig as a symbol of world peace, was once the centerpiece of the WTC's Austin J. Tobin Plaza. One of the few art objects to survive, it was reinstalled in Battery Park on March 11, 2002, as an interim WTC memorial.

Max Bond, was announced on January 6, 2004. An online exhibition of all submissions opened the following month.

In the aftermath of the attacks on the Pentagon in Arlington, Virginia, the capital was awash with flags and other patriotic displays. Virginia produced a popular special-edition license plate that featured a graphic of the Pentagon, the Twin Towers, and a 9/11 logo. However, one problem for grieving Washington area residents was that the Pentagon is isolated from the general population for security reasons. With the exception of official ceremonies, there was no spontaneous forum for a public expression of solidarity at the site, which inhibited the communal processing of emotion such as occurred in Manhattan.

What made Flight 93 unique was the resolution made by its passengers after they learned from urgent midair phone calls that theirs was likely the fourth in a quartet of suicide attacks: They decided to fight back. With passenger Todd Beamer's cry "Let's roll!" they stormed the cockpit to thwart the hijackers, thought to have been heading the plane for the White House or the Capitol. Their self-sacrifice was the opening chord in a newly defiant national chorus and, according to President Bush, "the first counteroffensive in the war on terror." Because the crash occurred in an isolated spot—an abandoned coal field in Shanksville, a town of 245 people located sixty miles southeast of Pittsburgh—and the cleanup was relatively straightforward, local officials in Somerset County, with the National Park Service, quickly began work to establish a memorial to the thirty-three passengers and seven crew members who died.

Opposite page, main photo One hundred sixty feet tall, the steel façade of One World Trade Center that remained upright after the blast was disassembled into twenty-five pieces weighing forty tons apiece so it could be stored for future exhibitions. This photograph is a reminder of how utterly beyond human scale the towers were.

Inset photo, top Numerous filmic commemorations included 9/11, a documentary by French brothers Jules and Gédéon Naudet; *Rudy,* a television docudrama about the role of Mayor Rudolph Giuliani; and *Faith and Doubt at Ground Zero,* a documentary that examined 9/11's impact on religious belief. *Here Is New York,* an exhibition of five thousand photographic images, was hastily mounted in a SoHo storefront within two weeks of 9/11 and culminated in a book of the same name.

Inset photo, center *Remote Control* by Nebojsa Seric Shoba (b. 1968) was one of four posters commissioned by Time to Consider: The Arts Respond to 9.11 and sniped in Manhattan from February 11 to 18, 2002. Shoba's image of a remote control device capable of life-or-death decisions addressed the heightened sense that one's destiny was in the hands of others.

Inset photo, bottom Union Square, though not an officially designated public place of mourning, became one because it was the farthest south most people could go once the streets below Fourteenth Street were closed. By early November, the primary place of spontaneous memorial moved to St. Paul's Chapel, a block from the World Trade Center.

Below On the first anniversary, New Yorkers awoke to the music of bagpipers streaming downtown through the five boroughs. Family members gathered at Ground Zero, where 2,801 names—beginning with "Gordon M. Aamoth Jr." and ending with "Igor Zukelman"—were read from the city's official list of the dead. Showings of the colors, concerts, interfaith services, and candlelight vigils were held in every state. There were more unconventional commemorations as well. Surfers in California paddled out to sea and sprinkled dust from Ground Zero in the ocean; in Lincoln, Nebraska, twenty immigrants were naturalized; and the Rolling Requiem, a worldwide choral performance of Mozart's *Requiem* by some fifteen thousand singers, began at the International Date Line and soared from time zone to time zone for twenty-four hours.

Right A steel beam bonded in the crash with a molten piece of airplane was one of many crosses—massive crossbeams—that were found in a section of the WTC dubbed "God's House." Dozens of construction workers were tattooed with the cross's image to commemorate the brotherhood they experienced on the site. Working twenty-four hours a day in acrid smoke—filled with toxins, pulverized concrete, and human remains—amid fire and hazardous site conditions, firemen and police, engineers, and unionized construction laborers efficiently cleared the ruins in ten months.

At all three locations, surviving family members were involved in the memorialization process from the outset. Their desire to express their loved ones' individuality reflects the larger trend toward personalized commemoration; the era of collective memorialization in which one column could stand for thousands is over. Other than the incorporation of all the 9/11 victims' names in the New York memorial, the three key memorials have been planned as stand-alone commemorations that are unrelated visually, symbolically, or geographically. Lost was any opportunity to create a tripartite memorial that would have made clear the historical connection of the three sites and reflected in microcosm the nation's participation in the event and the recovery operations that followed.

The thousands of cell phone calls made on September 11 revealed what is most essential in the face of eternity. Every message, it seemed, had only one thing to say—*I love you*—and those three words filled the air like a litany, embraced over and over again, until the telephones went silent. For all the complexity and worldly accomplishments of those in the towers, at the Pentagon, and on the planes, it all came down to love. Pitted against the horrific dimensions of murderous religious zeal plotted for years was the pure connection of one to another. Despite the day's uncountable toll, love itself was not betrayed.

Although there have been larger incidents of sudden, wholesale death at the hands of nature and man, and destroying buildings for political reasons is nothing new, what set September 11 apart was its unfolding before millions in real time. Like a giant photograph developing with inexorable speed, the event delineated a pitiless snapshot of humanity. An instant revealed a portrait of ourselves that had never been shown to so many at once. Framed was our full measure as a species, one with an extreme capacity for both love and hate. The attacks polarized these emotions, and yet portrayed them as they mysteriously coexist within ourselves, together bound, eternally hand in hand.

1973
Watergate defendants plead guilty; John Dean implicates President Nixon

The memorial incorporates a standing stone inscribed with a cross of arks—a cross within a circle, possibly a pre-Christian or early Christian symbol. Such stones are used in Ireland to mark places of pilgrimage.

1973

Vietnam War cease-fire agreement signed (Jan. 23); U.S. losses from 1965 to 1973 are 45,948 combat deaths, 10,298 noncombat deaths, 303,640 wounded

1973

U.S.S.R. agrees to abide by the terms of the Universal Copyright Convention

Irish Hunger Memorial

TO HAUNT IRISH HOMES, BUT FOR MILLIONS OF OUR FELLOW HUMAN BEINGS, ITS DEADLY MARC

LOCATION	DEDICATION	DESIGNER	COMMEMORATION
New York City	2002	Brian Tolle	Irish famine and migration of 1845–1852

On the banks of the Hudson River in Lower Manhattan is an unconventional memorial to the famine that ravaged Ireland in the nineteenth century and the panicked exodus that followed. The Irish Hunger Memorial replicates the past in exquisite, life-sized detail, and includes a reconstructed fieldstone cottage from County Mayo in a half-acre landscape of fallow potato furrows and indigenous plants.

The memorial is a veritable laboratory for multiple contemporary commemorative concerns. As sculpted by Brian Tolle (b. 1964), it offers moments of poignancy and commemorative insight and has enjoyed popularity beyond measure with the Irish and non-Irish alike. Embedded in an urban landscape, the monument manipulates nature for civic ends. That topological power, together with the trust it places in the viewer to interpret its multiple meanings, assures its commemorative longevity.

"An Gorta Mór," the Great Hunger, was the last major famine in Europe and the defining event in modern Irish history, occurring in successive years from 1845 to 1852, peaking in "Black '47." The famine was caused by a blight—specifically, a fungus called *Phytophthora infestans* that kills potatoes, a staple of the Irish diet—that swept through Europe and hit Ireland hardest. It is estimated that more than a million starved to death,

1974

Gasoline shortage in U.S. throughout winter months; year-round daylight-saving time adopted to save fuel (later repealed)

and another 1.5 million fled aboard ships bound for North America; all told, the Hunger affected one in four living in Ireland at that time. Coffin ships, so called because of the legions who died on board, deposited their desperate cargo on the docks of Lower Manhattan, where the survivors—impoverished and unwelcome—rolled up their sleeves and began a new life by dint of sheer muscle. Subsequently, the tragedy also had enduring impact on America, where one in eight claim Irish ancestry.

From the first it was intended that the memorial would use the historic famine to focus on the fact that people continue to starve today. Whether and how the Hunger related to the actual food supply in Ireland has been bitterly contested over the past fifteen decades, especially by Irish Americans, whose collective memory of their homeland relies on the vagaries of stories passed down over the years. What's not debatable, as noted by famine historian Cormac Ó Gráda, is that we have lost our ability to be shocked by unfathomable numbers of dead, whether in nineteenth-century Ireland, twentieth-century Poland, or Africa today.

The memorial makes no immediate connection to the idea of hunger. Indeed the cheerfulness of its rose-covered foundations and emerald topography obliterates thoughts of death. Consider the emaciated Giacomettian figures, usually darkly patinaed bronzes, that typify the hunger memorials erected in Dublin (1967 and 1998), Cambridge, Massachusetts (1997), Boston (1998), Chicago (1999), Ardsley, New York (2001), and Philadelphia (2003), to name a handful of sesquicentennial commemorations. It is equally easy not to "see" sculptures of this awful hyperrealism, since the typical viewer from disassociates depictions of extreme horror. Tolle cleverly seduces us with primroses and tumbled stones into a closer look. That closer look, literally the dark limestone underbelly of the elegiac landscape, reveals line after line about hunger's long reach.

Its unlikely site in Battery Park City in Lower Manhattan, on some of the world's costliest real estate, was chosen because of its proximity to Castle Clinton, once called Castle Garden, where Jenny Lind made her American debut and tens of thousands of Irish landed after 1855, when it closed as an opera house and reopened as an immigrant depot. It is also near what was once Five Points. That mythic slum, now buried beneath Chinatown and Foley Square, was inhabited primarily by Irish Catholics, and described in 1842 by Charles Dickens as "reeking every where with dirt and filth. . . . Debauchery has made the very houses prematurely old."

A memorial will always look like the people who manage it. Unlike many memorials that are presented to seem more durable and stronger than the lives of the people who built them, this memorial has been made to be as integrated, vulnerable, and sensitive as the people who maintain it. This memorial is aware that it could die. Its vulnerability is most evident in the landscape's need for constant maintenance, a key issue when considering memorials, and particularly apropos here in a work that exists precisely because of lands that were difficult to cultivate and ultimately decimated because of political action or inaction.

The ever-changing landscape endures, because it is a living thing, the life of this memorial about death. Writing in *The New Yorker,* historian Simon Schama said, "By having the landscape virtually enact the story, Tolle neatly sidestepped the figurative-abstract dilemma facing designers of historical memorials," and avoided the ambiguity of abstract monuments whose "symbolic forms are too rarefied to trigger memories, of dates, places, and people."

The memorial has two faces. From the west, it looks like an abstract concrete sculpture somewhat reminiscent of Gaudí's eccentric Parc Güell in Barcelona. From the east, the emphasis is on the landscape, which is strewn with stones and plants native to Ireland, such as heather, bulrushes, and blackthorn. There's not a single potato planted there, and perhaps that is the point, but to suggest that crop, the landscape is sculpted with rippled potato furrows that still characterize Ireland's topography. Half of the monument, a quarter-acre, consists of fallow fields, in reference to the infamous Gregory Clause, a trigger for the Hunger, that stipulated that no person occupying land of more than one-quarter acre was eligible for relief. Because these postage-stamp lots could not sustain crops other than potatoes, families were wholly dependent on the one crop, which failed. Tolle's measurement subtly makes the small size of these famine farms concrete.

The landscape cantilevers out over a wedge-shaped base made of alternating bands of glass and fossil-flecked Kilkenny limestone. This cross-section view recalls the cliffs along Ireland's western coast. The compressed space below the plinth evokes an intense physical sensation of vulnerability like that experienced when walking underneath the massive capstones of dolmens, the altarlike standing stones found in Celtic countries. Conveniently, the overhang also provides protection from the rain.

the ethereal text implies the inevitable aging of any memorial, and also works against the tradition of gravestone rubbing. Of the text, Tolle has said, "I didn't want it to become an object, a souvenir that people could walk off with. I wanted the text to exist in the mind."

An underground passageway leads visitors from the street, through a wall of sound composed of broadcasts about world hunger, and deposits them into a nineteenth-century rural landscape. This brilliant transition makes possible a complete break with the present. Its drama is enhanced by the passageway that telescopes toward the parallelogrammatic entrance that frames the main event: the skeletal ruins of a two-room cottage.

The base functions as a massive open book, encompassing stories, songs, parliamentary reports, diary entries, and other facts about the Hunger and about world hunger. Culled from global sources and presented in nonchronological order to give a sense of the breadth of hunger issues, the text juxtaposes an 1845 first-person account of starvation in Ireland, for instance, against a contemporary statistic about obesity in American children. The lettering is silk-screened on Plexiglas panels through which light shines: The letters are actually shadows. Conceptually,

One enters the memorial through a street entrance that leads to a two-room stone cottage, seen just left of center, and an open field. The landscape provides a commemoration experience that emphasizes life's fragility as well as its tenacity.

Built in the 1820s, the cottage was dismantled in Ireland and painstakingly reconstructed in New York. It is typical of the famine-era houses that are being torn down regularly in Ireland in the face of the country's current prosperity. The stone shelves and fireplaces are barren and the sole visual reminder that this is a memorial about hunger. The roofless structure recalls on rainy days the fate bestowed by weather, and, in a schizophrenic juxtaposition, allows views of the luxury highrises in Battery Park City.

A number of houses in Ireland were considered for the project. Serendipitously, relatives of Tolle's partner, Brian Clyne, had a famine-era cottage on their property in Carradoogan in County Mayo in the parish of Attymass—the place where the first report of death from starvation in Ireland had been recorded. The home in which Mary Slack, Clyne's grandmother, was born turned out to be the perfect house. When measured, it varied only four inches from the proposed memorial footprint. The cottage was not altered, with the exception of the removal of the eastern entry wall.

The Famine is a collective memory of impoverishment that is alive and well within the Irish community but has little correlation with the many

More than two miles of historical and contemporary quotations—a literary and political ticker tape—are wrapped around the memorial's base. No quote is more than one line long, to avoid big panels of didactic text and to allow an ahistorical perspective to emerge.

What would it mean to put a landscape into motion and watch to see how it negotiated its place? What would it mean to transplant something from its place of origin, to act on that colonial impulse to move things from, say, Egypt and display them in Central Park?

—Brian Tolle, interview with the author, 2005

accomplishments of Irish Americans. During planning meetings, descendants of Irish immigrants asked Tolle to give them "a piece of the auld sod." Tolle realized these comments were equally legitimate memorial fodder, and so he allowed the piece to address these sentiments as well.

Consequently, with its quaint cottage, shamrocks, fieldstone walls, and scalloped silhouette, the memorial teeters on the edge of kitsch. Tolle is comfortable with the comparison. Of architects' reactions, he said, "If they try to evaluate this as a building, then they're going to have a problem with it. People who understand that this is coming out of art, not architecture, appreciate the subtle play between kitsch and nostalgia, and genuine resonance and power. You have to let yourself surrender to the idea that this is art. . . . The fact that you can have an 1820s ruin dropped on something that looks like a spaceship is more akin with a sculptural tradition than an architectural one."

A potent concoction of reality and simulacra, the memorial is a "folly," a type of architectural bonbon born in sixteenth-century Italy that also has deep roots in Britain. Toying as it does with the historical imagination, Tolle's folly might be mistaken for a remnant of New Amsterdam. It is artifice set upon artifice—the 92-acre landfill it occupies did not exist before 1966, when acres of land, itself landfill from an earlier era, were excavated to form the foundations of the World Trade Center complex and dumped west of that site to create Battery Park City.

As much as the memorial's meaning depends on the literal re-creation of a typical Irish farm, it relies far more on the powerful icons that surround it. Tolle's economy of means is vividly apparent as one emerges from the cottage into the landscape and becomes a player in the historical drama.

One walks uphill through vignettes of rock and daisy, toward a simple platform enclosed by a parapet. At this vantage point comes the memorial's most inspired moment: an unobstructed sightline across the Hudson to the Statue of Liberty and Ellis Island, legendary symbols of emigrant hope.

The parapet view evokes a mental voyage that underscores the power of memory and place. The connection is made between the Famine and immigration, the old world and the new, despair and faith, and sums up the journey from Ireland to New York, its purposes, hopes, and outcome. We are simultaneously amidst the dead potato fields of nineteenth-century Ireland, in the hold of a miserable coffin ship crossing the Atlantic Ocean, about to enter a strange city crammed with buildings of unimaginable height, and in the heart of what is currently the mightiest financial center on earth.

Does this memorial work? It is hard to say, and that reluctant categorization makes it worth studying. When viewed from the sidewalk, the memorial is visually awkward, galloping as it does in all directions, and yet the artist has not willfully obstructed beauty as much as allowed the piece to be what it wanted to be, in all its many dimensions. It is visually abrasive—courageously so—and its lack of regard for convention makes it compelling. One wishes that all this memorial encompasses could have been expressed more simply, but life doesn't always work that way.

The Irish government wanted to contribute stones from each of the country's thirty-four counties. The artist agreed, with the stipulation that they be of a certain size, typical of their region, and without inscriptions. Nevertheless, fearing the stones would be confused, the government inscribed them with the names of each county. When they arrived, Tolle had no choice but to use them. He insisted on placing them where and how they would look best, which explains why some county names are upside down, some prominent, others half buried. Word got out that the memorial contained a rock from every county. That became a drawing card for thousands of Irish Americans, who swarmed over the site looking for specific county names. Once they were found, visitors kissed, rubbed, and photographed the rocks with an ardor ordinarily reserved for the Blarney Stone—and inadvertently destroyed the landscape. Indicative of Tolle's willingness to allow the work to be what it wanted to be, he relocated the stones to increase their visibility and protect the landscape from the rock hunters. This photograph shows the stone from County Derry.

1986
U.S. NASA space shuttle *Challenger* explodes 73 seconds into flight, killing the crew of six (Jan. 28)

1989
Fall of the Berlin Wall (Nov. 9); originally built Aug. 13, 1961; persons killed on Wall trying to escape East Germany: 192; Brandenburg Gate opened (Dec. 22, 1989); Germany reunited (Oct. 3, 1990)

The Heavenly City

Where do buildings, bridges, and other structures go when they have outlived their usefulness to us? We may save a brick or a fireplace mantel, like preserving a lock of a loved one's hair. However, the remainder of their fabric returns to the earth. But not their souls—they rise up and establish a new landscape. An eighteenth-century cottage may alight beside a twentieth-century theater, or a formerly urban denizen may move apart and obtain more elbow room than it previously had. Whatever the arrangement, they all flourish in their new surroundings— the Heavenly City.

—Frances White,
The Heavenly City, 2004

We seldom admit our attachment to buildings, preferring instead to focus our attention on the people who inhabit them and the events that transpire within their walls. Recalling the neighborhoods we have known and the mental maps of them we carry for a lifetime, however, makes it clear that architecture has an emotional resonance and identity beyond its physical dimensions. The larger, deeper meaning of a building exists apart from its structure. It is found in its location, the way it hides in gloom or basks in sunlight, its portals and ornament, its sounds and scent, and its relationship to its surroundings. *The Heavenly City* is a unique painted memorial that commemorates nearly five dozen buildings, each as distinct as an individual, that have been lost to history but not to memory.

Washingtonian Mark G. Griffin, a lawyer and real estate developer, is passionate about preserving the architectural fabric of the capital. In 2002, he asked himself, What happens to buildings when they die? So began a series of inspired conversations with artist Peter Waddell (b. 1955) and architectural historian James M. Goode about the Washington that didn't exist anymore. Architecture's impact is especially evident in the capital, where every edifice and landscape feature has been designed in relationship to existing federal buildings and national monuments. From a lengthy list of works designed by celebrated as well as anonymous builders, the trio culled a final group of fifty-eight buildings that would recall some of the capital's best-loved structures. The result, *The Heavenly City,* is a heroically scaled, 6-foot-square (1.83 m) oil-on-linen painting created by Waddell in 2004.

1990

The space shuttle *Discovery* deploys the Hubble Space Telescope 350 miles above the Earth

1990

In Geneva, Switzerland, British scientist Tim Berners-Lee (b. 1955) creates Hyper Text Markup Language (HTML), a computer program that facilitates information sharing, and births the World Wide Web

Working from original plans and descriptions and aided by old prints and photographs, Waddell recreated the structures in historically accurate and exquisitely rendered detail. His atmospheric and expansive painting recalls the enormously influential works of the French visionary architects Etienne-Louis Boullée (1728–1799) and Claude-Nicolas Ledoux (1736–1806). Boullée and Ledoux created imaginary places that embody reason and emotion, and couple a majestic physical presence with a sense of sublime emptiness. This same concept is central to *The Heavenly City*, which, like a traditional monument carved in stone, looks back to an idealized time and expresses permanence, mystery, and beautiful workmanship on which a good deal of money and thought has been expended. Employing the kind of logic used by town planners, Waddell populated the landscape with buildings dating from the capital's earliest history. He situated them aesthetically rather than by original location. Rock Creek snakes down the left-hand side of the painting, passes under the P Street Bridge, flows by the Key Bridge, over which runs a canal, and enters the Potomac River in the foreground. A charming pavilion (c. 1870) that stood on the grounds of the Department of Agriculture Building is placed on a high bluff overlooking boats similar to those that once plied the Potomac. Women and children promenade on the quay lying along the river. Fragments of the city, such as the wisteria vines that grace the façade of Wisteria House (1863–1924) and the awnings on Metzerott Hall (1851–94), create a parallel world that seems real by virtue of such authentic touches.

A snapshot history of the fifty-eight buildings is given in the Heavenly City catalogue, published in conjunction with the painting. The structural types run the gamut from churches to markets to jailhouses. Highlights include the First Unitarian Church (1822–1906) by Charles Bulfinch, third architect of the United States Capitol; Brentwood (1817–1919), considered to be the finest residence designed by Benjamin Henry Latrobe; and Primary Hall (1858–1916), a school building at Gallaudet College for the deaf. One building is not gone, but merely lost: The Key House (c. 1802–1948), where Francis Scott Key wrote "The Star-Spangled Banner," was razed so that the Key Bridge could be built. To appease those who protested its demise, the government had it dismantled, brick by brick, crated, and warehoused; unfortunately, no one today can recall where it was stored!

For all of its veracity of detail and nostalgia for what once was, the Heavenly City never did exist, at least not as shown in this portrayal. Like all monuments, its truth is found not in mere recapitulation of the past but in the ideals it espouses and its capacity to redirect our sights to those buildings that still stand among us.

1990
The Dycam Model 1, the first completely digital consumer camera, is released

Texas A&M University Bonfire Memorial

LOCATION	DEDICATION	DESIGNER	COMMEMORATION
College Station, Texas	*2004*	*Overland Partners Architects*	*Those who died in the 1999 bonfire collapse*

By responding sensitively to a specific event and local culture, the Texas A&M University Bonfire Memorial has transcended its regional roots and achieved a place in the national commemorative coda. Designed by Overland Partners Architects of San Antonio, the monument conjures a mythic landscape that evokes fundamental ideas about the nature of sacred ground.

One cannot overestimate the devotion of "Aggies," as Texas A&M students are called, to their school and its myriad traditions, many of which center on football, a singular passion for most of the university's forty-four thousand students and alumni. The first football game was held in 1892, almost two decades after the Agricultural and Mechanical College of Texas, as it was then known, opened in 1876. In 1894, they lost their first game against the Texas Longhorns in a 38–0 rout; eight seasons would pass before they beat their soon-to-be archrivals. The teams' first Thanksgiving Day match took place in 1919, won by A&M, and, incidentally, said to be the first football game covered in a play-by-play radio broadcast. The Thanksgiving game between A&M and Texas soon became a regional and national classic: Thirty-five thousand fans attended the 1924 game in Austin.

In 1909 the rivalry gave rise to a new A&M tradition—an annual bonfire built to symbolize the Aggies' "burning desire" to beat Texas. The early bonfires were made from whatever was at hand—trash, boxes, tree limbs—a glorified junk pile that evolved into a defining event. The first log center pole bonfire was built in 1946. By 1995, an estimated five thousand students, under the supervision of an elite handful of seniors and juniors called "red pots," expended more than 125,000 hours to cut, gather, and stack thousands of logs into a six-tiered wedding-cake configuration more than five stories tall. For safety reasons, a height limit of 55 feet was set in 1970 after reaching almost 110 feet, an all-time high, in 1969.

An Aggie chestnut explains, "From the outside looking in, you can't understand it. From the inside looking out, you can't explain it." This spirit, manifested in the school's many traditions, was most visible at the November bonfire, when tens of thousands returned to campus to witness its burning. Although burning bonfires to boost team spirit and warm fans on chilly autumnal nights is a long collegiate tradition, A&M's bonfire was by far the nation's largest. The A&M bonfire was unique too in the long months required for its construction, a shared work experience that has bonded generations of Aggies. The annual ritual made a sprawling campus small and imparted a sense of belonging in a culture that is increasingly untethered from familial, societal, and geographic roots.

On November 18, 1999, twelve Aggies were killed and at least twenty-seven were injured when the bonfire logs they were stacking fell apart and scattered like matchsticks. The tragedy captured international attention and shook the A&M community to the core. Why were so many lives lost to a sporting event? most asked, incredulously. The bonfire tradition with its codified, yet largely hermetic ritual was not well understood outside Texas.

Gig 'em, Aggies!

Aggies sacrificed time, grades, and everything else to create the largest bonfire in the world. An outhouse, known as the "t.u. tea room" or "t.u. frat house," built by sophomores in the Fightin' Texas Aggie Band, sits atop the completed bonfire.

1995

The 6.9 magnitude Hanshin-Awaji earthquake devastates Japan on January 17, killing 5,000 and affecting more than 4 million; the Nojima Fault Museum is built in Hokudan to preserve a section of the earthquake's fault line

1995

Alfred P. Murrah Federal Building, Oklahoma City, bombed, killing 168 people (Apr. 19)

The TAMU administration asked Houston businessman Leo E. Linbeck, Jr., to chair an independent commission to determine what caused the collapse. Their May 2002 report said the accident was caused by a fatal combination of physical and organizational factors. Structurally, it collapsed because of the "excessive internal stresses driven primarily by aggressive wedging of second-stack logs into the first stack"; in other words, the bottom stack was stuffed to bursting with logs from the upper tier, and the wire that bound the stacks together wasn't strong enough. Steel cables, used previously, were not used in 1999. Organizationally, the collapse was rooted in behaviors that had evolved over decades, including a strong "cultural bias impeding risk identification." There were no adequate guidelines or engineering controls for the construction of a complex structure—the design was maintained through oral tradition. As a result, "Bonfire was never built the same way twice even though the accepted basis for safe design was 'we have always done it this way and it always worked.'"

"Vanities of the Bonfire," an investigative essay by engineer Henry Petroski, pins the colossal structural failure on the Icarusian drive to build ever

bolder, and the blinding hubris caused by those attempts. Ironically, Petroski says, one reason the potential danger was ignored was because of the bonfire's long tradition, which, instead of being a source of "institutional memory about the dangers and pitfalls associated with such a major structural undertaking, was in fact an impediment to safe practice" that encouraged the ad hoc way in which the two-million-pound tower of logs was built. For now, there are no plans to reinstate the bonfire tradition.

Five years to the day, before a weeping, cheering crowd of some fifty thousand people, a monument that remembered the dead and injured and celebrated "Aggie Spirit" was dedicated.

The memorial consists of three distinct elements—Tradition Plaza, History Walk, and Spirit Ring—made primarily of granite and bronze and spread over a ten-acre site. The stone elements speak to the abstract ideas of spirit, history, and time, while those cast in bronze recall the students who were involved in the accident.

Behind a wall inscribed "the story that can ne'er be told," one enters Tradition Plaza, a transitional

1997
Design for the Oklahoma City National Memorial by Torrey and Hans Butzer, and Sven Berg, selected (June 23–24)

1997
Oklahoma City National Memorial becomes the 376th National Park (Oct.)

Amber-colored LCD lighting illuminates the path leading to the memorial's center and its perimeter and subtly recalls the glow and warmth of the bonfire.

Students wore safety helmets or "pots" that were painted various colors to designate the hierarchy of bonfire construction jobs.

2000
Oklahoma City National Memorial dedicated (April 19)

The design of the commemorative portraits of the twelve who died was guided by a question, "How do you know people?" and its answer, "You know them by their face, their name, and their signature, which is as unique as a fingerprint. You know them by what they thought and by what others thought about them."

Shown top to bottom, the twelve who died were Jerry Self, Scott West, Lucas Kimmel, Miranda Adams, Bryan McClain, and Jeremy Frampton; facing page, top to bottom: Jamie Hand, Chad Powell, Christopher Breen, Michael Ebanks, Christopher Heard, and Timothy Kerlee, Jr.

space between the parking lot and memorial proper that is minimally fitted with concrete seating and shade trees. A second wall is inscribed with "The Last Corps Trip," the poem that was always recited before the bonfire was lit. The poem provides a way to learn about the bonfire tradition, while the act of reading creates mental focus and physically slows down the heartbeat in preparation for the journey to the memorial's center.

History Walk is a 300-foot (91.4 m) gravel path that links the entrance plaza and central ring. The bonfire's history is presented in the abstract as eighty-nine granite blocks that are notched to mark the years it was held, from 1909 through 1998. The one exception is 1963, the year President John F. Kennedy was assassinated and the bonfire was dismantled, marked by a subtle gap in the timeline wall. Three previous bonfire-related deaths also are remembered along the path.

The memorial's centerpiece is the granite Spirit Ring, 170 feet (52 m) in diameter, that is situated where the bonfire once burned. Arranged along its perimeter are twelve granite portals that face the hometowns of those who perished in the collapse. An encompassing granite circle, at bench height so visitors can sit and linger, is marked with bronze inlays that honor the twenty-seven injured. At the circle's center is a black granite compass rose placed where the bonfire stack's center pole once stood and engraved with the time of the collapse: 11-18-1999 2:42 A.M.

The twelve gateways, each consisting of an outer stone gateway and an inner bronze one, presented formidable technical challenges. The outer portals are cut from pale, fine-grained granite quarried in China. Standing 16 feet (4.8 m) and weighing eighteen tons each, they are the largest pieces of

cut stone in the Americas. Since the stone was set without mortar to achieve a powerful, monolithic look, each slab had to be cut precisely. Dressing the stone was further complicated by the need to accommodate its movement; stone may seem static, but with constant expansion and contraction, it is very much alive.

Complicating matters further, the local climate in College Station, called the "belt buckle of the rain belt," required the construction of subterranean drainage systems. Engineering impresario Guy Nordenson devised a suspended foundation system that could absorb the movement of the stone portals, which, because of their tremendous weight, could not be set into the wet, expansive soil.

In a school permeated with traditions including Elephant Walk, Fish Camp, Ring Dance, Muster, and Midnight Yell, one of the most meaningful is that of the Twelfth Man, which speaks to supporting your friends by stepping in when they can't. As the story goes, while playing against Centre College in 1921, Aggie injuries forced Coach Dana X. Bible to ask E. King Gill, a sophomore who had never played, to suit up. Gill's readiness to play spurred the Aggies' 22–14 victory and birthed the hallowed "Twelfth Man" tradition of standing during the entire football game, thus signifying one's willingness to jump in if needed. Today, tens of thousands of Aggies in maroon and white stand throughout the game. Because visitors can enter the memorial's central area only through one of the portals, thus temporarily and symbolically filling the void left by a fallen Aggie, one becomes a metaphoric "Twelfth Man."

Twelve. It was almost inevitable. As alumna Martha Raney recalled, even as Aggies anxiously awaited news, many sensed the final count of the dead would be twelve, a number embedded in school legend and a formative influence on its culture. The number twelve—considered by numerologists, theologians, and mathematicians, among others, to be one of the most potent and mystical numbers—has inherent commemorative currency.

Each of the lost students is memorialized in one of the inner portals, which contain a cast bronze

2001
Timothy McVeigh dies by lethal injection (June 11)

2001
The first book is ceremonially placed in the new Bibliotheca Alexandrina in Egypt, located approximately on the site of the ancient Library of Alexandria; included among the first volumes are a handwritten seventh-century Qur'an, a Bible, and the Microsoft Excel 2000 handbook (Aug. 1)

It was bigger than necessary and defied reason and possibility, but we would not have it any other way. While it would have been more efficient to use modern technologies and equipment, we chose to do it as it was done for ninety years: with sweat, blisters, grunts, groans, teamwork, axes, machetes, ropes, chains, wire, oversized nails, pliers, steel-toed boots, Carhartt jackets, generous donations, left-handed skyhooks, FFE semis, muddy pickups, mufflerless tractors, scarecrows, and perimeter pole fires. . . . The cadets, nonregs, brownpots, yellowpots, buttpots, crew chiefs, centerpolepots, pinkpots, redpots, bonfire buddies, and randoms who had invested thousands of hours of sweat equity in that stack of wood knew that the only reason we burned it was to clear the Polo Fields so that we could do it all over again next year.

—Milton "Chip" Thiel, remarks at the Bonfire Memorial dedication ceremony, November 18, 2004

The central area is a sacred precinct, but it is not a sacred lawn, and visitors are encouraged to stroll, sit, and gather there.

cameo portrait sculpted by Erik Christianson as well as the student's signature and snippets of e-mail, poetry, and other text remembrances gathered by the families. The signatures, as it turned out, were the hardest items to locate.

To cover the astronomical costs of a dozen monumental bronze castings, consulting sculptor Stephen Daly came up with an ingenious method of welding plate stock with cast bronze elements to create what appears to be a seamless casting. More than a hundred patinas were tested to obtain the right color finish for the bronze; several new patinas and methods of applying them were developed in conjunction with this project.

Overland recognized the commemorative authority that would flow from building on the Polo Fields where the bonfire once stood. Every tool of art, architecture, and landscape was used to mitigate various site challenges, including an adjacent parking lot for several thousand cars that was visually jarring. The designers retained the field's wide-open feeling, but built a berm, a cradling mound of earth, that situated the memorial and blocked the view of the parking lot.

The encircling berm creates a dynamic interaction between the memorial's constructed and natural elements. As one approaches the center, the walkway veers to the left, quite subtly, and draws the visitor into the larger cosmic circle that arises from the berm's deft placement and grading. There is a palpable, physical sensation of having left ordinary time and entered an eternal dimension.

No one who has made a monumental installation of stone in the landscape is free from the gestalt of Stonehenge, the ceremonial circle dating from 3000 B.C. In form and scheme, the A&M portals recall such ancient megaliths, menhirs, cairns, dolmens, and other giant standing stones whose original meaning has been lost to history. Such stones still enthrall our imaginations, not so much for their romantic, lichened masses as for their mute ability to confirm time itself, a time when humanity had compelling, unknown reasons to order the world by arranging stones of impossible size. Whether old or new, such stones consecrate a cyclical ordering of time as it has always been marked, and affirm that the present moment, along with what once was and will be, is part of the sacred continuum. They reassure us that the seasons, along with reason and hope, endure.

2001

Al Qaeda forces crash two planes into the World Trade Center towers, New York; a third plane into the Pentagon, Washington, D.C.; a fourth plane crashes in Shanksville, PA; over 2,800 people from 92 countries are killed (Sept. 11)

2001

The U.S. war in Afghanistan begins (Oct. 7)

The "Tower of Faces" is a three-floor-high permanent exhibition at the U.S. Holocaust Memorial Museum in Washington, D.C. It consists of photographic portraits of the Jewish community of Eisiskes, Lithuania, who were massacred by the German Einsatzgruppe and their Lithuanian auxiliaries in 1941.

If any of the artists among us woke up one morning to find that the rest of humanity had disappeared overnight, then I suggest that that person would no longer make pictures.

—Richard Benson, *Notes on Pictures*, 2002

2002

Tribute in Light illuminated in Manhattan until April 13 to honor those killed in the World Trade Center attack (Mar. 11)

2002

The last girder from Ground Zero is removed in a somber ceremony, marking the end of recovery efforts at the World Trade Center site (May 28)

The former Iraqi president Saddam Hussein's sons, Uday and Qusay, were killed in 2003 in a military ambush in Mosul. Within hours, the American government released graphic photographs of the two brothers' bloodied heads, paired with images of them taken while alive. Here, the world was told, is incontrovertible proof of their deaths. It wasn't enough. Skepticism about the photographs' veracity grew to a collective scream for the head of John the Baptist on a platter. Additional photographs followed in rapid-fire succession, but did not quench demand for proof. New photos showed the brothers wiped clean and shaved, with faces heavily reconstructed by plastic surgery. Ignoring the reality that current surgical techniques can make anyone look like someone else, it was accepted, finally, that Uday and Qusay were dead.

Memento Mori

No one believes photographs tell the absolute truth anymore. When the Hussein images were first released, even Iraqi farmers paused in their fields and said, *Wait, that's not them, we need better evidence.* Early reverence for photography's mystical ability to recreate the world has long since evaporated to reveal its inherent fictionality and our increasingly relativistic approach to authenticity. But there's a lingering Victorian hangover about the reality expressed by a photograph, or a monument, for that matter. We want to believe we are looking at the truth as they express it, and have to force ourselves to acknowledge that the image, whether of paper or stone, is merely a fragment of a larger, and potentially much different, picture.

Photographs present a highly subjective version of reality. Photographers have always known this. The general public has clung to the notion of the camera's infallibility, its accurate and impartial rendering of the physical world. Although that belief was eventually unseated by the idea that the photogra-

pher, and not the medium itself, was the authority, the photograph's mythic veracity lingered because it required at least one witness at the scene to frame the hard evidence. With the rise of digital photography, the necessity of a witness has gone the way of the darkroom.

As family albums attest, photographs have been an important means of remembering since their invention. But now, able to be altered digitally in ways not imaginable less than a decade ago, visual images are suspect messengers of truth and hence of memory. Here a contradiction, new and quite marvelous, arises. Recent discoveries about how the brain retrieves memories reveal that the creation and distribution of digitally manipulated photographs mimic to an uncanny extent the evanescent nature of memory as well as the physical process of remembering.

Two early types of photographs are germane to a discussion of the interrelationship of photographs

A daguerreotype portrait of a seamstress made around 1853 is encased in a filigreed case. Early photographs such as this one elevated individuals of ordinary circumstances and memorialized them for eternity.

2002
The Lower Manhattan Development Corporation and Port Authority announce six proposals for a new layout of the World Trade Center site that are rejected by the public that same month (July)

2002
The Lower Manhattan Development Corporation announces that it will conduct a worldwide design competition to offer new ideas for the World Trade Center site (Aug. 14)

and monuments. Jacques Louis Daguerre's 1839 discovery of how to permanently record an image made possible the first commercially viable photographs. Daguerreotypes, one of a kind and not reproducible, were an astonishment. They were a "new type of magic," as John Szarkowski writes in *Photography Until Now*, "that preserved for its owner something that almost passed as a fragment of the real world." Contained in filigreed cases, they were "little reliquaries that, if opened in the right light and addressed from the right vantage point, revealed an image of exquisite subtlety and perfection."

It was common practice in the nineteenth century to make daguerreotypes of the dead, particularly of young children, to provide a treasured keepsake for their bereft families. Photographs of the deceased taken while they were living were also reprinted and distributed to mourners. Like medieval memento mori, visual admonitions to "remember death" that depicted skeletons or the Grim Reaper, postmortem photographs reminded the living that death was inevitable, but in their realism also defeated death. They were not merely portraits of the loved one, they *were* the loved one, talismans that could be held, spoken about, and passed down. The deceased, if not wholly alive, neither was released into the vagaries of memory.

Cartes de visite, miniature photographic portraits on paper of the good, the great, and the merely familial, had roughly the size and use of business cards. Introduced in Paris by 1857, and soon available in the United States, they were lightweight, easily reproduced, and inexpensive. The corollary appearance of the photographic album—no fewer than fifteen album patents were issued in America between 1861 and 1865—spurred a collecting craze dubbed "cartomania."

Cartes of family and acquaintances, as well as those of celebrities and politicians, exotic travel views, and architectural landmarks such as monuments, were snapped up by the popular market and formed a common cultural denominator. Their production thrived during the Civil War, when middle-class families wanted parting keepsakes of their sons, and also after the war when, as noted by historian

Keith F. Davis, newly expanded transportation and communication networks encouraged a shared familiarity with contemporary issues and personalities. Glued side by side in photo albums, the same-size images formed a new democracy, one in which the boundaries between the familiar and the infamous were blurred, if not leveled.

The nature of photography is to bring replicas of itself into being. An image, printed in thousands of newspapers and periodicals worldwide, is clipped and collected by the public. Still others are photocopied. Digital images, which can be collected and redistributed instantaneously, make replication easier still. Photos are resurrected again when they are reprinted in a book, such as the one you are holding; even the letters that form these words are photographs.

Certain iconic photographs have literally made history, and many have influenced monument design. Nick Ut's photograph of Kim Phuc, a nine-year-old girl scorched with napalm and running screaming down a Vietnamese road, was shown during hearings about the Vietnam Veterans Memorial as testimony as to why literal representation was not appropriate for that monument's design. The photo by Joe Rosenthal of the raising of the flag at Iwo Jima was sculpted into the most recognizable memorial in the nation. The World War II Memorial in Washington appears to have been conceived entirely from a photographic standpoint: Its razor-sharp planes and telegenic siting on the lush green Mall ensure that it will be experienced primarily in two dimensions, that is, in photographs.

Photographer and printer Richard Benson, discussing the peculiar place the medium occupies between reality and illusion, related a story about a woman pushing her grandchild in a carriage. Two of her friends arrive and say, "Oh, look at the baby. That baby is so wonderful!" And the proud granny replies, "Yes, and you should see his picture!"

What Susan Sontag has described in *On Photography* as a "chronic voyeuristic relation to the world" has shaped a new memorial phenomenon. Photographs of victims and grieving survivors, and of the tragedy itself, raise the question of what should be observed and, more blatantly, what we believe we are entitled to observe. The rise of the spontaneous memorial—the practice of leaving mementos at locations where tragedy has occurred—is directly related to the ubiquity of photography and reaches back still further to the cartomaniacal blurring of the distinctions between the individual and the celebrity. Vested in the minute details of a stranger's life—and none are deemed too intimate by the "If it bleeds, it leads" press corps—we sympathize with the victims of tragedy and their families, possess them and their stories, and so feel entitled to mourn them. Photography abets the spontaneous memorial itself by reproducing its image, which inspires yet another segment of the population to make a therapeutic deposit at the growing mountain of offerings.

Just as photography freed painters in the nineteenth century from the need to re-create the factual world, digital photography has separated itself from traditional darkroom photography and the expectation of veracity. Digital images are suspect holders of memory because they are so easily manipulated and distributed, and yet, paradoxically, their quixotic mutability parallels the way our brains actually recall people and events.

How we remember is one of the last great mysteries. Memories were once thought to be stored in individual brain cells and retrievable in their entirety, like photographs in an album. Now it is known—to oversimplify egregiously—that memory is fragmented, biochemically so, and exists in the synaptic connections between nerve cells. With each recall, we do not retrieve, but remake the memory anew. Memory is not static, but creative, surprisingly chaotic, and subtly different each time it is conjured. It's not uncommon for individuals—siblings recalling a childhood event, for instance—to remember the same event in radically dissimilar ways. When we remember an experience, our brain reimagines it by making new connections, an activity that is comparable to the sites, pages, and hyperlinks in cyberspace that remain in virtual storage until retrieved but emerge fully updated and ordered. Memory, you could say, is as fickle as a photograph.

Photography no longer merely documents reality; in many cases, it is reality. Digital photography heightens, proves, and extracts its own version of truth. Every computer is now a darkroom where images can be manipulated to suit a preferred reality. The digital medium begs for its own distortion.

My neighbor Michelle routinely inserts images of her beloved late grandparents into photographs of family gatherings, her rationale being that they would have attended if they had been alive. She is crafting a reality that, if not true in the realm of linear time, has its own satisfying emotional legitimacy. "The morality of art consists in the perfect use of an imperfect medium," wrote Oscar Wilde. The difference between digital and still photography is comparable to the gap that exists between a monument and its precipitating event.

Monuments and photographs serve the same god. Just as a pristine war memorial bears no trace of the bloody sacrifice it honors, nor the disagreements that accompanied its construction, a photograph encourages us to forget whatever has fallen outside its frame. Monuments and photographs distill the essence—always subjective, often idealized—of an instant in time, and contain it in physical form so that we, and future generations, can repeatedly scrutinize its message. Because both stop time, they are inherently elegiac, and turn a negative into a positive—the photograph literally, the monument figuratively. More than static conjurers of the past, monuments and photographs also shape the future by creating agreement about what in the present moment is worth preserving.

Monuments, like their photographic counterparts, are tangible gatekeepers of the intangible realm of memory. Born of memory and its preservation, they exist wholly apart from it, and in this paradox lies their compelling seduction. Once disconnected from the events and ideologies that inspired its creation, a monument, like a snapshot removed from a family album, becomes an anonymous, disembodied entity. The meaning of both memorial and photograph relies rather precariously on the continuum of memory, itself a fluid and illusive creature.

Since the Renaissance, the term *vanitas*, Latin for "vanity," has been used to denote life's brevity and the related appreciation of its pleasures and their inevitable loss. In Western art, particularly seventeenth-century Dutch still lifes, the vanitas was a visual reminder of mortality and final judgment. In these paintings, artists expressed life's temporality by including images of flowers, overripe fruit, snuffed candles, skulls, and hourglasses. American artist Steve Miller (b. 1951) has updated traditional portraiture and the vanitas oeuvre in works that literally allow us to look beneath human flesh. Using an electron microscope, the artist has photographed images of his blood and combined them with X-rayed icons of vanitas. In *Self-Portrait Vanitas, #27* (1998), shown above, an X-ray of French tulips is juxtaposed with the artist's red blood platelets and an HIV-positive blood cell that floats in the "sky" of this biological landscape.

2003

Bill Mauldin, the Army sergeant who created Willie and Joe, the cartoon characters who became symbols of the American infantrymen in World War II, dies (Jan. 23)

2003

Space shuttle *Columbia* breaks up during its landing approach, killing all six crew members (Feb. 1)

Luminous Manuscript

LOCATION	DEDICATION	DESIGNER	COMMEMORATION
Center for Jewish History, New York City	*2004*	*Diane Samuels*	*The breadth of Jewish history*

According to a beloved Jewish folktale, an angel whispered to the sixteenth-century mystic Isaac Luria that living in the mountains near Tiberias was a man whose prayers were particularly efficacious. Luria found the man, a poor farmer, and asked him why his prayers were so powerful. The simple man replied that since he could not read, he prayed the entire alphabet with all his strength, over and over again, and asked God to form the letters into prayers.

Variations on this story that emphasize giving with a full heart, or that it is possible to learn something from people from whom one doesn't think one can learn anything, float in the collective memory, are recounted across cultures, and endure over centuries. Numerical values are placed on each letter in the Hebrew alphabet that, when added together, convey special meaning. Other mystical Judaic traditions, such as the Kabbalah, hold that letters have creative power. It is said too that scribes of old counted each letter in the Bible, some six hundred thousand of them, one for every Jew in the Exodus. Traditionally, Jewish children are named using the first letter of the name of a deceased loved one. All forms of oral and written tradition—stories and songs, poems and prayer are the foundation on which Jewish culture has been built and has survived.

2003
Master plan by architect Daniel Libeskind selected for the World Trade Center site (Feb. 27)

2003
Lower Manhattan Development Corporation announces international competition to design World Trade Center site memorial (Apr. 28)

Luminous Manuscript (2004) is a wondrously intricate array of letters and numerals that looks capable of telling every story in the world. The monumental stone and glass tablet is located in Manhattan's Center for Jewish History (CJH), one of the largest repositories of Jewish cultural history. It was created by artist Diane Samuels, who has worked with the Isaac Luria story since 1993. That story forms the basis, sometimes visible, occasionally hidden, but always there, of many of her public sculptural works and artist's books. With monastic intensity, Samuels reworks the themes of history and memory, explicating them in materials and processes that align conceptually with the breadth of language and the written word. Of the enduring significance of the book, she said, "You can hold a book in your hand and inside there's an entire world that someone has created."

By reordering the symbols of language, Samuels's acentric relief illuminates the fragmentary and elusive nature of memory and thus history, and how we grasp, lose, and refashion our stories—individually, in community, and over time. Hers is not a mere exercise in retelling. In a note to the artist, the German historian Roland Deigendesch wrote, "it doesn't make much sense to preserve and to look back just for the sake of preserving and just for the sake of looking back. The task of the historian is (in my eyes) to help position human society in the present. In situations like now, which have no easy solutions, no easy answers, what do we need more than art?"

The staggering presence of hundreds of thousands of letters, numbers, symbols, words, and equations

Luminous Manuscript suggests daytime, and the dark hues of *Biblical Species* (2000), an inlaid terrazzo floor piece by Michele Oka Doner, suggest nighttime. *Luminous Manuscript* is hard to capture in a photograph. The work's cobweb delicacy and fine sensibility can only be conveyed by seeing it in person, and by touching it.

2003

5,201 people from 62 countries submit designs for the World Trade Center memorial competition, making it the largest design competition in history (June 30)

2004

"Reflecting Absence," a memorial for victims of 9/11 designed by architect Michael Arad and landscape architect Peter Walker, is chosen for the World Trade Center site (Jan. 6)

in *Luminous Manuscript* testifies to fundamental emotion expressed by the marks made by the human hand. The potency of the human hand is underscored by the tiny hands scattered over the surface, which are imprints of the hands of 3,100 children that were scanned, reduced, and

I wanted to make the artwork rich and full, not in a baroque or decorative sense, but really full, fuller than you can imagine, the way the Center's archives are full. All those books, boxes, and objects on the shelves that I saw, those hundreds of thousands of things, made me want to include hundreds of thousands of elements in this artwork, and I wanted each one to be individually polished, ground, sandblasted, touched, handled, and looked after in the same way that material is cared for at the Center.

—Diane Samuels, conversation with the author, 2005

engraved into the glass surface. A lively combination of both symmetry and chaos, the piece is adamantly not machine-made.

From a distance, *Luminous Manuscript* looks like a shimmering page from the Talmud. It is in fact organized by the format of that sacred book: A central column of text is flanked on the left and right by two columns of commentary. The multilayered relief consists of 80,500 pieces of clear Starphire glass (tesserae), ranging in size from ³/₄ inch (1.9 cm) wide to 1³/₄ inches (4.4 cm) high, that were affixed to 440 Jerusalem stone panels arranged on a 22-foot-high x 20-foot-

wide (6.7 x 6 m) grid. Engraved into both faces of the glass and into the stone panels underneath are some 170,000 numerals, alphabetic characters, and handwritten documents from the CJH archives. The wall support is a honeycomb panel hung with Z-type clips that was designed by the architectural firm of Beyer Blinder Belle.

Samuels began gathering handwriting samples at a 2003 dinner celebrating Paul Steinberg's bar mitzvah in the Great Hall named for his grandparents. She also involved the public, eventually collecting handwritten letters representing fifty-seven languages and writing systems ranging from Hindu to Italian to stenography, which were sandblasted onto glass tiles. Additionally, more than 33,000 pieces were etched with numerals from 0 to 7000, representing dates in the Gregorian and Jewish calendars that extend far into the future.

Translating the characters from ink on paper to glass and stone involved a mind-numbing production sequence that included digitally scanning and laying out individual characters that were then cut from vinyl. Letters were hand-picked from the vinyl stencils, applied to the final surface, and then sandblasted, cleaned, and polished. The archival documents were scanned, engraved into the reverse side of the glass, spray-painted in silver, and then scraped so that only the handwriting remained silver; each document on glass was subsequently cut by water jet into tiny rectilinear pieces that were then sandblasted with single characters. It has been estimated that by the time they had been peeled, scrubbed, ground, polished, and hand assembled, each piece was handled at least ten times. Bordering the columns are 23,200 narrow glass strips that recall the faint laid lines in handmade paper. The ochre-colored Jerusalem stone includes fossils and mineral veins that, along with the alphabet characters engraved into them, were lightly stained to create further visual depth. Curator Dara Meyers-Kingsley compared the variations in the limestone to "lines that evoke the look of a map, or a system of veins and arteries—a bloodline, perhaps—and yet another visual representation of the Jewish people's connection to each other throughout time and history."

2004

Astronomers unveil the Hubble Ultra Deep Field, a composite photographic portrait of the deepest view of the universe ever taken that reveals the first galaxies to emerge in the first half billion years after the Big Bang (Mar. 9)

2004

Photographs of American soldiers abusing prisoners at Baghdad's Abu Ghraib prison surface (Apr. 28)

Luminous Manuscript reflects the artist's long involvement with the CJH site, staff, and archives that allowed her to make many small adjustments over time that shaped the work perfectly to its location. Samuels sat for hours in the Great Hall, observing the flow of staff and visitors and wondering how to make a memorial that wouldn't become invisible and ignored once its newness faded. After affixing full-scale printouts to the wall, Samuels realized that if she could see the elements from across the room, "there was no reason to come up close and look at the piece," and so she made them smaller.

The work culminates in an eighteenth-century drawing that is positioned low on the wall at child's eye level. Fittingly, it shows an angel sprinkling Hebrew characters on the heads of children to help them learn the alphabet and carry forth into the world their own prayers and stories.

The 170 archival documents incorporated into the wall include copies of Albert Einstein's scribbled notations; Emma Lazarus's 1883 sonnet, "The New Colossus," which is inscribed on the pedestal of the Statue of Liberty; an Auschwitz prisoner's registration form; and a page from Nobel laureate Isaac Bashevis Singer's manuscript "Must Yiddish Literature Disappear?" Most are more mundane documents that emphasize that history is written day by day by everyone. At the very top are a piece

2004

The 9/11 Commission releases its final report that says the September 11, 2001, terrorist attacks resulted from "deep institutional failings" (July 22)

2004

Boston Red Sox end the "Curse of the Bambino" by winning their first World Series in eighty-six years (Oct. 27)

of Yiddish music and a cookbook recipe. "I loved starting with music and food," said Samuels.

For all its joyful explication, the wall is hermetic as well, closing in on itself, perhaps hiding its secrets, or at least not surrendering them easily. It is difficult to read the documents beneath the glass (although the adjacent touch-screen information kiosk makes them easily identifiable and retrievable from the archival collections), but that very blurring speaks of the rich-ness of Judaic history and the myriad writers, theologians, musicians, and scientists represented by the selected documents. Much of the piece is beyond the viewer's gaze and cannot be seen without climbing scaffolding—intentionally so, to suggest the one hundred million documents and half a million library books stored on the twelve floors above the Great Hall. Paradoxically, the piece's meaning grows out of the unique human mark and yet would not have been possible without the electronics necessary to

digitize handwriting samples, scan copies of archival documents and children's hands, and cut the vinyl stencils and glass tesserae.

Photographs can only approximate the work's delicacy and texture, how light emanates from its center, the way the hieroglyphic layers dissolve into pure abstraction. One's gaze shifts constantly between the magnitude and complexity of the work overall and the individual tiles. Because the tiles were placed by hand, there are infinitesimal variations in the relief's surface that cause them to catch light and sparkle like crystal, like shattered glass, like water dappled by sunlight, like tears brimming in the eyes, like any one of a billion stars that are so numerous that most are numbered and not named.

The idea of reconstructing something new from something broken is the basis of another Isaac Luria story about *tikkun olam,* or the "repair of the world." The Kabbalist taught that all was once holy darkness and, to create the world, God poured divine light into cosmic vessels that catastrophically shattered and sent out innumerable sparks of light that now exist inside every aspect of creation. Embodied in *Luminous Manuscript,* the story also recalls Kristallnacht, the "Night of Broken Glass," November 9, 1938, when countless synagogues and Jewish businesses throughout Germany were destroyed. Samuels's craftsmanship is so meticulous that it comes as a shock to detect two tiles, less than an inch wide and barely visible, that were cracked in transit. The artist decided not to replace them, perhaps seeing in their imperfection the acknowledgment that no work of human hands can ever be perfect.

Samuels takes handwriting—intensely personal and yet universal, composed of characters that are spidery, heavy, cursive, childlike, sophisticated, or tentative, each having individual flourishes, pressure, and slant—and weaves it into a cosmology, the complexity of which underscores the subtle yet profound bonds that exist between human beings and celebrates the infinite number of ways we express our common humanity.

Visual complexity has long been employed as a metaphor for one's innermost being as well as the entirety of creation. That of *Luminous Manuscript* is comparable to the sumptuous detail found in the stained-glass windows of medieval cathedrals, Islamic ceramics, and Buddhist mandala paintings, to provide archetypal examples of exponential multiplicity as a reflection of the Creator's hand.

Jewish culture is reflected in preserved ruins, museums, and memorials throughout the world that commemorate its breadth, depth, and freighted political history. These sites have kept alive crucial debate about fundamental commemorative issues, including the nature and function of memorials, where and how the demands of memory and politics intersect, and the necessity of keeping unresolved issues such as racial hatred and genocide at the forefront of the global conscience.

Luminous Manuscript's unfathomable scale exists in the realm of those abstractions, like eternity, that can be grasped only viscerally, and not by standard ledgers. Like the peasant's prayers, it gathers humanity's ordinary and most noble enterprises in a form that doesn't so much speak as whisper a reminder of what is best in human nature.

Opposite The word "manuscript," defined as a document produced by hand or handwriting itself, was chosen deliberately by Samuels, shown working, so the piece's title would reflect its unique manufacture.

Opposite, inset The work's format is based on page 24a of *Tractate Megillah* from the Schottenstein edition of the Babylonian Talmud. Samuels selected the page for its visual attributes but, in a felicitous twist, this particular page comments on who is permitted to read the Talmud and in what order.

Luminous Manuscript is located in the Paul S. and Sylvia Steinberg Great Hall of the Center for Jewish History. Diane Samuels (b. 1948) was chosen in 2002 in an international invitational competition organized by independent curator Dara Meyers-Kingsley and judged by leaders in the arts and the Jewish scholarly community. The competition and creation of this artwork was sponsored by Joseph S. and Diane H. Steinberg in honor of his parents, for whom the hall is named. Considered the "Jewish Library of Congress," the Center is a unique repository for Jewish scholarship, history, and art, the largest such collection outside of Israel, that is held by five partner institutions: the American Jewish Historical Society, American Sephardi Federation, Leo Baeck Institute, Yeshiva University Museum, and YIVO Institute for Jewish Research.

While many messages have been sent from Earth into deep space, receiving a signal from a civilization circling another star would be an event unprecedented though long imagined. If extraterrestrials were to contact us, should we reply? And what should we say? In anticipation, researchers are developing responses that question the assumption that E.T. will understand the laws of nature and math as they are formulated here on earth. Scientists and artists are working in collaboration to expand the range of potential message formats—whether images, music, logic, or algorithms—as well as their content. Beyond simple anatomical representation of human beings, they are seeking to express the breadth of human experience, and in the process are asking the same philosophical questions posed by monument makers throughout history: What are our highest aspirations, and how are they best conveyed?

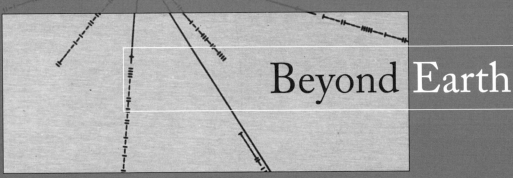

Beyond Earth

The *Pioneer 10* and *11* spacecraft were launched into deep space on March 2, 1972, and April 5, 1973. *Christian Science Monitor* writer Eric Burgess, along with two other journalists, proposed that Earth's first emissaries should "carry into Infinity a literal 'Message from Mankind.'" Consequently, a cosmic postcard designed by astronomer Carl Sagan and astrophysicist Frank Drake, and drawn by Sagan's wife, Linda Salzman Sagan, was bolted to the two spacecrafts. The trio had to devise a message that was independent of language and culture and would be understandable by a disparate species. As described by Sagan, the 6 x 9-inch (15.25 x 22.8 cm) plaque was etched with "a drawing that describes something of the epoch and locale of our civilization, portrayed in a scientific language we hope is comprehensible to a scientifically literate society with no prior knowledge of our planet or its inhabitants."

Hydrogen, the most common element, is illustrated schematically in the left-hand corner of the *Pioneer* plaque and provides a universal "yardstick" of both time and physical length. Earth's location is given relative to its position among fourteen pulsars—stellar rarities that emit powerful radio pulses that would better indicate Earth's position than the sun, which is not distinguishable from a billion other such stars—that were mapped in a starburst pattern.

Two odd figures, which we read as a man and a woman, are the plaque's only shred of human information. According to NASA, their ethnically neutral physiognomy was "determined from results of a computerized analysis of the average person in our civilization," although visually they are direct descendants of the classical tradition in Western art. Their nudity aroused the usual repercussions; some complained it was insufficiently explicit, while others castigated it as "smut."

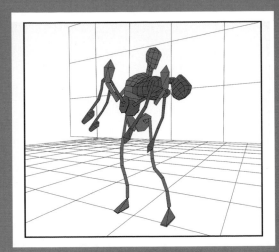

Left Dr. Douglas Vakoch of the SETI Institute is developing interstellar images that define humanity in terms of altruism. The figures are sexually neutral to emphasize the basic physical form of all humans and highlight commonality, and are colored red and blue to avoid representing any specific race.

Top right On August 20 and September 5, 1977, *Voyagers I* and *II* were launched into space from Cape Canaveral bearing an exterior gold-coated phonograph record of Earth's images and sounds.

Bottom right Clockwise from upper left: the *Voyager* record cover shows a top and side view of the record player and stylus; directions on how to construct pictures from the recorded signals, which are shown as vertical lines; a circle in a box—the first picture on the record; a drawing of a hydrogen atom; and a pulsar map of the Earth's location previously sent on *Pioneer 10* and *11*.

Pioneer 10 was a true pioneer—after it passed Mars in 1973 and then Pluto a decade later, it ventured where nothing made by human hands had gone before. Originally designed for a twenty-one-month mission, it spent more than three decades in space. It last called home, from some 7.6 billion miles away, on January 22, 2003. The final transmission from *Pioneer 11* was received on September 30, 1995. Now a ghost ship, *Pioneer 10* will continue to coast into interstellar space, headed toward the red star Aldebaran, about sixty-eight light-years away, where it will arrive in about two million years.

NASA planned a more ambitious message for *Voyagers I* and *II*, which were launched in 1977. Sagan again created a message that would describe life on earth. An effort was made this time to describe humanity in terms larger than those of the *Pioneer* spacecraft: We were not individuals so much as a cooperative, communal species. Frank Drake made the critical suggestion that the message be etched into the grooves of a phonograph record for longevity's sake. It remains the most extensive message sent thus far.

The *Voyager* record, identical copies of which were affixed to both spacecraft, is made of copper sheathed in aluminum. It holds almost ninety minutes of music, an audio essay composed of ambient sounds, greetings in fifty-five languages, and 118 photographs encoded in the audio spectrum. *Murmurs of the Earth* by Sagan and his colleagues, the definitive work about the *Voyager* record, lists its contents in full.

Voyager's mix of photographs, drawings, and graphs included pictures of the earth, human anatomy, flora and fauna, farmland, and cities. Some, like the diagram of a circle in a box, were simple to read; others, such as the scene of a woman sampling grapes in a supermarket's produce section, might be harder for aliens to decipher. Depictions of religious structures or rituals were not included because of the sheer number of possibilities. Notably lacking were any images of poverty or war, something Sagan's group debated at length before omitting them on the grounds that they might be construed as a threat. Overriding all was the feeling that humanity should be depicted positively. First impressions do count. Because our civilization has flowered from books, they added a photograph of a page of Sir Isaac Newton's *System of the World* that depicts, for the first time, the correct procedure for launching an object into orbit.

Voyager's greetings include one in ancient Sumerian, which is no longer spoken, and others, like that of an American boy, that are spoken by millions. All are short, some are formal, and others, such as the message in Mandarin Chinese,

2006

The United States Air Force Memorial, located in Arlington, VA, opens (Oct. 17)

2006

Flags of Our Fathers, Clint Eastwood's film about the fates of those who raised the American flag on Iwo Jima, opens (Oct. 20)

are impromptu—"Hope everyone's well. We are thinking about you all. Please come here to visit us when you have time." The twelve-minute auditory essay is a montage of sounds of the earth that cover the gamut from the familiar (a kiss) to the geologic (a rumbling volcano) to the technical (an EEG recording). Music includes classical works and a global choir of sound encompassing Javanese gamelans, Peruvian panpipes, Senegalese percussion, a Navajo Night Chant, a Northern Indian raga, Louis Armstrong coaxing "Melancholy Blues" from his jazz trumpet, and Chuck Berry wailing "Johnny B. Goode."

The *Pioneer* figures share the idealized proportions of the masterful Riace Bronzes (c. 460–450 B.C.), two bronze warriors with bone and glass eyes, silver teeth, and copper lips and nipples that were cast in ancient Greece. The pair were recovered in 1972 from a shipwreck off the coast of Riace, Italy, and are held now in the Museo Nazionale della Magna Grecia in Reggio Calabria.

While the technological effectiveness of SETI has increased by over a trillion times in the past forty years, only modest progress has been made in developing messages that would be intelligible to other species. Many SETI researchers believe that response to such contact, long anticipated by science fictionists, is too important to leave to chance. While contending with the cosmic silence, they are considering how best to respond should E.T. phone.

The *Pioneer* figures draw on a long artistic tradition in which physical perfection is a metaphor for the possession of a host of less tangible, highly

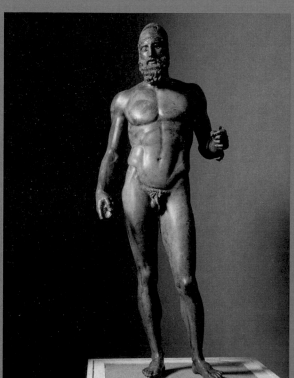

Interstellar messages—even though intangible, inaudible, and invisible to us—may be much more solid monuments to the human condition than fragile artifacts made of mere stone and cement. Once sent to the stars, traversing the silence of space, our messages become impervious to the vicissitudes of human actions on Earth.

—Douglas Vakoch, SETI Institute, August 2, 2003

desirable virtues. In Western art, this idea is exemplified by masterworks such as the two Greek males known as the Riace Bronzes, which are sensuously muscled to lustrous perfection and authority. The archetypal ideal formulated by the ancient Greeks continues to determine how men and women are depicted in monumental portraiture. "Beauty brings copies of itself into being," as Elaine Scarry writes in *On Beauty*. A glance at any newsstand will confirm that the equation of physical beauty with superior intellect, wealth, and morals still holds.

Large-scale searches for extraterrestrial intelligence (SETI) are under way at several locations worldwide. Scientists at the California-based SETI Institute, which conducts the world's most sensitive search for radio signals from extraterrestrials, have been listening for other civilizations rather than attempting to send messages. Listening, far less expensive than transmitting, is logical, since, cosmically speaking, our civilization is still in our "terrestrial twos." The assumption is that older planetary species are more capable of transmission.

In this context, SETI Institute scientists are drafting messages that present a portrait of humanity that differs from those of the past. Dr. Douglas Vakoch, the SETI Institute's Director of Interstellar Message Composition, is studying how Earth's reply messages can more fully express what it's like to be human. In collaboration with scholars globally, Vakoch is developing messages that define us as being far more than a head, two arms, and two legs. What defines our humanity, according to many biologists and humanists, is our capacity for altruism.

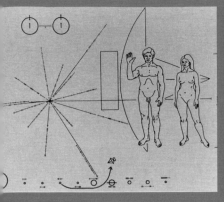

Although altruism is a somewhat arbitrary starting point for stating the breadth of human experience, it is a logical one. It is a concept understood across cultures, and can be expressed in mathematical language. Given the formidable technology needed to communicate over vast distances, SETI Institute founder Frank Drake believes that such messages could be transmitted only by organized civilizations with a complex technological infrastructure. Since optimistic estimates place the nearest space civilization some thousand light-years away, establishing that infrastructure would require altruism greater than the simple evolutionary self-interest described by Darwin. It would require that trait's higher manifestation: the willingness to set aside individual desires in favor of the whole and the motivation to construct ever more complex technology for society's benefit.

Only an altruistic society would attempt interstellar communication, and would do so with the realization that their transmissions to distant others may provide no benefit to themselves. As Drake as written, "Any signal we discover will not only reveal the existence of an altruistic civilization, it will be altruism's direct result."

According to Vakoch, the notion of altruism can be expressed and transmitted readily in Lincos, short for Lingua Cosmica, a mathematical language developed in 1960, some of which was used to formulate previous deep space messages. Using a series of simple signals, Lincos can express complex concepts of time and space. Vakoch has devised three-dimensional animated images of human interaction that can be viewed from any angle to increase their legibility to aliens. He views these messages as "interstellar morality plays, in which aliens would come to understand the meaning of our spiritual principles by seeing them acted out."

One of Vakoch's images shows a human figure holding another to represent "support and caring." Though this particular image will not be transmitted, it is intended to encourage discussion of what sorts of messages might be. If they were sent, writes Vakoch, "one approach would be to describe the individual points in each frame of an animation sequence as vectors, by using, for example, Lincos or a related language as the basic mathematical language." Because no one is sure which, if any, formats would be understood by extraterrestrials, identical messages in multiple formats could be sent.

Two immediate questions arise. Can we convince extraterrestrials of our higher nature? After all, fifty years of television and radio transmissions sent out at the speed of light have revealed our wars and scandals, not to mention reruns of *Gilligan's Island*. And is it possible to communicate anything more than our intention to communicate? Even on earth, a picture's meaning changes from culture toculture. The dazzling circles, squiggles, and dots of an Australian Aboriginal Dreamtime painting, for example, are read as cosmological maps of the lands peopled by ancestral spirits—if you're an Aborigine. To others, it's great abstract art.

While it may be optimistic to expect an extraterrestrial message any time soon, or presume too much about the decoding abilities of our potential addressees, speculation on what could be said fosters greater understanding of the issues that have underscored the creation of more earthbound monuments since the first stone was put on stone. It is valuable to contemplate the expansiveness of the human spirit and to consider too that the barriers that separate us will seem inconsequential, if not evaporate entirely, should extraterrestrials arrive.

Interstellar messages draw their power from the recognition of the eternal bonds that exist between human beings by simple virtue of our fundamental shared reality: We are born, we love, and we die. The past can be re-created only in imagination and memory. The future, similarly intangible and unknowable, rides on a limitless tide of speculation and hope—though it never quite manages to look like our dreams of it when it arrives. Whether commemorated in monument or in mind, both past and future intersect in the present, the only moment, ultimately, that we can claim as our own. Life's hour is always now.

Left Both the *Pioneer 10* and *11* spacecraft, launched into deep space in 1972 and 1973, carried a gold-anodized aluminum plaque attached to the spacecraft's antenna support struts that indicated what we look like, our location, and the date when the mission began.

Acknowledgments

Steve Miller, *Calla Lily,* from the *X-Ray Flowers* portfolio (2002), iris print on paper.

Monuments unfolded over a six-year period. From the start, after proposing this book on September 10, 2001, the book made it clear to me that it had its own time frame. At first, I labored slowly in the foggy ethers of the dead, shouldering what seemed an unbearable weight of sadness and feeling inadequate to the task of finding words that could honor the memory of several million souls.

Then, in February 2003, came a turning point. In the snowy woods of the MacDowell Colony in Peterborough, New Hampshire, in the glad company of many gifted artists, I realized that *Monuments* was not about death but about life. There, I put aside my writing one day and borrowed a spade to dig a grave, needing to physically experience my thoughts. The snow, which was hard enough to bear my weight, allowed me to choose a spot deep in the evergreens. I cut into it with lapidary precision, meticulously measuring and digging out a 3 x 6-foot block, about 4 feet deep. Completed, it looked like a perfect small swimming pool.

Afterward, I sat on the edge, legs dangling into the hole, unexpectedly at peace. Subsequently, I learned that I had by chance assigned to the sepulcher the same measurementas the space typically alloted to a prisoner at Auschwitz, where I later traveled to understand the horrific legacy of World War II borne by many Americans. Ultimately, what I remember best from that day-long excavation is the image of an evergreen branch that I threw into the snowy pit at the last moment to relieve its bleakness. Life continues.

A number of architects, artists, conservators, and historians graciously agreed to interviews, and my text has been enriched exponentially by their insights into the process of planning, executing, and maintaining monumental works. They include Thomas Antenen, New York City Department of Correction; Michael Arad; John E. Benson; Nicholas Benson, John Stevens Shop; Richard Benson; Meredith Bergmann; Hans and Torrey Butzer, Butzer Design Partnership; Michael G. Conley, American Battle Monuments Commission; Bernard Cywinski, Bohlin Cywinski Jackson; Paul DiPasquale; John A. Doerner, Little Bighorn Battlefield National Monument; Sarah Shields Driggs; Captain Eliza N. Garfield, AMISTAD America; Romaldo Giurgola; Mark G. Griffin, Esq.; Hugh Hardy; Daniel Libeskind; Thomas Luebke, U.S. Commission of Fine Arts; Cesar Pelli; Julie Rhoad, NAMES Project Foundation; Diane Samuels; Judith Shea; Robert Shemwell, Overland Partners Architects; Friedrich St. Florian; Barry Strauss; Jane Thomas and Kari F. Watkins, Oklahoma City National Memorial; Brian Tolle; Douglas Vakoch, SETI Institute; Peter Waddell; and Meg Winslow, Mount Auburn Cemetery.

I am grateful to the MacDowell Colony as well as the New York Foundation for the Arts, the New York State Council on the Arts, and the Garrison Art Center for their support.

I am indebted to the many photographers whose work graces this book. In particular, I thank Karen Ostrom, Roger Straus, Ann Kilbourne, and Lee Sandstead, for the gift of their artistry, collaboration, and friendship.

To Ted Goodman, colleague and friend, thank you for your diligent research and perennial good cheer. My agent, Alice Martell, collects, among other rarities, scarab beetles, which the Egyptians considered symbols of regeneration and new life. Now I know why. Thank you, Alice, for your steadfastness in seeing this book to completion.

Ten years ago I had the good fortune to collaborate with the designer Allison Russo. Time and motherhood have only deepened the rare and happy alchemy that we share, which is reflected in Allison's elegant and lively design. Thank you, Allison, for loving books as much as I do.

Random House's thoughtful editorial assistance and expert production assistance, apparent on every page, was provided by Dana Isaacson, Lea Beresford, Julia Cheiffitz, Stacy Rockwood-Chen, Richard Elman, Carole Lowenstein, Lisa Feuer, Benjamin Dreyer, Emily DeHuff, and Vincent La Scala. Gina Centrello, who has made Random House an extraordinary home for writers, has my admiration and gratitude. To Nancy Miller, best of editors, thank you for your friendship, generosity, meticulous eye, and unwavering belief that Jesse's enthusiasm would be shared by many.

The joyful and compassionate presence of my friends and colleagues at Yale Divinity School and Yale Institute of Sacred Music is an ongoing inspiration. A.M.D.G. My friends Elizabeth Abbott, Leslie Cecil, Regina Clarkin O'Leary, Linda Figg, Laurie Foos, Cathy Hemming, Danette Koke, Mary Lazin, Lily Prigioniero, and Dale Wilhelm, are the wellspring of my life. For a hundred reasons of the heart, thank you.

To my family, the spirited Duprés and Wilsons, and especially my sisters, Cynthia, Susan, and Lisa, thank you for your love, laughter, and abiding delight in a good story well told. My lovable sons, Brendan and Emmet, weathered *Monuments*'s long season with grace, and remind me daily that memory is stronger than death, and love is stronger than both.

Many others vetted these pages, offered hospitality, and shared their wisdom, professional expertise, and photographs, all of which allowed me to realize a small piece of a large subject. Thank you all:

Terry Adams, National Park Service; Nina Akamu; Erik Amkoff; Gretchen Bank; Mary Banks; Steven McLeod Bedford; Achim Bednorz; Jonathan Berger; Dianne Bilyak; Ken and Cara Blazier; Sophie Body-Gendrot; Lance Jay Brown; Kate Brubacher; David Brussat; Sarah Taft Carter; Anthony Catarella; Claire Lennon Clayton; Joy Collins, AMISTAD America; Michael Conner, Bohlin Cywinski Jackson; Michael J. Crosbie; Colleen Cutschall; Jeanmaire Dani; Greg Daugherty; Jacqueline Decter and Vadim Strukov; the Dionne family; the Donilon family; Michael Elmgreen and Ingar Dragset; Ann Farrington; David Finn; Fraenkel Gallery, San Francisco; Lee Friedlander; Noriko Fujinami, Robert Graham Studio; Wayne Furman, New York Public Library; Roger Gentile; Ralph Granata; Michael Graves; Bernice Green; Joan Grott and the staff of the Mamaroneck Public Library; Barbara Hall; Frances Halsband; James and Juhee Lee Hartford; John Henley; Peter Himler; Historic American Buildings Survey and the Historic American Engineering Record; Robin Holland; Ann Hunt and Laurie Ozelius; Tim Hursley; Michelle Ianarelli; Stu Jenks; Nan Jernigan and Ted Danforth; Miriam Kadar; Scott Kale and William Gaske; Barbara Kasten; Marylin Kingston; Cesia and Morrie Kingston; Keith and Susan Kroeger; Eleanor Krolian; Laura Kurgan; Rodney Leon, AARRIS Architects; Meg Lindsay; Rollin La France; Jeffrey Laner, Henry Davis, Sidney Druckman, Battery Park City Authority; Edward Linenthal; Robert and Paula Loffredo; Stephen Lorenzetti and Robert J. Karotko, National Park Service; Beth Griffin Matthews; Polyxeni Mastroperrou; Maureen McClave; Ellen McCloskey; Ann Breen Metcalfe; Dara Meyers-Kingsley; Steve Miller; Carolann Morrissey; Margaret Morton; Dean Motter; Overland Partners Architects; Dong-il Pak; Thomas Palmer; Jennifer Pierson; Steven Pierson; Gigi Price, National Park Service; Martha Raney; Richard Rhodes, Rhodes Architectural Stone; Jonathan F.P. Rose; Frank J. Scaturro, Grant Monument Association; Paul G. Seldes; Pete Shaver; Lisa Grischy Shelton; Molly Shields; Pamela and Mike Smith; Whitman D. Smith; Eileen Smyth; Will Spence; Bruce Springsteen; Roy Spungin; William Stanley and Ivenue Love-Stanley; Louise Scott Steele; Steven and Diana Steinman; Erica Stoller; Hudson Talbott; TATS CRU; Audrey T. Tepper, National Park Service, Technical Preservation Services Branch; Alina Tugend and Mark Stein; Tom Tugend; Wojtek Wacowski; Joy Caruolo Welshman and the Caruolo family; Richard Whelan, International Center of Photography; Alice Wingwall and Donlyn Lyndon; Carol Pezzelli Wise; Ben Wurtmann; and Jo-Ann C. Yozura.

Bibliography

To make the text as accessible as possible, references within the essays are limited to very specific citations. The bibliography acknowledges my many intellectual debts and provides a reading list for those who would like to explore the monuments in further detail. Every effort was made to provide accurate information; to this end, whenever possible, an essay about a given monument has been read for factual accuracy by those entrusted with its legacy and maintenance.

General Reference

Burrell, Brian. *The Words We Live By: The Creeds, Mottoes, and Pledges That Have Shaped America.* New York: Free Press, 1997.

Choay, Françoise. *The Invention of the Historic Monument.* New York: Cambridge University Press, 2001.

"Constructions of Memory." *The Harvard Design Magazine,* Fall 1999, no. 9, whole issue.

"Crowding the Mall: On the National Memorial Dilemma." *The Harvard Design Magazine,* Fall 1999, no. 9, 32–37.

Flanner, Janet. *Men and Monuments.* Essay Index Reprint Series. Freeport, NY: Books for Libraries Press, 1970.

Friedlander, Lee. *The American Monument.* New York: Eakins, 1976.

Galison, Peter Louis. *Einstein's Clocks and Poincaré's Maps: Empires of Time.* New York: W. W. Norton, 2003.

Gayle, Margot, Michele Cohen, Art Commission of the City of New York, and Municipal Art Society of New York. *The Art Commission and the Municipal Art Society Guide to Manhattan's Outdoor Sculpture.* New York: Prentice Hall Press, 1988.

Goode, James M. *The Outdoor Sculpture of Washington, D.C.: A Comprehensive Historical Guide.* Washington, D.C.: Smithsonian Institution Press, distributed by G. Braziller, 1974.

Jackson, J. B. *The Necessity for Ruins, and Other Topics.* Amherst: University of Massachusetts Press, 1980.

Linenthal, Edward Tabor. *Sacred Ground: Americans and Their Battlefields.* Chicago: University of Illinois, 1991.

Miller, Sara Cedar, and Central Park Conservancy. *Central Park, An American Masterpiece: A Comprehensive History of the Nation's First Urban Park.* New York: Harry N. Abrams, 2003.

Ockman, Joan, and Temple Hoyne Buell Center for the Study of American Architecture. *Out of Ground Zero: Case Studies in Urban Reinvention.* New York: Temple Hoyne Buell Center for the Study of American Architecture, Columbia University; Munich: Prestel, 2002.

Petruccioli, Attilio, ed. "Water and Architecture." *Environmental Design: Journal of the Islamic Environmental Design Research Centre.* 1985, no. 2, whole issue. http://archnet.org/library/documents/onedocument.tcl?document_id=6312 (May 2, 2004).

Placzek, Adolf K., ed. *Macmillan Encyclopedia of Architects.* New York: Free Press; London: Collier Macmillan, 1982.

Platt, Richard. *Smithsonian Visual Timeline of Inventions.* New York: Dorling Kindersley, 1994.

Reynolds, Donald M. *Monuments and Masterpieces: Histories and Views of Public Sculpture in New York City.* New York: Thames and Hudson, 1997.

Rieth, Adolf. *Monuments to the Victims of Tyranny.* New York: Frederick A. Praeger, 1969.

Turner, Jane, ed. *The Dictionary of Art.* New York: Grove's Dictionaries, 1996.

Withey, Henry F. *Biographical Dictionary of American Architects.* Detroit: Omnigraphics, 1994.

Yarwood, Doreen, and Suhail Butt. *International Dictionary of Architects and Architecture.* Detroit: St. James Press, 1993.

Yates, Frances Amelia. *The Art of Memory.* Chicago: University of Chicago Press, 1966.

Foreword

Author interview with Daniel Libeskind on June 17, 2003.

Harrison, Robert Pogue. *The Dominion of the Dead.* Chicago: University of Chicago Press, 2003.

Haub, Carl. "How Many People Have Ever Lived on Earth?" *Population Today,* November/December 2002, vol. 30, no. 8, 3–4.

Lake, Matt. "An Art Form That's Precise But Friendly Enough to Wink." *New York Times,* May 20, 1999, G.11.

Rosenblatt, Roger. "How We Remember." *Time,* 155, no. 22 (2000), 26–30.

Rugoff, Ralph. *Monuments for the USA.* San Francisco: California College of the Arts, Wattis Institute for Contemporary Arts, 2005.

Russell, James S. "Crowding the Mall: On the National Memorial Dilemma." *Harvard Design Magazine,* Fall 1999, 32–37.

The Evolving Monument

Author interview with Cesar Pelli on May 16, 2003.

Author correspondence with Judith Shea, March–April 2004.

Albrecht, Donald. "Remembering Women." *Architecture,* February 1998, vol. 87, no. 2, 90–97.

American Public Transportation Association. "National Transit Tribute to Rosa Parks Day." http://apta.com/rosa/ (December 5, 2005).

"A Permanent Arch; The St. Nicholas Club Subscribes $1,000 Toward That Object." *New York Times,* May 4, 1889, 5.

"Art Gossip." *Brooklyn Eagle,* July 23, 1899, 19.

Bergmann, Meredith. *American Arts Quarterly,* Summer 2005, vol. 22, no. 3, 24–29.

Dibner, Bern. *Moving the Obelisks: A Chapter in Engineering History in Which the Vatican Obelisk in Rome in 1586 Was Moved by Muscle Power, and a Study of More Recent Similar Moves.* Cambridge, Mass.: M.I.T. Press, 1970.

Elsen, Albert E. *Rodin.* New York: The Museum of Modern Art and Doubleday & Co., 1963.

Forgey, Benjamin. "A Memorial Passes Muster." *Washington Post,* October 18, 1997, C1.

"Gallery and Studio, The MacMonnies Quadriga for the Memorial Arch." *Brooklyn Eagle,* August 21, 1898, 22.

Kelly, Tom, and Mercedes Padilla. "MTA Honors Memory of Rosa Parks." Press release. Metropolitan Transit Authority, State of New York, November 30, 2005.

Mumford, Lewis. *The Culture of Cities.* New York: Harcourt Brace and Company, 1938.

"New Groups by MacMonnies." *New York Times,* February 12, 1899, IMS2.

Phillips, Claude. "Auguste Rodin." *Magazine of Art,* March 1888, vol. 11, no. 26, 138–144.

Ramsden, E. H. "Burghers of Calais: A New Interpretation." *Apollo,* NS, no. 91, 235–37.

Richman, Michael. *Daniel Chester French: An American Sculptor.* New York: The Metropolitan Museum of Art, 1976; reprint, Washington, D.C.: Preservation Press, 1983, 39–40.

Senie, Harriet F. "A Difference in Kind: Spontaneous Memorials after 9/11." *Sculpture,* July/August 2003, vol. 22, no. 6, x.

"Vietnam Veterans Memorial Visitor Center Authorization" (Public Law 108–126), United States Statues at Large, November 17, 2003, 1349.

"The Washington Memorial Arch." *Century Illustrated,* August 1889, vol. 38, no. 4, 635.

"The Washington Arch of New York." *Scientific American,* July 6, 1889 , vol. 61, no. 1, 8.

The Liberty Bell

Author interview with Bernard Cywinski, Bohlin Cywinski Jackson, March 22, 2006.

Corbin, Alain. *Village Bells: Sound and Meaning in the 19th-Century French Countryside.* New York: Columbia University Press, 1998.

Davis, Allen F. "Liberty Bell Center." *The Journal of American History,* December 2004, vol. 91, no. 3, 963–66.

Hampton, Tudor. "Park Service Preps Liberty Bell for Relocation in September." *Engineering News-Record.* April 14, 2003, vol. 250, no. 14, 17.

Infield, Tom. "Liberty Bell Replica Dedicated in Town near Normandy." Knight Ridder Tribune News Service, June 7, 2004, 1.

Kashatus, William C. "Liberty Meets Slavery in Philadelphia." *American History,* October 2002, vol. 37, no. 4, 8.

Klein, Julia M. "Letting Freedom Ring True." *Preservation: The Magazine of the National Trust for Historic Preservation,* September/October 2003, vol. 55, no. 5, 16–17.

Lopez, Michael. "Silent Bell, Loud Voices Won Women the Right to Vote." *Times Union,* February 14, 1999, A3.

Meneely, Clinton. "The Musical Quality of Bell Tones." Paper presented at Schenectady, N.Y., to the American Mechanical and Electrical Engineers societies. February 28, 1935.

Olin, Laurie. "Giving Form to a Creation Story—The Remaking of Independence Mall." *Places,* vol. 13, no. 3, 52–59.

Raphael, Michael. "Re-creating Historical Artifacts: First Digital Copy of the Liberty Bell Allows for Exact Reproduction." Press release. Direct Dimensions, June 9, 2005.

Saffron, Inga. "Part of Cityscape? Only in Its View." *Philadelphia Inquirer,* October 9, 2003, A1.

Salisbury, Stephan. "Past Imperfect Comes Alive For 'We The People'—All Of Them." *Philadelphia Inquirer,* October 14, 2005, B1.

Schaffer, Michael D. "Bell's Crack Arrived Early, Iconic Status Came Later." *Philadelphia Inquirer,* October 5, 2003, A15.

"Suffrage Liberty Bell." *New York Times,* March 31, 1915, 6.

Turner, Rob. "Independent View: A New Home for the Liberty Bell Cuts Modern Intrusions out of the Historic Picture." *Metropolis,* November 2003, vol. 23, no. 3, 64.

Mount Auburn Cemetery

Bigelow, Jacob. *A History of the Cemetery of Mount Auburn.* Boston: James Munroe and Company, 1860.

Heywood, Janet, and Cathleen, Lambert Breitkreutz. "Mount Auburn Cemetery: A New American Landscape." http://www.cr.nps.gov/nr/twhp/wwwlps/lessons/84mount auburn/84mountauburn.htm (August 2, 2005).

Jackson, Kenneth T., and Camilo J. Vergara. *Silent Cities: The Evolution of the American Cemetery.* New York: Princeton Architectural Press, 1989.

Johnson, Thomas H., ed. *Emily Dickinson: Selected Letters.* Cambridge, Mass.: The Belknap Press, 1985.

Linden-Ward, Blanche. *Silent City on a Hill: Landscapes of Memory and Boston's Mount Auburn Cemetery.* Columbus: Ohio State University Press, 1989.

Murphy, Katherine, and Kristen Rohde. "'This Embellishment of Nature': The 19th Century Picturesque Landscape, Worcester's Rural Cemetery." http://college.holycross.edu/projects/worcester/growth/ landscape.htm (August 2, 2005).

"Official Website of Mount Auburn Cemetery." http://www.mountauburn.org (August 2, 2005).

Orr, J. Robert. "Tomb with a View: Mount Auburn, Oak Hill and the Rise of Rural Landscape Cemeteries in America." *Smithsonian Preservation Quarterly,* Summer/Fall 1995.

Story, Joseph. "An Address Delivered on the Dedication of the Cemetery at Mount Auburn, September 24, 1831." Boston: Joseph T. & Edwin Buckingham, 1831.

The Alamo

Author correspondence with Alice Wingwall, December 2005–January 2006.

Davis, William C. *Three Roads to the Alamo: The Lives and Fortunes of David Crockett, James Bowie, and William Barret Travis.* New York: HarperCollins Publishers, 1998.

Garner, John C., Jr., "Mission San Antonio de Valero, Convent, Alamo Plaza, San Antonio, Bexar County, TX." Historic American Building Survey HABS TX-318-B. Washington, D.C.: National Park Service, U.S. Department of the Interior, 1968.

Gould, Stephen Jay. "Jim Bowie's Letter & Bill Buckner's Legs: Analysis of Events at the Alamo Siege, 1836." *Natural History,* May 2000, vol. 109, no. 4, 26–40.

Harrigan, Stephen. "My Own Private Alamo." *Texas Monthly,* March 2000, vol. 28, no. 3, 100ff.

Nelson, George. *The Alamo: An Illustrated History.* Dry Frio Canyon, Tex.: Aldine Press, 1998.

"San Antonio Missions: A Historical Guidebook to the Missions of San Antonio." Catalogue. San Marcos, Tex.: Southwest Texas State University, 2000.

Thompson, Frank T. *The Alamo: A Cultural History.* Dallas, Tex.: Taylor Publishing, 2001.

Thompson, Frank T. *Alamo Movies.* Burbank, Calif.: Old Mill Books, 1991.

Winders, Richard B. *Sacrificed at the Alamo: Tragedy and Triumph in the Texas Revolution.* Abilene, Tex.: State House Press, 2004.

Freedom Schooner *Amistad*

Voluminous documents relating to the *Amistad* are available online. The Mystic Seaport Library contains more than five hundred primary documents including court records, journal entries, and newspaper stories that can be viewed in the original print or handwriting and in transcription.

Adams, John Quincy. "Argument before the Supreme Court of the United States in the Case of the United States, Appellants, vs. Cinque and Other Africans Captured in the Schooner Amistad" (delivered February 24 and March 1, 1841). New York: W. W. Benedict, 1841.

Brecher, Jeremy. "The Amistad Incident." *Amistad America.* http://www.amistadamerica.org/index.cfm?fuseaction=ho me.viewpage&page_id=98921E0B-F174-016C-D15314B1F5FC2A97 (April 10, 2005).

Day, George E. "Narrative of the Africans." *New York Journal of Commerce,* October 10, 1839.

Jones, Howard. *Mutiny on the Amistad: The Saga of a Slave Revolt and Its Impact on American Abolition, Law and Diplomacy.* New York: Oxford University Press, 1987.

Mystic Seaport, The Museum of America and the Sea. "Exploring Amistad: Race and the Boundaries of Freedom in Antebellum Maritime America." http://amistad.mysticseaport.org/main/welcome.html (August 2, 2005).

Smithsonian Archives of American Art. "Oral History Interview with Hale Woodruff and Al Murray, November 18, 1968." http://www.aaa.si.edu/collections/oralhistories/ transcripts/woodru68.htm (April 2004).

Spielberg, Steven. *Amistad* (DVD). DreamWorks, 1997.

Gettysburg National Military Park

Author correspondence with Dion Neutra, June 2003.

"A Problem of Common Ground." Washington, D.C., Advisory Council on Historic Preservation Advisory Council statement, May 10, 1999.

Blight, David W. *Race and Reunion: The Civil War in American Memory.* Cambridge, Mass.: Belknap Press of Harvard University Press, 2001.

"Brady's Photographs." *New York Times,* October 20, 1862, 5.

Burns, Ken. *The Civil War: A Film by Ken Burns.* (VHS). 1990.

Craven, Wayne, and Milo Stewart. *The Sculptures at Gettysburg.* New York: Eastern Acorn Press, 1982.

Davis, Keith F. "A Terrible Distinctness." *Photography in Nineteenth-Century America.* Fort Worth, Tex., and New York: Amon Carter Museum; H. N. Abrams, 1991.

Desjardin, Thomas A. *These Honored Dead: How the Story of Gettysburg Shaped American Memory.* Cambridge, Mass.: Da Capo Press, 2003.

Foote, Shelby. *The Civil War: A Narrative.* New York: Random House, 1963.

Frassanito, William A. *Gettysburg: A Journey in Time.* New York: Scribner, 1974.

"Gettysburg; The Proposed Meeting of the Federal and Confederate Generals." *New York Times,* July 31, 1869, 2.

Hawthorne, Frederick H. *Gettysburg: Stories of Men and Monuments as Told by Battlefield Guides.* Gettysburg, Pa.: Association of Licensed Battlefield Guides, 1988.

Henry, Patty. "19 New Historic Landmarks Considered for Designation." *National Historic Landmarks Network,* Winter 1999, vol. II, no. 2, 1.

Hine, Thomas. "Which of All the Pasts to Preserve?" *New York Times,* February 21, 1999, 48.

Holzer, Harold, and Mark E. Neely, Jr. "The Gettysburg Cyclorama." *American History,* 2003 Supplement, 54.

Horwitz, Tony. *Confederates in the Attic: Dispatches from the Unfinished Civil War.* New York: Pantheon Books, 1998.

Howe, Ward Allan. "A Date to Recall." *New York Times,* June 9, 1963, 451.

Huyck, Dorothy B. "Gettysburg's Gain." *New York Times,* May 6, 1962, 411.

Letter to Fran Mainella, Director of the National Park Service, from Richard Longstreth, Society of Architectural Historians, regarding the appeal of the National Historic Landmark Ruling by the National Parks Advisory Board on the Cyclorama Building, Gettysburg National Military Park, February 24, 2004.

McPherson, James M. *Hallowed Ground: A Walk at Gettysburg.* New York: Crown Journeys, 2003.

"Our Gettysburg Correspondence." *New York Times,* July 15, 1863, 2.

Slaiby, Barbara E., and Nora J. Mitchell. *A Handbook for Managers of Cultural Landscapes with Natural Resource Values.* Woodstock, Vt.: Conservation Study Institute, 2003.

Warren, Robert Penn. *The Legacy of the Civil War: Meditations on the Centennial.* New York: Random House, 1961.

Weeks, Jim. *Gettysburg: Memory, Market, and an American Shrine.* Princeton, N.J.: Princeton University Press, 2003.

Wills, Garry. *Lincoln at Gettysburg: The Words That Remade America.* New York: Simon & Schuster, 1992.

Hart Island

Author interview with Thomas Antenen, Deputy Commissioner, New York City Department of Correction, on Hart Island, October 8, 2003; author correspondence with T. Antenen, September–November 2003.

Baldwin, Hanson W. "First 2 Nike Nests Almost Ready In Supersonic City Defense Ring." *New York Times,* January 7, 1955, 9.

"City Reformatory on Hart's Island Is Affected by Harlem Colored Amusement Park Site." *Bronx Home News,* June 4, 1925, 17.

Corn, Leslie. "New York City's Potter's Field: A Visit to Hart Island's City Cemetery in Bronx County." *New York Genealogical and Biographical Society Newsletter,* Summer 2000.

Ellison, Michael. "Only the Lonely." *The Guardian,* June 5, 1999, T24.

Grossfeld, Stan. "They Never Had A Chance." *Boston Globe,* December 29, 1994, A6.

Horwitz, Tony. "Necropolitan Diary: New York's City of Unclaimed Dead." *Wall Street Journal,* August 26, 1998, A1.

Hunt, Melinda, and Joel Sternfeld. *Hart Island.* Zurich: Scalo, 1998.

"Purchase of Hart's Island." *New York Times,* February 27, 1869, 8.

Santora, Marc. "An Island of the Dead Fascinates the Living." *New York Times,* January 27, 2003, B5.

Seitz, Sharon, and Stuart Miller. *The Other Islands of New York City: A Historical Companion.* New York: W.W. Norton, 1996.

Vanderbilt, Tom. "When Nike Meant More Than 'Just Do It'." *New York Times,* March 5, 2000, C14.

Little Bighorn Battlefield National Monument

Author correspondence with Colleen Cutschall, memorial sculptor, December 2005. Interview of John A. Doerner, Chief Historian, Little Bighorn Battlefield National Memorial, by Ann Kilbourne. June 2005.

Ambrose, Stephen E. *Crazy Horse and Custer: The Parallel Lives of Two American Warriors.* Garden City, N.Y.: Doubleday, 1975.

Collins, John R., and Alison J. Towers. Indian Memorial Competition Design Statement. October 1996.

Cutschall, Colleen. *Little Bighorn Aboriginal Monument.* http://www.sisterwolf.com/sculpture/index.html. August 1, 2005.

Doerner, John A. "So That the Place Might Be Remembered." *Research Review: The Journal of the Little Big Horn Associates,* vol. 14, no 2 (2000).

Ethier, Eric. "Custer: How Today's Historians Rate Him." *American History,* vol. 32, no. 5 (1997), 22.

Fox, Richard Allan, Jr. *Archaeology, History, and Custer's Last Battle.* Norman and London: University of Oklahoma Press, 1993.

Harjo, Suzan Shown. "Indian Country Today." *Knight Ridder/Tribune Business News.* June 29, 2003.

"Indian Memorial Dedication Officially Scheduled for June 25, 2003." News release. National Park Service, U.S. Department of the Interior. October 3, 2002.

"Little Bighorn Battlefield." Pamphlet. National Park Service, U.S. Department of the Interior. 2002.

"Memorial Dedication Ceremonies June 25, 2003." Press release. Department of the Interior, National Park Service, Little Bighorn Battlefield National Monument. April 24, 2003.

National Park Service. "Strategic Plan, Little Bighorn Battlefield National Monument, October 1, 2001–September 30, 2005." http://www.nps.gov/libi/pphtml/documents.html (June 22, 2005).

"Peace Through Unity." Indian Memorial Dedication program, National Park Service, Little Bighorn Battlefield National Monument. June 25, 2003.

"Peace Through Unity: The Indian Memorial at Little Bighorn Battlefield National Monument." Pamphlet. Tucson, Ariz.: Western National Parks Association, 2003.

Perrottet, Tony. "Little Bighorn Reborn." *Smithsonian,* vol. 36, no. 1 (2005), 90.

Solnit, Rebecca. "The Struggle of Dawning Intelligence: On Monuments and Native Americans." *Harvard Design Magazine, Harvard University Graduate School of Design,* Fall 1999, 54–56.

Utley, Robert M. Statement "Before the Subcommittee on National Parks and Public Lands," Committee on Interior and Insular Affairs, House of Representatives, on H.R. 847, H.R. 848, and H.R. 770, Relating to Custer Battlefield National Monument, Montana, April 23, 1991.

Utley, Robert M. *The Lance and the Shield: The Life and Times of Sitting Bull.* New York: Henry Holt and Company, 1993.

Viola, Herman J. *Little Bighorn Remembered: The Untold Indian Story of Custer's Last Stand.* New York: Times Books, 1999.

"Visual Artist Designs Sculpture for National U.S. Monument." Press release. Brandon University, Brandon, Manitoba, Canada. November 19, 2002.

Welch, James, and Paul Stekler. *Killing Custer.* New York: W. W. Norton, 1994.

———. *Killing Custer.* New York: Penguin Books, 1995.

Washington Monument

Allen, Thomas B. *The Washington Monument: It Stands for All.* New York: Discovery Books, 2000.

Board of Managers, Washington National Monument Society. Resolution of 6 July 1836. Records of the Washington National Monument Society, Records of the Office of Public Buildings and Grounds, Record Group

42, National Archives; Society and Congressional Publications Concerning the Monument and Society, Box 33, RG 42, NA: Harvey, 25–26.

Bryan, John M. *Robert Mills: America's First Architect.* New York: Princeton Architectural Press, 2001.

"The Completion of the Washington Monument." *The Manufacturer and Builder,* March 1885, vol. 17, no. 3, 66.

Duffus, R. L. "Shaft Symbolic of the Nation's March." *New York Times,* February 17, 1935, SM4.

Forgey, Benjamin. "The Monument's New Winter Coat; Temporary Transformation of Obelisk Is Quite a Treat." *Washington Post,* January 23, 1999, C1.

Gallagher, H. M. Pierce. *Robert Mills: Architect of the Washington Monument, 1781–1855.* New York: Columbia University Press, 1935.

Goldberger, Paul. "Postmodern Pillar." *New Yorker,* October 4, 1999: 81.

Jacob, Judith M. "Conservation Treatments for the Washington Monument Commemorative Stones." *Cultural Resource Management,* 1999, v. 22, n. 7, 16-18.

Kamin, Blair. "Elegant Scaffolding on Washington Monument Captivates Capital City." *Chicago Tribune,* July 4, 1999, 1.

"Marking a People's Love, Dedication of the Washington Monument." *New York Times,* February 22, 1885, 3.

"A Monumental Task." *News Hour with Jim Lehrer,* March 2, 1999, transcript.

National Park Service. "Washington Monument Scaffold Concept Announced." Press release, October 17, 1997.

"Setting the Capstone." *New York Times,* December 7, 1884, 7.

"The Tallest in the World." *New York Times,* July 28, 1884, 8.

Torres, Louis. *The United States Army Corps of Engineers and the Construction of the Washington Monument.* Honolulu: University Press of the Pacific, 2001.

"The Washington Monument." *New York Times,* February 22, 1885, 6.

"The Washington Monument." *New York Times,* October 6, 1888, 5.

"The Washington Monument and Mr. Story's Design." *Atlantic Monthly,* April 1879, vol. 43, no. 258, 524–527.

Yardley, Jonathan. "On the Mall, Entrenched Thinking." *Washington Post,* May 6, 2002, C2.

Statue of Liberty

Bartholdi, Frédéric-Auguste. "The Statue of Liberty Enlightening the World." *North American Review,* 1885.

"Bartholdi's Statue of Liberty." *American Architect and Building News,* 1883, vol. 14, 126, 137, 284.

Burns, Ken. *Statue of Liberty* (DVD). Florentine Films Production, 1985.

Fisher, Thomas. "Liberty Update." *Progressive Architecture,* March 1985, vol. 66, no. 3, 95–99.

"France to America." *Scribner's Monthly,* June 1877, vol. 14, no. 2, 129–136.

"France's Gift Accepted." *New York Times,* October 29, 1886, 1.

"The Inauguration of the Statue of Liberty." *Scientific American,* November 6, 1886, no. 19, 288.

Levine, Benjamin, and Isabelle F. Story. *Statue of Liberty National Monument,* Bedloe's Island, New York. Washington, D.C.: *National Park Service Historical Handbook,* no. 11, 1954.

McIntire, Mike. "Visitors Can Go Underfoot, but Not to Liberty's Crown." *New York Times,* August 3, 2004, B4.

Moreno, Barry. *The Statue of Liberty Encyclopedia.* New York: Simon & Schuster, 2000.

Rawls, Walton H. *Wake Up, America! World War I and the American Poster.* New York: Abbeville Press, 1988.

Shapiro, Mary J., and Huck Scarry. *How They Built the Statue of Liberty.* New York: Random House, 1985.

"Statue of Liberty." National Park Service. http://www.nps.gov/stli/ (November 2, 2005).

"The Statue Unveiled." *New York Times,* Oct. 29, 1886, 2.

"The Statue of 'Liberty'" *Harper's Weekly,* Feb. 12, 1884, 450–51.

"The Statue of Liberty: A Final Appeal from the Pedestal Committee." *New York Times,* Mar. 23, 1885, 8.

"They Enter a Protest; Woman Suffragists Think the Ceremonies an Empty Farce." *New York Times,* Oct. 29, 1886, 8.

"To Liberty." *Brooklyn Eagle,* Aug. 5 1884, 4.

Trachtenberg, Marvin. *The Statue of Liberty.* New York: Viking Press, 1976.

Monument Avenue

Author interview with Sarah Driggs, April 20, 2005.

Driggs, Sarah Shields, Richard Guy Wilson, Robert P. Winthrop, and Historic Monument Avenue and Fan District Foundation. *Richmond's Monument Avenue.* Chapel Hill: University of North Carolina Press, 2001.

DuPriest, James E., and Douglas O. Tice, Jr. *Monument and Boulevard: Richmond's Grand Avenues.* Richmond, Va.: Richmond Discoveries Publications, 1996.

Finn, Robin. "Arthur Ashe, Tennis Star, Is Dead at 49." *New York Times,* February 8, 1993, B9.

Forgey, Benjamin. "Richmond's Happy Median." *Washington Post,* December 1, 1996, G1.

Kneebone, John T. "Location, Location, Location: The Arthur Ashe Monument and Monument Avenue." *Cultural Resource Management Online,* 1999, http://crm.cr.nps.gov/archive/22-9/22-09-o1.pdf (April 2, 2005).

"The Lee Statue Unveiled: Thousands of Veterans Honor His Memory." *New York Times,* May 30, 1890, 1.

Spodek, Jonathan C. "Map of Monument Avenue." *Washington, D.C.: Historic American Buildings Survey,* National Park Service, 1991.

"Tennis Legend Arthur Ashe's Statue Unveiled in His Hometown." *Jet,* July 29, 1996, vol. 90, no. 11, 46.

Tooley, J. A. "Boulevard of Broken Dreams." *U.S. News & World Report,* November 11, 1991, vol. 111, no. 20.

Adams Memorial

Author correspondence with Steven Pierson, February and March 2004.

Adams, Henry. *The Education of Henry Adams: An Autobiography.* Boston: Houghton Mifflin, 2000.

Adams, Marian, and Ward Thoron. *The Letters of Mrs. Henry Adams, 1865–1883.* Boston: Little, Brown and Company, 1936.

"Adams Memorial Restored." *Sculpture,* September 2002, vol. 21, no. 7, 16.

Dryfhout, John. *The Work of Augustus Saint-Gaudens.* Hanover, N.H.: University Press of New England, 1982.

Friedrich, Otto. *Clover.* New York: Simon & Schuster, 1979.

Kirstein, Lincoln. *Memorial to a Marriage: An Album on the Saint-Gaudens Memorial in Rock Creek Cemetery Commissioned by Henry Adams in Honor of His Wife, Marian Hooper Adams.* New York: Metropolitan Museum of Art and Harry N. Abrams, 1989.

Lash, Joseph P. *Eleanor and Franklin.* New York: W.W. Norton, 1971.

O'Toole, Patricia. *The Five of Hearts: An Intimate Portrait of Henry Adams and His Friends, 1880–1918.* New York: Clarkson Potter: Distributed by Crown Publishers, 1990.

Gallagher, Joseph. "A Wordless, Anonymous Memorial: The Story Behind a Masterpiece." *New York Times,* December 1, 1985, A31.

Hunter, Marjorie. "Adams Memorial Draws Responses." *New York Times,* June 7, 1983, B6.

Mills, Cynthia, J. "Casting Shadows: The Adams Memorial and Its Doubles." *American Art,* Summer 2000, vol. 14, no. 2, 2–25.

"The One American Sculptor of World Rank." *Current Opinion,* March 1, 1914, 216–17.

Richard, Paul. "Cloaked in Mystery." *Washington Post,* November 25, 2001, G1.

Scheyer, Ernest. "The Adams Memorial by Augustus Saint-Gaudens." *Art Quarterly,* Summer 1956, vol.19, 178–97.

Schulte, Bret. "Sunlight and Shade." *Washington Post,* June 13, 2002, C1.

General Grant National Memorial

Author correspondence with Frank J. Scaturro, Grant Monument Association, April 2004 and March 20, 2005.

"A Nation at a Tomb." *New York Times,* August 9, 1885, 1.

"At Gen. Grant's Tomb." *New York Times,* April 28, 1897, 2.

"Benches at Grant's Tomb Getting Mosaic Touch." *New York Times,* Sep. 12, 1973, 49.

Colimore, Edward. "Grave Mission." *Philadelphia Inquirer,* February 16, 1995, G1.

"Competition Designs for Grant's Tomb by John H. Duncan, Carrere & Hastings, John Ord, C. H. Clinton, and J. A. Schwenfurth." *The American Architect and Building News,* October 18, 1890, 41–42.

Ennis, Thomas W. "Mosaic Murals at Grant's Tomb Dedicated." *New York Times,* May 27, 1966, 1.

"Gen. Grant's Monument: Architect Duncan Describes the Plan Adopted." *New York Times,* September 13, 1890, 8.

"Grant Tomb Accepted." *New York Times,* April 28, 1897, 1.

Grant, Ulysses S. *Personal Memoirs.* New York: Modern Library, 1999.

Hevesi, Dennis. "No One in Grant's Tomb Unless It's Fixed, Family Warns." *New York Times,* October 16, 1994, 39.

"The Last Days of General Grant." *Harper's Weekly,* August 15, 1885, 538.

McFeely, William S. *Grant: A Biography.* New York: W.W. Norton, 1981.

Onishi, Norimitsu. "Ceremony at Grant's Tomb Notes Gadfly's Triumph." *New York Times,* April 28, 1997, B3.

Reinert, Eric A. *Grant's Tomb.* Fort Washington, Pa.: Eastern National, 1997.

Scaturro, Frank J. *President Grant Reconsidered.* Lanham, Md.: University Press of America, 1998.

Smith, Jean Edward. *Grant.* New York: Simon & Schuster, 2001.

"Ulysses S. Grant, The Career of a Soldier." *New York Times,* July 24, 1885, 3.

Shaw Memorial

Author interview with Richard Benson on September 23, 2003, in New Haven, Connecticut.

Atkinson, Edward, William A. Coffin, and Thomas W. Higginson. "Shaw Memorial and the Sculptor Saint-Gaudens." *The Century,* June 1897, vol. 54, no. 2, 176–200.

Barnes, James. "The Shaw Memorial." *Harper's Weekly,* May 29, 1897, 546.

Benson, Richard, Lincoln Kirstein, and Augustus Saint-Gaudens. *Lay This Laurel: An Album on the Saint-Gaudens Memorial on Boston Common, Honoring Black and White Men Together, Who Served the Union Cause with Robert Gould Shaw and Died with Him July 18, 1863.* New York: Eakins Press, 1973.

Blight, David W. *Beyond the Battlefield: Race, Memory and the American Civil War.* Amherst: University of Massachusetts Press, 2002.

Boime, Albert. *The Art of Exclusion: Representing Blacks in the Nineteenth Century.* Washington, D.C.: Smithsonian Institution Press, 1990.

"Boston Honors Col. Shaw." *New York Times,* June 1, 1897, 4.

Burchard, Peter. *One Gallant Rush; Robert Gould Shaw and His Brave Black Regiment.* New York: St. Martin's Press, 1965.

Greenthal, Kathryn. *Augustus Saint-Gaudens, Master Sculptor.* New York: Metropolitan Museum of Art, 1985.

"The Hero." *The Century,* June 1897, vol. 54, no. 2, 312–14.

Marcus, Lois Goldreich. "The Shaw Memorial by Augustus Saint-Gaudens." *Winterthur Portfolio,* Spring 1979, vol. 14, no. 1, 1–23.

"Memorable Words." *The Century,* August 1897, vol. 54, no. 4, 634–36.

Murray, Freeman H. *Emancipation and the Freed in American Sculpture: A Study in Interpretation.* Freeport, N.Y.: Books for Libraries Press, 1972.

"Saint Gaudens, Sculptor, Is Dead." *New York Times,* August 4, 1907, 7.

Shackel, Paul A. *Myth, Memory, and the Making of the American Landscape.* Gainesville: University Press of Florida, 2001.

Savage, Kirk. *Standing Soldiers, Kneeling Slaves: Race, War, and Monument in Nineteenth-Century America.* Princeton, N.J.: Princeton University Press, 1997.

Lincoln Memorial

Anderson, Marian. *My Lord, What a Morning: An Autobiography.* New York: Viking Press, 1956.

"Attilio Piccirilli, Sculptor, 77, Dies." *New York Times,* October 9, 1945, 21.

Boney, Leslie N. "Henry Bacon's Magnificent Temple." *American Institute of Architects Journal,* May 1974, vol. 61, 54–55.

Brown, Katherine Stanley. "Architecture at the Nation's Capital." *Architect and Engineer,* January 1936, vol. 124, 27ff.

Cram, Ralph Adams. "The Lincoln Memorial, Washington, D.C." *Architectural Record,* April 1923, vol. 53, 478–508.

Fernandez, Manny. "King's Words Echo During Dedication." *Washington Post,* August 23, 2003, B1.

"French the Sculptor to Make Statue of Lincoln for Washington Memorial." *New York Times,* December 19, 1914, 8.

Gray, Christopher. "Six Brothers Who Left Their Mark as Sculptors." *New York Times,* October 17, 1999, 47.

"Harding Dedicates Lincoln Memorial; Blue and Gray Join." *New York Times,* May 31, 1922, 1.

"Harding Lauds Work of Lincoln Architect." *New York Times,* May 19, 1923, 15.

Karlowicz, Titus M., ed. "American Expositions and Architecture." *American Society of Architectural Historians Journal,* December 1976, vol. 35, no. 4, 272–279.

Larson, Erik. *The Devil in the White City: Murder, Magic, and Madness at the Fair that Changed America.* New York: Crown Publishers, 2003.

Lincoln, Abraham. "Second Inaugural Address." March 4, 1865 (endorsed by Lincoln, April 10, 1865). Abraham Lincoln Papers at the Library of Congress. Transcribed by the Lincoln Studies Center, Knox College, Galesburg, Illinois.

Lincoln Memorial Documentation Project. Library of Congress, Prints and Photographs Division. Historic American Buildings Survey, 1993.

Lombardo, Josef Vincent. *Attilio Piccirilli: Life of an American Sculptor.* New York, Chicago: Pitman Publishing Corporation, 1944.

Mellon, James. *The Face of Lincoln.* New York: Viking Press, 1979.

National Park Service. *Lincoln Memorial: A Guide to the Lincoln Memorial, District of Columbia.* Washington, D.C.: U.S. Dept. of the Interior, 1986.

Neely, Mark E. *The Last Best Hope of Earth: Abraham Lincoln and the Promise of America.* Cambridge: Harvard University Press, 1993.

Peterson, Merrill D. *Lincoln in American Memory.* New York: Oxford University Press, 1994.

Richman, Michael. *Daniel Chester French, an American Sculptor.* New York: Metropolitan Museum of Art for the National Trust for Historic Preservation, 1976.

Rosenbaum, Alvin. "Opposing Views: Rediscovering America at the 1893 World's Columbian Exposition." *Blueprints,* Winter 1993, vol. XI, no. 1, 2–7.

Tepper, Audrey T. "Restoration of the Lincoln Memorial Murals." *Cultural Resource Management,* no. 7, 1999, 35–37.

Thomas, Christopher A. *The Lincoln Memorial and American Life.* Princeton, N.J.: Princeton University Press, 2002.

"$2,000,000 Memorial to the Memory of Lincoln." *New York Times,* February 9, 1913, SM3.

Wills, Garry. *Lincoln at Gettysburg: The Words that Remade America.* New York: Simon & Schuster, 1992.

Balto

Adams, Mildred. "Dogs That Rank as Heroes." *New York Times,* January 5, 1930, SM7.

"Balto, Nome Hero, Dead." *New York Times,* March 16, 1933, 20.

"For Monument to Balto." *New York Times,* February 7, 1925, 5.

"Frederick Roth, Sculptor, Was 72." *New York Times,* May 22, 1944, 19.

"His Effigy Unveiled, Balto Is Unmoved." *New York Times,* December 16, 1925, 20.

"Lauds Rescue Dogs in Senate Speech." *New York Times,* February 7, 1925, 5.

Olmsted, Frederick Law. *Documents of the Board of Commissioners of the Central Park for the Year Ending April 30, 1859,* doc. no. 5, May 31, 1858, 6.

Riddles, Libby, and Tim Jones. *Race Across Alaska: First Woman to Win the Iditarod Tells Her Story.* Harrisburg, Pa.: Stackpole Books, 1988.

"Serum Arrives Frozen." *New York Times,* February 3, 1925, 1.

"Tells How Lead Dog Got Serum to Nome." *New York Times,* February 4, 1925, 3.

Thomas, Robert McG., Jr. "Edgar Nollner, 94, Dies; Hero in Epidemic." *New York Times,* January 24, 1999, 41.

Château-Thierry Monument

Author correspondence with Michael G. Conley, American Battle Monuments Commission, March 2006.

American Battle Monuments Commission. http://www.abmc.gov/home.php (November 6, 2004).

Castellucci, John. "The Man Behind the WWI Monument." *Providence Journal–Bulletin,* January 29, 1996, C1.

"Chateau-Thierry Monument." American Battle Monuments Commission. http://permanent.access.gpo.gov/websites/dodandmilitaryejournals/www.abmc.gov/am_basc.pdf (February 10, 2005).

Coombs, Rose E. B. *Before Endeavors Fade: A Guide to the Battlefields of the First World War.* London: Battle of Britain International, 1994.

"Dr. Paul Cret Dies: A Noted Architect." *New York Times,* September 9, 1945, 47.

Grossman, Elizabeth G. "Architecture for a Public Client: The Monuments and Chapels of the American Battle Monuments Commission." *Journal of the Society of Architectural Historians,* May 1984, vol. 43, no. 2, 119–43.

———. *The Civic Architecture of Paul Cret.* New York: Cambridge University Press, 1996.

"Monuments to the Deeds of the A.E.F.: Chapels and Battle Memorials Will Soon Mark the Spots Where the Americans Fought." *New York Times,* July 17, 1927, SM14.

Nicholson, J. W. "Off the Beaten Path." *Army,* November 2005, vol. 55, no. 11, 40–42, 44.

"Pershing to Consult on War Monuments." *Washington Post,* March 20, 1927, M6.

Sherman, Daniel J. "Bodies and Names: The Emergence of Commemoration in Interwar France." *American Historical Review,* 1998, vol. 103, no. 2, 443–66.

"3 War Memorials to be Built for U.S. on Soil of France." *Washington Post,* July 3, 1927, 4.

Winter, J. M. *Sites of Memory, Sites of Mourning.* Cambridge; New York: Cambridge University Press, 1995.

Tomb of the Unknowns

Allen, Donald G. "A Point of Honor and Pride; Guards of the Unknown Soldiers." *Officer Review Magazine,* December 2004, vol. 44, no. 5, 12–13.

"Award of Design for Tomb of Unknown Soldier." *American Architect,* January 5, 1929, vol. 135, 29–30.

Bretherick, Jill. "Honor of Sacrifice: The Evolution of Arlington National Cemetery." *Modulus,* 1984, no. 17, 106–119.

"Completion of the Tomb of the Unknown Solider, Arlington; Report of the Jury, with Five Designs and Plot Plans." *Pencil Points,* January 1929, vol. 10, 46–57.

Duffus, R. L. "America's New Symbol of Memorial Day." *New York Times,* May 29, 1932, SM6.

Hershey, Robert D., Jr. "One of 58,012 Vietnam Dead Joins the Unknowns." *New York Times,* May 29, 1984, A1.

Kennicott, Philip. "Memorials Set History in Stone." *Washington Post,* May 30, 2004, B1.

"The Tomb at Arlington." *New York Times,* May 27, 1934, SM14.

"Tomb of the Unknown Soldier and Approaches, Arlington, VA." *Architecture,* May 1933, vol. 67, 255–60.

"The Unknown Soldier." *New York Times,* November 11, 1921, 10.

Mount Rushmore National Memorial

Borglum, Gutzon. "Moulding a Mountain." *Forum,* October 1923, vol. 60, no. 4, 2019ff.

"Borglum Is Ousted at Stone Mountain; Warrant Is Issued." *New York Times,* February 26, 1925, 1.

Carter, Robin Borglum. *Gutzon Borglum: His Life and Work.* Austin, Tex.: Eakin Press, 1998.

Conderacci, Greg. "After 25 Years' Work, Sculptor Chips Away at a Monumental Task: Korczak Ziolkowski Calls It a Tribute to the Indians; But Some Call Him a Fraud." *Wall Street Journal,* April 20, 1973, 1.

"The Confederate Soldiers Memorial at Stone Mountain." *American Architect,* April 5, 1926, vol. 129, 415–19.

Fite, Gilbert C. *Mount Rushmore.* Norman; London: University of Oklahoma Press, 1952.

Frazier, Ian. *Great Plains.* New York: Farrar, Straus and Giroux, 1989.

Johnson, Gerald W. *The Undefeated.* New York: Minton, Balch & Company, 1927.

Marshall, Edward. "New York a Sieve for Art Junk." *New York Times,* January 24, 1915, SM10.

McMurtry, Larry. *Crazy Horse.* New York: Viking Penguin, 1999.

"Mountain a Monument; Gutzon Borglum Proposes to Carve the Solid Granite of Stone Mountain into a Wonderful Confederate Memorial." *New York Times,* January 2, 1916, SM1.

Romero, Librado. "Crazy Horse Writ Large and Dream to Match." *New York Times,* August 25, 2004, E1.

Shaff, Howard, Gutzon Borglum, and Audrey Karl Shaff. *Six Wars at a Time: The Life and Times of Gutzon Borglum, Sculptor of Mount Rushmore.* Sioux Falls, S.D.; Darien, Conn.: Center for Western Studies; Permelia Publishing, 1985.

Smith, Rex Alan. *The Carving of Mount Rushmore.* New York: Abbeville Press, 1985.

Taliaferro, John. *Great White Fathers: The Story of the Obsessive Quest to Create Mount Rushmore.* New York: Public Affairs, 2002.

Therrien, Khiota. "Will Reagan Be Chiseled Out?" *Washington Post,* February 15, 1999, A27.

Jefferson Memorial

Airman, Duncan. "Capital Becomes Art Battleground." *New York Times,* April 18, 1937, 12.

Bedford, Steven. *John Russell Pope: Architect of Empire.* New York: Rizzoli, 1998.

Bolles, Blair. "Jefferson Memorial a Storm Center." *New York Times,* April 17, 1938, 6.

"Discussion of Public Architecture and Monuments Conducted by the American Federation of the Arts." *Architectural Record,* August 1937, 52–57.

Ellis, Joseph J. *American Sphinx: The Character of Thomas Jefferson.* New York: Alfred A. Knopf, 1997.

Ellis, Joseph J., et al., and Library of Congress. *Thomas Jefferson: Genius of Liberty.* New York: Viking Studio in association with the Library of Congress, Washington, D.C., 2000.

Fanning, Kay. "On Kimball and the Jefferson Memorial." Paper delivered at Fiske Kimball: Creator of an American Architecture. Symposium. November 19, 1995. University of Virginia, Charlottesville.

Howard, Hugh. *Thomas Jefferson, Architect: The Built Legacy of Our Third President.* New York: Rizzoli, 2003.

Hudnut, Joseph. "The Last of the Romans." *Magazine of Art,* April 1941, 169–73.

Jefferson Memorial Documentation Project. Library of Congress, Prints and Photographs Division. Historic American Building Survey, 1994.

"Jefferson Memorial Raises Stormy Discussion." *Architectural Record,* June 1937, 24–26.

"Jefferson Temple Is Still in Dispute." *New York Times,* March 27, 1939, 13.

Kimball, Fiske. Letter to the editor. *Magazine of Art,* November 1941, vol. 34, 316–318.

Peterson, Merrill D. The Jefferson Image in the American Mind. *New York: Oxford University Press,* 1960.

"The Proposed Jefferson Memorial." *Pencil Points,* April 1937, vol. 18, 233–34.

"Roosevelt Curbs Tree 'Rebellion.'" *New York Times,* November 19, 1938, 19.

"Roosevelt Lauds Jefferson's Deeds." *New York Times,* December 16, 1938, 3.

Shalett, Sidney. "Roosevelt, Hailing Jefferson, Looks to Gain in Liberty." *New York Times,* April 14, 1943, 14.

Stanton, Phoebe. "A Note on John Russell Pope." *Baltimore Museum of Art Annual 4,* 1972, 60–69.

Remembering World War II

"Allied Armies Land in France in the Havre-Cherbourg Area; Great Invasion Is Under Way." *New York Times,* June 6, 1944, 1.

Bradley, James, and Ron Powers. *Flags of Our Fathers.* New York: Bantam Books, 2000.

Brown, Patricia Leigh. "'Rosie the Riveter' Honored in California Memorial." *New York Times,* October 22, 2000, 16.

Capa, Robert. *Images of War.* New York: Grossman Publishers, 1964.

Dunlap, David W. *Abyssinian to Zion: A Guide to Manhattan's Houses of Worship.* New York: Columbia University Press, 2004.

Frank, Benis M. "The Man Who Took the Picture on Iwo Jima." Letter to The *New York Times,* November 16, 1991, 18.

Goldstein, Richard. "Joe Rosenthal, Photographer Who Captured the Flag-Raising at Iwo Jima, Dies at 94." *New York Times,* August 22, 2006, C11.

Hallissy, Erin. "Riveting Memories for Rosies." *San Francisco Chronicle,* June 15, 2005, B5.

Harvey, Sheridan. "Rosie the Riveter: Real Women Workers in World War II." Library of Congress. http://www.loc.gov/rr/program/journey/rosie.html (March 8, 2006).

Lenihan, Daniel J., ed. "Submerged Cultural Resources Study: USS *Arizona* Memorial and Pearl Harbor National Historic Landmark." No. 23, 1989. http://www.nps.gov/usar/scrs/scrs0a.htm (March 1, 2005).

Livingston, Paul. "Monument Pays Tribute to Shipyard." *Portland Press Herald,* December 18, 2003, 7G.

Marling, Karal Ann, and John Wetenhall. *Iwo Jima: Monuments, Memories, and the American Hero.* Cambridge: Harvard University Press, 1991.

"Memorial in Normandy Dedicated to U.S. Dead." *New York Times,* July 20, 1956, 5.

Metcalfe, Jack. "Sentimental Journey to Beaches of Normandy." *New York Sunday News,* June 1, 1969, 2, 84–85.

Miller, Mike. "Pearl Harbor 30 Years Later." *New York Times,* December 5, 1971, 1.

Normandy American Cemetery and Memorial. Arlington, Va.: American Battle Monuments Commission, undated.

Roosevelt, Franklin Delano. "Declaration of War, December 8, 1941." Handwritten changes to final speech. Franklin D. Roosevelt Library Digital Archives.

Slackman, Michael. *Remembering Pearl Harbor: The Story of the USS Arizona Memorial.* Honolulu: Arizona Memorial Museum Association, 1984.

Smith, Rex Alan, and Gerald A. Meehl. *Pacific Legacy: Image and Memory from World War II in the Pacific.* New York: Abbeville Press, 2002.

Thompson, Chuck. *The 25 Best World War II Sites—Pacific Theater: The Ultimate Traveler's Guide to Battlefields, Monuments and Museums.* San Francisco: Greenline Publications, 2002.

"USS *Arizona.*" Report BB-39, HAER No. HI-13. *Historic American Engineering Record,* 1986.

World War II Memorial

Author interview with architect Friedrich St. Florian, November 6, 2003.

Author interview with architect Hugh Hardy, Chairman, WW2 Memorial Architect-Engineer Evaluation Board, October 3, 2003.

Author interview with Nick Benson on October 29, 2003, on the site of the National World War II Memorial, Washington, D.C.; author correspondence, October–December 2003.

Benson, John Howard, and Graham Carey. *The Elements of Lettering.* New York: McGraw-Hill, 1950.

Crosbie, Michael J. "World War II Memorial: Classic Design for Sacred Ground." *Hartford Courant,* May 30, 2004, C4.

Fishkin, Joseph. "Anatomy of an Eyesore: Monumental Error." *The New Republic,* September 2000, vol. 25, no. 4, 471.

Forgey, Benjamin. "Leaving a Mark on Washington." *Washington Post,* April 6, 1997, G1.

———. "An Overdue Honor for WWII Veterans Once Again Is Unjustly in the Line of Fire." *Washington Post,* May 5, 2001, C1.

———. "War and Remembrance." *Washington Post,* April 25, 2004, N1.

Goldberger, Paul. "The National World War II Memorial." *The New Yorker,* May 31, 2004, vol. 80, no. 14, 82–84.

Hedges, Michael. "140,000 attend dedication of World War II Memorial." *Houston Chronicle,* May 30, 2004, 1.

Janofsky, Michael. "An Academic Touches the Masses with War Memorial." *New York Times,* May 26, 2004, E2.

———. "Veterans Gather to Dedicate World War II Memorial." *New York Times,* May 30, 2004, A22.

Mauldin, Bill. *Up Front.* New York: Henry Holt and Company, 1945.

Mills, Nicolaus. *Their Last Battle: The Fight for a National World War II Memorial.* New York: Basic Books, 2004.

Mulligan, John E. "A Tribute in Stone." *Providence Journal-Bulletin,* November 11, 2003, 1.

Neuman, Johanna. "Memorial Dedicated Amid Tears, Joy." *Los Angeles Times,* May 30, 2004, A1.

"A New Memorial." *Washington Post,* May 1, 2004, A20.

Puente, Maria. "WWII Monument Should Please Veterans, but It Disappoints Architects and Historians." *USA Today,* May 20, 2004, A1.

Reel, Monte. "WWII Memorial Opens." *Washington Post,* April 29, 2004, A1.

Shribman, David. "Congress Considers a Statue Statute for Nation's Capital: Monument Curb Is Necessary, Backers Say, to Halt Glut." *Wall Street Journal*, July 7, 1986, 1.

Martin Luther King, Jr., National Historic Site

Applebome, Peter. "Coretta Scott King, a Civil Rights Icon, Dies at 78." *New York Times*, February 1, 2006, A1.

"Atlanta Games Day 16 Guide, Art in the Streets." *Atlanta Journal-Constitution*, August 3, 1996, S37.

Duke, Lynne. "Blueprint of a Life: Architect J. Max Bond Jr. Has Had to Build Bridges to Reach Ground Zero." *Washington Post*, July 1, 2004, C1.

Dewan, Shaila K. "Civil Rights Battlegrounds Enter World of Tourism." *New York Times*, August 10, 2004, A1.

———. "Disarray at Center for Dr. King Casts Pall on Family and Legacy." *New York Times*, January 14, 2006, A1.

Dupré, Judith. *Churches*. New York: HarperCollins, 2001.

King, Dr. Martin Luther, Jr. "Nobel Prize Acceptance Speech, December 10, 1964." http://www.nobelprizes.com/nobel/peace/MLK-nobel.html (February 1, 2004).

"Martin Luther King, Jr., National Historic Site." Brochure. Washington, D.C.: National Park Service, U.S. Department of the Interior, 1999.

"Our Opinions: A Legacy Squandered: Financial, Physical Upkeep of King Center Cannot Be Left in Hands of the Civil Rights Leader's Family." *Atlanta Journal-Constitution*, February 9, 2005, A14.

Tucker, Cynthia. "Heirs Will Bury King Legacy." *Atlanta Journal-Constitution*, January 4, 2006, A11.

Windsor, Shawn. "Bus at Center of Civil-Rights Movement Restored." *San Diego Union-Tribune*, February 9, 2003, A18.

Vietnam Veterans Memorial

Author conversations and correspondence with James F. and Dolores Caruolo, James J. Caruolo, Anthony Catarella, Joe Cichon, Clarice Dionne, Curt Dionne, Michael Dionne, Ellen Donilon, Robert E. Dupré, Matthew Higgins, and Joy Caruolo Welshman, July–August 2003.

Allen, Thomas B. *Offerings at the Wall: Artifacts from the Vietnam Veterans Memorial Collection*. Atlanta: Turner Publishing, 1995.

Berdahl, Daphne. "Mythical Realities at a National Shrine: The Vietnam Veterans Memorial in Washington, D.C." *Kritische Berichte*, 1996, vol. 24, no. 3, 13–19.

Blum, Shirley Neilsen. "The National Vietnam War Memorial." *Arts Magazine*, December 1984, vol. 59, no. 4, 124–28.

Burwell, Wayne. Letter to Dolores Caruolo, April 16, 1966.

Campbell, Robert. "An Emotive Place Apart." *AIA Journal*, May 1983, vol. 72, no. 5, 150–51.

Carhart, Tom. "Insulting Vietnam Vets." *New York Times*, October 24, 1981, 23.

Clines, Francis X. "Tribute to Vietnam Dead: Words, a Wall." *New York Times*, November 11, 1982, A1.

———. "Vietnam War Memorial: Rancor, Tears and Song." *New York Times*, November 11, 1982, B7.

Danto, Arthur. "The Vietnam Veterans Memorial." *The Nation*, August 31, 1985, 152—55.

Friedman, D. S. "Public Things in the Modern City: Belated Notes on Tilted Arc and the Vietnam Veterans Memorial." *Journal of Architectural Education*, November 1995, vol. 49, no. 2, 62–78.

Goldberger, Paul. "Vietnam Memorial: Questions of Architecture." *New York Times*, October 7, 1982, C25.

———. "Vietnam Wall Memorial to Capture Anguish of a Decade of Doubt," *New York Times*, June 6, 1981, 7.

Hass, Kristin Ann. *Carried to the Wall: American Memory and the Vietnam Veterans Memorial*. Berkeley: University of California Press, 1998.

Howett, Catherine M. "The Vietnam Veterans Memorial: Public Art and Politics." *Landscape*, 1985, vol. 28, no. 2, 1–9.

Hubbard, William. "A Meaning for Monuments." *Public Interest*, Winter 1984, no. 74, 17–30.

Karnow, Stanley. *Vietnam: A History*. New York: Viking Press, 1983.

Katakis, Michael. *The Vietnam Veterans Memorial*. New York: Crown, 1988.

Krauthammer, Charles. "Memorials." *New Republic*, May 16, 1981, vol. 184, no. 2, 43.

Lin, Maya Ying. *Boundaries*. New York: Simon & Schuster, 2000.

———. "Interview with Lilly Wei." *Artforum*, April 1983, vol. 21, 76–77.

———. Vietnam Veterans Memorial Competition, design submission presentation board, 1980 or 1981.

Marling, Karal Ann, and Robert Silberman. "The Statue Near the Wall: The Vietnam Veterans Memorial and the Art of Remembering." *Smithsonian Studies in American Art*, Spring 1987, vol. 1, no. 1, 4–29.

Maya Lin: A Strong Clear Vision, directed by Freida Lee Mock (VHS). American Film Foundation, Sanders & Mock Productions, Santa Monica, Calif., 1995.

McCarthy, Dave. "Fallen Heroes Not Forgotten." *Providence Journal*, March 4, 2003, C1.

Menand, Louis. "The Reluctant Memorialist." *The New Yorker*, July 8, 2002, 54–65.

Molotsky, Irvin. "Changes Set in Vietnam Memorial." *New York Times*, October 14, 1982, C17.

Moreno, Elena Marcheso. "Proposed Additions to Vietnam Memorial Spark Controversy." *Architecture: The AIA Journal*, May 1988, vol. 77, no. 5, 48–49.

Morrow, Lance. "A Bloody Rite of Passage; Viet Nam Cost America Its Innocence and Still Haunts Its Conscience." *Time*, April 15, 1985, 3.

O'Brien, Tim. *The Things They Carried*. Boston: Houghton Mifflin, 1990.

Ochsner, Jeffrey Karl. "A Space of Loss: The Vietnam Veterans Memorial." *Journal of Architectural Education*, February 1997, vol. 50, no. 3, 156–171.

"Proposed Viet Sculpture Shown as Architects Fight Additions." *AIA Journal*, October 1982, vol. 71, no. 12, 22–27.

Reel, Monte. "Wall Evolves but Still Enthralls." *Washington Post*, November 3, 2002, C1.

Roberts, Roxanne. "Honoring the Women; New Vietnam Memorial Readied on Mall." *Washington Post*, November 2, 1993, A1.

Trilett, Bill. "Judging The Wall." *The VVA Veteran*, Online Commemorative Issue, November 2002, http://www.vva.org/TheVeteran/2002_special/judging.htm.

Webb, James H., Jr. "Reassessing the Vietnam Veterans Memorial." *Wall Street Journal*, December 18, 1981, 22.

Weinraub, Bernard. "Carter Hails Veterans of Vietnam in Signing Bill for a War Memorial." *New York Times*, July 2, 1980, A14.

———. "Ground Broken in Capital for Memorial on Vietnam." *New York Times*, March 27, 1981, 1.

Wolfe, Tom. "Art Disputes War: The Battle of the Vietnam Memorial." *Washington Post*, October 13, 1982, B3.

AIDS Memorial Quilt

I thank Jonathan Berger, Jan Chase, and Jack Hitt for some of the ideas in this essay.

Author interview with Julie Rhoad, Director, NAMES Project Foundation, Atlanta, Georgia, May 20, 2005; correspondence with Julie Rhoad, May–June 2005.

"AIDS Treatment: A Focus on '3 by 5.' Fact sheet published by UNAIDS, February 2, 2004.

Baker, Rob. *The Art of AIDS*. New York: Continuum, 1994.

Common Threads: Stories from the Quilt. Directed by Robert Epstein and Jeffrey Friedman. VHS. Telling Pictures and the NAMES Project Foundation, 1989.

Crichton, E. G. "Is the NAMES Quilt Art?" *In Critical Issues in Public Art*, edited by Harriet F. Senie and Sally Webster. Washington, D.C., and London: Smithsonian Institution Press, 1992.

Fuchs, Elinor. "The Performance of Mourning." *American Theater*, January 1993, 15.

Green, Jesse. "When Political Art Mattered." *New York Times Magazine*, December 7, 2003, 68.

Hepworth, Kate. "Beyond the Closet Door: Mapping Queer Space in the Urban Environment." *Architectural Theory Review: Journal of the Department of Architecture, University of Sydney*, November 1999, vol. 4, no. 2, 93.

Heredia, Christopher. "AIDS Quilt to be Stored in Atlanta." *San Francisco Chronicle*, February 6, 2001, A3.

———. "Rip in the Quilt." *San Francisco Chronicle*, July 20, 2002, A11.

Jones, Cleve, and Jeff Dawson. *Stitching a Revolution: The Making of an Activist*. San Francisco: HarperSanFrancisco, 2000.

Mainardi, Patricia. "Quilts: The Great American Art." *In Feminist Art History: Questioning the Litany*, edited by Norma Broude and Mary D. Garrard. New York: Harper and Row, 1982.

Political Funerals. January 30, 2004. ACT UP, AIDS Coalition to Release Power. February 26, 2004. http://www.actupny.org/diva/polfunsyn.html. (Accessed May 30, 2004.)

Ruskin, Cindy, and Matt Herron. *The Quilt: Stories from the Names Project*. New York: Pocket Books, 1988.

Sommer, Richard M. "Time Incorporated: The Romantic Life of the Modern Monument." *Harvard Design Magazine*, Fall 1999, 38.

Staples, Gracie Bond. "AIDS Quilt Preparing to Find Home in Atlanta." *Atlanta Journal and Constitution*, February 9, 2001, 1E.

Sturken, Marita. *Tangled Memories: The Vietnam War, the AIDS Epidemic, and the Politics of Remembering*. Berkeley: University of California Press, 1997.

Wojnarowicz, David. "Postcards from America: X-Rays from Hell." *Witnesses: Against Our Vanishing, Catalogue, Artists Space*, November 16, 1989, to January 6, 1990. Organized by Nan Goldin.

———, Barry Blinderman, and Illinois State University. David Wojnarowicz: *Tongues of Flame*. Normal, Ill.: University Galleries, Illinois State University, 1990.

———, Dan Cameron, Amy Scholder, and New Museum of Contemporary Art. *Fever: The Art of David Wojnarowicz*. New York: Rizzoli, 1998.

Manzanar National Historic Site

June Otani interview with Meg Lindsay, Irvington, New York, July 28, 2002.

Adams, Ansel. *Born Free and Equal: Photographs of the Loyal Japanese-Americans at Manzanar Relocation Center, Inyo County, California*. New York: U.S. Camera, 1944.

Boxall, Bettina. "Reassembling a Sad Chapter of History." *Los Angeles Times*, December 11, 2002, 1.

Burton, Jeffrey F., Mary M. Farrell, Florence B. Lord, and Richard W. Lord. *Confinement and Ethnicity: An Overview of World War II Japanese American Relocation Sites*. Report no. 74. Tucson: Western Archaeological and Conservation Center, 1999, rev. 2000.

Davidov, Judith Fryer. "The Color of My Skin, the Shape of My Eyes: Photographs of the Japanese-American Internment by Dorothea Lange, Ansel Adams, and Toyo Miyatake." *The Yale Journal of Criticism*, vol. 9, no. 2, 1996, 223–44.

"Fancy Chalet Monikers." *Manzanar Free Press*, vol. 1, no. 1, April 11, 1942, 2.

Gordon, Linda, and Gary Y. Okihiro. *Impounded: Dorothea Lange and the Censored Images of Japanese American Internment*. New York: W. W. Norton & Company, 2006.

Hamilton, William L. "Places That Tell America's Diverse Story." *New York Times*, July 10, 2005, TR3.

Houston, Jeanne Wakatsuki, and James D. Houston. *Farewell to Manzanar: A True Story of Japanese American Experience During and After the World War II Internment.* Boston: Houghton Mifflin, 2002.

Kluger, Steve. "Play Ball!" *Los Angeles Times,* August 7, 2002, 11.

"Manzanar's Salvage Gives Homes to GI's." *New York Times,* December 2, 1946, 34.

Moley, Raymond. "The Japanese and Their Migration: The Mass Evacuation of One Hundred Forty Thousand Japanese Presents Stiff Problem." *Wall Street Journal,* April 8, 1942, 6.

Pearlstine, Norman. "The 'Quiet Minority.'" *Wall Street Journal,* August 8, 1972, 1.

Robinson, Gerald H. *Elusive Truth: Four Photographers at Manzanar.* Nevada City, Calif.: C. Mautz, 2002.

Unrau, Harlan D. *The Evacuation and Relocation of Persons of Japanese Ancestry During World War II: A Historical Study of the Manzanar War Relocation Center.* U.S. Department of the Interior: National Park Service, 1996.

Winks, Robin. "Sites of Shame." *National Parks,* March/April 1994, vol. 68, no. 3/4, 22.

Korean War Veterans Memorial

"Architects File Suit Over Changes in Korean War Memorial Design." *Architecture,* February 1991, vol. 80, no. 2, 26–27.

Finn, David. "Korean War Veterans Memorial." *Sculpture Review,* Spring 1998, vol. 46, no. 4, 22–25.

Forgey, Benjamin. "A March to Remember." *Washington Post,* July 22, 1995, D1.

Johnson, Jory. "Granite Platoon." *Landscape Architecture,* January 1990, vol. 80, no. 1, 69–71.

"Korea War Memorial." U.S. Department of the Interior. Washington, D.C.: National Park Service, publication 432-903/60375, 1998.

Lewis, Roger K. "Washington Monuments: Battles Over the Mall." *Architectural Record,* January 1996, vol. 184, no. 1, 17, 19, 21.

Lucas, Veronica Burns, et al. "Korean War Memorial (letter)." *Progressive Architecture,* November 1989, vol. 70, no. 12, 11.

Sun, Lena H. "Korea Remembered." *Washington Post,* July 28, 1995, A1.

Franklin Delano Roosevelt Memorial

Author correspondence with John E. Benson, various dates, 2003, 2004.

Black, Conrad. *Franklin Delano Roosevelt: Champion of Freedom.* New York: Public Affairs, 2003.

"Capital Monument Plan For F. D. Roosevelt Set." *New York Times,* November 24, 1958, 57.

Checkman, Louis. "Design for Roosevelt Memorial Is Rejected by Fine Arts Panel." *New York Times,* February 22, 1962, 27.

Clinton, Bill. "Dedication of the Roosevelt Memorial: Tributes of Triumph to Their Generation." *Vital Speeches of the Day,* June 1, 1997, vol. 63, no. 16, 482–84.

Creighton, Thomas H. *The Architecture of Monuments.* New York: Reinhold Pub. Corp., 1962.

Dillon, David. *The Franklin Delano Roosevelt Memorial Designed by Lawrence Halprin.* Washington, D.C.: Spacemaker Press, 1998.

Forgey, Benjamin. "A Natural Choice to Honor FDR: Landscape Architect Lawrence Halprin Planted an Idea That Blossomed." *Washington Post,* April 30, 1997, D1.

Franklin Delano Roosevelt Memorial Commission Report to Congress: December 15, 1997. Washington, D.C.: The Commission, 1997.

Furman, Bess. "A Shrine Chosen for Roosevelt." *New York Times,* December 31, 1960, 1.

Gabor, Andrea. "Even Our Most Loved Monuments Had a Trial by Fire." *Smithsonian,* May 1997, vol. 28, no. 2, 96.

Goodwin, Doris Kearns. *No Ordinary Time: Franklin and Eleanor Roosevelt: The Home Front in World War II.* New York: Simon & Schuster, 1994.

Halprin, Lawrence. *The Franklin Delano Roosevelt Memorial.* San Francisco: Chronicle Books, 1997.

Hunter, Marjorie. "Five Roosevelts Oppose Memorial." *New York Times,* June 26, 1964, 31.

Huxtable, Ada Louise. "Breuer to Shape Roosevelt Shrine: Selection by Memorial Unit Ends 5 Years of Debate." *New York Times,* June 9, 1966, 39.

———. "If at First You Don't Succeed." *New York Times,* January 1, 1967, 75.

Hyman, Isabelle. "Marcel Breuer and the Franklin Delano Roosevelt Memorial." *Journal of the Society of Architectural Historians,* December 1995, vol. 54, no. 4, 446.

McKinzie, Richard D. *The New Deal for Artists.* Princeton, N.J.: Princeton University Press, 1973.

Moses, Michael Valdez. "A Rendezvous with Destiny." *Reason,* April 2001, vol. 32, no. 11, 52.

Peduzzi, Kelli, and Diane Smook. *Shaping a President: Sculpting for the Roosevelt Memorial.* Brookfield, Conn.: Millbrook Press, 1997.

"Roosevelt Foundation Forms to Preserve His Ideals Through 'A Living Memorial.'" *New York Times,* November 2, 1945, 13.

Thompson, J. William. "Notes from Underground." *Landscape Architecture,* September 1997, vol. 87, no. 9, 40.

Will, George F. "Don't Hide His Source of Strength." *Washington Post,* May 9, 1996, A23.

The *New York Times* Capsule

Brown, Peter G. "Back to Work." *Sciences,* vol. 40, no. 1 (2000), 2.

Dean, Kathy. "Time Capsule's Digital Divide." *Wired News,* 2001. http://www.wired.com/news/business/0,1367,43400,00.html. (September 19, 2003.)

"Design Is Selected for Times Capsule." *New York Times,* December 2, 1999, E3.

Hawking, Stephen W. *A Brief History of Time: From the Big Bang to Black Holes.* New York: Bantam, 1988.

Hitt, Jack. "How to Make a Time Capsule." *New York Times Magazine,* December 5, 1999, 114–120.

Ivy, Robert. "Calatrava Speaks..." *Architectural Record,* July 2000, 70–91.

Kershaw, Sarah. "Time Capsule Mystery Stumps Portland, Ore." *New York Times,* May 18, 2003, 30.

Larson, Soren. "Calatrava Wins Times Capsule Competition with a Steel Design Based on Folded Spheres." *Architectural Record,* vol. 188, no. 1 (2000), 36.

Oklahoma City National Memorial

Author interview, Hans and Torrey Butzer, April 29, 2003; author correspondence, Hans Butzer, January-May 2003, February 2004.

Author interview with Collections Manager Jane Thomas, Oklahoma City National Memorial, April 30 and May 30, 2003.

Author interview with Executive Director Kari F. Watkins, Oklahoma City National Memorial, April 30, 2003.

Anderson, Lisa. "U.S. Executes Its Worst Terrorist, Some Feel Cheated by 'Easy' Death." *Chicago Tribune,* June 12, 2001, 1. (Also see similar articles of same date in *New York Times, Denver Post, Boston Globe,* and *St. Louis Post-Dispatch.*)

Bush, George W. "Remarks at the Dedication of the National Memorial Center Museum in Oklahoma City, Oklahoma." *Weekly Compilation of Presidential Documents,* vol. 37, no. 8 (2001), 312–13.

———. *Weekly Compilation of Presidential Documents,* vol. 36, no. 16 (2001), 880.

Collyer, Stanley. "The Search for an Appropriate Symbol: The Oklahoma City Memorial Competition." *Competitions,* vol. 7, no. 3 (1997), 4–15.

Dillon, David. "Oklahoma City Memorial Recognizes Individuals, Moment." *Architectural Record,* July 2000, 28.

Goldberger, Paul. "Requiem; Memorializing Terrorism's Victims in Oklahoma." *The New Yorker,* January 14, 2002, 90.

Katz, Jessie. "Inspiration Sought in Horrors, Oklahoma Wants Memorial Designers to Feel Bomb Victim's Pain." *Los Angeles Times,* January 7, 1997, A5.

Linenthal, Edward Tabor. *The Unfinished Bombing: Oklahoma City in American Memory.* New York: Oxford University Press, 2001.

McAllister, Bill. "Designs Infused with Loss and Hope Are Finalists for Murrah Memorial." *Washington Post,* May 12, 1997, A17.

Melcher, Katherine A. "Preserving Our Changing Memories." *Landscape Architecture,* vol. 91, no. 11 (2001), 136.

Memorial Mission Statement, Oklahoma City Memorial Foundation, Murrah Federal Building Memorial, Inc., March 26, 1996.

"Oklahoma City National Memorial Act of 1997." S. 871 / Public Law 105-58. *Weekly Compilation of Presidential Documents,* vol. 33, no. 41 (1997), 1554.

Oklahoma City National Memorial Trust. Scope of Collections Statement, Effective As of 12 May 2002.

Patient, Michelle. "Oklahoma City Dedicates Bombing Memorial." *Architecture,* vol. 89, no. 6 (2000), 32–33.

Project Statement, Butzer Design Partnership, August 2000.

Romano, Lois. "Turning Point for Survivors in Oklahoma; Gore Breaks Ground at Bombing Shrine." *Washington Post,* October 26, 1998, A4.

Russell, James S. "Who Owns Grief? An Interview with Edward T. Linenthal." *Architectural Record,* vol. 190, no. 7 (2002), 120–23.

Scales, Ann. "'This Place Is Such Sacred Ground'; Oklahoma City Site Dedicated." *Boston Globe,* April 20, 2000, A3.

Serrano, Richard. "McVeigh Execution Stayed." *Los Angeles Times,* May 12, 2001, A1. (Also see similar articles of same date in *New York Times, Denver Post, Houston Chronicle,* and *San Francisco Chronicle.*)

Stowers, Carlton. "Not to Be Forgotten." *Houston Chronicle,* April 9, 2000, TM8.

Twardy, Chuck. "The Mourning After." *Metropolis,* vol. 20, no. 1 (2000), 30, 48.

Uhlenbrock, Tom. "This City is OK." *Houston Chronicle,* September 8, 2002, 2.

Yardley, Jim. "5 Years After Terrorist Act, a Memorial to the 168 Victims." *New York Times,* April 20, 2000, A20.

———. "Uneasily, Oklahoma City Welcomes Tourists." *New York Times,* June 11, 2001, A1.

The Temporary Memorials of 9/11

Author correspondence with Margaret Morton, May–June, 2004.

Author interview with Michael Arad, December 19, 2005.

Adamson, Jeremy. "Documenting the Present for Posterity: 9/11 Acquisitions at the Library of Congress." Paper delivered at the Art Libraries Society of North America conference, April 17, 2004.

Arad, Michael, and Peter Walker. "Reflecting Absence." Statement, January 14, 2004. http://www.wtcsitememorial.org/fin7.html (May 9, 2004).

Barry, Dan. "A New Account of Sept. 11 Loss, With 40 Fewer Souls to Mourn." *New York Times,* October 29, 2003, A1.

———. "Minutes of Silence and Shafts of Light Recall New York's Dark Day." *New York Times,* March 12, 2002, A1.

———. "Remembering What a City Can't Forget." *New York Times,* August 13, 2003, B1.

Batchen, Geoffrey. "Requiem." *Afterimage,* vol. 29, no. 4, January/February 2002, 5.

Benjamin, Daniel. "The 1,776-Foot-Tall Target." *New York Times,* March 23, 2004, A23.

Bernstein, Fred. "At the Pentagon, Visions of 184 Pieces for the Missing." *New York Times,* December 22, 2002, 2.43.

Berry, Gene. "Special Editions, Newspapers Worldwide Reflect Shock and Horror." *Library of Congress Information Bulletin,* September 2002. http://www.loc.gov/loc/lcib/0209/worldnews.html (accessed May 1, 2004.)

Civic Alliance to Rebuild Downtown New York. "Listening to the City Participant Guide." Report of July 20 and 22, 2002, proceedings, at the Jacob Javits Center, New York City.

Clark, Mary L. "A Fresh Start at Ground Zero." *New York Times,* May 5, 2004, A27.

Darton, Eric. *Divided We Stand: A Biography of New York's World Trade Center.* New York: Basic Books, 1999.

Dunlap, David W. "24 Are Appointed to Set Details of Museum at Ground Zero." *New York Times,* April 9, 2004, B4.

———. "Curators Battle Elements to Preserve Pieces of a Terrible History." *New York Times,* April 3, 2004, B1.

———. "In a Space This Sacred, Every Square Foot Counts." *New York Times,* April 29, 2004, B3.

———. "In Depths of Ground Zero, Historic Notice Can't Wait." *New York Times,* February 8, 2004, A27.

———. "New Partners for Architect of Memorial at 9/11 Site." *New York Times,* April 25, 2004, A35.

———. "Oh, The Stories These Mute Pieces Could Tell." *New York Times,* March 31, 2004, G1.

———. "Opinions Vary on Treating Remnants at Ground Zero." *New York Times,* March 6, 2004, B3.

———. "Who Owns Ground Zero? Don't Expect a Simple Answer." *New York Times,* April 22, 2004, B2.

Dupré, Judith. "Transcending the Tragedy, New Glass Construction at Ground Zero." *Building Design & Construction,* September 2002, 42–43.

Forgey, Benjamin. "Buildings That Stood Tall as Symbols of Strength." *Washington Post,* September 13, 2001, C1.

———. "The Pentagon's Path of Memory." *Washington Post,* March 4, 2002, C1.

Glanz, James. "High Anxiety." *New York Times,* March 14, 2004, B1.

Glanz, James, and Eric Lipton. *City in the Sky: The Rise and Fall of the World Trade Center.* New York: Times Books, 2003.

Gopnik, Adam. "The City and the Pillars." *The New Yorker,* September 24, 2001, 34.

Heritage Preservation, Inc. "Cataclysm and Challenge: Impact of September 11, 2001, on Our Nation's Cultural Heritage." Report by Heritage Preservation on behalf of the Heritage Emergency National Task Force, 2002.

Jacobson, Louis. "A 9/11 Memorial in Pennsylvania." *Planning,* June 2002, vol. 68, no. 6, 33–34.

Junod, Tom. "The Falling Man." *Esquire,* September 2003, 177.

Kamin, Blair. "Icons Look Like Targets in Wake of Attack." *Chicago Tribune,* September 13, 2001, 1.

Kaseman Beckman Amsterdam Studio. "Pentagon Memorial Design Description." Kaseman Beckman Amsterdam Studio statement, 2003.

Kimmelman, Michael. "Ground Zero Finally Grows Up." *New York Times,* February 1, 2004, B1.

Langewiesche, William. *American Ground: Unbuilding the World Trade Center.* New York: North Point Press, 2002.

Leland, John. "Letting the View Speak for Itself." *New York Times,* January 3, 2002, F1.

Levine, Samantha. "Shanksville, Pa.; In the Sky, a Heroic Struggle Aboard Hijacked United Flight 93. This Is Where It Ended." *U.S. News & World Report,* November 11, 2001, 72.

Lipton, Eric. "Surplus History from Ground Zero Rusts in a Hangar." *New York Times,* December 19, 2003, B1.

Lower Manhattan Development Corporation. "Governor Pataki, Mayor Bloomberg and the Lower Manhattan Development Corporation Unveil Plans for an Interim Memorial for the Victims of September 11th and the 1993 World Trade Center Bombing." Press release, March 5, 2002.

———. "LMDC Announces Launch of Virtual Exhibition of All 5,201 Submissions Received for the International Competition to Design the World Trade Center Site Memorial." Press release, February 19, 2004.

McEwan, Ian. "Only Love and Then Oblivion. Love Was All They Had to Set Against Their Murderers." *The Guardian,* September 15, 2001. http://www.guardian.co.uk/comment/story/0,3604,552398,00.html (May 16, 2004).

Muschamp, Herbert. "At Ground Zero, an Architectural Void No Longer." *New York Times,* August 1, 2003, B7.

Pew Internet & American Life Project. "The Commons of the Tragedy: How the Internet Was Used by Millions after the Terror Attacks to Grieve, Console, Share News, and Debate the Country's Response." A report of the Pew Internet & American Life Project, an initiative of the Pew Research Center for People and the Press, funded by the Pew Charitable Trusts, October 10, 2001.

Sanders, James. "Honoring the Dead in the City that Never Weeps." *New York Times,* August 31, 2003, B19.

Scott, Janny. "Closing a Scrapbook Full of Life and Sorrow." *New York Times,* December 31, 2001, B6.

Scharnberg, Kirsten. "Tattoo Unites WTC's Laborers." *Chicago Tribune,* July 22, 2002, 18.

Sella, Marshall. "Missing: How a Grief Ritual Is Born." *New York Times,* October 7, 2001, 48.

Slackman, Michael. "Plan to Preserve Sept. 11 Remains Leaves Open Future Identification." *New York Times,* August 25, 2003, 1.

Sorkin, Michael, and Sharon Zukin. *After the World Trade Center: Rethinking New York City.* New York: Routledge, 2002.

Voorsanger, Bart. "Artifacts, Memories and Memorials." Paper delivered at the Art Libraries Society of North America conference, April 17, 2004.

Whitney, Helen, and Ron Rosenbaum. *Faith and Doubt at Ground Zero.* A Frontline Co-production with Helen Whitney Productions, WGBH Educational Foundation. Airdate: September 3, 2003.

Zimmerman, Elyn. "The World Trade Center Memorial, 1993." September 11th: Art Loss, Damage, and Repercussions. Proceedings of an IFAR Symposium on February 28, 2002.

Irish Hunger Memorial

Author interview with memorial designer Brian Tolle, June 2, 2005.

Davidson, Cynthia. "The Artist Brian Tolle, With 1100 Architect, Gives a Twist to Known and Nostalgic Elements in the Design for the Irish Hunger Memorial in Lower Manhattan." *Architectural Record,* vol. 191, no. 7 (2003), 102.

Dunlap, David W. "Memorial to the Hunger, Complete With Old Sod." *New York Times,* March 15, 2001, E1.

Frankel, David. "Hunger Artist." *Artforum,* Summer 2002, 35.

Kelleher, Margaret. "Hunger in History: Monuments to the Great Famine." Lecture, Boston College. http://fron-trow.bc.edu/program/kelleher/#programnotes (April 27, 2003).

Klinkenborg, Verlyn. "The Great Irish Hunger and the Art of Honoring Memory." *New York Times,* July 21, 2002, A12.

Macken, Walter. *The Silent People.* New York: Macmillan, 1962.

Nobel, Philip. "Going Hungry." *Metropolis,* vol. 22, no. 3 (2002), 82, 84.

Ó Gráda, Cormac. *Black '47 and Beyond: The Great Irish Famine in History, Economy, and Memory.* The Princeton Economic History of the Western World. Princeton, N.J.: Princeton University Press, 1999.

Ó Gráda, Cormac, and Economic History Society. *The Great Irish Famine.* Cambridge University Press, ed. New Studies in Economic and Social History. Cambridge; New York: Cambridge University Press, 1995.

Richardson, Lynda. "Like Potato Fields, His Memorial Lies Fallow." *New York Times,* May 14, 2003, B2.

Sen, Amartya Kumar. *Poverty and Famines: An Essay on Entitlement and Deprivation.* Oxford and New York: Clarendon Press; Oxford University Press, 1981.

Schama, Simon. "A Patch of Earth." *The New Yorker,* vol. 78, no. 24 (2002), 58.

Smith, Roberta. "A Memorial Remembers the Hungry." *New York Times,* July 16, 2002, C1.

Woodham Smith, Cecil. *The Great Hunger: Ireland 1845–1849.* New York: Harper & Row, 1962.

The Heavenly City

Author interview with Mark G. Griffin and Peter Waddell on February 24, 2006.

Allen, William C. *History of the United States Capitol.* Washington, D.C.: U.S. Government Printing Office, 2001.

Goode, James M. *Best Addresses.* Washington, D.C.: Smithsonian Institution Press, 1989.

———. *Capital Losses: A Cultural History of Washington's Destroyed Buildings.* Washington, D.C.: Smithsonian Institution Press, 1979.

Waddell, Peter. "Peter Waddell." http://www.peterwaddell.com/ (February 25, 2006).

White, Frances. *The Heavenly City.* Washington, D.C.: Mark G. Griffin, 2004.

Texas A&M University Bonfire Memorial

Author interview and correspondence with memorial designer Robert L. Shemwell, Overland Partners, September 2004–August 2005.

"Aggie Bonfire Memorial." Pamphlet. Texas A&M University, Office of University Relations, 2004.

"Anatomy of the Texas A&M Bonfire." *Austin American Statesman,* November 19, 1999, A8.

Dethloff, Henry C. *A Pictorial History of Texas A&M University, 1876–1976.* College Station, Tex.: Texas A&M University Press, 1975.

"The Eternal Spirit, A Special Report." *Bryan-College Station Eagle,* Tuesday, November 18, 2004, 1–12.

Jacobs, Homer. *The Pride of Aggieland: Spirit and Football at a Place Like No Other.* New York: Silver Lining Books, 2002.

Loupots, J. E. *Aggie Facts and Figures.* College Station, Tex.: Loupot's Bookstores, 2004.

Moreno, Sylvia. "Texas A&M to Honor Victims of Bonfire Collapse." *Washington Post,* November 7, 2004, A2.

Petroski, Henry. "Vanities of the Bonfire." *Pushing the Limits: New Adventures in Engineering.* New York: Knopf, 2004.

Phillips, Glenn Allen. "Bonfire Memorial." Texas A&M University, Class of '99 Newsletter, June 2005, vol. 6, no. 1, 8–9.

Shemwell, Robert. "The Story of the Bonfire Memorial." Lecture. Texas A&M University, November 17, 2004.

Special Commission on the 1999 Texas A&M Bonfire. Final Report, May 2, 2000.

Thiel, Milton "Chip." Remarks at Bonfire Memorial Dedication Ceremony. College Station, Texas, November 18, 2004.

Yardley, Jim. "Aggies, Shaken by Accident, Cling to Pride and Tradition." *New York Times,* November 20, 1999, A1.

Memento Mori

Author interview with Richard Benson, September 23, 2003.
Author correspondence with Steve Miller, March–April 2004.

Benson, Richard. *Notes on Pictures.* Self-published monograph. August 2002.

Davis, Keith F. "A Terrible Distinctness," in *Photography in Nineteenth-Century America.* Fort Worth, Tex., and New York: Amon Carter Museum; H. N. Abrams, 1991.

Evans, Walker, and Museum of Modern Art. *Walker Evans.* New York: Museum of Modern Art; distributed by New York Graphic Society, Greenwich, Conn., 1971.

Macfarquhar, Neil, and Neela Banerjee. "Army Is Reluctant to Flaunt Photos of Hussein's Sons." *New York Times,* July 24, 2003, A1.

Meinwald, Dan. "Memento Mori: Death and Photography in Nineteenth Century America." *California Museum of Photography Bulletin,* vol. 9, no. 4.

Newhall, Beaumont. *The History of Photography, from 1839 to the Present Day.* New York: Museum of Modern Art; distributed by Doubleday, 1964.

Ruby, Jay. "Post-Mortem Portraiture in America." *History of Photography,* vol. 8, no. 3 (1984), 201–22.

———. *Secure the Shadow: Death and Photography in America.* Cambridge: MIT Press, 1995.

Sandweiss, Martha A., Alan Trachtenberg, and Amon Carter Museum of Western Art. *Photography in Nineteenth-Century America.* Fort Worth, Tex.; New York: Amon Carter Museum; Harry N. Abrams, 1991.

Sontag, Susan. *On Photography.* New York: Farrar, Straus and Giroux, 1977.

Shadid, Anthony, and Sullivan, Kevin. "Photos of Slain Husseins Issued; 3 U.S. Soldiers Killed; Officials Hope Images Wipe Out Skepticism." *Washington Post,* July 25, 2003, A20.

Szarkowski, John, Museum of Modern Art, and Cleveland Museum of Art. *Photography Until Now.* New York, Boston: Museum of Modern Art; distributed by Bulfinch Press, 1989.

Luminous Manuscript

Author interview with artist Diane Samuels, July 1, 2005.

Author correspondence with curator Dara Meyers-Kingsley, May–July 2005.

Author correspondence with Diane Samuels, February–July 2005.

Author correspondence with Center for Jewish History curator Brian Shuman, July 2005.

Borum, Jennifer P. "Toward a Visionary Aesthetic." *Visual Glossolalia.* New York: Luise Ross Gallery, July 15, 2005.

Diane Samuels, Inscription. Exhibition catalogue. Pittsburgh: Carnegie Museum of Art, September 15, 2001–February 24, 2002.

Kahn, Howie. "The Writing on the Wall." *ARTnews,* vol. 103, no. 7, 40.

Making Luminous Manuscript (DVD). New York: Center for Jewish History and Diane Samuels, 2004.

Meyers-Kingsley, Dara. "Diane Samuels: One Letter at a Time." *Lifestyles,* vol. 33, no. 195 (2005), 56–59.

———. "Luminous Manuscript, Diane Samuels; Biblical Species, Michelle Oka Doner: Two Site-Specific Artworks at the Center for Jewish History." Catalog. New York: Center for Jewish History, 2004.

Samuels, Diane. "Luminous Manuscript Final Proposal." Center for Jewish History, June 2003.

Schwartz, Howard. "The Precious Prayer," *Gabriel's Palace: Jewish Mystical Tales.* New York, Oxford: Oxford University Press, 1993. 86–87.

Beyond Earth

Author correspondence with Douglas Vakoch, July–August 2003; March–April 2004.

Burgess, Eric. By Jupiter: *Odysseys to a Giant.* New York: Columbia University Press, 1982.

Cowen, Robert C. "Earthly Greetings from Emissaries to Stars." *Christian Science Monitor,* March 11, 1992, 15.

Drake, Frank. "Altruism in the Universe?" September/October 2001. The SETI Institute. March 31, 2004. www.seti.org/seti/our_projects/interstellar_messages/overview/drake_altruism.html (accessed May 30, 2004).

Fimmel, Richard O., James Alfred Van Allen, Eric Burgess, Ames Research Center, and United States National Aeronautics and Space Administration. Scientific and Technical Information Office. *Pioneer, First to Jupiter, Saturn, and Beyond.* Washington, D.C.: Scientific and Technical Information Office, National Aeronautics and Space Administration, 1980.

National Aeronautics and Space Administration. "Pioneer 10 Spacecraft Sends Last Signal." Press Release (03-082HQ), February 25, 2003.

Overbye, Dennis. "When It's Not Enough to Say 'Take Me to Your Leader.'" *New York Times,* March 5, 2002, F1.

Rayl, A.J.S. "Pioneer 10 Signs Off—This Time It's for Real." The Planetary Society, February 27, 2003. www.planetary.org/html/news/articlearchive/headlines/2003/pioneer10_last-signal.html (accessed May 30, 2004).

Sagan, Carl. *Murmurs of Earth: The Voyager Interstellar Record.* New York: Random House, 1978.

Sagan, Carl, Linda Salzman Sagan, and Frank Drake. "A Message from Earth." *Science,* March 1972, 274–277.

Vakoch, Douglas. "Growing Up with ET." SETI: Search for Life. November 15, 2000. http://www.space.com/searchforlife/vakoch_seti_001115.html (accessed May 30, 2004).

———. "Le Sacrifice de Soi: Une Composition Interstellaire." *Anomalie Digital Arts,* no. 4 (2003), 201–2.

The Louisiana State Memorial (1971) by Donald De Lue reflects the contemporary styling of the later, Confederate monuments erected at Gettysburg.

Illustration Credits

A: AARRIS Architects, PC: xiv (top); Peter Aaron/Esto, courtesy Bohlin Cywinski Jackson: 15 (inset), 16b, 19 (main); ANA-MPA/Pantelis Saitas: xi; Ansel Adams/Library of Congress: 166-169, 192-193; Terry Adams/National Park Service: 54, 88, 92b, 114, 129, 152, 154 (inset), 172 (inset), 176; Nina Akamu: 12l; Courtesy the Alamo: 26, 27bl; American Battle Monuments Commission: 100 (inset), 123t, 126l; American Public Transportation Association: 13; Michael Arad: 199; Reproduced from the Schottenstein Edition of the Talmud, with permission of the copyright holders, ArtScroll/Mesorah Publications, Ltd.: 226; Simona Aru, courtesy Center for Jewish History: 225 (inset). **B:** John B. Bachelder/Library of Congress Geography and Map Division: 38-39; Achim Bednorz, bed-norz-images.com: 11; Courtesy Nicholas Benson and the John Stevens Shop: 139l, 140, 141; Richard Benson and the Eakins Press Foundation: 80, 82, 83, 85; Meredith Bergmann, 2003: 10br; Andrea Booher/FEMA News Photo: 202-203 (main); Jack E. Boucher, Historic American Buildings Survey/Library of Congress: 8t, 52 (inset), 62-63, 115, 156; David Brussat: 86t. **C:** Courtesy Santiago Calatrava: 183; Robert Capa, Omaha Beach, Normandy coast, France, June 6, 1944, the first wave of American troops landing on D-Day, gelatin silver print, copyright Cornell Capa, courtesy International Center of Photography: 124; Courtesy the Caruolo Family: 157; Anthony Catarella: 159; Frederick Charles, fcharles.com, courtesy Center for Jewish History: 222, 223, 225 (main); Crazy Horse Memorial Foundation, Korczak, Sculptor: 111; Michael J. Crosbie: 132-133 (main), 138b; Cushing Memorial Library and Archives, Texas A&M University: 213; Colleen Cutschall, designer/John R. Collins and Christopher S. Collins, sculptors, 2002: 51b; Bernard Cywinski, courtesy Bohlin Cywinski Jackson: 16 (inset). **D:** Doug Demmon, National Mall and Memorial Parks, National Park Service: 90-91; Judith Dupré: endpapers, iv-v, xvi (inset), 1, 3, 6, 9, 12r, 24 (inset), 25, 26 (inset), 27l, 30bl, 52b, 70, 71, 79, 98, 100-101, 101 (inset), 103, 104, 118-119, 125t, 125b, 126-127, 131, 132t, 136tr, 136tl, 137l, 137 second from l, 137c, 137r, 138t, 139r, 143r, 145, 146b, 149, 153, 155, 162, 168, 178-179, 180b, 181, 186 (inset), 187, 188-189, 188l, 189b, 191l, 201, 204, 207 (inset), 209. **E:** Courtesy Elmgreen & Dragset and Tanya Bonakdar Gallery, New York: xv; G. Jill Evans, 2001, courtesy Oklahoma City National Memorial Foundation: 190. **F:** Federal Emergency Management Agency (FEMA): xi (inset); Courtesy FIGG

Engineering Group: xiii; David Finn/Library of Congress: 194l; Lee Friedlander, courtesy Fraenkel Gallery, San Francisco: xii. **G:** Alexander Gardner/Library of Congress: 34t, 35t, 36t; Alexander Gardner, Meserve Collection, restored by Richard Benson for *The Face of Lincoln* (Viking Penguin, Inc., 1979): 95; Gettysburg National Military Park: 42, 43; Courtesy Robert Graham Studio: 2, 173; Ralph R. Granata: 20-23; Courtesy Michael Graves & Associates: 56; Collection of Mark G. Griffin: 210, 211; Bill Guy: 10bl. **H:** John Henley: 67r; Historic American Engineering Record, National Park Service, delineated by Robert R. Arzola, Amy L. Darling, Ellyn P. Goldkind, Lynne E. Holler, Dana L. Lockett, Mark Schara, Jose Raul Vazquez/Library of Congress: 112; Historic American Engineering Record, National Park Service, profiles drawn by Jerry L. Livingston after Farley Watanabe and Larry V. Nordby, 1984, bird's-eye view drawn by Larry V. Nordby, 1986/Library of Congress: 123r; Historic American Engineering Record, National Park Service, delineated 1986, edited by Ann Wheaton and Craig Strong, 1995/Library of Congress: 63r; Timothy Hursley: 186, 218, 219 (inset). **I:** David Iliff: 110t; Irish Hunger Memorial, copyright 2001 Brian Tolle, courtesy of Stan Ries Photography: 205, 207 (main), 208, 234. **J:** Stu Jenks: 64 (inset), 66, 146t. **K:** David J. Kaminsky, Historic American Buildings Survey/Library of Congress: 144 (inset); Alan Karchmer: 182 (inset), 184; Ann Kilbourne: 49t, 50. **L:** Rollin R. La France: 18b; Richard Latoff 2004/American Battle Monuments Commission: 133 (inset), 134, 135, 136bl, 137 second from r; Nic Lehoux, courtesy Bohlin Cywinski Jackson: 14, 18t, 19 (inset); Erich Lessing/Art Resource, NY: 230; Courtesy Provincial Government of Leyte through Gov. Carlos Jericho L. Petilla: 129 (inset); Library of Congress, Prints and Photographs Division: xx-xxi; 27br, 51r, 52 (inset), 53, 57, 58, 60tr, 64b, 69, 74 (inset), 75, 87 (inset), 92t, 120-121, 130t, 142, 147, 148, 156, 200lc, 219b; Library of Congress, Rare Book and Special Collections Division: 17; Jane Lidz: 113; Jet Lowe, Historic American Buildings Survey/Library of Congress: xix, 58 (inset), 59, 60b, 60tl. **M:** Copyright 1944 by Bill Mauldin, courtesy of the Mauldin Estate: 130br; Courtesy Steve Miller and Laumont Editions: 232; Steve Miller, courtesy Universal Concepts Unlimited, NY: 221; Margaret Morton, Ombra Luce LLC, 2001: 194-198. **N:** Courtesy The NAMES Project Foundation: 160, 161, 164, 165; National Aeronautics and Space Administration (NASA): 228, 229r, 231; National Anthropological

Archives, Smithsonian Institution (Ms. 2367A, inv. 08569200): 49b; National Archives: 55; Photograph No. 520748, "Flag Raising on Iwo Jima, 02/23/1945," Still Picture Records, Special Media Archives Services Division, National Archives: 128; Produced by Westinghouse for the War Production Coordinating Committee/National Archives: 130bl; National Park Service: 51l; National Park Service, Mount Rushmore National Memorial: 106-107, 108, 109; National Park Service, Mount Rushmore National Memorial, MORU 4498: 110b; Harrison Northcutt, courtesy Stanley, Love-Stanley, P.C.: 143t, 144 (main). **O:** Courtesy Oklahoma City National Memorial Foundation: 191r; Illustration by Lawrence Ormsby, reprinted from *Peace Through Unity* (2003) published by Western National Parks Association: 51 (inset); Timothy O'Sullivan/Library of Congress: 33 (inset), 35b; Courtesy Overland Partners Architects, Martha Raney, Elizabeth Day: 212, 214-217. **R:** Michael Ragsdale Flyer Collection, (g25.tif), The September 11 Digital Archive http://911digitalarchive.org: 200tr; Henry Reese, courtesy Diane Samuels: 226 (main); Richard Renner, Renner and Woodworth: 130cr; Michael Rieger/FEMA News Photo: 202-203 (inset); Cervin Robinson/Library of Congress: 74 (main); Bri Rodriguez/FEMA News Photo: 200 (main); Franklin D. Roosevelt Presidential Library and Museum: 181. **S:** Charlie Samuels: 194br; Art Historian Lee Sandstead: iii, vi-vii, viii, x, xiv (bottom), 4-5, 9b, 67l, 67lc, 67c, 67rc, 73, 86-87 (main), 93, 102, 117, 154 (main), 170, 172-173, 174, 175, 177b, 180t; Paul G. Seldes, Vero Beach, Florida: 200bl; Courtesy SETI Institute: 229; Brett Seymour, National Park Service-Submerged Resources Center: 120 (inset), 121r, 122; Judith Shea: 10tl; SmithGroup: 125c; Diane Smook: 177t; Spodek, Jonathan C. "Map of Monument Avenue." Washington, D.C.: Historic American Buildings Survey, National Park Service, 1991/Library of Congress: 65r; Roger W. Straus III: 8b; 32, 33, 34b, 36b, 37, 40-41, 41b, 44-45, 46, 47, 76, 77, 96, 130cl, 242; Curt Suplee, National Science Foundation: 15. **T:** Courtesy 2006 TATS CRU: xviii. **U:** U.S. coin image from the United States Mint: 116; U.S. Commission of Fine Arts: xvi-xvii. **V:** Valentine Richmond History Center: 65. **W:** Wojtek (Voytec) Wacowski: 28, 29, 30 (main), 30br, 31; Wesleyan University Library, Special Collections & Archives: 89b; Dale Wilhelm: 251, 252 (inset); Alice Wingwall: 24 (main); Courtesy Krzysztof Wodiczko and Galerie Lelong, New York: 7; Courtesy the Women's Memorial: 9tl.

Index

"I WENT TO THE WOODS BECAUSE I WISHED TO LIVE DELIBERATELY, TO FRONT ONLY THE ESSENTIAL FACTS OF LIFE. AND SEE IF I COULD NOT LEARN WHAT IT HAD TO TEACH AND NOT, WHEN I CAME TO DIE, DISCOVER THAT I HAD NOT LIVED." THOREAU

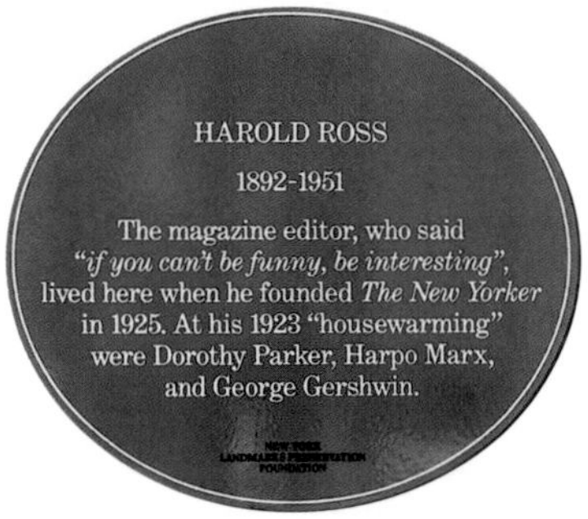

HAROLD ROSS
1892-1951
*The magazine editor, who said
"if you can't be funny, be interesting",
lived here when he founded The New Yorker
in 1925. At his 1923 "housewarming"
were Dorothy Parker, Harpo Marx,
and George Gershwin.*

NEW YORK
LANDMARKS PRESERVATION
FOUNDATION

Woodworth Associates, 130, 131
Woodworth, Brad, 131
Woolworth Store, Greensboro, NC, 147
Works Progress Administration (WPA), 78; Federal Art Project, 74, 176
World AIDS Day, 164
World Trade Center Memorial Competition, 6, 150, 199, 201

These signs and floors below are part of the surviving structure of the World Trade Center

Judith Dupré's international bestselling books, *Skyscrapers, Bridges,* and *Churches,* explore the worlds of art, photography, and architecture in ways that delight and educate. Born in Providence, Rhode Island, into a family of historic preservationists, she learned the transformative power of architecture at an early age. She subsequently received degrees in English and Studio Art from Brown University, and studied at the Open Atelier of Design and Architecture in Manhattan. For two decades, she developed visual arts programs for the public. Currently, as the Dominique de Menil Scholar at the Institute of Sacred Music at Yale Divinity School, she is investigating the influence of time, memory, and beauty on sacred architecture. She lives with her family outside of New York City. For more information, visit www.judithdupre.com.

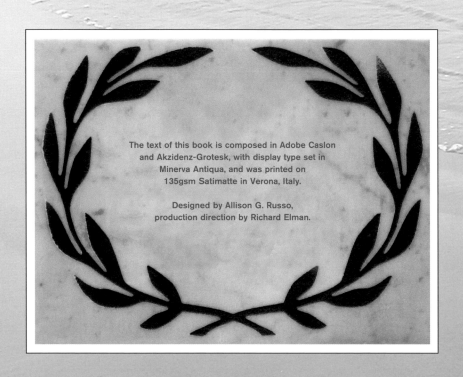

The text of this book is composed in Adobe Caslon
and Akzidenz-Grotesk, with display type set in
Minerva Antiqua, and was printed on
135gsm Satimatte in Verona, Italy.

Designed by Allison G. Russo,
production direction by Richard Elman.